China and Latin America

Development, Agency and Geopolitics

Chris Alden and Álvaro Méndez

BLOOMSBURY ACADEMIC
LONDON • NEW YORK • OXFORD • NEW DELHI • SYDNEY

BLOOMSBURY ACADEMIC
Bloomsbury Publishing Plc
50 Bedford Square, London, WC1B 3DP, UK
1385 Broadway, New York, NY 10018, USA
29 Earlsfort Terrace, Dublin 2, Ireland

BLOOMSBURY, BLOOMSBURY ACADEMIC and the Diana logo
are trademarks of Bloomsbury Publishing Plc

First published in Great Britain 2023
Reprinted in 2024

Copyright © Chris Alden and Álvaro Méndez, 2023

Chris Alden and Álvaro Méndez have asserted their right under the Copyright, Designs and Patents Act, 1988, to be identified as Authors of this work.

Cover design by Adriana Brioso
Cover image: Chinese New Year celebrations in Lima, Peru, 2019.
(© Manuel Medir/Getty Images)

All rights reserved. No part of this publication may be reproduced or transmitted in any form or by any means, electronic or mechanical, including photocopying, recording, or any information storage or retrieval system, without prior permission in writing from the publishers.

Bloomsbury Publishing Plc does not have any control over, or responsibility for, any third-party websites referred to or in this book. All internet addresses given in this book were correct at the time of going to press. The author and publisher regret any inconvenience caused if addresses have changed or sites have ceased to exist, but can accept no responsibility for any such changes.

A catalogue record for this book is available from the British Library.

Library of Congress Cataloging-in-Publication Data
Names: Alden, Chris, author. | Méndez Álvaro author.
Title: China and Latin America: development, agency and geopolitics / Chris Alden and Álvaro Méndez.
Description: London; New York: Bloomsbury Academic, [2023] | Includes bibliographical references and index.
Identifiers: LCCN 2022032018 (print) | LCCN 2022032019 (ebook) | ISBN 9781786992536 (hardback) | ISBN 9781786992529 (paperback) | ISBN 9781786992550 (epub) | ISBN 9781786992543 (pdf) | ISBN 9781350236950
Subjects: LCSH: Latin America–Foreign economic relations–China. | China–Foreign economic relations–Latin America. | Latin America–Commerce–China. | China–Commerce–Latin America. | Investments, Chinese–Latin America. | Latin America–Economic conditions–21st century.
Classification: LCC HF1480.5.Z4 C6238 2023 (print) | LCC HF1480.5.Z4 (ebook) | DDC 337.5108–dc23/eng/20220727
LC record available at https://lccn.loc.gov/2022032018
LC ebook record available at https://lccn.loc.gov/2022032019

ISBN:	HB:	978-1-7869-9253-6
	PB:	978-1-7869-9252-9
	ePDF:	978-1-7869-9254-3
	eBook:	978-1-7869-9255-0

Typeset by Integra Software Services Pvt. Ltd.
Printed and bound in Great Britain

To find out more about our authors and books visit www.bloomsbury.com and sign up for our newsletters.

China and Latin America

Chris
I dedicate this work to my family for all their support.

Álvaro
I dedicate this book to the memory of my best friend and father,
Dr. Álvaro Méndez Peñaranda.
Mon Pere – "I love you all the time"

Chris Alden
London School of Economics (LSE)

Álvaro Méndez
ESIC University, Madrid Spain
London School of Economics (LSE)
Fudan University, Shanghai, China

Contents

Introduction: Global China, Latin America and the Winds of Change	1
Silver, Railroads and Migrants	4
China Rising, Latin America Swooning – Development, Agency and Geopolitics	6
Development	7
Agency	9
Geopolitics	12
Our Approach	13
Book Outline	15
1 Silver, Railroads and Migrants – Imperial China and the Making of Latin America	17
The Silver Mountain and the Chinese Emperor's Treasury	17
La Trata Amarilla and Latin American Development	27
Chinese Communities in Latin America	31
Conclusion: The Chinese Legacy in Shaping Latin America	33
2 From Comrades to Capitalists – China's Cold War in Latin America and Its Rise as a Global Economic Power	35
China's Cold War in Latin America	35
Diplomatic Recognition and the 'Two Chinas'	36
The Sino-Soviet Split and Latin America	38
Maoism and Latin American Revolutionaries	40
The End of China's Revolutionary Phase	42
China Goes Global	42
China's 'Going Out' Policy and Latin America	46
Conclusion	48
3 Chile, Peru and Argentina – Riding the Tiger	51
Chile	51
History and Diplomacy	52
Economic Ties	54
Chinese Firms in Chile, Chilean Firms in China	57
Renegotiating and Extending the FTA	58

	Peru	59
	History and Diplomacy	60
	Trade and Investment	63
	Peruvian Chinese Community	66
	Argentina	67
	History and Diplomacy	68
	Economic Ties	69
	Elite Consortium, Development Finance and China's Expanding Interests	72
	Macri and the 'Recalibration' of Argentina-China Relations	73
	Return of the Peronists	75
	Conclusion: Chile, Peru and Argentina	76
4	Venezuela, Ecuador and Bolivia – Incautious Embrace	79
	Venezuela	80
	Building the Bolivarian Republic of Venezuela	81
	China-Venezuela – Diplomacy, Trade and Development Finance	82
	After Chávez and Oil	86
	Opposition Politics, Regime Collapse and Risk Mitigation	87
	Ecuador	90
	Ecuador and China Embrace – Rebalancing in the Era of *'Buen Vivir'*	90
	Trade, Development Finance and Infrastructure Projects	92
	Chinese Development Models and *Buen Vivir*	95
	Future Imperfect	96
	Bolivia	97
	Trade and Investment	99
	Playing the China Card	101
	Conclusion: Venezuela, Ecuador and Bolivia	103
5	Brazil – Partnership to Populism	105
	Brazil and China – From Imperial Relations to Emerging Powers	106
	Lula and the Era of Expansive Cooperation – Trade, Investment and Competition	107

	Trade and Investment in the Building of a Comprehensive	
	Strategic Partnership	110
	Focus on the Agricultural Sector	115
	Focus on the Manufacturing and Technology Sector:	
	Aviation and Automobiles	117
	Focus on the Energy Sector	118
	Brazilian Companies in China, Chinese Companies in Brazil	120
	Global and Regional Diplomatic Dimension of Brazil-China Ties	121
	Bolsonaro – From Rejection to Rebooting the Relationship	123
	Conclusion	125
6	Mexico – Competition and Cooperation	127
	Mexican-Chinese Diplomatic Relations	128
	Evolving Economic Ties – Between Competition and	
	Collaboration	129
	Trade and Investment: Spotlight on Infrastructure	131
	Trade and Investment: Spotlight on Special Economic Zones	132
	Trade and Investment: Spotlight on the Retail Sector	133
	Mexican Companies in China, Chinese Companies in Mexico	133
	Trump, NAFTA 2.0 and Trade Wars	135
	Conclusion	137
7	Central America and the Caribbean – Dollar Diplomacy and	
	Development	139
	Economic Engagement: Development Financing for	
	Infrastructure, Resources and Tourism	139
	Dollar Diplomacy	145
	Focus on Costa Rica	149
	Focus on Panama	153
	Focus on Jamaica	157
	Conclusion	161
8	Global China, the United States and the New Geopolitics	
	of Latin America	163
	Institutionalizing China and Latin America's Common Destiny:	
	From Strategic Partnerships to Regional Forums	164

CELAC and 1+3+6	164
Next Steps: White Paper on China and Latin America and the Caribbean 2016	165
Autumn of the Patriarch? US Response to China in Latin America and the Caribbean	166
Strategic Competitor	167
The New Geopolitics of Latin America	168
Development Reframed	168
Agency Reconsidered	170
China Re-evaluates Risk in Latin America and the Caribbean	171
Geopolitics Ascendant – Huawei and Covid Diplomacy	172
Resources, Railroads and Migrants Redux – Global China's New Silk Road and the Remaking of Latin America	174
Appendices	**178**
Appendix A: Trade Figures – China and Latin America	178
Table A.1 Imports, Exports and Total Trade between Latin America and China	178
Figure A.1 Bar Chart – Trade between Latin America and China 2000–2019	179
Appendix B: Foreign Direct Investment Figures	179
Figure B.1 LAC: FDI Inflows from China and Hong Kong 2000–2019	180
Appendix C: Diplomatic and Geopolitical Matters	180
Table C.1 PRC – Diplomatic Relations with LAC (1960–2022)	181
Table C.2 Diplomatic Allies of Taiwan in LAC as of July 2022	182
Table C.3 LAC Countries that have endorsed the BRI as of July 2022	182
Notes	**184**
Further Reading	**260**
Index	**263**

Introduction: Global China, Latin America and the Winds of Change

It was a moment resplendent with the most potent kind of symbolism. In the lobby of the Maritime Authority of the Panama Canal on 8 May 2018, the country's elites gathered together with Chinese officials to mark the countdown to the entry into force of the *Panama-China Maritime Agreement*.[1] Festooned with red paper fans and flanked by young Panamanian women in colourful *pollera* and stylish *cheongsam* dresses, Panamanian and Chinese managers mingled, while senior officials delivered speeches extolling the virtues of their countries' cooperation. At the appointed hour, Panamanian and Chinese officials jointly pulled a curtain to reveal a placard with the number ten etched in bold black ink. Outside there was a thunderclap of sound as the beating of drums echoed across the complex, Chinese lion dancers leapt and shouted in celebration at the front of the building, while beaming bureaucrats, cooled by air conditioning inside, looked on.

Out on the original canal, working in the boiling heat of that same midday, a Chinese inspection team surveyed the workmanship of American engineers and construction firms on the Miraflores lock built over a hundred years ago. Methodically, they measured the width of the canal walls, walked the length of the lock and studied the displacement of brackish canal water as it flowed into the enclosure. They were not, however, the only Chinese visitors to Panama's man-made wonder and principal economic resource – the 'goose that laid the golden egg' for the United States, as an American politician once put it. Panama and its famous canal had already become a high-end destination for discerning Chinese tourists some years back, drawn by the beaches, casinos and well-developed ecological tourist sites.

The next morning in the bustling heart of Panama City, a Chinese trade delegation arrived at an auditorium packed with Panamanian business representatives, jostling with one another to meet the Chinese delegates from industries as diverse as engineering and automotive manufacturing. Zhang Yujing, the distinguished-looking head of the China Chamber of Commerce for Import and Export of Machinery and Electronic Products (CCCME), told the assembled group that Panama was the 'natural extension of the silk road and a gateway to Latin American markets'.[2] At the same gathering, the principal Panamanian trade negotiator fretted nervously to anyone who would listen about the pending commencement of discussions with his Chinese counterpart over a formative Free Trade Agreement aimed at locking in concessions with the global trading giant. Around him, the freewheeling chatter of business representatives making small talk about export markets and expanded earnings threatened to drown out his carefully chosen words.

Later that evening, slick media packages capturing the day's events were streamed into the homes of Panamanians across the narrow isthmus. *Diario Chino Latinoamericano*, a newspaper for the local Chinese immigrant community, splashed the story across its banner headline. For many Panamanians watching the news reports on television, reading newspapers and browsing online, China was not an alien presence but rather one with which they had long-standing familial ties. Panamanians of Chinese origin could claim ancestry from Cantonese and Hakka migrants who had come to work on the railroad in the mid-nineteenth century. Their sweat and blood, like that of their contemporaries in Peru, Mexico and the United States, contributed to the building of Panama's formative infrastructure.[3] With 10 per cent of its population of Chinese heritage, it is no surprise that one of Panama's national dishes is itself a variation on the classic Cantonese 'chaufan'.

Once the cornerstone of Washington's commercial and imperial aspirations in Latin America,[4] the canal cuts across the Panamanian isthmus linking the Atlantic and Pacific oceans and allowing trade to flow from industrial factories and farming communities in the United States to points up and down the Western Hemisphere and beyond. Built and occupied by the US military between 1904 and 1914, the Panama Canal stood unchallenged as a symbol of American hegemonic determination to dominate Latin America, and concurrently its emergence as a global power.[5] During the Cold War, South Command, one of the US military's key regional nodes, was headquartered in Panama. Although President Jimmy Carter negotiated the withdrawal of US forces in 1977 and agreed to hand over the canal to the Panamanian government after twenty years, this did not stop the US from launching a controversial invasion in 1989 which toppled the autocratic rule of General Manuel Noriega. By 2007, the Panamanian authorities undertook an expansion of the canal, funded through an internationally syndicated loan and completed in June 2016.[6] At the opening of the new locks, in a sign of China's rise as a global trading power, it was a Chinese merchant vessel named 'Cosco Shipping Panama' that first traversed the isthmus.[7] The initial phase of the $900 million deal signed in 2016 to build a deep-water port on the Atlantic side of the canal by China's Landbridge Group was officially launched in June 2017,⁸ a few days before Panama declared it was breaking diplomatic ties with Taiwan in favour of China on 13 June 2017.⁹ A century of American dominance of the canal was suddenly on the cusp of being swept away, overshadowed by the radiance of Chinese power and money.

What has happened in Panama since the announcement of diplomatic relations may well have assumed iconic proportions, but it was by no means an isolated phenomenon in Latin America and the Caribbean (LAC). Running up and down the spine of the Andes mountain range to the tip of South America are countries like Peru and Chile that have sought to embrace China's economic expansion through Free Trade Agreements and open investment regimes. Successive governments in Argentina, struggling to raise vital finance on global capital markets as the peso collapsed and shut out of IMF lending, turned to China for help through a series of currency swaps and the short-term liquidity they provide,¹⁰ even while increasing Argentina's indebtedness by financing hydroelectric dams.¹¹ The self-styled Bolivarian republics of Venezuela, Ecuador and Bolivia all saw in China the alternative to a century of US dominance, although notably (or perhaps deliberately) misconstruing its single party Communist system as one aligned to the ideologies of the Latin American left. Their governments welcomed Chinese investment as a mix of grants, zero-interest, concessional and non-concessional loans,¹² largely uncritically, even as some local communities complained about corruption, labour disputes and environmental degradation at the hands of Chinese firms. Remarkably, the same embrace was eschewed by the hard-nosed pragmatists in Havana, who kept Chinese economic interests at bay as they courted other investors. Meanwhile, Central American and Caribbean states, many of them still diplomatically tied to Taiwan, watched opportunistically as they positioned themselves to reap the benefits of the two-way contestation between Beijing and Taipei.¹³

Mexico, one of the key countries of the region, has been among those most heavily impacted by China.¹⁴ Mexican manufacturers of textiles, footwear and electronics found themselves in direct competition with Chinese producers for access to the lucrative US market, and many Mexican firms found it more cost effective to relocate to southern China in the late 1990s. This trend reversed after 2008, when rising costs of labour in China began to price its producers out of these sectors, and companies started moving back to Mexico. Interestingly, Chinese attempts to penetrate the Mexican economy exhibit distinctive features, making it more in keeping with the patterns seen in industrialized and regulated economies in Europe and Southeast Asia. The publicity surrounding the failed high-speed railway project exemplifies the problems Chinese firms have had in breaking into sectors traditionally open to them in other parts of Latin America.[15]

For the behemoth that is Brazil, occupying the wide Atlantic coast and much of the vast expanse of the Amazon, deepening engagement with China had been a national priority since the election of Lula Da Silva back in 2002.[16] Two-way trade soared from $6.7 billion in 2003 to $36.9 billion by 2009, with Chinese demand for Brazilian agricultural products fuelling expansion and Chinese financing of Brazilian infrastructure development promising further growth.[17] Brazil's global ambitions received a boost with Beijing's endorsement of its bid for a permanent seat on the UN Security Council and the invitation to become a founding member of BRICs (Brazil, Russia, India, China).[18]

Within a few years, however, the Brazilian business community was complaining about competition from low-cost Chinese imports at the same time that Chinese officials were grumbling about barriers to realizing rapid profits from their investments in steel. Moreover, battered by the fall in commodity prices in the aftermath of the global financial crisis, the Brazilian government struggled to raise capital to fund its mounting debt burden. The result was an unprecedented surge in Chinese-financed mergers and acquisitions by its state-owned enterprises, making Brazil the third largest recipient of Chinese foreign direct investment (FDI) in 2016.[19] Once vaunted as a source of national pride, Petrobras, the oil parastatal that symbolized Brazil's technological capacities and global aspirations, turned down Chinese bids for an equity stake in 2009, only to have to borrow $5 billion in exchange for oil shipments, as the Brazilian economy reeled closer to depression.[20] The election of former military captain Jair Bolsonaro to the presidency in 2018 was propelled in part by his appeal to growing anti-Chinese sentiment amongst Brazilians. 'China is not buying in Brazil,' Bolsonaro railed, 'it is buying Brazil.'[21]

Silver, Railroads and Migrants

For most observers, China's appearance in Latin America is a new phenomenon, something commensurate with the remarkable rise of the Chinese economy and its globalization in the twenty-first century. But its roots are much deeper than that: in fact, China is intimately bound up in the expansion of European colonialism in the region in ways that have profoundly shaped Latin American economies, state formations and societies down to the present day.

Spanish conquistadors, who brutally overthrew the indigenous empires and reconfigured their economies to serve as sources of precious metals and captive markets for Spanish goods exported from Cadiz, were part of the Crown's larger endeavours to open up trade routes to Asia. Recognizing the mineral wealth of their newly conquered territories, the Spanish Empire embarked on the forging of a grand trade network – the Silver Route (*Via de la Plata*) – which linked mining interests in Peru and New Spain (Mexico) to the galleon trade through the Spanish entrepôt of Manila. From there, Spanish, Dutch and Portuguese merchants transhipped these cargoes to the Portuguese colony of Macau where, at the Cantonese warehouses just over the border, Chinese Imperial officials logged the import of silver and its exchange for silks and porcelain. At its peak from the midpoint to the end of the sixteenth century, upwards of five million silver pesos – half of Peru's entire annual production – were shipped to China.[22] One incredibly rich network of silver arteries buried inside Potosí, a mountain high in the Andes in a territory known as Upper Peru (today, Bolivia), provided the bulk of the silver extracted for export during this period. In fact, between 1500 and 1800 a handful of mines in Peru and Mexico accounted for 80 per cent of the total global trade in silver, with a third of their production being directed to the Chinese market.[23]

The steady flow of vast quantities of silver into the Chinese Imperial treasury served to back their paper money, and when that collapsed, silver itself became the empire's key medium of exchange domestically and internationally. It made fortunes for the Huai and Jin merchant clans operating out of Canton, and planted the green shoots of modern capitalism in the rigid feudalistic Chinese political and social order. But this dependency on Latin American silver also had the perverse effect of triggering deleterious inflationary cycles that destabilized the Chinese economy and eventually contributed to the fall of the Ming Dynasty.

On the other side of the globe, the slow decline of the Spanish Empire and the growing turmoil across Latin America ushered in a new phase of relations between China and the region. The republics of Peru, Mexico and Colombia, having gained independence in the early part of the nineteenth century, began national programmes to expand their infrastructure into the interior. Heavily leveraged with foreign debt, these governments built railroads in virgin jungle and through mountain passes, or along the coastal littoral, as they sought to open up regions, build new roads and improve harbour facilities. Labour consignments, beginning in the 1840s, brought thousands of Cantonese and Fujianese immigrants to Latin America and the Caribbean to take up so-called 'coolie' employment in these development projects. It was a process not without controversy, inspiring an international campaign that brought together anti-slavery abolitionists, Qing Dynasty officials and the British Navy to forcibly end the 'coolie trade' by the 1880s. Settling in cities like Lima, Tijuana, Panama City and Havana, these Chinese migrants set up small businesses as their communities grew over the next decades.[24] Xenophobia reared its head at times, with 25,000 Chinese expelled from Sonora state in Mexico in 1931, following a concerted campaign to fan fears amongst the local unemployed.[25]

Today, Chinese communities from Santo Domingo in the Dominican Republic to São Paulo in Brazil are emerging from the shadows of this past and celebrating their common heritage as migrants from one of the world's great powers. Panama – a sliver of a territory bridging the strategically important Atlantic and Pacific oceans – hosts one of the most vibrant Chinese communities in the region.[26] It is a trend that is surging again as the Chinese population in Latin America continues to expand into the millions. The Overseas Chinese Affairs Office has very conservatively estimated the total number of Chinese in Latin America at two million in 2011, but by now that figure is likely to be much higher, especially as some scholars have calculated that in Peru alone it could be between 1.5 and three million.[27] Embracing Chinese culture, this time through the prism of state-funded Confucius Centres and *putonghua* (or 'Mandarin') language learning, is setting the stage for a new phase in Chinese-Latin American communities.

China Rising, Latin America Swooning – Development, Agency and Geopolitics

The encounter of Chinese trade diplomats with their Latin American counterparts at the annual summits of the newly formed Asia-Pacific Economic Cooperation (APEC) sparked mutual recognition of economic opportunities realizable in building closer ties. In November 2004 China's new leader Hu Jintao used the APEC Summit in Chile as a starting point for ground-breaking diplomatic visits to Brazil, Argentina and Cuba. The steady surge in economic involvement, with China surpassing the US as the principal trading partner for many of the leading regional economies in 2010, set the stage for a more comprehensive economic engagement. As one Chinese academic, Song Xiaoping, put it a few years later:

> Today, China's traditional markets – the United States, European Union, Japan and the countries and territories of Southeast Asia – are essentially saturated. Furthermore, the major developed economies find themselves in a state of inertia and China's trade with these markets has dropped sharply. Thus, China has devised a strategic plan to diversify its export market, with an emphasis on emerging economies, which include the main countries of Latin America.[28]

Echoed in the Chinese Foreign Ministry's White Papers on Latin America published in 2008 and 2016, Beijing's approach to the region can be understood as driven primarily by economic purposes, which sees tying down vital natural resources and opening new markets in Latin America as crucial to growth and stability at home. At the same time, China's economic outreach and diplomatic forays appeal to the development aspirations of a Latin America intent on seeking new sources of finance, unencumbered by the strictures imposed by US-led neo-liberalism and alignments that broaden commercial and diplomatic opportunities. Embedded within deepening Chinese involvement, however, are local communities, environmental activists and economic nationalists in Latin America, who increasingly challenge the 'win-win' deals struck by their elites, pushing back for greater gains from trade and improved social outcomes. China's commitment, made in January 2014 at the newly formed China-CELAC Forum (CELAC stands for *Comunidad de Estados Latinoamericanos y Caribeños*), to expand two-way trade to reach $500 billion annually and investment stock to $250 billion over the next ten years, symbolized the ambitions Beijing and its Latin American partners had for the relationship.[29] Finally, the ongoing power transition towards Asia with China at its centre is manifesting as a realignment of the global economic system away from Western dominance. In this context, China's ambitious Belt and Road Initiative (BRI) presents a geo-strategic vision of development whose implications and global reach has simultaneously enthused, perplexed and, over time, troubled officials in Latin America's capitals, not to mention those residing in Washington, DC. Three broad themes, therefore, emerge from our study of China's engagement with Latin America, namely, development, agency and geopolitics.

Development

The rising fortunes of Latin America and the Caribbean over the last decades have launched an economic and social transformation every bit as consequential as the onset of democratization in the region two decades earlier. The position of Latin America as a perpetually low-growth, inward-looking region with limited innovation and outreach beyond its borders is being set aside, as political and business leaders in Brazil, Mexico, Chile and Colombia break into new markets at home and abroad. Foreign investment has risen exponentially in some sectors, trade is booming and incomes have risen significantly over the last few decades; while Latin American MNCs or so-called *multilatinas* are becoming global players in traditionally Northern economies as well as in the emerging markets of the South.

And yet against this positive picture are economic problems that continue to bedevil the region, from income inequality and the middle-income trap, to the infrastructure backlog and endemic corruption, which, if not addressed, threaten Latin America's development prospects well into the twenty-first century. Current events in countries like Venezuela and Argentina underscore the fragility of institutional commitments to democracy and markets. Vast gaps in income render the recent development gains in Brazil and elsewhere vulnerable to shocks that could instigate social unrest at a time when some countries' dependency on commodities for earnings is actually increasing.

Into this evolving situation comes a new powerful actor, China, whose dynamism and competitiveness are transforming the international political economy. Latin America's largest trading partner since 2010, the combination of China's strategic singleness of purpose, its seemingly bottomless financial reserves and its state-owned and private firms' aggressive pursuit of resource and market opportunities, are all beginning to have a major impact on the region. Having reached $268 billion in total two-way trade in 2017,[30] Beijing's stated ambitions to increase trade to $500 billion and FDI to $250 billion by 2024 are a reflection of the economic importance which the region is assuming in China's calculus and of the dependency relationship in the making.[31] Indeed, Chinese demand for Latin American resources is probably the key element in Latin America's positive economic growth trajectory in the past decade. While Chinese demand is, for example, absorbing over 40 per cent of Brazilian soya exports, import of China's competitively priced finished goods is challenging the market position of Latin American firms as well as their established development gains in sectors as diverse as textiles and aviation. Chinese state-owned enterprises are buying up equity stakes in Latin American firms, investing in joint ventures in the resource sector, and even providing large-scale loans to Latin American governments and their parastatals. Initiatives like the mammoth 'Two Oceans Railway', which was supposed to cut across the Andes to link Brazilian markets directly with the Pacific coast, though now defunct through political infighting, at least demonstrated Beijing's readiness to realize some of Latin America's long-standing development aspirations.

For some analysts, in fact, Latin America's growing dependency on the export of commodities to China merely replicates the disturbing trade patterns of the past.[32] Riding the sustained surge in commodity prices driven by China's (and other emerging powers') appetite for resources, Latin American economies were participating in a commodity 'supercycle' that has seen prices for energy and minerals double and food products rise by 75 per cent between 2003 and 2008.[33] Others note the changing profile of Chinese FDI, which since 2010 has been moving beyond the resource sector into high-tech and employment-generating areas like telecommunications and automobile assembly.[34] This movement from an exclusive focus on resource and market-seeking conduct to using FDI to source innovation and technology is coming to characterize a new direction in investment.[35]

Behind the startling success of Chinese penetration of Latin American markets is its skilful employment of economic statecraft. Mobilizing financial reserves of $3.22 trillion dollars,[36] Beijing has been able to secure access to local resources through large-scale loans aimed at major infrastructure projects in Latin America. Often tied to these loans are provisions for the employment of Chinese firms, labourers and suppliers, providing much-needed sources of capital for investment-starved developing countries in Latin America and at the same time a way for Beijing to underwrite the expansion of its own firms overseas. In aggregate, lending by Chinese policy banks overtook the total combined value of loans provided by the World Bank and the Inter-American Development Bank (IDB) in 2010, with 87 per cent of it aimed at financing infrastructure, a sector which traditional lenders had largely ignored.[37]

Linked to this has been an effort to put the economic relationship with Latin America on a longer-term, sustainable footing. The signing of three bilateral Free Trade Agreements (FTAs) with Chile (2006), Peru (2009) and Costa Rica (2011) – with other bilateral and regional FTAs at various stages of discussion – has opened the door to expanded trade and greater investment in these economies, while concurrently opening up market access in China for Latin American products. At a more pedestrian level, the FTAs have paved the way for Chinese small and medium-sized enterprises (SMEs) to start ventures in light manufacturing, services, agricultural production and the retail sector in these countries, while their Latin American counterparts have in the main struggled to gain a foothold in China's domestic market.

Agency

The advent of a global power transition offers unprecedented prospects for less-powerful states to exercise greater policy autonomy through strategic policy engagement. With structural features of the Western-dominated international system in flux, signalled by the weakening of international institutions and the softening of traditional international regimes of conduct, the ability of these states to forge opportunities with this soft systemic clay is much enhanced. For Latin Americans whose development trajectories and domestic politics have been defined by their relationships with the US government and Wall Street finance for the last century – even when casting themselves as definitively in opposition to Washington – the struggle for state autonomy is one of asserting diversity over the logic of external primacy.

Agency can be seen as running along two axes: one essentially defined by diplomacy and economic statecraft and the other through the interests of a panoply of sub-state and societal actors within states. In this context, agency has many policy expressions, captured in the work of Russell and Tokatlian on relational autonomy, including strategic alignment with great powers ('coupling'), balancing and hedging against great powers ('accommodation' and 'limited opposition'), collective action ('challenging') and pursuing autarky ('isolation').[38] For instance, agency can be seen in strategic choices whereby a government positions itself in alignment with a foreign power – Colombia's 'invitation to intervention' to the United States or Cuba's alignment with the Soviet Union come to mind.[39] Agency can be observed in collective action: the seemingly perpetual drive for regionalism which galvanizes Latin American governments and academics (sometimes even publics) whose aim is to mobilize the combined forces of states and markets to improve trade policy outcomes and reduce dependency on great powers. It also can be found in the policies of governments determined to break their dependency on great powers altogether – self-determining development – as pursued by past Peruvian military regimes during the Cold War and still recognizable in muted form in the impulses of Morales's Bolivia.[40]

These depictions of agency, however, are situated at the level of state action and ignore another facet that involves elites and civil society in mobilizing great power resources to serve localized interests. Elites, whether ensconced within governments or occupying powerful positions in the commercial sphere, can utilize the state apparatus to engage with external powers to pursue narrow parochial agendas.[41] By way of contrast, civil society – a term loosely defining myriad actors, including trade unions, consumer groups and environmental activists – can play a significant part in shaping ties with external actors through their resistance strategies to specific initiatives.[42] For instance, the Somoza family's control over key sectors in the Nicaraguan economy starting in the 1940s led to decades of state policies geared towards extracting diplomatic, financial and security resources from the US which strengthened their dominant position.[43] In a different vein, the protests by indigenous communities and environmental activists in Ecuador in the 1990s aimed at disrupting the construction of roads through Amazonian forest forced the withdrawal of US oil companies from that sector and, concurrently, a hardening of policies from Washington. This represents another kind of bottom-up agency.[44]

In this respect, Beijing's arrival in the region was recognized by Latin Americans as an opportunity to exercise their own agency in pursuit of greater autonomy from the US in an era in which unipolarity and neo-liberalism dominated the Western Hemisphere. The failure of the US-led Free Trade Area of the Americas (FTAA) to win passage in 2005 marked a turning point, as Bonilla and Millet observe, creating 'the conditions that have allowed other international actors to become active in the region'.[45] China's confidence in developing closer ties with the region was captured in the publication of its first ever White Paper on Latin America and the Caribbean in 2008.[46]

China's expanding power can certainly be measured by the surge in aggregate trade after this date, as well as by the onset of loans and investment. But China also features as an alternative source of *ideas, financial resources and practices of development*. For many Latin American governments, the first expression of this ongoing global transformation was the effect that China had in loosening the strictures of neo-liberalism in the development debate. Freed of the catechism of neo-liberal dogma, Latin American policymakers, reflecting on the East Asia experience of state-led development and increasingly China's interpretation of its own experience, were encouraged to reconsider their own development pathways. This allowed a revival of infrastructure-led growth, buoyed by soaring commodity prices, and gave impetus to local policies of 'neo-extractivism' (see Chapter 3). The promulgation of the 'Chinese development model' through the twinning of development finance with ambitious infrastructure projects, inspired fast-track improvements in a long-neglected sector, as well as the twinning of commercial interests with nation-building imperatives. For the self-styled Bolivarian republics, the proximity of enlightened technocratic leadership and authoritarian rule in China validated their instinctive preference for one-party rule as a means of achieving efficiencies in allocation of resources. That this extension of the development experience into forms of illiberal democracy and even authoritarianism would spill over into opportunism and corruption was perhaps inevitable, as time would tell.

All of this was happening against the backdrop of significant disruptions to the liberal international trading system, coupled with the active pursuit, led by the most developed economies (minus the US under Trump), of a host of trans-regional trade and investment initiatives like the Trans-Pacific Partnership (TPP),[47] and of more localized initiatives like the Pacific Alliance. Almost unnoticed in this process was the impact China was having on traditional hegemons in the region, producing a quiet economic marginalization of the United States, along with other developed economies like Europe and Japan. This paved the way for a reconsideration of Chinese intentions in Latin America and the Caribbean, one of which is beginning to have a significant effect on China's position in the relationship.

Geopolitics

Geopolitics, defined by Parker as 'the study of international relations from a spatial or geographical perspective', focuses on analysis of the interaction between geographical entities and an international or global dimension, and their utilization to pursue political advantage.[48] Seen through this wide-ranging lens, China's economic endeavours in Latin America and the Caribbean are reflective of larger power transformations in the international system: in that context, Beijing's assertive application of economic statecraft and its policy initiatives in diplomacy and security are contributing factors in accelerating US marginalization from the region. For instance, rising debt tallies owed to China by Ecuador, Jamaica and Argentina are expressions of 'debt-trap diplomacy' designed, as some US analysts and their Latin American counterparts believe, to ensnare these governments into crippling dependency on Beijing by giving huge loans with strings attached.[49] Local concerns, moreover, resound across the region that Chinese engagement replicates its approach to acquiring African resources, stirring worries over de-industrialization as well as more primordial racist narratives.[50] Alarmist accounts of Chinese intentions, read through bilateral discussions of security cooperation or the onset of military training programmes, add fuel to incendiary speculation.

In fact, Beijing has shown caution in its diplomatic engagement with Latin America and the Caribbean, especially in sensitive cases like Venezuela and Ecuador, precisely in order to allay US concerns. However, the enthusiasm with which Latin American governments have embraced China as a southern partner and alternative to the US – and the lack of any preventive reaction from Washington – has taken even the Chinese by surprise, and has tended to force the pace of deepening ties (see Chapter 3). So, too, has the volatility of the regional policy environment, with resource nationalism and the revival of populism introducing unexpected risks to Chinese investments and loans in the region. Moreover, the deepening exposure of Chinese firms and Chinese citizens to hazards in Latin America highlights the need to enhance the security of these interests.[51] Both of China's White Papers on Latin America, published in 2008 and 2016, call for closer bilateral cooperation between police forces, judiciaries and militaries to combat transnational crime and to improve the safety of Chinese interests.[52]

In the US, the soporific combination of historical dominance and neglect continues to play out in how different presidential administrations see Chinese involvement in Latin America. For a generation of American policymakers, the very idea that China might be challenging the US pre-eminent position through its commercial expansion into Latin America was nonsensical (see

Chapter 7 and 8).⁵³ The bulk of scholarship, echoing these views, suggested that the fundamentally economic content of Chinese involvement should be understood as fitting in with the broader ambit of US-led globalization.⁵⁴ Now some are becoming less sanguine, with Pham pointing to the erosion of US influence in the region and Ellis arguing that Chinese support for left-wing populism in countries like Venezuela sets the stage for local advocates with hostile intent towards US interests.⁵⁵ The launching of China-CELAC Forum in 2014, an organization consisting of China, Latin America and the Caribbean – and notably without the US or Canada – marked a bold departure from the cautious approach of Hu Jintao. Even within China itself there are debates over the implications of China's intentions towards the region with some scholars calling for retaliation against US actions in the South China Sea by opening up a diplomatic front in 'America's own backyard'.⁵⁶ Other scholars describe how Chinese analysts, given America's continuing preponderance of power in the Western Hemisphere, see 'caution and prudence'⁵⁷ as the best avenue to implement foreign policy in the region.

The unexpected election of Donald Trump in November 2016, the launch of the 'trade war' and his administration's formal designation of China as a 'strategic competitor' in the US National Security Strategy two years on were all portents that this period of ambiguity has come to an end.⁵⁸ Indeed, against the background of bipartisan consensus on challenging China on trade, there is growing concern voiced within the US security establishment about the inroads that China has made into the Western Hemisphere through the Latin American and Caribbean 'backdoor'.⁵⁹ Equally, other observers have suggested that Trump's 'America First' policies have acted as an own-goal, effectively undermining US influence in the region.⁶⁰ Although once having assumed it to be motivated by development and commerce, Washington is now reframing the China-LAC relationship through the logic of geopolitics.

Our Approach

Understanding the global transformation, its manifestations in trade, investment, diplomatic and even geopolitical settings is crucial to charting a future for Latin America. Four features in particular are significant in the relationship with China:

- the changing trade and investment patterns from North-South to South-South, with China leading – and its implications for resource trade, new markets, de-industrialization, employment and social stability
- the new assertiveness of select Latin American states and multinationals on the global economic stage

- the centrality of democratic institutions and market economies, some embedded but others more fragile, to Latin American development
- the creeping dislodgement of the US as the privileged economic, political and security actor in the region.[61]

These are deeply important transformations which are generally poorly understood and analysed by scholars of contemporary Latin American studies and by policymaking and corporate circles both inside and outside the region. For instance, what are the interests, strategies and practices of China, the incoming economic power? Does Beijing's approach to Latin America differ in significant ways, as is often claimed by Chinese leaders, from its approach to other developing regions like Africa? How proactive have Latin American leaders been in managing China while pursuing their own interests? How influential are business and civil society in promoting their concerns to China? What are the implications for Latin American development aspirations in the context of the decline of one hegemon and the arrival of another potential one? How has the rising tide of Chinese migration to the region impacted on Latin American perceptions and policies towards China?

The academic literature on the subject focuses almost exclusively on the interplay and competition between great powers in transition on a global stage, in which Latin America is but one terrain of the struggle; *or* on the development impacts of Chinese trade and investment on different sectors of selected Latin American economies. Less effort has been made either to detail the actual areas of contestation and cooperation, which are fundamentally bilateral, or to assess the geo-strategic implications of the new engagement. Our approach in this book is to extend this line of inquiry towards a more focused set of comparative treatments between China and key Latin American countries, and, based on extensive fieldwork and analysis, to frame these in terms of three broad questions:

- *What motivates Chinese interests in Latin America and how has this shaped its approach to the region?* More specifically, why have Chinese firms invested in Latin America and how has this state-driven outreach affected investment decisions, modalities of engagement in local economies and commercial outcomes? How has competition between Chinese state actors (as well as the private sector) influenced the choices of investment? Studies ranging from analysis of Chinese enterprise conduct and policy bank lending to analysis of CPC party congress documents provide new insights for assessment of Chinese engagement with the region.[62]

- *How have Latin American governments, firms and societies responded to China's deepening economic and political involvement in their region?* Countries have reacted in distinctive ways to China's economic arrival; for instance, the pattern of engagement with local elites or the impact of Chinese financing and the conduct of its firms on unfamiliar terrain. A particular focus is the degree of local agency at play in the context of China-Latin America relations, where that agency is located and how it is exercised in the service of material interests and even ideology. Alves' and others' work provides a framework for understanding how local political and regulatory regimes – alongside the role of elites, networks and social groups – help shape the responsiveness of governments, businesses and civil society to the myriad experiences of China and the Chinese.[63]
- *Given the rising global competition between China and the US, how have geo-strategic considerations begun to impinge on the China-Latin America relationship?* Understanding geo-strategic interpretations of Chinese intentions in the region, and how these views have changed over time, especially since the onset of the US administration's designation of China as a 'strategic competitor' in 2018, is important for developing a picture of this new phase in China-Latin America relations.[64]

Book Outline

This book will examine the content and trajectory of China's relationship with Latin America in a series of eight interrelated chapters. Chapter 1 positions the relationship in its proper historical context, providing insights into the formative role that China had in shaping the economies of the Spanish and Portuguese Empires as well as the independent states of Latin America and the Caribbean that succeeded them. Chapter 2 focuses on China's involvement in Latin America during the Cold War and the lingering influence of ideology in local politics, as well as the rise of Global China. Building on this foundation, Chapter 3 examines the contemporary relations between Chile, Peru and Argentina, three of the most active and in some cases forward-looking economies in the region. Chapter 4 looks at cases of Chinese engagement with Bolivarian nationalism in Venezuela, Ecuador and Bolivia and its aftermath. Chapter 5 foregrounds the region's leading economic giant, Brazil, and how ever-closer political and economic ties under Lula produced contrary reactions in business, labour and eventually domestic politics. Chapter 6 examines how cooperation and competition shape the complex relationship between Mexico and China. Chapter 7 looks at the countries of Central America and the Caribbean, with special attention paid to Costa Rica, Panama and Jamaica. Chapter 8 turns to the question of the United States and how it has perceived and responded to the expansion of Global China's commercial interests and foreign policy activism in a region often characterized as 'America's backyard'. More broadly, the chapter reflects on the nature of the US-China relationship against the backdrop of history, economic ties and, in the context of geopolitics, what the likely shape of its future might be.

1

Silver, Railroads and Migrants – Imperial China and the Making of Latin America

The roots of China-Latin America ties are every bit as deep as the fabled Silk Road that stretched across the steppes of Eurasia, and every bit as formative for the integration of China with the New World in the emerging network of global trade. The seductive power of Chinese products like silk and porcelain for European consumers mirrored the lure of silver doubloons for the Ming treasury, putting Latin America at the centre of this three-way exchange. Tens of thousands of nautical miles between the three continents proved to be no barrier, as accelerating annual trade in goods between Canton, Manila, Acapulco, Havana and Cadiz carried with it the exchange of material riches, but also ideas and peoples. The collapse of the Ming and Hapsburg dynasties brought the Manila galleons to a halt by the dawn of the nineteenth century, but in less than thirty years another phase commenced, with the newly independent Latin American republics recruiting contract labourers ('coolies') from southern China to work on plantations and build railroads. In their wake came a trickle of Chinese migrants who established businesses and developed communities as they struggled to make a life in Latin America.

Far from being esoteric or even exotic, the contemporary relationship between China and Latin America is built upon a profound and near-continuous history, one in which China has played a fundamental role in shaping the politics of empire, the regional economy that emerged in the postcolonial period and even the multicultural societies that are the bedrock of Latin America. In short, it is, as scholars have pointed out, in so many different aspects 'a history hidden in plain sight'.[1]

The Silver Mountain and the Chinese Emperor's Treasury

The lure of spices, silks and porcelain from the East spawned dreams of fabulous wealth, mesmerizing the royal courts and merchant houses of Europe, a continent in the throes of a commercial and cultural renaissance since the fourteenth century.² With Catalan, Genoese and Venetian merchants controlling the lucrative trade in the eastern Mediterranean Sea, finding a direct trade route to India and the ancient kingdom of Cathay became a central preoccupation of Western European governments, merchants and elite consumers for generations. The possibilities of opening up trade routes to Asia via oceanic links, thereby circumventing the time-worn dependency on middlemen, lay behind the burst of Iberian exploration starting in the mid-fifteenth century.³ The profits to be had were phenomenal. Vasco de Gama's initial voyage from Lisbon, around Africa and onwards to India in 1497 may have cost a third of the participants' lives, but it generated a staggering 600 per cent return on one ship-load of spices, and another flotilla was hastily organized in its wake.⁴ The Portuguese quickly went on to establish a network of fortified enclaves stretching from coastal Africa, Ormuz on the Persian Gulf, Goa off of the Indian subcontinent, Malacca in Southeast Asia, to Macau in southern China to secure their trading position.

Under the auspices of the Portuguese monarchy, an annual flotilla of *carracks* (later supplanted by larger galleons) was sent out from Lisbon from 1515 onwards to trade Portuguese-sourced silver for Chinese wares.⁵ Macau, the Portuguese entrepôt established in 1557, became a key focal point of Western European trade with the Chinese market for the next 150 years. This exchange of 'silk for silver' came to dominate the trade with China, with Macau serving initially as a waystation between China and Japan, and subsequently for New World silver.⁶ From there Portuguese, Spanish and eventually other European merchants shipped these cargoes onward to Cantonese warehouses on the mainland where the precious metal was exchanged for silk and porcelain.

The Crown of Castile and Aragon, as the Spanish monarchy was then known, had been awarded the right to explore and colonize the Western Hemisphere west of 46°30′ W by the terms of the Tordesillas Treaty of 1494, which ratified the Portuguese claims to Brazil as well as, theoretically, all of Africa and Asia. In the early sixteenth century Spanish conquistadors savagely overthrew the indigenous empires and reconfigured these economies to serve as sources of precious metals and captive markets for Spanish goods exported from Cadiz. Recognizing immediately the mineral wealth of these newly conquered territories, the Spanish empire embarked on forging a grand trade network – the Silver Route (*Via de la Plata*) – which linked mining interests in Peru and New Spain (Mexico) to the galleon trade through Macau and onward to Chinese markets.

The Western European dilemma of gaining direct access to China may appear to have been addressed by the establishment of long-distance sea voyages to Asia. This did, however, raise an equally challenging set of problems, centred on the fact that the Ming Dynasty remained intent on restricting foreign access to the Chinese market to the Portuguese enclave of Macau, and, through their base in Macau, the Portuguese were as assuredly intent on maintaining their monopoly on access to the Canton-based 'hongs' (factories).[7] Spanish, Dutch and later French and English merchants were obliged to trade via the Portuguese-controlled territory, which constrained their ability to fully exploit commercial opportunities. In Loire valley chateaux, in merchant houses in Amsterdam and Cadiz, and even in ducal palaces in Savoy, rooms would be decorated in the Chinese style and filled with Asian furnishings, Ming vases and *longban* ceramic plates on display for the pleasure and prestige of their owners. Western Europeans' demand for *chinoiserie* continued unabated, fuelled by elite consumption of exotic imports from the East in societies that were expanding through trade and the initial phases of industrial production. Local imitations of Chinese 'kraak' porcelain sprung up like the Dutch-manufactured Delft blue and white pottery produced in the early seventeenth century (or 'bone china' subsequently developed by Wedgwood in Gloucestershire in the late eighteenth century). It satisfied some of that growing domestic appetite in Europe and its colonies, but failed to achieve the variety and sophistication of the originals.

Fortunately, as the Spanish authorities were soon to discover, Imperial China's own appetite for silver turned out to be boundless as well. Gold's value as an export from the Spanish colonies in the New World to Spain had, by 1530, already been outpaced by the demand for silver. It was, as Flynn and Giráldez point out, 'the Chinese demand for silver ... (that) elevated the value of the commodity and provided the impetus for trade around the globe'.[8] Silver mined in upper Peru and New Spain was forged into ingots and 'pieces of eight' (Spanish dollars contained 25 per cent pure silver) in local mints, then transported out of Acapulco to Macau via Guam (and later to Manila), and from there to the Canton factories.[9] Behind this rising demand were shifting policies by the Imperial treasury, which made it mandatory from 1581 that local taxes be paid in silver, forcing increasing numbers of Chinese into cottage silk production for export as a means of obtaining this precious commodity.[10] The result was that the demand for silver escalated, with households and nascent factories alike engaged in frantic efforts to produce more Chinese silk that was so universally prized outside the country. This economic exchange had the knock-on effect of compelling the entire trading network of the Chinese tributary system in Asia to adopt silver as its principal means of exchange by the mid-sixteenth century.[11]

The Imperial treasury's silver policy was initially aimed at securing the precious metal from the Japanese market in exchange for Chinese silk, and in this respect Macau played a key role in the trade as middleman (along with Fujianese merchants). This Sino-Macau-Nagasaki trade route continued mostly uninterrupted (in the interim the Dutch secured exclusive trading rights in Dejima island off of Nagasaki after the ouster of the Portuguese in 1639) until the mid-seventeenth century when the Japanese mines became depleted.[12] At the same time, the exploitation of New World silver offered opportunities to tap into new sources and penetrate the Chinese market. Recognizing this as early as 1527, Hernan Cortes – conquistador and entrepreneur – ordered a flotilla of three Spanish galleons filled with silver bullion to sail from Acapulco on the Pacific coast to exchange for Chinese silks, porcelain and lacquerware.[13] Though operating within the constraints of Chinese regulations and Portuguese control of Macau, Cortes's initiative was a sufficient threat to domestic interests in Spain that the Crown moved to shut down direct access to Asian markets by its colonies.

The founding of a Spanish colony in the Philippines in 1571, on the heels of initial incursions in 1564, was a seminal event in structuring the relationship between Latin America and China.[14] The Spanish colony in Manila, serving as a trade outpost for the region effectively run by the Viceroy of New Spain, was charged with securing goods from China and other parts of Asia in exchange for silver carried by chartered ships from Acapulco.[15] In Manila, the pealing of church bells signalled the arrival of the Spanish galleons in the fortified port of Cavite, gathering people to the harbour to see the ships being unloaded.[16] The *Sangley*, Chinese migrants who settled in Manila in response to the trading opportunities, set up an emporium called the Parian, which served as the hub of exchange between the Spanish colony and the Portuguese enclave of Macau and, when possible, illegal ports in coastal China. Other regional destinations included Batavia, Nagasaki, Malacca and Calcutta, sources of spices and other exotic goods that were carried on Spanish galleons to the Western Hemisphere.

Across on the eastern side of the Pacific, the arrival of the *Não de China* in the port of Acapulco was also greeted with the pealing of church bells and a runner was despatched along el camino de China to take the news to Mexico City.[17] Goods were brought to the 'Parian' in the central plaza of Mexico City, named after its counterpart in Manila and exclusively devoted to the exchange of products from Asia. The English priest Thomas Gage reported finding a street of renowned gold- and silversmiths who had honed their craft through working with what he called immigrant 'Chinese Christians'.[18] Above all, the *chinos* – sometimes referred to as *indios chinos* but as likely to be people of Japanese, Malay or even other South Asian origin as they would Chinese – traded in silk and raw and finished products for which there were no parallels produced in Europe.[19] In Mexico City, goods were exchanged between merchants from other Spanish colonies like Peru and New Granada. Finally, the consignments of silks, porcelain and lacquerware were transported across eastern Mexico to Veracruz, where they were shipped onward to Spain and from Cadiz and Seville onward to other European markets.

What emerged was a royal monopoly on commerce with Asia called the 'Manila galleon trade' (also known variously as the '*Não de China*' or '*Não de Acapulco*' depending on which way across the Pacific Ocean one was sailing), centred around the annual departure of generally two Spanish galleons from Cadiz bound for the Western Hemisphere and coordinated to coincide with the arrival of another royally commissioned flotilla in Acapulco from across the Pacific. For Spain it became a vital source of revenue maintaining its ambitious continental and global presence and subsidizing the monarchy's expenditures on military adventurism in northern Europe, Italy and the eastern Mediterranean.[20] And at its heart was silver for silk, as one scholar put it, 'the raison d'être for the Manila trade' linking the Spanish colonies in the Western Hemisphere with China.[21]

The main source of the Spanish galleons' annual cargoes of silver was a mountain high in the Andes in a territory known then as Upper Peru (today, Bolivia).[22] Potosí was a small village situated at over 4,000 metres in what the Spanish named the Cerro Rico Mountains where, as legend has it, a local native shepherd obliged to seek shelter in a cave in 1545 found its craggy walls lined with glittering silver ore.[23] Indeed, so fabulously rich was the mountain at Potosí that just one of its mines provided the bulk of the silver extracted for export during the first hundred years of its operation. The discovery of what ultimately turned out to be four deep veins of silver ore buried underground within sight of Potosí sparked a delirious scramble for stakes in the mines.

Mining the ore, however, required an enormous investment in capital and labour, and the village of Potosí grew into a city of 160,000 colonists and 30,000 natives, making it larger than Madrid or London at the time. Silver-refining factories were set up to process the ore, and the first mint in the Western Hemisphere was established to stamp it into imperial-weighted coins. Over the next 250 years, the indigenous population was employed in mining, with many of them conscripted under the old Incan Empire's *mita* system, which compelled them to provide their labour to the Crown, and redeployed by the Viceroy Francisco de Toledo in 1575 to Potosí. Up to thirteen thousand natives were conscripted annually, although numbers generally stood at four thousand, and these joined an equivalent number of contract labourers already working the mines.[24] Hundreds of thousands died in the arduous extraction of the precious ore from the honeycomb of mines deep inside the mountainside and, when numbers fell precipitously, African slaves were brought in to bolster the work force.

The discovery of significant deposits of mercury in the village of Huancavelica in the mountainous region of eastern Peru, a substance traditionally used for extracting silver from the mined ore, and one which before had had to be sourced directly from Spain, provided Potosí with a steady supply of this vital catalyst.[25] From 1563 onwards mercury was carried by mules and llamas on a 1,200 kilometre trek across the Andes to Potosí. Thereafter, incremental improvements in the *patio* process of amalgamation introduced from Europe contributed to lower onsite production costs and simultaneously to speed up production, on the one hand keeping Potosí competitive on the global market, while on the other, exacting a huge human cost.[26] Mercury poisoning became commonplace amongst those working in this hazardous profession, which involved crushing the ore by hand (and feet), adding to the prevalent dangers of pneumonia and underground collapse faced by the labourers. So dire were the conditions for those labourers working in the mines at Potosí, that it was nicknamed 'the mountain that eats men'.

Twelve million silver pesos (or 128 tons) were shipped from the Vice-Royalty of Peru via New Spain to China in 1597, averaging six million silver pesos annually or half of Peru's total silver production.[27] In fact, between the years 1500 and 1800 only a handful of mines in Peru and Mexico accounted for 80 per cent of total global trade in silver, with a third of their production being directed to the Chinese market.[28] Silver ingots and coins minted at Potosí were shipped by sea from Callao in Peru via Panama City on the west coast while cargoes destined for Spain were taken overland to the Isthmus of Darian (Panama) and via Porto Bello on the east coast to the Caribbean.[29] The discovery of silver in Zacatecas in the central highlands of New Spain in 1548 made a contribution but it was Potosí that remained the world's single largest source of silver for a hundred years. By 1610, the fabulous silver lode had peaked and gradually production declined, so much so that by 1714 its output had fallen by 83 per cent.[30] As a result, the silver lode in Zacatecas (and a lesser one in Guanajuato) in New Spain assumed greater importance in supplying bullion to the Asian market. Some scholars suggest that the trade between New Spain and China was worth two million pesos per annum, though these figures most certainly disguise the rampant illicit trade encouraged by corrupt colonial officials in the Western Hemisphere and their counterparts in Macau and Manila.[31]

For the Chinese Imperial treasury the silver trade was absolutely crucial to the economy and, despite the cycle of inflation and crisis that accompanied its dependency, the Ming Dynasty persisted with its use. For one thing, the steady flow of vast quantities of silver into the Imperial treasury served to back the circulation of paper money, and when that collapsed, became the empire's key medium of exchange domestically and internationally. Spanish silver ingots and coins became accepted currency within China itself, amongst its trading partners and across much of Europe. In the trading hub of Canton, it made fortunes for the Huai and Jin merchant clans whose accumulation of capital even challenged the rigid feudalistic Chinese economic and social order. These merchants accrued such wealth that they came to flaunt the conventions of the social hierarchy where they were near the bottom of the scale, and carried themselves after the fashion of Imperial officials ('mandarins' to use the term devised by the Portuguese, or, loosely translated, 'those who give orders').[32]

Corresponding to the Chinese appetite for New World silver was the demand for Chinese-produced silks in New Spain and Peru, which provided the impetus driving direct two-way trade. Colonial authorities tried importing Moorish artisans and mulberry trees from Granada to be planted in New Spain to create their own silk industry.[33] But silk production in Mixteca was not up to Chinese standards and the inferior quality of Spanish-produced silks meant that, when imported into the Spanish colonies, they were rejected as too 'oily'.[34] *Sangley* and *mestizo* merchants in the two Parian emporiums in Manila and Mexico City developed trading networks that moved goods like silk back and forth with the regularity of the annual Manila galleons. The *chinos* residing in Mexico City even earned an exemption from sales tax from the Spanish Crown, subject to their commitment to not wholesale silk from China or Spain.[35] By 1600 competition from imported Chinese silk gradually stifled and eventually killed off this nascent domestic silk production in New Spain. Imports of raw silk increased, however, bringing about the establishment of factories in Mexico City that at their peak employed 14,000 labourers to weave the material into reams of cloth.[36]

Other industries thrived through the Manila galleon trade as well. Shipbuilding featured from the outset of the Spanish conquest, with Cortez having thirteen shallow-draft *bergantines* built for the invasion force that targeted the Aztec capital of Tenochtitlan.[37] Construction of ships for the Pacific fleet took off in the port city of Guayaquil (in modern-day Ecuador), which by the early seventeenth century was building two 200-ton galleons a year from local materials suited to the conditions of the Pacific crossing.[38] Garcia de Palacio's shipbuilders' guide, published in Mexico City in 1587, details the specific requirements for galleons built for the 'South Seas' (the Pacific).[39] On the back of growing demand for the Pacific trade, other shipyards sprung up in Panama City, Iztapa (Guatemala) and Acapulco.[40] In Puebla (Mexico), where a sizable Asian community had settled, kilns were established with the sole purpose of producing imitations of Chinese *qingbai* (blue and white) pottery for the local market in New Spain.⁴¹ The casting of cannons used to defend the port city of Veracruz was done in Manila by the skilled *Sangley* smiths.⁴² Intricate wrought iron gates, carved ivory Madonnas and Chinese vases with Christian motifs used to adorn the cathedral in Mexico City and numerous churches and chapels alike were mass-produced in Macau, Canton and Zhangzhou to supply demand in New Spain and Europe.⁴³

The Spanish Crown, at the behest of merchants in Cadiz and Seville facing stiff competition from these Chinese goods, periodically attempted to shut down the trade between New Spain and China. According to one scholar, 'The royal plan was to wall off Mexico and prevent Chinese merchandise from ruining Spanish markets in other colonies (in the New World). It failed.'⁴⁴ Acapulco remained the China trade hub for the Spanish colonies. Peru's own short-lived foray into direct trade with Manila, with galleons departing the port city of Callao in 1581 and 1582, was blocked by a series of royal edicts that forbade the ports of Callao, Guayaquil, Porto Bello and Nicaragua to engage in the galleon trade with Manila.⁴⁵ According to Spanish commissioners secretly sent to report on compliance to royal edicts prohibiting trade with China outside of the annual Manila galleons, Chinese porcelain was sold openly in the markets of Lima, and Chinese silks were worn in public in towns and cities from Panama to Chile.⁴⁶ Moreover, elites in both Spain and the colonies preferred the quality and variety of silk products coming out of China to those produced under monopolistic conditions in the mother country. Within a few short years, the import of Chinese silks into the Spanish colonies and directly into Spain itself forced factory owners in Valencia to shut down a quarter of their looms and sack twelve thousand artisans.⁴⁷

The outbreak of unrest in the Spanish colonies from the eighteenth century onwards was fuelled by local elites whose grievances extended from the Crown's restrictions on trade to the *quinto real* (a Crown tax of a fifth of all earnings) to a growing desire for self-government. Merchants colluded with local officials in a cat-and-mouse game, systematically skirting the law through stratagems such as exporting silver overland across the Andes Mountains to the frontier port of Buenos Aires and thence to Manila. Royal efforts in 1634 to stamp out the unregulated silk trade between New Spain and Peru had the unintended consequence of damaging silver output in northern Mexico which had become increasingly dependent on Peruvian mercury supplies.⁴⁸ Back in Spain the circulation of so much silver and gold had the perverse effect of generating rapid inflation (as was the case in China), undermining the economy and driving up the costs of local production. These periodic economic crises were compounded by the serial failure of the Hapsburg Dynasty to rule effectively.

When change finally came, it was partial, reformist and ultimately insufficient to address the root problems of the Spanish Empire. The advent of a new ruling dynasty coupled with a belated recognition of the debilitating impact of Hapsburg administration brought on a set of reforms in the late-eighteenth century that aimed both to address colonial grievances and to broaden, if not fully liberalize, trade across the Spanish Empire. The *Reglamento para el comercio libre* propagated in 1778 under the new Bourbon monarch Charles III designated the Caribbean possessions as an open trading system, but restrictions on trade with non-Spanish ports remained in place for the colonies of New Spain and Peru.[49] One of the reforms tried to emulate the success of other royally sanctioned companies by putting private investors at the helm, like the British East India Company. The Royal Company of the Philippines was created in 1786 out of the ashes of the short-lived Caracas Company to import cotton merchandise from Asia via the Cape of Good Hope and re-export it to the Latin American markets.[50] It failed through a combination of chronic mismanagement and rapacious speculation.

Meanwhile, continuing Chinese economic dependency on Latin American silver periodically triggered deleterious cycles of rampant inflation that destabilized the Chinese economy and eventually sped up the fall of the Ming Dynasty. In 1644, sensing the empire's weakness, the northern Manchus' 'banner armies' marched on Beijing, ousting the ailing emperor and sweeping away nearly three hundred years of Ming rule. From the outset, the new Qing emperors were determined to learn from the failings of their predecessors. They reviewed the loosely managed trading arrangements with foreign barbarians and restricted contact between Western merchants and the populace, a process that was eventually formalized in the 'Thirteen Factories' system at Canton in 1757. During this same period, demographic changes in China saw the population double from an estimated 150 million to 300 million between the seventeenth and eighteenth centuries. According to scholars, this was in no small part thanks to the introduction of crops indigenous to Latin America, like maize (corn) and potatoes, by foreign traders, which, ironically, put more pressure on the rural economy.[51]

By 1799, however, the high point of the Qing Dynasty had already passed with the death of the Qianlong emperor (the last of the Three Great Emperors). Domestic economic distress piled up, with the price of silver mounting steadily as sources of ore in Latin America dried up, making it ever more difficult for the Chinese population to meet taxation demands.[52] Rising expenditures on costly wars and an extravagant imperial lifestyle, coupled with rampant corruption by trusted senior officials like Heshen, led the country from a healthy surplus of 79.3 million silver taels in the Imperial treasury at the start of the Qianlong emperor's reign in 1775 to a massive deficit of approximately that amount at his death.[53]

The impact of these deteriorating circumstances on the Chinese economy began to be felt more acutely across the country as a succession of weak rulers further undermined Imperial authority. Unrest broke out on the borderlands of the empire in the north, as well as in Burma and Tibet, forcing the Qing to undertake costly military campaigns, while the rapid population growth and crop failures all combined to heighten instability at home. Western merchants, seeking an alternative to silver coinage as their trade imbalance with China continued to mount, shifted their exchange goods to include opium from the late eighteenth century. By 1825 there was a net outflow of silver from China to meet the skyrocketing demand for the drug which, on top of the inflationary impact of excess silver imports on the Chinese currency in the eighteenth century, now added a scarcity of silver to the disruptive effects.[54]

Economic distress, coupled with feeble Imperial rule, deepened social unrest across the country. Millenarian movements grew out of the desperation of the peasantry, and a period of near continuous civil wars commenced in southeast China that culminated in the Taiping Rebellion (1851-1865) in which thirty million people are said to have died.[55] The catastrophic displacement of millions of Chinese during this period sparked an outflow of thousands of migrants to Southeast Asia and, at more modest levels, a push to seek out opportunities for emigration to far-flung destinations like the Western Hemisphere.

Far more worrisome for the Spanish authorities in colonial Latin America was the Túpac Amaru rebellion in November 1780, which evolved from a localized protest against the corrupt practices of the *corregidor* in the Cuzco highlands of Peru to one that mobilized indigenous peoples to execute colonial officials. Rising instability in the colonies was exacerbated by an enervated economy in Spain, which fell further behind as the industrial revolution in northern Europe began to outpace it. Economic change brought with it liberal ideals, and the onset of the settler revolt in Britain's North American colonies added to the political ferment in France. The catalyst of the French Revolution sowed the seeds of radical Republicanism and then, in the wake of its collapse, Napoleonic rule. The French conquests first of Portugal in 1807 and then Spain in 1808, forcing the abdication of the royal families, were the final catalyst for wholesale revolution against the Spanish Crown in 1810. Led by Simon Bolivar, an army officer, independence was declared in New Spain, Peru and New Granada. Following defeat at the hands of these rebels, the Spanish authorities had no choice but to formally end the annual Manila galleons, the key source of revenue for the Crown and the backbone of the trading network that had linked China, the Western Hemisphere and Europe for 250 years.

La Trata Amarilla and Latin American Development

The slow decline of the Qing empire, the withdrawal of Spain from most of its territories in the Americas and the growing turmoil across Latin America ushered in a new phase of relations between China and the region. The nascent republics of Peru, Mexico and Colombia, having all gained independence in the early the nineteenth century, began national programmes to develop plantation agriculture, open up new mining opportunities and build infrastructure into the interior of their territories. Increasing production of cash crops like sugar cane and sisal for export required more cheap labour. At the same time, heavily leveraged governments launched a series of ventures aimed at opening up regions, building new roads and improving harbour facilities. These ambitious development programmes depended on capital from the expanding trade in resources, large-scale loans from European and US financiers and, crucially, the introduction of low-cost, productive Chinese workers.

Latin Americans' turn to the Chinese was initially a strategy by plantation owners seeking an alternative to African slave labour.[56] The British Royal Navy's interdiction of slaving ships on the high seas and the freeing of its occupants, following from the policy to end slavery within the British Empire in 1807 and its implementation in 1832, cut by half the numbers of new slaves imported into countries like Peru.[57] For those with foresight in the Spanish and Portuguese territories, the eventual end of the Atlantic slave trade meant that new labour sources were needed to maintain production levels. South Asians and Chinese were contracted by plantation owners across British colonies to replace slaves and the transition to new sources of labour influenced Latin America and the Caribbean.[58]

Underlying the choice of Asian labour were Western perceptions that South Asians and Chinese were more passive and obedient than the restive Afro-Caribbean slaves.[59] Chinese migrants were exclusively male and came from Fujian and Canton provinces, with port cities like Canton (Guangzhou) and Chuanchow (Quanzhou) providing a steady stream of overseas migrants for well over a hundred years.[60] The ongoing instability in China, periodic famines and other crises contributed to the uptick in migration throughout the nineteenth and into the early twentieth century.

One of the first contingents was two hundred Cantonese brought to Trinidad in 1806 to replace the African slaves who had left after being given their freedom.[61] Soon afterwards, more were brought to the plantations in Jamaica. Labour consignments, beginning in the early 1840s, expanded upon these initiatives and brought thousands of Cantonese and Fujianese contract labourers to Latin America and the Caribbean to take up *kuli* ('coolie') employment. In the early days of this system, Chinese worked alongside African slaves on plantations in Cuba and Peru, although the plantation owners sought to separate their accommodation and distinguish practices like punishments.

In Cuba, which was restored to the Spanish Empire after the Treaty of Paris in 1763, *la trata amarilla* ('the yellow traffic'), as it was often called, was in the beginning conducted in tandem with the slave trade which, while legal in Cuba until 1886, had become increasingly difficult after 1807 under the British policy of interdiction against slave ships on the high seas.[62] As in other parts of Latin America, Chinese-indentured labourers were initially brought in to replace or supplement the use of African slaves on the sugar plantations in Cuba. Some were recruited by labour brokers who falsely promised high wages and good conditions, made to sign contracts and taken to *baracoons* to await shipment abroad. Others were kidnapped by Cantonese pirates and sold on to the labour brokers.[63] According to contemporary accounts, Chinese arriving after a two-month journey in cramped conditions disembarked in Havana and went straight to the city's slave market, la Regla, to be contracted to local buyers. From there, they were herded by foot across the island to the patchwork of farms and plantations to begin their arduous tenure in near-slave conditions.

In its first decade, the Republic of Peru had limited financial capital to begin its ambitious development plans, and so the new demand in European markets for guano-based fertilizer and refined sugar proved to be a godsend. Chinese labour migration was a crucial factor in generating revenues needed at this phase in Peru's development. Firms like Carnevarao and Compañía became involved in the lucrative guano and coolie trade in 1846 (later joined by the British mercantile group W. R. Grace and Company), recruiting the first Chinese to mine guano on islands off the coast of Lima.[64] Backbreaking work in isolation drove some labourers to commit suicide rather than suffer the onerous conditions they found themselves in. From there, plantation owners took to recruiting more Chinese to work alongside slaves on the sugar plantations in the Paramonga region north of Lima. The use of opium was widespread, supplied by the Peruvians to control their workers and numb them to the dire conditions they faced, as well as to encourage docile behaviour. Some of these Chinese did escape, creating communities in the floral density of the Amazon far outside of the reach of the state.[65] In 1854, the liberal party took over the Peruvian government and abolished slavery, concurrently passing legislation that allowed for a greater influx of indentured labourers from China to replace freed slaves on sugar and cotton plantations.

Other Latin American governments followed suit. In 1855, the Costa Rican government, perceiving Chinese migration in neighbouring British Honduras to be a success and recognizing that they had failed to encourage sufficient European immigration to meet economic demands, turned to Chinese contract labour as the solution to raise agricultural output.[66] To the south, in Dutch Surinam and French Guyana, colonial authorities pursued similar policies, anxious to replace plantation slavery with contract labour from China.[67]

Echoing its mission in West Africa, from 1856 onwards the British Royal Navy was authorized to interdict ships in the international waters off of China suspected of carrying 'coolie labour'.[68] Typically, a cruiser operating out of Hong Kong would hail a suspect vessel – often on the authority of the British consul in one of the coastal towns like Amoy – obliging it to stop and be boarded by British sailors. The Chinese labourers crammed in the hold would be brought up on deck and quizzed by the British as to their recruitment, the conditions they were experiencing, expected destination and wages. If the labourers identified recruitment practices that amounted to undue compulsion or expressed any reservations, the British navy took it upon themselves to return them to China. No less a notable than Charles Dickens voiced his concern in the *Anti-Slavery Reporter* in July 1860 that such missions disclosed that 'there was not much difference in their treatment once on board, both [Chinese labourers and African slaves] being kept barred down between decks, and only allowed to come up in detachments, existing alike on rice and water'.[69]

As word trickled back to the Imperial government in Beijing, seconded by the pamphleteering of anti-slavery societies in Britain and elsewhere, Chinese authorities began to feel pressure to crack down on the coolie trade. Local officials in ports like Swatow (Shatou), Amoy (Xiamen) and Canton (Guangzhou) wavered between collusion with labour brokers and compliance with Imperial edicts to block the trade. Pressure from London (and later Washington) on the Imperial government to regulate the trade generated a flurry of official commissions looking into the matter. For instance, the Chinese Commission of Enquiry set up in 1873 to investigate conditions in Cuba, noted in its final report that the Chinese labourer 'cannot be regarded as occupying a position different from that of the [enslaved, ed.] negroes'.[70] In the aftermath of the Commission's findings, the contract labour scheme came to a formal end (though slavery continued on until being banned in 1886). In 1887 the governments of Peru and Imperial China established a similar joint commission to investigate the condition of indentured Chinese labourers. The findings were as damning, and efforts were made to improve the terms of recruitment and the conditions in which Chinese labourers worked.

Concurrent with closer scrutiny of the 'coolie trade' in the agricultural sector, Peruvian President Manuel Prado began in 1878 a massive railroad-building programme, turning to Ernest Malinowski, a Polish immigrant, to design and construct the high-altitude network of tracks, tunnels and bridges across the Andes mountains, while the controversial US financier Henry Meiggs agreed to fund it. W. R. Grace and Company, long active in Peru in the guano trade and owners of sugar plantations, agreed to organize the transport of Chinese.[71] Chinese labour brokers were engaged and the first consignment of contract workers were offloaded at the port of Callao and taken to the hinterlands where they were set to work on the national railway linking Lima with the towns of La Oroya and Huancayo in the interior.

Panama's interest in Chinese labour began in 1853 with the recruitment of two thousand labourers from Canton to work on the final stages of the Panama railway.[72] Far from finishing the job, hundreds fell ill from tropical diseases while others succumbed to opium addiction and suicide.[73] Successive efforts at building a canal across the isthmus brought renewed demand for contract labourers, although by the early 1900s discriminatory legal provisions made it increasingly difficult to recruit from China.[74]

In Mexico the strongman Porfirio Diaz turned to Chinese labourers to assist his government in realizing its ambitious development plans. He sought out capital from the US and Europe to fund the construction of railroads and expansion of agriculture, but looked to China for labour. In 1899 Diaz's government signed the Treaty of Amity and Commerce with the Imperial Chinese government, laying the legal foundation for Chinese migration to the plantations and the railroads.[75] Regulating the coolie trade and immigration more generally had an impact on Chinese migration to the Western Hemisphere. The Chinese exclusion laws in California in 1882 and thereafter, for example, diverted voluntary migrants southward to Mexico and beyond.

All in all, from 1847 to 1874 nearly 225,000 Chinese males were imported as part of *la trata amarilla*.[76] Hundreds died on the four-month journey from Canton to Callao, and thousands more in the truly dire conditions in which they found themselves in Latin America. Beatings, whiplashing and punishments for slight infringements were found to be routine by the various joint commissions investigating the coolie trade. Local labourers outside the plantations surmised that Chinese labour was designed to undercut their wages; consequently there were protests and outbreaks of violence against them. When it was finally stopped – the outcome of a sustained international campaign as ardently pursued by liberal governments in Europe and the Western Hemisphere as the abolitionist movement had been decades before – Latin America was changed forever. Roads, railways and canals cut through the jungles and mountains, much of it the product of Chinese labour and often at a terrible human cost. What remained, however, was a small Chinese and *mestizo* population that, supplemented over time by immigration from China, laid the basis for one of Latin America's most dynamic communities.

Chinese Communities in Latin America

Against a backdrop of literally hundreds of years of uninterrupted commerce between Latin America and China, it should be no surprise that Latin American society has been significantly influenced by migration from Asia, much of it from China. A census conducted in Lima in 1613 found that numerous 'Indians from Manila and China' (as well as 'Indians of Portuguese India' and 'Indians of Japan') made up part of the city's population of twenty-five thousand (the official moniker 'Indian' being equivalent to today's use of 'Asian').[77] Chinese migrants were noted by officials in New Spain in 1635, where their numbers were sufficient to cause local businessmen to complain about Chinese business practices.[78]

To put this in context, according to one study, a total of 139,000 Spanish and 93,000 Portuguese migrated to the new colonies in the Western Hemisphere between 1500 and 1580.[79] This fell from a combined annual immigration rate of 5,400 a year to an annual immigration of 4,200 between 1580 and 1700. The big surge in Chinese immigration to Latin America began from the late nineteenth century onwards. Settling in cities like Lima, Tijuana, Panama City and Havana, these nineteenth-century Chinese immigrants moved into their own barrios and soon set up small businesses that throve as the community grew in the next decades.[80] By 1876, a decade after contract labourers were brought into Peru, Chinese migrants made up 10 per cent of Lima's total population of two million.[81]

The onset of racist restrictions targeting Chinese (and later Japanese) immigrants to North America, starting with laws passed in California in the 1870s and subsequently expanded to federal law through the Chinese Exclusion Act in 1882, as well as a host of legislation in the 1920s, closed down decades of this movement of people. For a time, this pushed Chinese migration southward into Latin America, where restrictive legal barriers accompanied social barriers to make life increasingly constrained in Panama, Costa Rica and even Peru. During this period, ethnic cleansing, every bit as cruel as those incidents in the United States and Canada occurring at the same time, took place with growing frequency. In 1911, 303 Chinese men, women and children were murdered by an armed mob in Torreón in northern Mexico. Twenty years later, following a concerted campaign by Mexican politicians to fan xenophobic fears amongst the unemployed, over twenty-five thousand Chinese were expelled from Sonora state.[82] In 1918, Jamaicans rioted across the country to protest the dominance of the Chinese in the retail trade and rising tensions over racial politics, followed by attacks against Chinese in Kingston in 1938 and again in 1965.[83]

In spite of these setbacks, Chinese communities continued to reside in the region, sometimes in urban enclaves but increasingly integrating into the fabric of society in countries like Peru as well as others like Panama and the Dominican Republic. Chinese immigrants and established Chinese alike formed associations as self-help organizations, providing assistance in getting settled in the new country or establishing a business, building networks and serving as a venue for social gatherings. Conversion to Catholicism helped bridge gaps between themselves and other Peruvians. The *tusan*, a local Peruvian term for people of mixed Chinese origin, grew in prominence in Lima as their businesses expanded, and by the early twentieth century their concerns involved, like other middle-class Peruvians, their children's education, marriage brokering and society dances as part of their enriched cultural life as Peruvians.[84] Even national politics, once the preserve of the colonial and *mestizo* elites, saw the rise of politicians of Chinese origin elected to office. Past presidents of Guyana and Trinidad and Tobago can trace Chinese ancestry in their backgrounds.[85]

The imprint of Chinese culture, often assimilated to other Asian cultures like Japanese or Filipino for Latin Americans unaware of distinctions, is felt across the region.[86] In Mexico '*la China poblana*' is a folkloric figure of gentle naiveté who comes from the countryside and is apparently rooted in an historical figure of Asian origin, Catarina de San Juan from the seventeenth century.[87] A Brazilian expression for a favourable business deal is '*negócio de China*'. The *chifa* restaurant serving localized versions of Chinese food is ubiquitous across contemporary Peru.

Today, this historical impact of China and the Chinese diaspora continues to shape contemporary Latin America. For instance, Panama hosts one of the most vibrant Chinese migrant communities in the region.[88] In the former Dutch colony of Surinam in coastal South America, 10 per cent of the population can claim Chinese ancestry. It is a trend that is surging again as the Chinese population in Latin America expanded. The Overseas Chinese

Affairs Office has very conservatively estimated the total number of Chinese in Latin America at two million in 2011, but by now that figure is likely much higher.[89] In Venezuela, for instance, the Chinese community was estimated to be sixty thousand in 2000 and eighteen years later – according to the president – had grown to half a million immigrants.[90]

Conclusion: The Chinese Legacy in Shaping Latin America

While differing in terms of scale and modality, the Chinese legacy in shaping Latin America is nearly as profound as that of the Spanish and Portuguese colonial empires. The original rationale behind the Iberian expeditions was to seek out and establish trading relationships with Asia. The discovery of vast lodes of precious metals in New World territories incited campaigns of violent conquest which, even before the Spanish had fully subjugated indigenous peoples and assumed control over their territories, had begun to settle into trading patterns of New World silver for Chinese silk. Two hundred years later, this pattern of commodity exports still dominates Latin American economies and the elites still turn to foreign capital and Chinese labour to drive their countries' development. Thus, at formative moments and in key sectors – namely, the Chinese Imperial state interacting with the Iberian empires; China as a vast market for Latin American resources and traded goods; China as the origin of contract labour and migrants for Latin American infrastructure; and, finally, China as a source of culture and community – China has played a crucial role in the development of Latin America.

Though largely neglected in mainstream accounts of Latin American history, this restoration of the place of China and the Chinese in history provides a context in which we can better appreciate the past and assess its meaning for contemporary relations. We will now turn to the twentieth century to assess how modern China, riven by decades of civil war that culminated in the establishment of the People's Republic of China in 1949, exerted influence on Latin America and the Caribbean during the Cold War and beyond.

2

From Comrades to Capitalists – China's Cold War in Latin America and Its Rise as a Global Economic Power

In keeping with the previous three centuries, China's involvement in Latin America and the Caribbean in the Cold War reflected the dominant trends of the era. During the Cold War, the newly established Peoples Republic of China sought to enhance its diplomatic standing at the expense of its rival claimant, Taiwan, and promote itself as a font of revolution and a leader of the Third World. Increasingly out-manoeuvred by the Soviet Union and its Cuban ally by the 1970s, China's influence in the region waned in the wake of the destructive impact of the Cultural Revolution and Mao Zedong's death. Maoism, however, and the cult of revolution, was to cast a long shadow in countries like Peru.

Two decades later, China's radical shift towards market liberalism engineered a dramatic transformation in its domestic economy and set it on the road to becoming a leading economic power. These changing circumstances at home accelerated its growing integration into global value chains and, with that, a search for vital resources and new markets. Latin America and the Caribbean were to be an ideal target for this emerging economic behemoth, Global China.

China's Cold War in Latin America

China's involvement in Latin America during the Cold War has been curiously neglected by historians, politicians and publics alike. Until recently, it was possible to read leading scholarship on Chinese foreign policy that said virtually nothing about China-Latin America relations during this period.[1] In contemporary political circles, beyond an approving invocation of Beijing's anti-imperialist credentials by the Bolivarist leaders in Venezuela and others on the Left, the role that China played in the Cold War is conveniently forgotten by the business-minded politicians of today.

And yet, closer analysis demonstrates that for a time China occupied an important part in the volatile struggles of the early Cold War in the region.

China's Cold War in Latin America revolved around three main themes: i) the continuing contestation between the People's Republic of China (PRC) and the Republic of China (ROC); ii) the divisive impact of the Sino-Soviet split on China's position in Latin America; and iii) Maoism's appeal to Latin America's 'New Left' which, when domesticated into local conditions, proved to be a powerfully influential political – and even revolutionary – force in some countries.

Diplomatic Recognition and the 'Two Chinas'

The civil war in China, pitting the Nationalist Party (Kuomintang or KMT[2]) against the Communist Party of China (CPC), profoundly shaped China's conduct during the Cold War. Notwithstanding their agreement to combat the invading Japanese in the 1930s, the CPC's triumphant ousting of the KMT and the establishment of the People's Republic of China in October 1949 was followed by extensive diplomatic battles over official recognition.

In fact, political competition between the KMT and the CPC was itself embedded in an even older, time-bound tradition of diaspora politics in Latin America and the Caribbean. From the dawn of the twentieth century, overseas Chinese communities were entrenched in the domestic politics of China, serving alternatively as a refuge for dissidents, a supplier of recruits and a source of funding. For instance, Sun Yat-sen, the 'father' of China's republic, toured the Chinese diaspora communities in the Hawaii territory, California and Japan to spread awareness of republican ideas, win backing for the patriotic campaign to overthrow the Imperial court and eventually to raise funds for the Nationalist Party.[3] As the Chinese civil war raged at home, benevolent societies amongst overseas Chinese communities – including those in Latin America and the Caribbean – came to represent different factions and tendencies in the political struggle between the KMT and the CPC.[4]

This carried on after 1949 in the form of diplomatic contestation between the People's Republic of China (PRC, or China) and the Republic of China (ROC, or Taiwan). The United Front strategies of the Communist Party during the Cold War sought to identify and align with like-minded political parties in Latin America, connections with whom could undergird broader forms of cooperation. Winning Latin American support for ousting the ROC from the UN Security Council seat remained, however, the critical objective.[5]

For instance, in October 1952 twelve countries from Latin America and the Caribbean had an early encounter with the PRC when 110 delegates from the region were sent to attend the Asian and Pacific Regions Peace Conference in Beijing. None of these countries had recognized the PRC diplomatically, but were keen to learn more about China, particularly as it was a generous invitation by Beijing.⁶ The Conference is an early example of cultural diplomacy by the PRC to promote its agenda and ideas. Bilateral relations were developed through organizations like the Chile-China Cultural Association founded in 1952, following on a sponsored visit of Chilean poet Pablo Neruda.⁷ A number of illustrious visitors from Chile followed, notably Salvador Allende in 1954.⁸ He was key in fostering unofficiual ties between the PRC and Chile untile the establishment of formal diplomatic relations in 1970.⁹

This agenda-seeking early recognition continued and in 1954 the PRC created the Chinese People's Association for Friendship with Foreign Countries (CPAFFC), a putatively unofficial agency 'to carry out foreign relations work ... [and to] serve as a link in the friendly relations between the Chinese people and ... the world'.¹⁰ The work of CPAFFC was effective all over the world because it enabled China to promote its official agenda in a manner that did not generate friction in host countries lacking formal diplomatic recognition with the PRC. Six years after its creation, CPAFFC sponsored the inauguration of the China-Latin America and Caribbean Friendship Association (CHILAC) on 6 March 1960.¹¹ During this period, in the absence of formal diplomatic ties, China's Xinhua News Agency offices opened in Latin American countries, which would often serve as the first informal point of contact between locals and Chinese officials.¹²

At this point not a single country in Latin America and the Caribbean recognized the PRC diplomatically, a situation that was to change on 28 September 1960, when Cuba became the first country in the region to recognize Beijing. Subsequent years saw the founding of chapters in almost every Latin American country, and these Friendship Associations played an important role in driving private and public sector interest toward Beijing, and while not the only factor, certainly, an important one in Beijing's winning diplomatic recognition of many countries in the region.¹³

It is important to note that, while diplomatic contestation predominated as a driver of policy in China during the revolutionary phase, Beijing concurrently pursued economic engagement with the region. The establishment of the China Council for the Promotion of International Trade in 1952 was designed to foster trade ties with countries with whom Beijing did not have diplomatic relations.¹⁴ China's first trade agreement involving copper and nitrates was signed with Chile that same year while trade deals were secured with Mexico and Argentina in subsequent years. Two-way trade between China and Latin America grew from $1.9 million in 1950 to a peak of $475.7 million in 1975.

Following the surprise summit between US President Richard Nixon and Mao Zedong in 1972 and the switch to formal diplomatic recognition by Washington in 1979, many Latin American countries changed their own bilateral diplomatic ties to the PRC. By the end of the Cold War, despite a small but steady accretion of diplomatic victories by Beijing, Latin American and Caribbean states remained the largest regional stronghold of Taiwan's formal diplomatic representation in the world.

The Sino-Soviet Split and Latin America

The Sino-Soviet split was another area that came to define China's foreign policy relationship with Latin American countries and their political parties during the Cold War.[15] Mao Zedong, China's paramount leader and architect of the CPC's guerrilla struggle, became increasingly dissatisfied with Soviet leadership of the communist bloc under Nikita Khrushchev whose anti-Stalinist position at home and ambivalent support for China's nuclear programme had opened up a rift between the two allies.[16] This came to a head with Moscow's conduct over the Cuban missile crisis in 1962, viewed by Beijing as a dangerous capitulation by Khrushchev, and encouraged Mao to redouble his efforts to forge China's own path to global leadership with like-minded developing countries.

Cuba, despite being an important ally for the Soviet Union in the region, had steadily closer ties with China in the years following the opening of an embassy in 1960. After October 1962, Castro became a frequent visitor to the Chinese embassy and for a time, Chinese commitments to greater economic assistance and trade at favourable non-market rates were making inroads into the staunch Soviet ally.[17] Indeed, by 1964 China had provided a $60 million loan to Havana on concessional terms to Cuba while trade (mainly in rice and sugar) grew to a peak of $224 million in 1965.[18] At the same time, Castro was being courted by Moscow (in the aftermath of Khrushchev's ousting), whose willingness to provide extensive economic assistance to an increasingly bereft Cuban economy proved to be an important lure. Some signs, however, soon emerged that suggested that Havana's newfound friendship with Beijing was in trouble. For instance, fifty days of negotiations with Beijing for a full reinstatement of annual rice shipments to Cuba in late 1964, which had been suspended due to an alleged shortage, went nowhere.[19] China's continual distribution of pro-China propaganda on the island too was increasingly a matter of dispute with the Cuban government.

By January 1966, ties between Cuba and China had deteriorated to the point where Castro, speaking before six hundred delegates from eighty-one countries at the all-important Tricontinental Conference held in Havana, openly criticized China's diminishing assistance to Cuba. In March the same year, Castro launched another stinging public attack on China for its role in undermining international solidarity against Western imperialism and likening Mao to a 'senile idiot'.[20] The break with China was complete and mutual estrangement was to last until the 1990s.

Thereafter, the growing proximity between the Soviet Union and Cuba, underwritten by flourishing economic and military aid from Moscow since 1965, proved over the long term to be critical to Soviet success in winning over allies in Latin America. Facilitating this process was the newly elected Chilean President Salvador Allende who played an important part in reintegrating Cuba into a region still wary of Castro's revolutionary interventionism.[21] Allende, who had opened diplomatic ties with Beijing in 1970, negotiated hard to get Cuba's inclusion at the UNCTAD Conference held in Chile in 1971. Castro's vocal support for the Soviet Union while touting a revolutionary line – which, being at the outer edge of Moscow's official position on peace coexistence, bordered on criticism – helped sideline China's radical appeal to established communist parties in Latin America.[22] At the same time, Beijing's decision to maintain diplomatic relations with the military regime that overthrew Allende in 1973, following from the logic of Sino-Soviet conflict, did not sit well with the Latin American left.

Throughout this period, China continued its attempts to counter Soviet gains and win support amongst developing countries in Asia, Africa and Latin America. According to Mao's 'Three Worlds Theory' of international relations espoused at the time, these regions were natural allies of China against those of the two superpowers (first world) and industrialized economies like Japan, Canada and Europe (second world).[23] Deng Xiaoping's presentation of the Three Worlds theory at the Special Session on the New International Economic Order held at the UN General Assembly in New York in April 1974 underscored Beijing's bid for leadership of the 'Third World'. However, the disclosure that China supported an armed faction in the Angolan civil war in 1975–1976 which itself was underwritten by the American CIA and apartheid South Africa's military, at the same time that over thirty thousand Cuban troops and Soviet advisers were backing the governing MPLA, did untold damage to Chinese revolutionary credentials in Latin America and beyond. With the death of Mao in 1976 and Deng Xiaoping's shift towards the West and the focus on domestic development, China effectively withdrew from active political engagement in the politics of Latin America and the Caribbean.

Maoism and Latin American Revolutionaries

While Mao had died and China's policies increasingly aligned with the United States, the influence of Maoism lived on in parts of Latin America. This was particularly the case amongst leftist intellectuals and political activists, for whom Maoism and its focus on the revolutionary role of peasantry proved to have an enduring appeal. In this regard, the work of organizations like the aforementioned CHILAC along with sponsored visits for everyone from politicians to cultural artists exercised considerable influence on Latin American politics at home. Indeed, one study at the time suggests that at least 1,500 Latin Americans were invited to China to take part in formal visits, training seminars and exchange programmes between 1959 and 1969 (and more certainly in the years up to 1976).[24]

The impact of these visits was evident in the party politics playing out across the region. As one scholar says, 'Beijing had been very active in creating Maoist splinter parties in Latin America, and the Moscow-oriented parties had spent much of the last five years (since 1960) fending off Chinese-inspired attacks.'[25] According to Rothwell:

> By 1963, the Chinese called on their international followers to break with parties dominated by supporters of the Soviet line. Already in 1959, the Chinese began to prepare the ground for this split by sponsoring training schools for foreign communists from the developing world that sought to propagate Chinese positions within the international communist movement.[26]

The results were seen in a fragmenting of the Left across Latin America in communist parties in Bolivia, Mexico, Peru and Chile.

In the late 1960s, students drawn to Maoism's radical vision expressed through the Cultural Revolution became another source of support for China's interests in the struggle for leadership of the international left.[27] Splinter factions within the local communist parties led by Maoist adherents emerged and broke off to form competing political parties that fought ideological battles that spilled over into violent skirmishes between activists. In some cases, Maoism was 'domesticated' – that is to say, it was adapted by its adherents to fit local conditions and contribute to local agendas – and in this way transformed into a powerful tool for political mobilization.[28]

In Mexico, for instance, communist party leader and union activist Vincente Lombardo Toledano visited Beijing as part of an international conference on trade unionism held in late 1949, only a few months after the founding of the PRC. His advocacy of China reflected his understanding of the aspirations and apparent success of its socialist development model while fellow Mexicans like Arturo Gámiz and Florencio Medrano drew inspiration from Mao's treatises on revolutionary warfare. Lombardo's activism took place largely within the confines of established national politics while Arturo Gámiz launched an ill-fated attack on military barracks in Chihuahua state. In Medrano's case, he broke off from mainstream leftist politics to form a revolutionary armed insurrection on the border of Oaxaca and Veracruz states starting in 1973 that lasted for five years.[29]

Undoubtedly, the most dramatic and thoroughgoing example of Maoist influence in Latin America was that of Abimael Guzmán and the *Sendero Luminoso* or 'Shining Path'. Originating in the Peruvian highlands of Ayacucho in the 1970s, under Guzmán's leadership the movement came to have operational cells across most of the rural communities in the country by the late 1980s. According to Rothwell:

> The influence of Chinese revolutionary politics in Peru did not come about spontaneously or somehow by chance. The top leadership of the Shining Path, and many other pro-Chinese communists from competing organizations, travelled to China and studied Maoism there. Not unlike Catholic priests taking special classes in Rome, in China they honed their ideology and developed a more consolidated, and more sophisticated, understanding of their mission. And they returned imbued with the authority of having studied in Beijing ... (A)s rival Maoist organizations emerged in the 1960s, they fought polemical battles with the ferocious zeal of rival inquisitors. What the Maoists forged in Peru, culminating in the Shining Path's insurrection of the 1980s and 1990s, was the product of strenuous effort.[30]

Guzmán was a secondary figure within the Peruvian Communist Party who, after two inspiring trips to China in 1965 and 1967, was deeply impressed by the crowds marshalled in support of the Cultural Revolution and the concomitant shattering of the CPC's bureaucratic apparatus in the service of idealism.[31] Back in Peru, he used his senior position at Ayacucho's Universidad Nacional de San Cristóbal de Huamanga (UNSCH) to build a network of revolutionary activists working in tandem with local communities which formed the backbone of the Shining Path. Academic faculty at UNSCH were frequent visitors to China in this period, with an estimated quarter of all 120 staff having undertaken official visits to the country, while Maoist organizations like 'Red Fatherland', fuelled by a steady stream of Chinese propaganda, were a dominant presence in the miners' and teachers' unions.[32] The Shining Path's 'Peoples War' was launched in 1980 and, though the revolutionaries soon lost much local support under the weight of security force crackdowns, the Shining Path's guerrilla war techniques enabled it to continue as a destabilizing force until its defeat in 1992 (see Chapter 3 for further details).

The End of China's Revolutionary Phase

While the onset of the Cultural Revolution in 1966 inspired intellectuals and student activists in Latin America, by 1969 the battle between Mao's youthful Red Guards and the establishment over power was making the country virtually ungovernable. Armed clashes between the Chinese and Soviet militaries along their common border threatened the outbreak of war, including even the possibility of nuclear strikes.[33] The ongoing turmoil saw a further retrenchment of China's involvement abroad, with closure of Chinese embassies in many developing countries and, as the internal power struggle finally drew to a close in 1975, the reduction in already limited provisions for Chinese aid.[34] Mao's death the following year and the ascension of Deng Xiaoping as paramount leader marked the beginning of experimental market reforms that were to catalyse China's economic transformation over the next thirty years.

For Latin America and the Caribbean, this turning away from the ideological sources of engagement with China ushered in an era of relative quietude in relations. Deng Xiaoping's suspension of revolutionary activism abroad and the introduction of reformist economic policies at home brought about a deepening alignment with the West and, concurrently, an inward-looking focus within China. It would be another two decades before the region would again experience Chinese activism but this time of a very different kind.

China Goes Global

China's rapid domestic growth, built upon the gradualist application of market reforms in the four special economic zones and the agricultural sector in the early 1980s, paved the way for sustained double-digit growth and a rise in per capita income.[35] As the reforms (*gaige kaifang*) were extended across the country and into additional sectors, China's position as the manufacturing hub of a globalizing world economy became more dominant as did its accumulation of capital. Rapid growth and liberalization contributed to continuous socioeconomic improvements and, for some, the desire for further opening of the political process.

The onset of peaceful protests by university students in 1988, culminating in the state's crackdown at Tiananmen Square in June 1989, sent a shockwave across China and the world. The imposition of sanctions by Western governments produced strenuous debate within the CPC as to the direction of economic policy and its impact on nascent political liberalization, seemingly paralyzing the process for a time. The ousting of Zhao Ziyang in particular, General Secretary of the CPC and ardent reformist who had supported the students, seemed to signal that the period of liberalization was over. However, in early 1992, Deng Xiaoping undertook a widely publicized tour of the special economic zones in southern China and used this as a platform to call for a revival and intensification of economic reforms.[36]

The decision by Deng Xiaoping to 'double down' on the opening and reform policy in 1992, despite opposition from hardliners within the CPC still reeling from student protests at Tiananmen Square and the international backlash at their suppression, inspired a new phase of economic liberalization. The linchpin of Deng's policy would be a radical step: to lock in market liberalization through joining the newly formed World Trade Organization (WTO), a process that would demand comprehensive restructuring of the Chinese domestic economy to demonstrate adherence to the strict criteria required to become a member.[37] Moreover, and this increasingly preoccupied policymakers in Beijing, unrestricted opening of the domestic economy to foreign firms implied in full compliance to the WTO could potentially pave the way for powerful Western multinational corporations and financial interests to occupy a dominant position within China and effectively sideline nascent Chinese firms in their own domestic market.[38] The recent collapse of the Soviet Union and the predatory actions of Western governments and its businesses in rapidly dismantling the state sector as well as assuming key positions within the domestic economy provided salutary lessons for Chinese policymakers in this regard.

Careful planning, led by the National Development Reform Commission (NDRC), was recognized to be crucial to ensuring that China would be able to absorb and respond to the anticipated economic changes. While Chinese negotiators began what turned out to be a lengthy nine-year process of tough discussions with US counterparts on the exact terms of Chinese membership to the WTO, the NDRC led a comprehensive restructuring of the country's state-owned enterprises (SOEs) to prepare them for global competition at home and abroad.[39] With tens of thousands of SOEs in every sector and every region of the country employing hundreds of millions of Chinese workers the task before officials was monumental. Starting in 1992, the Chinese government began a process of going sector by sector to review and consolidate SOEs, weeding out the weakest actors and creating new organizational frameworks and mandates for their replacements. For instance, in the petroleum sector the Ministry of Petroleum was broken up into three state-owned companies, the China National Overseas Oil Company (CNNOC), China National Petroleum Company (CNPC) and Sinopec with different positions in the extraction, refinement and retail process within the sector.

The costs of this reformist push of breaking up and restructuring SOEs to Chinese society in the 1990s should not be underestimated. Over forty-five million jobs were cut, putting tens of millions out of work, forced to retire or having to seek employment in the emerging private business sector.[40] Moreover, these radical measures were accompanied by the winding down of social security benefits and access to free public services such as health care. What scholars have called the 'breaking of the iron rice bowl' represented a shock to ordinary Chinese and one that contributed to massive shifts in rural to urban migration.[41] At the same time, the opening up of opportunities for private entrepreneurship unleashed productive forces on the mainland which, when coupled to finance, management and knowledge from overseas Chinese investors, generated rapid if sometimes manic forms of production and capital accumulation that further accelerated growth.

Concurrently, the Chinese government introduced radical reforms to the state-owned financial sector in order to prepare it for a strategic role in this process. In 1994, the People's Bank of China was divided into the Bank of China, the China Export-Import Bank and the China Development Bank, gearing these last two institutions up to play a leading part in financing international trade expansion and infrastructure projects in external markets.[42] Offices were opened in faraway locations such as South Africa, France and Russia to facilitate and manage new lending. Oversight and decision-making structures were to evolve, with the Administration Commission (SASAC) initially over SOEs.[43] China's state-owned commercial banks, led by Industrial and Commercial Bank of China (ICBC), followed in the wake of the policy banks and the SOEs to seek business opportunities abroad. This was to set the stage for more assertive policies in this sector in the years to come, such as ICBC's take over of Standard Bank's office in Argentina in 2012 and China Construction Bank (CCB)'s purchase of Brazil's BicBanco in 2013.[44]

SOEs newly reconstituted into 'national champions' along sectoral lines aiming to compete with Western multinational corporations became the cornerstone of China's 'going out' (*zou chuqu*) strategy.[45] Utilizing finance from the policy banks, sometimes in combination with their own capital resources, SOEs sought out long-term access to energy, mineral and agricultural resources through competitive bidding, acquiring leases and outright purchases of resource companies around the world.

Underpinning strategic planning for SOEs was a series of studies commissioned by the State Council to assess China's current resources and projected needs as the economy grew. Updated every few years, the reports on the energy, mineral and agricultural sectors continually emphasized the necessity of having national strategic plans in light of scarcity, demand and international market volatility. For instance, successive reports on energy where officials outlined in 2008 the significance of that sector to its development aspirations, exuding confidence in SOEs' penetration of international markets to supply China's needs:

> China is currently the second [largest] energy producer and consumer in the world. The continuous growth of [domestic] energy supplies has provided important support for economic and social development. The rapid growth of energy consumption has created a broad development space for the world energy market. China has become an indispensable and important part of the global energy market and is playing an increasingly important and positive role in maintaining global energy security.[46]

By 2012, however, the sanguine tone in the report had been replaced by alarm:

> The energy security situation is grim. In recent years, (China's) energy dependence has increased rapidly, especially oil dependence from 32% in 2000 to 57% currently. The safety risk of oil maritime transportation has increased, and the necessity to secure cross-border oil and gas pipelines cannot be ignored. Price fluctuations in the international energy market make it more difficult to ensure domestic energy supply. The scale of energy reserves is small, and the emergency response capacity is relatively weak.[47]

The review of the mineral sector in 2008 reflected on the progress and continuing necessity of:

> Implement(ing) a strategic mineral reserve system to enhance the country's ability to respond to emergencies and resist challenges in the international market. Promot(ing) the establishment of mineral resource reserves for key resources such as petroleum, special coals, scarce coals, copper, chromium, manganese, tungsten, and rare earths.[48]

In 2016, the national report focused on the following issues:

> Due to the world's economic downturn, decrease in demand, energy restructuring, and the release of production capacity in light of high-intensity investment in the early stages, the global supply of mineral products is generally characterised by oversupply, and prices have fallen sharply. Domestic mineral prices are not competitive, mining enterprises generally face difficulties in operations, and there is a serious overcapacity in the coal, iron and steel, cement, and other sectors.[49]

Equivalent strategic planning documents in the agricultural sector in 2000 warned that:

> China's economy and society will certainly have greater development, and higher requirements will be put forward for the development of agriculture. With the increase in economic flows, the international competition for agricultural products will become increasingly fierce. All Party members must be aware that China's agricultural foundation is still not solid and cannot be relaxed at any time.[50]

The 2003 report elaborated upon strategies for expanding Chinese agri-industrial firms presence in overseas markets:

> The foreign trade development fund should promote the export of agricultural products, mainly to support enterprises in developing new products and technologies, open up international markets, participate in international certification, and support export-oriented production. Encourage and guide agricultural export processing enterprises to enter/be part of export processing trade zone.[51]

Fortified by this analysis of the changing conditions in these key sectors, coupled with industry assessments by individual SOEs and the state's imperative for high octane economic growth, the push to position Chinese firms abroad became doctrine. The wheels were set in motion for the great expansion of Global China beyond its boundaries and the familiar trading partners in the West.

China's 'Going Out' Policy and Latin America

China's entry into Latin American markets was propelled by two economic rationales that were reflected in the national planning strategy documents produced for key sectors.[52] The first trajectory was based on the search for resources and the second trajectory was driven by the search for markets.

The first policy imperative generated a drive into marginal sites or sectors long neglected by Western multinationals and financial institutions in the region while the second policy imperative sought out trade opportunities in lower- and middle-income economies in the region.

Concurrently, Beijing sought to employ economic statecraft to secure gains in other areas such as formal designation of China's status as a market economy, a condition tied to virtually all of its bilateral trade agreements. The acceptance of China's status as a market economy by Latin American countries (and by extension, other countries) was an important policy position of both symbolic and substantive value to Beijing. In the first instance, it had been agreed from the outset that China would be granted market economy status fifteen years after joining in 2001. Subsequent disputes over interpretation of the clause outlining this and how to measure adherence caused Western efforts to block China. Adding fuel to the fire, the US granted other non-market economies like Russia market economy status starting in 2003.[53]

Practically speaking, although the designation itself is open to interpretation, it nonetheless had been used by the US, Japan and the EU – as well as Brazil and Argentina – to penalize China through costly arbitration at the WTO. Behind their actions were fears that by achieving market economy status, China would be in a position to increase export volumes significantly, further skew trade balances with China's favour and in the process displace industrial production in these countries.[54] Gaining formal support for recognition of it as a market economy from a coalition of developing countries would strengthen pressure on Western governments to accept a single party-controlled economy as a peer and dilute the liberalizing principles underlying WTO membership.

Some of the earliest manifestations of China's new global expansion into regions like Latin America and the Caribbean were forays by SOEs in mining and oil operations. Behind some of the initiatives were contacts fostered at the Asia Pacific Economic Conference (APEC). Established in 1989, APEC is composed of leading industrialized economies like the US and Japan as well as a myriad of developing economies from around the Pacific Rim. APEC's annual summits attended by national leaders and top business officials were sites for opening up dialogues with Latin America's top economies and, as such, played an important part in exposing Chinese policy makers to the region.

The bold move by China's SOE Shougang to invest in Peru's mining sector in 1992 represents the earliest such effort and for a long time the largest investment abroad (see Chapter 3). China's pursuit of energy proved successful in Venezuela not the least because of the persistence of its leadership in seeking out Beijing from 2001 onwards (see Chapter 4). In 2005, Ecuador became the main site of oil exploration in South America by Chinese firms when China National Petroleum Company (CNPC) bought EnCana's Ecuadorian holdings from Canada. The trend continued and in 2012 Tiptop Energy (a subsidiary of Sinopec) also bought an important stake of the operations owned by Spanish firm Repsol.[55]

Efforts by Baosteel to secure a stake in Brazil a decade later were summarily turned down by Brazilian CVRD (later renamed Vale) before another more considered offer for a joint venture was put forward (see Chapter 5). Attempts to gain a foothold by Chinese SOEs to Chilean copper in 2005 were, however, stymied by regulatory regimes on environment and court action (see Chapter 3). One of China's leading port and harbour construction firms, China Harbour Engineering Company, approached the Jamaican government in 2013 with a mega-project that sought to reposition the island as a global transhipment hub in the Caribbean (see Chapter 6). Tackling entry into Latin American markets turned out to be tantalizing in its possibilities but complex in its operationalization.

Other manifestations of China's interest in the region for its own subsistence can be found in the agricultural sector. This interest is exemplified by Beijing's purchase of land in Latin America as long ago as 1996 when it bought 8,259 hectares for rice farming in Cuba.[56] Agricultural exports have not been as strong as mining and oil due to high tariffs on these products.[57] This trend, however, has slightly changed and China's imports of foodstuff from the region are on the increase. Soyabeans and soyameal make a very important component of Brazilian and Argentinian exports to China (see Chapter 3 and Chapter 4).[58]

Conclusion

As Manriquez and Alvarez remind us, 'China only fully engaged Latin America after the end of the Cold War'.[59] And yet there is, as this chapter demonstrates, strong evidence to show that China's involvement in Latin America and the Caribbean during the Cold War was both significant and consequential before the onset of its role as a global economic actor in the region. It was significant in that the diplomatic recognition contestation resulted in a regional bulwark of international support for the ebbing power of Taiwan, even with the loss of recognition in most of South America after 1972. It also brought the Sino-Soviet dispute for international leadership into the domain of local politics, dividing the Left, producing internecine conflict and weakening the Left's overall impact in domestic politics. Finally, Maoism itself was a source of inspiration for intellectuals and revolutionaries, contributing in the cases of Mexico and Peru to the development of guerrilla warfare, which for a time played a major part in destabilizing these countries.

Following the Cold War and in the wake of China's gradualist application of market economy reforms, another face of China was revealed to the region. Twenty years of rapid economic growth under the guidance of liberal reformists in the CPC had laid the foundation for an expansion into Latin American resource sectors and markets, led by its SOEs and underwritten by national policy banks. It was this 'Global China', awash with cash and brimming with confidence that was to lead another transformative phase in China-Latin America relations.

3

Chile, Peru and Argentina – Riding the Tiger

Chile and Peru, two very different countries, are at the forefront of the changing global realities in which China has played a central role over the past forty years. Their contrasting approaches to engaging China speak to the distinctive characteristics of their overall approach to globalization and to managing their national resource endowment, while at the same time reflecting the changing political dynamics within both countries. Conversely, Argentina's successive financial crises belie its growing economic significance for China and Argentine elite efforts to leverage Chinese financial resources to serve their interests. Unpacking the sources driving foreign and development policy in Santiago, Lima and Buenos Aires, coupled with the challenges facing Chinese policymakers and state-owned enterprises operating in these new environments, offers insights into the strategic choices made and experiences undergone in pursuing closer ties with China.

Chile

Chile's relationship with China reflects its determination to align its foreign and economic policies within the overarching structures of globalization. This fundamentally pragmatic, commercially minded and non-ideological approach to international relations in some ways echoes Beijing's own evolution from an ideologically driven foreign and economic policy under Mao to the gradualist market reforms crafted by Deng Xiaoping and his successors. It also coheres with Chile's long-standing self-image as a Pacific power, one with strong roots in the navy, trade and the Chilean elites stretching back to the mid-nineteenth century.[1] The result can be measured by a number of Chilean achievements as a 'first mover' in reaching out to Beijing. At the same time, some early indicators of the limitations and barriers to deepening economic ties between the two countries are also visible.

History and Diplomacy

Official diplomatic relations between Chile and the People's Republic of China began in December 1970, shortly after the election of leftist president Salvador Allende.[2] This built on long-standing relations between the Chilean Communist Party and the Chilean Socialist Party, including the opening of a Chile–China Cultural Association in Santiago in 1952 to promote 'people to people' relations and in that capacity to organize visits and study tours to China.[3] Allende himself spent two months in China in 1954, and five weeks in 1963, expressing admiration for Mao's achievements.[4] Beijing provided Chile $63 million in export credits in 1963 – China's second largest financial disbursement to a Latin American country (Cuba being the first)[5] – followed by negotiations over further loans which were cut short by the 1973 coup. Trade, principally in copper, commenced in earnest after 1965 with the opening of a commercial office in Chile, only to be effectively shut down by the disruptive impact of the Cultural Revolution.[6] Formal diplomatic recognition followed in the wake of Allende's election as leader of a coalition of progressive parties, flourishing despite periodic misgivings expressed by Beijing as to the role of its rival, Moscow, with numerous delegations exchanged and their revived mutual economic interests given considerable media attention in China.[7]

Following the military coup that ousted Allende in September 1973, Beijing opted to maintain diplomatic ties, unlike most communist governments in the Cold War period, following on US President Richard Nixon's opening of diplomatic links with China in 1972. Beijing's tacit recognition of the military regime in Santiago, even as far as denying asylum to Chilean leftists, paved the way for continuing diplomatic relations with General Augusto Pinochet.[8] Thereafter, only consistent diplomatic exchanges defined the relationship in its first two decades, with China's nascent experiment in capitalism preoccupying its leadership at home and the Chilean dictatorship's enthusiastic application of the Chicago School's economic prescriptions consuming its attention. Indeed, despite high-profile visits like Chinese President Yang Shankun's in 1990 under Patricio Aylwin's government, and General Pinochet's two visits as Commander-in-Chief of the Army in 1993 and 1997, there was little concrete to show for the two countries except trade in copper and demonstrable good will.[9]

Pinochet's departure from office in 1990 brought about no significant change in relations, in keeping with the pragmatic tenets that have guided Chilean foreign policy; however, within ten years both sides saw opportunities in expanding economic ties. Behind this new enthusiasm was the domestic development achieved by both countries, with Beijing's state-directed policy of 'opening and reform' successfully transforming China into the world's leading manufacturer and exporter in search of new resources and markets. For its part, the Chilean state's support under Pinochet for capitalism through mechanisms like soft loans and other policy incentives, however underplayed in the literature, continued and was crucial to its economic success.[10] In particular, the cultivation of entrepreneurs – 'empresarios' – was transformative, creating a new elite capable of navigating the challenges of expanding exports beyond Chile's natural resources base. The result was evident: Chile's economy grew and diversified over time, paving the way for its formal recognition by the OECD as a fully developed economy in 2010, and coinciding with a search for new markets and investment opportunities across the Pacific.

The result was reflected in intensifying diplomatic exchanges, beginning with President Jiang Zemin's tour of South America in 2001, which included Chile, followed by President Ricardo Lagos's visit to Beijing the same year. Out of this exchange came negotiations leading to a formal 'Cooperative Partnership', signed during President Hu Jintao's visit to Chile in 2004, which laid the foundation for a free trade agreement. Chile's leading position in China's relations with Latin America is evident in other areas as well, with President Michelle Bachelet invited to China's flagship 'Boao Asia Forum' in 2008.[11] Annual visits by members of the Chilean National Assembly deepened the exposure of lesser politicians to China, while from 1990 to 2013 Chile hosted a succession of Chinese leaders on nearly an annual basis.[12]

The Chileans' sense of their importance to Beijing in the regional context turned out to be misplaced, however. Neither had their China market-access dreams been realized.[13] For one former foreign minister, the fact that the Chinese president did not even visit Chile on his last two regional tours signalled that 'we've lost sight of the strategic importance of China' and, consequently, that they needed to redouble efforts to attract Beijing's attention.[14] Given the US summary withdrawal from the Trans-Pacific Partnership (TPP) early in the Trump administration, and Chilean determination to work with other Asia-Pacific states for the TPP's passage, a reset of ties with Beijing became necessary. Arguably, these factors influenced President Bachelet's decision to participate in the BRI Summit in May 2017 as one of only two Latin American leaders, as a way of signalling the country's continuing interest in strengthening relations with China.

Befitting the long-standing role of the military in Chile's government, bilateral ties between the armed forces were cordial throughout this period. Pinochet, under the auspices of his role as president until 1990, and as head of the military until 1998, forged a closer relationship than what would have been expected, given the ideological differences that divided China and Chile in that period.

Expanded Chile-China military cooperation was under discussion when the respective ministers of defence held talks in Beijing in 2011.[15] Regular naval visits had commenced as early as 1972 with the Chilean tall ship and training vessel *Esmeralda* docking at the port of Shanghai, while the Chinese navy made a tour of the Pacific states in 1997.[16] Training programmes, involving middle-ranking Chilean officers being selected and sent to China, were conducted periodically.

Given the long-standing relationship between Chile and China, one that developed substantively under the leadership of the Chilean armed forces, it would be no surprise if close military cooperation ensued; however, despite frequent exchanges of personnel and the participation of Chilean officers in training programmes administered by the Defense Studies Institute in Changping upwards of twice a year since 2005, the relationship remains cordial but not close.[17] This is particularly evident when comparing Chile's ties with the US or Britain, where frequent exchanges and training are the norm, bolstered by the sale of significant armaments to Chile. Interestingly, in a pattern that was to be repeated across the Latin American and Caribbean region, China's military exchanges and training programmes led to meetings at the behest of Chinese authorities with their arms manufacturers. According to one former foreign minister, Chilean officials concluded that this was outside their interests and they refused.[18] The fixed budget allocation to the Chilean military of 10 per cent of copper sales by the state-owned mining company Codelco has allowed it to continue to make high-quality weapons purchases from the US and Europe.[19]

Beyond the diplomatic and commercial ties outlined here, China's involvement in Chile's national educational system has expanded over time, with Chile hosting two Confucius Centres and Mandarin becoming one of the most popular languages to study in the school system.[20] Tourism is picking up as nearly twenty-three thousand Chinese tourists visited Chile in 2016.[21]

Economic Ties

The commencement of diplomatic relations in 1971 coincided with that of trade relations, initially peaking at $110 million in 1974 – which represented 38 per cent of China's total trade with Latin America at the time – but was only fully restored to this level after 1980.[22] China's imports of copper kept bilateral trade with Chile near the top of its balance sheet in Latin America until the dawn of the 1990s, when commercial trade was expanded to other parts of the region. Behind this prominence was China's growing demand for Chilean mineral resources, as it consumed over 40 per cent of the world's copper, while Chile was the third-largest producer of copper in the world.

The most defining feature of Chile's relationship with China to date, however, remains the decision to negotiate a Free Trade Agreement (FTA). This initiative came against the backdrop of Chilean negotiations to join the North American Free Trade Agreement (NAFTA), which started in 1994 and ultimately failed to materialize, though Chile and the US did sign an FTA in 2003; not to mention FTAs with Canada in 1996, Mexico in 1998 and South Korea in 2003. Initiated by the Chinese, the Chilean government responded by establishing a negotiating team with the mandate to secure for Chilean exports and FDI preferential access to the growing Chinese market in exchange for Chinese goods and, potentially, enhanced investment.

Underlying the Chinese interest in an FTA was a strategy of negotiating with small but sophisticated economies like Chile and New Zealand as a way of gaining experience in negotiating bilateral FTAs.[23] This built upon China's accession to the World Trade Organization (WTO) in 2001 and was in keeping with the policy of cautious learning to integrate into the liberal trading system that had characterized the Chinese approach to WTO negotiations from the outset. For Santiago, the interest in developing better market access to Asia-Pacific economies had already impelled it to collaborate with South Korea in negotiating an FTA as early as 2004; which had been followed up by intensive negotiations for an FTA with the US. In this respect, the FTA with China should be understood from the Chilean perspective as part of a broader outreach to the dynamic economies of the Asia-Pacific and, given the history of well-established relations, an opportunity to 'cash in' on Chile's 'first mover' advantage with China.

After intense negotiations, the Chile-China FTA was signed in November 2005, coming into force in October 2006. The agreement included tariff reductions on nearly ten thousand Chilean products, with immediate effect or phased-in at five or ten years in some cases, and provided detailed arrangements on matters like market access, trade barriers, phytosanitary rules and related measures.[24] This phased-in, zero-duty treatment eventually covered 97 per cent of all Chilean products. China's duty-free products covered a wide range of consumer goods as well as electronics, machinery and related items.

While innovative at the time, the FTA was framed within WTO rules and, as such, it left significant gaps in areas like services and investment. In particular, unregulated investment in the state-dominated extractive sector, a key export earner for the Chilean economy, was kept out of the agreement by design. The Chinese negotiators had pressed their Chilean counterparts to include this in the FTA but, according to a source from the Chilean negotiating team, Santiago was unwilling to open that critical sector to outside investors, and managed to convince the Chinese that there could be a separate agreement negotiated in the future. A supplementary agreement on services was indeed signed in 2008, and a further amendment on investment regulations was signed in 2012, but notably remained outside of the bilateral trade framework.

The impact of the FTA in Chile could be measured almost immediately, with total trade increasing from $8 billion in 2005 to $16.6 billion in 2008.[25] By 2010, total trade between the two countries had gone up to $32.4 billion.[26] Recent figures from 2019 still indicate an uptrend ($39.12 billion) where 32.39 per cent of all of Chilean exports went to the Chinese market.[27] With China as its top trading partner since 2009, the principal concern of the Chilean government has been to diversify exports beyond metals and minerals.[28] Overall, Chilean exports to China are still dominated by metals and mineral resources. In 2019, these resources amounted to 75 per cent of all the exports (copper being at the very top).[29] By contrast, Chinese exports are largely valued-added consumer goods, which have come to occupy a growing share of the consumer market in Chile.

Nevertheless, Chilean exports to China have diversified particularly within its agro-industrial sector. A good example of this is the success of the Chilean wine industry, which in capturing a significant market share of China's imports of wine has been notable. In 2000 $4.27 million worth of Chilean wine was imported to China, taking 10.13 per cent of the Chinese domestic market; by 2017 this had risen to 15 per cent.[30] Chile is now the second largest exporter of wine to China (after France).[31]

Other Chilean agricultural products like cherries, which have become a favourite for Chinese consumers during the Spring Festival celebrations,[32] have fared likewise; indeed, 80 per cent of Chile's production is exported to China. In 2016, Chile became the top fruit exporter to China 'by value (one out of every four fruits imported by China hails from Chile)'.[33] This seems to point the way to an area of comparative advantage for Chile, that is, agricultural production, and the central effort is now to ensure ever higher value-added products are being sold on to the Chinese market.[34]

But Chile's experience has also been marked by a distinctive deterioration in its domestic production of a range of manufactured goods and services. In textiles and apparel, for instance, Chinese imports had displaced 90 per cent of local production by 2011.[35] This was a far cry from the expected 'consolidation of Chile as [China's] productive business platform to South America', but was more that of a logistics hub en route to other Latin American markets.[36] The degree of integration into global value chains, as expressed in Chile's linkages to the Chinese economy at that time, represents the dominant role that copper plays in the production cycle in China. Studies undertaken in 2016 show that mining and base metal exports made up over 60 per cent of Chile's domestic content in Chinese exports by 2011, while during the same period Chilean supply to the services sector actually dropped from 35 per cent to 24 per cent.[37] This echoed the experience of most other Latin American economies engaged in substantive trade with China and, as such, it is a setback to these countries' development aspirations.

Chinese Firms in Chile, Chilean Firms in China

Chile's low corporate tax rate and open economy, coupled with its globally recognized role as a standard-bearer on financial accountability, has made it an attractive destination for foreign investors. One of the main expectations in top Chilean government and business circles was that the strengthening of bilateral economic ties would funnel Chinese FDI into Chile and vice versa.[38] In 2010 this expectation had yet to be realized, with only $685 million invested by Chinese firms in Chile and $212 million by Chilean firms in China[39] – at a time (2003–2016) when the Chinese were investing $71 billion in Brazil (sinking $17 billion in 2010 alone) and $18 billion in Peru. Chile received only $3 billion in Chinese FDI over the same period.[40] Mining is a sector that contributed anywhere from 12 per cent to 20 per cent of Chile's total earnings between 2006 and 2016.[41] The experience of Chinese firms attempting to invest in the Chilean mining sector in 2010 proved to be unsettling for both sides, as indicated in the section below, and produced a more cautious approach to investment. The experiences of Chinese state-owned enterprises in the Chilean mining sector, and Chilean firms seeking more production advantages and market opportunities in China, speak to the stagnation gradually settling over this sector in the economic relationship.

In 2005 the Chinese SOE Minmetals purchased a Chilean mining concession held by state-owned Codelco in the northern Antofagasto desert region, announcing it would fund the development of an existing open-cast Gaby mine to the tune of $500 million.[42] Under pressure from the trade unions, the Chilean government stopped Minmetals from exercising an option to buy the Gaby mine when it was disclosed that the agreement had involving fixing 5 per cent of copper exports at below market rates over a fifteen-year period.[43] Another firm, Hebei Wenfeng, found its plans to mine in Atacama, along with constructing transport infrastructure and port facilities on the coast, substantively delayed by environmental regulations.

While China's first forays into the Chilean market were encountering difficulties, Chilean firms were attempting to open up business in China. The Chilean company involved in the production of copper products set up a factory in China but within a year of starting production, the Chilean management noticed the disappearance of key inventory items and, before long, a local factory had sprung up producing virtually the same products at lower cost.⁴⁴ The Chileans decided to shut down their factory. While most major Chilean firms have offices in Beijing, the expectation that they would use this as a platform to establish local production facilities has been blunted by such experiences.

A notably different experience was that of Luis Schmidt, who combined entrepreneurial flair with his simultaneous tenure as ambassador to China and head of the Chilean Agricultural Association. With the support of the Foreign Minister, and bolstered by his own knowledge of the wine industry, Schmidt became a promoter of Chilean products in Chinese markets.⁴⁵ His personal role as a business figure played a part in his promotion of wine – he even went so far as to establish a small demonstration vineyard outside Beijing – as well as other Chilean agricultural products like cherries.⁴⁶ He noted that Chinese tastes in 1991, when he first visited the country, had changed dramatically, and as a result of this Chilean wine producers have been able to take advantage of that changing demand.⁴⁷

Renegotiating and Extending the FTA

This trend accelerated with the commencement of the updated amendment to the original FTA in March 2019. Initiated in 2016, the three rounds of negotiation took only a year and were designed to build on prior amendments in 2008 on trade and 2012 on services.⁴⁸ The final agreement provided Chinese investors with access to forty formerly excluded sectors, including construction and transportation, while Chile was allowed to set up distribution networks and legal services in China.⁴⁹ This opened up a new phase in China-Chile economic ties as Chinese firms began to look more closely at investment opportunities in these sectors.

Despite periodic setbacks to Chinese SOEs in Chile's resource sector, Minmetals revived its interest in the copper sector and launched negotiations in 2018 for a three-year deal to import sixty thousand tonnes of copper worth $900 million which was signed off in 2019.⁵⁰ Another firm, Tianqi Lithium, purchased a 24 per cent stake in Chilean fertilizer-maker *Sociedad Química y Minera de Chile* (SQM) from a Canadian firm for $4.1 billion in 2018.⁵¹ Initially blocked, first by the Chilean development agency, the Corporation for the Promotion of Production (Corfo), and then by Chilean shareholders who feared Tianqi would access strategic technology, the eventual purchase has enabled Tianqi to control 70 per cent of global lithium resources through its worldwide holdings.⁵² With demand for lithium batteries – used in electric vehicles – expected to grow exponentially, China was clearly positioning itself to lead in green technology. In a display of small-state agency, the Chilean government had insisted that firms tendering for a share in SQM must address the need for local production in the processing of lithium extracted under this deal and set up a special centre for energy production in Antofagasta in conjunction with Canadian firm Albemarle.[53]

In the telecoms sector, China's signature global company Huawei won the contract to build a submarine fibre-optic cable in the southern tip of Chile in 2017, while its retail position in the Chilean cellular phone market continued to expand. In September 2019 Huawei opened a data centre, declaring that Chile would be its gateway to the Latin American region.[54] Competitors in Europe and the US worried that this could pave the way for an Asian-Latin American trans-oceanic submarine fibre-optic cable linking the Asian mainland via China and via Chile to the rest of Latin America. In the end it was Japan that actually won that contract.[55]

And in the infrastructure sector, China Railway Group and two local companies put forward a proposal to build a high-speed railway between Santiago and Valparaíso. Blocked in January 2018 by the Ministry of Transportation, the proposal was revived under the new president, Sebastian Piñera, a few months later.[56] A Chinese firm won the bid for the construction of stations on the capital's metro while China Harbour Engineering Company secured contracts worth $210 million to expand the ports of San Antonio and San Juan.

There is no doubt that the renegotiated terms contained within the FTA played an important part in focusing Chinese interest in inward investment into Chile. Coupled with the Piñera government's decision to commit $2 billion to upgrading and expanding Chile's infrastructure over the next five years, these policy initiatives paved the way for greater Chinese involvement in the Chilean economy.[57]

Peru

Peru's contemporary position as China's gateway to the South American hinterland, symbolized by the planned route of the Trans-Oceanic Railway, an infrastructure project linking Brazil to the Peruvian port of Callao on the Pacific, had seemed to many Peruvians to have secured its special status within the constellation of top Chinese trading partners.[58] As a recipient of one of China's first investments in the region, the purchase of a debilitated iron ore mine by Shougang in Marcona in 1992, the Peruvian experience is in many ways indicative of the advantages of adopting a gradualist approach to developing closer ties with China. Additional investments in the mining sector, flowing in part from the FTA with China in 2009, coupled with infrastructure loans and expanding retail trade, signalled deepening bilateral economic ties. Yet the rising friction Marcona generated in the local community as more and more environmental, trade union and community activists criticized the company's conduct, and subsequent reactions by the Chinese government and firms, illustrate the challenges that emerge in this process.[59] Finally, the ongoing debates in Peru on the opportunities and consequences of greater Chinese involvement provide insight into the complexities of policy formulation that face local governments, particularly the impact on institutions and local politics.

History and Diplomacy

In terms of historical engagement with China, Peru ranks amongst a handful of countries in Latin America with a substantive and rooted Chinese community. Although there was a small 'Chinese' presence – more likely a mix of Asians, including Chinese – during the colonial period, it was in the mid-nineteenth century when Chinese labourers were recruited to work in agriculture, the guano trade and infrastructure projects like railways that this expanded into a full-fledged community.[60] Hailing primarily from Canton (Guangdong), men and later women settled in Lima, so that by 1883 the outlines of a 'Barrio Chino' had emerged in the capital city.[61] What followed was the founding of several Chinese associations and the first of many Chinese newspapers, along with popular retail establishments like *La Corporación Wong* and *La Corporación Yichang*.[62]

Peru opened official ties with Imperial China in 1875, motivated by the need for Peruvian officials to manage unrestricted migration from China. Persecution of Chinese in Peru followed an uprising by Chinese labourers working along the disputed southern border with Chile, and the incorporation of a Chinese battalion into the Chilean army during the War of the Pacific (1879–1884) between Peru and Chile.

After the fall of the Qing Dynasty, relations were re-established in 1911 with the Republic of China but were largely dormant due to continuing political strife in China up to the Japanese invasion of Manchuria. The politics of the Cold War had only a modest impact on Peruvian-Chinese relations, and consisted primarily of Lima's diplomatic censure of Beijing's actions at the UN on issues like the Korean War and the Sino-Indian border conflict. China's first declaration of an interest in Peruvian natural resources dates back to the CPC's solidarity with local leftist parties' calls for nationalization of its oil industry in the late 1950s.[63] Peru and the People's Republic of China negotiated a series of commercial agreements in 1964, 1965 and 1969 which marked the beginning of a modest bilateral commercial exchange.[64] Talks between Lima and Beijing on diplomatic recognition began in April 1971, anticipating the forthcoming switch at the UN, and culminated in formal recognition of the People's Republic of China on 2 November 1971.[65]

A succession of military regimes and economic crises in Peru followed, notable for the stability of diplomatic ties with Beijing for the duration (but without significant economic engagement). Indeed, throughout the Cold War, Peru's foreign policy abroad and economic policy at home swung wildly from seeking FDI and adopting open market policies under civilian President Fernando Belaúnde in the 1960s to General Juan Velasco's military regime with its agrarian reforms and nationalization policies (degenerating into unbridled authoritarianism), and many variations in between.[66] It was President Alberto Fujimori who finally put Peru's domestic development policy in line with wholesale accession to neo-liberalism, entailing tough macroeconomic stabilization policies that caused wrenching social dislocations. Peru negotiated write-offs and restructuring of its 'foreign-debt obligations by some $9.4 billion, more than a third of the total owed to foreign creditors',[67] and gradually macroeconomic stabilization was rewarded with improved growth and investment.[68] On the other hand, Fujimori was beset by internal security problems, which a Maoist insurgency and powerful narco-traffickers aggravated. In the end, he mobilized the military and suspended the constitution in 1992, which made the country a pariah in the region.[69]

The insurgency by the self-styled Maoist revolutionary movement *Sendero Luminoso* ('Shining Path'), based in the impoverished communities of the Andean highlands, instigated more than a decade of violence in the country. As outlined in Chapter 2, the leadership took inspiration from Mao's ideas and strategy of peasant revolution, demonstrating the enduring and quixotic attraction of 'revolutionary China' to Latin Americans of the Left.[70] The Fujimori government's aggressive embrace of neo-liberalism, combined with the military's harsh counter-insurgency strategy costing more than fifteen thousand lives, turned the tide by 1994.

Only after Fujimori was ousted and democracy restored with Alejandro Toledo's accession to power in 2001 did Peru actually complete aligning its development strategy, domestic political system and foreign policy to the prevailing unipolar, neo-liberal international system.[71] This intertwining of international with national interests, a manifestation of Peru's middle-power foreign policy activism, resulted in its growing participation in an array of regional and multilateral economic initiatives. With the primary impetus being to embolden Latin Americans in their international negotiations, Peru began as early as the 1990s to renew its call – a retread of the 1968 Andean

Pact, but this time discredited by Fujimori's *coup* – on the Andean states to negotiate common positions on trade and investment so as to strategically link these to Washington's transnational security concerns over issues like drug cartels.[72]

This period coincided with the opening of the Peruvian economy to global investment and, incidentally, greater exposure to China through regional bodies like the Asia-Pacific Economic Community (APEC) set up in 1989.[73] Though no formal 'China strategy' guided Peruvian foreign policy, it was nonetheless apparent that an evolving understanding of the country's interests vis-à-vis China was shared in policymaking circles over the next couple of decades.[74] This centred on the growing awareness of the impact of globalization on Peru that followed its promotion to the WTO in 1998 (having been a GATT member since 1951) and the new regionalism emerging through institutions such as APEC.

Peruvian diplomacy took a more prominent role in promoting liberal trade and investment policies internationally, underscored by Lima's hosting the APEC Summit in 2008 in the shadow of the global financial crisis.[75] The creation of the Pacific Alliance in 2011, which aimed to integrate the economic policies of Peru, Chile, Colombia and Mexico in order to promote regional development via private sector-led pragmatic convergence, ensued.[76] Ironically, this forthright commitment to consolidating the liberal international order, expressed by the Peruvian government at the 2008 APEC Summit, came at this turning point, which signalled China's arrival as a newly assertive economic giant on the global stage.

After the conclusion of the 2009 FTA, China's designation of Peru as a 'Comprehensive Strategic Partner' in 2013 reflected the strengthening bilateral ties, but also the ambitions Beijing had for this particular relationship. Eleven bilateral agreements were signed as part of Beijing's new designation of Peru as a strategic partner, including commitments to cooperate at ministerial levels in agriculture, science and technology, and education.[77] Anxious to expand ties with Beijing, President Pedro Pablo Kuczynski held talks with Xi Jinping in the Chinese capital in November 2016 aimed at 'optimizing' their FTA, a process that evolved into extended negotiations.[78]

With closer ties came efforts to enhance joint military cooperation between the two countries' armed forces. A tour organized for senior officials in the Peruvian Ministry of Defence to meet counterparts in China's PLA and PLAN in Changping left Peruvians with the impression that Chinese military equipment was essentially 'copies of Russian material'.[79] Blatant overtures to induce the Peruvian delegation to deal with Chinese arms manufacturers backfired when the Peruvians took offence at this breach of protocol.[80]

An area of growing concern for all Peruvians was a rise in a host of illegal activities by the Chinese, from undocumented migration to illegal fishing and other forms of exploitation of resources.[81] According to one source in the Peruvian military, the Chinese triads had become heavily involved in human trafficking and illegal migration from southern China to Peru, echoing government worries from more than a century ago.[82]

Trade and Investment

Peru and China's overall bilateral trade patterns resemble those of other Latin American countries, with Peru exporting primarily natural resources and importing manufactured goods, construction equipment, consumer goods and electronics from China.

Like its neighbour Chile, Peru's opening of negotiations for an FTA with China was preceded by a similar attempt with the US. Both were part of an array of FTAs that Lima was utilizing to bolster its regulatory and market reforms to the domestic economy.[83] Prior discussions with Chilean trade experts helped sharpen Peru's focus on clauses on investment and competition policy in negotiations with the Chinese.[84] After six rounds, the governments of Peru and China finally signed their FTA in 2009. It committed the signatories to putting over 85 per cent of Peruvian products on a zero-tariff basis with China, while all but 1 per cent of Chinese products were zero-rated.[85] There were clear expectations that minerals, petroleum and fisheries would be amongst the winners from the FTA, and it was recognized that local manufacturers in textiles, leather goods and metal production would suffer from the lifting of protective measures.[86]

The results were immediate, if not as spectacular as anticipated, with trade growing from $10.5 billion in 2010 to $15.9 billion in 2014.[87] It was only in 2018 that two-way trade reached $23.3 billion, up from $2 billion in 2004, when Peru decided to recognize China as a market economy,[88] and $7.3 billion in 2009, when the FTA was signed.[89] Over this time period the structure of trade remained roughly the same, with Peru importing a wide variety of Chinese products, ranging from electronics to automobiles, while copper and other minerals made up well over 70 per cent of Chinese imports from Peru. Growing penetration of Peru's market by Chinese SMEs, numbering one hundred according to China's NDRC, has exposed the gap in Peruvian businesses' ability to access Chinese consumers.[90] For instance, despite being a priority of the Peruvian government and its agricultural sector since the 2009 FTA, accessing Chinese consumers for a greater variety of fruit and new products like quinoa was a much slower process that accelerated only after the US-China trade war began in 2018.[91] The late 2018 negotiations to 'optimize' the FTA – including extending it beyond the extractive sector to include services, rules of origin, intellectual property and improving Peru's access to the Chinese market – signalled a new assertiveness on the part of Lima.

Behind the FTA update was the fact that the rising profile of bilateral trade has not prevented economic activity remaining fixated on the extractive sector. Over 95 per cent of Peruvian exports to China consisted of metals, minerals and fish or fishmeal products, with 84.9 per cent derived from mining.[92] China had invested $261.7 million in Peru by 2010, but that made it only Peru's fourteenth-largest investor, and virtually all of that was in the mining sector.[93] Excepting mineral resources, the Chinese petroleum SOE, CNPC, obtained the licence for one of Peru's offshore oil concessions in 1993 and in the Amazonian interior in 2003. Ten years later, Petrobras, Brazil's struggling oil SOE, sold its shares in the Amazon to CNPC to the tune of $2.6 billion to offset its mounting debt balance sheet and rising costs at home (see Chapter 5), making CNPC effectively the owner of 40 per cent of Peru's oil holdings.[94] Indigenous communities and environmental activists expressed dismay at the firm's environmental record and continued their campaign to challenge the legal basis of the award in light of the oil industry's decades-long damaging impact on forestry and public health.[95] Further afield, Hong Kong-registered firms purchased three Peruvian fishing companies and used these to fish in Peru's designated waters and export their catch to the Chinese market.[96] Since 2014 hundreds of Chinese fishing vessels have been reported illegally fishing for anchovies and even protected species in these waters.[97] Systematic overfishing by Chinese trawlers has diminished fish stocks, devastating communities in coastal Peru and damaging entire marine ecosystems.

It is China's conduct in the mining sector that has done more than any other factor to shape Peruvian domestic opinion and outsiders' views of Chinese commercial operations. Mining represents a significant component of the Peruvian economy, 62 per cent of Peruvian exports in 2017, a quarter of its tax revenue, and, according to Sanborn, one-third of its mergers and acquisitions.[98] With substantial reserves of copper, iron, coal, lithium and precious metals, Peru offered Chinese investors opportunities to develop both existing operations and greenfield projects.

One of China's largest overseas investment forays at the time was the SOE Shougang's 1992 acquisition of Hierro Peru for $120 million, an ailing Peruvian mining parastatal based in Marcona.[99] Shortages of iron ore in China coupled with rapid growth in the steel industry impelled Shougang to search for sources outside of China as far back as 1985.[100] Almost immediately upon starting operations in Peru, however, Shougang-Hierro

Peru found itself accused of violating labour laws, non-compliance with health and safety regulations and unfair dismissal of 50 per cent of the Peruvian workforce and their replacement with Chinese workers;[101] moreover, as part of its original agreement, Shougang-Hierro Peru had agreed to invest $150 million in the local community, but only put in $35 million and paid a $14 million fine instead. On the other hand, as Sanborn and Chon note, Shougang-Hierro Peru remains the only Chinese mining firm to make significant tax contributions to the local community.[102] As if to make up for the controversy and chronic setbacks of the past twenty-five years, Shougang-Hierro Peru announced a $1.5 billion expansion of capacity that would double its iron ore exports in 2018, only to have its operations suspended by Peruvian regulators in 2019 for failing to comply with environmental regulations.[103]

Chinalco, which originally promised an investment of $2 billion in 2008, ended up purchasing rights of $4.82 billion for the Toromocho copper mine in 2013. Unlike Shougang-Hierro Peru, Chinalco had commissioned a Canadian firm in 2010 to produce an environmental impact statement and created the *Fundo Social Toromocho* to support the local community in light of the SOE's decision to move the entire town of Morococha to a new location.[104] Like Shougang, Chinalco's search for resource security in minerals has been a driving force for its investment and operational expansion into Peru.[105] New Morococha, built nearby, boasts electrified houses with running water but apparently little employment.

In 2014 a Chinese joint venture involving Minmetals (MMG) and Jiangxi invested $2.5 billion in the mines near El Galeno. MMG went on to purchase the licence for Glencore's Las Bambas copper mine in 2014, the country's largest producer contributing 1 per cent to Peru's national GDP. Like the case of Toromocho, MMG moved the local community from Fuerabamba to a new town, Neuva Fuerabamba. Resistance by some in the community in 2015 spilled over into violence and police action resulted in three deaths.[106] Further controversy ensued, however, with protests erupting in March 2018, causing the government to declare another state of emergency, suspend the constitutional rights of protesters, send in the army and jail its leaders.[107] This is one of seven states of emergency declared in the same region, which have together undermined MMG's carefully cultivated image.

It is suggested by critics of Chinese mining firms in Peru that these problems all mirror the experience of Peru with US and European mining firms, whose conduct was rarely exemplary either, and came despite the steps Chinese firms took, like signing up to the Extractive Industries Transparency Initiatives (EITI) in 2014.[108] Firms like MMG drew up Corporate Social Responsibility plans and 'beneficiation' schemes at the behest of the Peruvian government, aimed at enhancing value-added production in the commodity-exporting sector, in vain.

China ExIm Bank and China Development Bank, China's policy banks, provided the financing for many of these projects and their offsets, such as transport infrastructure development, that featured in deals struck with the government. Chinese-Peruvian ambitions remain high: the proposed Chancay Port Terminal 50 km north of Lima, a joint venture between Chinese shipping giant Cosco and Peru's Volcan costing $3 billion, aims to build massive container facilities that would, according to Cosco's CEO, 'bring cargo directly from Asia and then distribute it around the region'.[109]

Peruvian Chinese Community

Against this background of expanding ties with China, the Peruvian Chinese community finds itself in an ambivalent position. While boosted by the growing attention and refracted prestige of a rising China, and celebrated in official statements as an important source of Peru's 'soft power' in its relations with Beijing, in fact there are only limited efforts by Peruvian officials and big business to involve them in the actual proceedings. The divisions within Chinese community associations reflect the historical position of a community composed of Cantonese, Fujianese and Haka immigrants from the late nineteenth and early twentieth centuries with ties to the Republic of China.[110] These divisions are said by Peruvian officials to restrict government outreach to local Chinese communities that would otherwise draw on their knowledge and resources to manage relations with Beijing.[111] Meanwhile, entrepreneurs like the owner of *La Corporación Sam* have given their own financial support to a Center for China at the Universidad del Pacifico.[112]

By contrast, the Chinese government itself has made an effort to mobilize the Chinese community in Peru through active involvement in key business and social associations like *Beneficencia China* if they will support its interests.[113] The Chinese embassy's funding for the Chinese-Peruvian Friendship Centre and its overt ties to the political party led by the late President Alan Garcia have also forged ties with Peruvian elite interests and politicians.[114] Despite pronounced differences in the Chinese community, there is evidence of a sense of pride and identification with these Chinese government entreaties. Even *tusans* are said to be increasingly attracted to China, proclaiming their Chinese roots more openly than in the past.[115]

Chinese media instruments, including CGTN, *China Hoy* (China Daily) and Xinhua, all have cooperative agreements with Peruvian national media, including training programmes for Peruvian journalists.[116] There are four Confucius Centres at leading universities in Lima and at regional universities as well as funded courses in Chinese language in a few secondary schools.[117]

Finally, the commercial spill over from greater understanding of Peru burgeoned after 2016. China's designation of Peru as an official tourist destination produced a small but steady rise in Chinese visitors holidaying in what the Chinese still see as an exotic destination. The visa-waiver programme of 2016 that provides Chinese tourists with cost-free visas to enter Peru as long as they can produce existing visas for North America, the UK, Australia or the Schengen countries of the EU, has boosted numbers by about 50 per cent, from 19,243 in 2015 to 31,405 in 2017.[118] As observers from the tourist-dependent Caribbean have noted and scholars have seconded, tourism is not immune from being used as a tool of economic statecraft.[119]

Argentina

The pendulum swings experienced as part of the Argentina-China relationship can be said to track the political shifts in the country from Peronist adherents to neo-liberal advocates. Peronist politicians on the centre-left found in China a partner with deep financial pockets, an appetite for risk – or certainly one which ignored the Western financial markets' consensus on Argentine economic woes – with a proven capacity to build big infrastructure projects that spoke to both its grandiose development ambitions and decoupling from US dominance. For the neo-liberal proponents on the centre-right, China's ideological predilections and the lack of transparency in loans, as well as its suspect intentions towards Argentina, contributed to caution, bordering at times on hostility, towards Beijing even when circumstances led to deeper commercial engagement.

The drivers of nationalism, necessity and profit as applied to Argentina-China ties produced multi-billion loan package for two major dams, two nuclear power plants, a burgeoning Chinese demand for Argentine soyabeans and other agricultural exports as well as investments in the resource sector, especially lithium. They also contributed to domestic debates around debt exposure and growing dependency on China, the disruptive effect of Chinese imports on local businesses, Chinese FDI in land and the systematic exploitation of Argentina's coastal marine riches by Chinese fishing fleet. Despite the differences between the two political trends, there were commonalities rooted in elite interests which gave continuity to the relationship with the Asian giant.

History and Diplomacy

China's relationship with Argentina began in the late nineteenth century, like other Latin American states, with diplomatic ties to the Republic of China and continued under the military junta after the coup in 1976.[120] The collapse of military rule was followed by the installation of democracy led by President Raúl Alfonsín in 1983. His successor, Carlos Menem, ran the country from 1989 to 1999 and, faced with the severe economic crisis upon taking office, abandoned Peronist precepts of his party to become the chief architect of Argentina's embrace of neo-liberalism. The economic shock of devaluation of the US dollar-linked peso and subsequent Argentine default in 2001–2002 was followed by the exposure of serial corruption scandals and a sharp rise in national poverty. The economic turmoil brought about a disavowal of 'Menemism' or neo-liberal policies with Peronist circles which shaped debates over the direction of state economic policy for the next two decades.[121]

The establishment of a strategic partnership declared by President Hu Jintao and President Néstor Carlos Kirchner during the latter's state visit to China in June 2004 put the contours of the relationship into place. Kirchner's populism and the gradual stabilization of the economy provide a more inviting economic context for cooperation with China. President Hu Jintao's follow-up visit to Argentina in November that same year and the announcement that Chinese investment worth $20 billion into the infrastructure and energy sectors was under discussion, including transport, high-speed trains and housing.[122] Argentina's recognition of China's official status as a market economy followed and, on the heels of that decision, protests from local businesses fearful of the impact of unrestricted Chinese imports.[123] Moreover, rumours that the agreement contained a secret clause in which the Argentine government agreed to limit its use of anti-dumping in the WTO angered some businesses.[124] The selective imposition of tariffs and other measures on Chinese goods sparked heated reaction from Beijing and the foreign minister, Rafael Bielsa, rushed to Beijing to explain the Argentine government's violation of the recent bilateral agreement.[125] Beyond these concerns, both countries' desire to expand value-added crushing capacity to produce soya oil and meal, which limited Argentina's ability to improve its trade balance with China, continued to generate diplomatic friction.

Under the presidency of Cristina Fernández de Kirchner, vice president under her husband who took over leadership in 2007 after his untimely death, the first serious economic investments and loan packages stemming from the 2004 MOU were initiated. Formal establishment of the institutional mechanism of a Strategic Partnership had to wait until 2013, with the signing of an MOU to set up a permanent Binational Commission for more regularized discussions.[126] A year later, the diplomatic relationship was cemented under President Xi Jinping with the upgrading of ties to that of a Comprehensive Strategic Partnership. This set in motion a further intensification of relations on more fronts, from a broadening of economic engagement to educational and military cooperation that was to continue to define the relationship. This was despite a hiatus in participation in these joint commissions in President Mauricio Macri's first year in office.

Economic Ties

China's growing appetite for resources and markets in LAC has led to multiple high profile visits to the region (four to Argentina): Jiang in 2001; Hu in 2004; and Xi in 2016 and 2018. Beijing's interest in a closer economic relationship with the region was also behind the launching of the China-Mercosur Dialogue Forum in 1998 which provided further exposure.[127] Ironically, though it was Peronists who pursued closer ties with China, it was the opening of Argentina's market under the auspices of neo-liberalism that paved the way for Chinese investment and trade policies towards the South American state. Argentine resources, with a focus on energy, minerals and agricultural products, were actively sought out while debt-financed infrastructure projects were mooted by the two governments.

Exports of soyabeans (whether or not broken) products grew exponentially and went from $90 million in 1998 to $4.1 billion in 2010.[128] With 56.2 per cent of all of Argentine soyabean exports going to the Chinese market in 2012, the possibilities for expanding into domestic production proved to be very attractive to Chinese agro-industry SOEs.[129] COFCO, through direct acquisitions in Argentina and through mergers and acquisitions internationally with global leaders like Noble Group, over time became the largest commodities broker in Argentina.[130] Other Chinese firms like Beidahuang Nongken from Heilongjiang struck a $1.5 billion agreement with the Rio Negro provincial government in October 2010 for 320,000 hectares in Patagonia which included the concession rights to build a terminal at the port of San Antonio Oeste.[131] According to the agreement, Beidahuang would not own the land outright but rather contract with Argentine farmers to develop and produce agricultural outputs.[132] The public outcry against these arrangements caused the Fernández government to conduct an audit of foreign ownership of land and set restrictions.[133]

Another critical aspect of Argentina's agricultural supply infrastructure has been the expansion of the 'grain superhighway' on the Paraná River and onward to the Atlantic. By dredging the river deeper and widening the channel at the port city of Rosario, where 80 per cent of Argentina's grain is exported, this would enable bigger Panamax cargo ships to load larger consignments of grains transported by rail from the Argentine interior as well as from sources in Paraguay and Brazil.[134] Along with the upgrading of the national railway network, this would allow Argentina to improve its international position as the primary exporter of soya and other grains to the world by raising trade volumes and lowering the cost of transit of agricultural products from the region. Indeed, every foot of river dredged reportedly allows cargo ships to carry an additional 1,800 to 2,200 tonnes of grain while the annual toll of $200 million on shipping companies would underwrite the continued clearance of the vital waterway.[135] Shanghai Dredging Company, a subsidiary of China Communication Construction Company (CCCC), sought to outbid a long-standing European dredging company contracted to maintaining Rosario's accessibility on the Paraná River. The sensitivity of the deal forced the Argentine government in July 2021 to postpone the tendering process for twelve months.[136] According to Myers, this was part of a larger Chinese strategy to 'invest across international agricultural supply chains to better control supply and pricing'.[137]

In the energy sector, Chinese oil giants CNOOC and Sinopec put in a bid for the ailing Repsol-YPF's stake in Argentina's offshore oil in 2009. Still smarting from the US government's blocking of CNOOC's purchase of US oil company UNOCAL in 2005, the fall of oil prices in the intervening three years meant that CNOOC was able to secure a 50 per cent stake along with its Argentine partner company, Bridas, for $3.1 billion in March 2010.[138] CNOOC's financial means and technical prowess were seen to be key to restarting the production which had become dormant under Repsol-YPF. However, by 2014, the Chinese firm was trying to offload its shares as the oil prices fell, chastened as the Argentine government forced through a partial nationalization of Repsol Argentina in 2012 (for which Repsol received $5 billion in government compensation). Eventually it was able to restructure its position through Repsol's subsidiary, Pan American Energy, and form a joint venture with BP in 2017. In another part of the energy sector, the Chinese firm China National Technical Import-Export Corporation was contracted to build a 50 km natural gas pipeline in the provinces of Entre Rios.[139]

Mineral resources commanded a great deal of attention from China as well. In 2007, China Metallurgical Corporation (CMC) purchased the Campana Mahuida copper mine in the province of Neuquén but, due to disputes with the local community and province over water rights, had to suspend operations in 2012.[140] CMC's other purchase of an iron ore mine fell victim to the collapse in commodity prices in 2016.[141] A major Chinese SOE, Shandong, with established interests in Africa and Asia, bought a 50 per cent share in Argentina's largest gold and silver mining firm in 2017 for $960 million.[142]

While these initial resource investments focused on existing mining operations, the Chinese interest in lithium as a crucial ore in the production of batteries for electric vehicles pointed to the future trajectory of bilateral resources exchange. Ganfeng purchased a 50 per cent stake in the Cauchari-Olaroz lithium mine in the high plains of the northern province of Jujuy for $160 million in 2019, committing to providing further investments as well as conducting exploration in neighbouring Salta province.[143] As China's largest firm involved in the extraction and processing of lithium, Ganfeng is also a major actor in the production and recycling of batteries, having invested in the Mexican border state of Sonora (see Chapter 6). Smaller Chinese firms have taken up positions in this sector, with Hanaq's investments in lithium in Salta and uranium exploration in central Chubut region standing out for its efforts to demonstrate ESG compliance.

Beyond mining resources, China's interest in building or refurbishing infrastructure was a critical component of engagement. In 1999, a consortium of union and corporate interests formed to sign a thirty-year lease on a large portion of Argentina's state-owned railway network. The Belgrano Cargas, a freight and logistics company, was chronically under-funded and its carrying capacity gradually reduced over time from 3.2 million tonnes of freight in 1998 to 500,000 tonnes in 2006.[144] As a consequence, given Argentina's export potential in agricultural and mineral resources, and China's recognized strengths in financing and construction, improved infrastructure could lower transport costs considerably. Railway, road and port projects were proposed as early as 2004 as potential areas of cooperation, and some tentative agreements were struck in that period.

Significantly, however, it was only in the aftermath of the elevation of ties to a Comprehensive Strategic Partnership in 2014 that the government in Buenos Aires began to agree to larger loans for infrastructure. Making good on an earlier multi-billion commitment by President Fernández de Kirchner in Beijing in 2010, the country began a concerted effort to mobilize Chinese capacity in conjunction with Argentinian counterparts to revitalize the country's transportation system. Repairs and new tracks, as well as upgraded logistics, were introduced through a phased approach to construction, which included provisions for significant local employment. For instance, the first phase of the San Martin infrastructure project – the 1,813-km freight line running from western provinces to Argentina's major ports – was to be constructed by CRCC, underwritten by a $2.6 billion loan and employing 16,830 locals.[145] The 911-km stretch of the Belgrano Cargas network from Jujuy in the north of the country to Buenos Aires and

Catamarca in the southeast, was scheduled to be built by China Machine Engineering Corporation (CMEC) through a loan of $815 million, with 65 per cent for construction and the remaining 35 per cent for rolling stock, and would create 6,202 jobs.[146] The impact of the renovation was significant: the travel time between Salta and Rosario was cut from eighteen to eight days, enabling exports in agricultural products to shoot up by 66 per cent year on year.[147] Light rail services were built around greater Buenos Aires, and were proposed for other major urban areas in the country.

Some of the biggest infrastructure projects and largest loan portfolios between Argentina and China were found in the hydropower sector. A $4.73 billion loan package from China Development Bank, People's Bank of China and ICBC was agreed in 2013 by the Cristina Fernández de Kirchner government to build two dams on the Santa Cruz River with the Gezhouba group leading a consortium that included Argentine partners.[148] Tapping into this source of energy would provide 5 per cent of the country's electricity needs while reducing its annual carbon emissions by 2.5 per cent.[149] Fallout from environmental activists critical of the opaque Environmental Impact Assessment brought a lawsuit to the Argentine Supreme Court, bringing the construction of the dams to a temporary halt in 2015. The court's ruling at the end of December 2016 opened up a process of review that included other affected provinces and the national legislature.

Elite Consortium, Development Finance and China's Expanding Interests

At the heart of the push to expand Chinese interests in Argentina was the formation of a business group drawn from amongst the country's leading business, trade union and political interests. According to Laufer, under the Néstor Kirchner government, a consortium called Shima formed by the Argentina business group led by Franco Macri, trade union leaders and Chinese SOE Sanhe Hopefull Grain & Oil from Hebei proposed a multi-billion dollar infrastructure programme for the country announced during Hu Jintao's visit in 2004.[150] These included electrification of key intra-city railways, construction of roads and ports as well as high-speed railways and housing. Macri, whose son was the mayor of Buenos Aires and went on to win the presidency in 2015, was appointed China's key investment adviser on Latin America in 2006 and, in addition to heading up two Sino-Argentine business associations, served as a middleman between CITIC and Chinese firms seeking investments in Argentina's energy sector.[151] China Exim Bank and China Development Bank underwrote most of the loans provided to cover infrastructure projects organized through Shima. Indeed, according to former energy secretary Jorge Lapeña, 'Projects are now decided based on political convenience (under Fernández de Kirchner). Then we have to deal with the problems when they have to be implemented.'¹⁵² But the controversy over the mingling of personal and commercial interests was one that would affect the politicians on the right as well.¹⁵³

Despite the growing economic ties, China's expanding position in Argentina periodically generated pushback from within elite circles but also from local constituencies, which elites sometimes could not ignore. For instance in 2010 the Cristina de Fernández government slapped anti-dumping tariffs on Chinese manufactured imports but, according to Oviedo, the real rationale resided in her government's concerns that China was developing soyabean crushing capacity that would reduce Argentina's value-added exports in soya oil products.¹⁵⁴

The elevation of bilateral relations to a Comprehensive Strategic Partnership in 2014 corresponded with the opening of discussions about the purchase of Chinese military hardware by Argentina. In 2015, it was announced that Argentina would buy over one hundred armed personnel carriers, 14 JF17/FC-1 fighter jets and five coast patrol boats. China donated policing equipment valued at $18.3 million to the federal and national police in advance of the G20 summit held in Argentina in 2018.¹⁵⁵ Regular training programmes and exchanges of military personnel were indicative of institutionalization of cooperation.¹⁵⁶

Beijing's desire to expand its interests went beyond sectors of the Argentine economy. In 2016, following bilateral discussions on loan repayment and restructuring, Buenos Aires agreed to grant China a fifty-year lease on an old military base in Patagonia.¹⁵⁷ There the Chinese military set up a satellite tracking station to monitor its space programme and communication satellites.¹⁵⁸ Chinese global ambitions in the Antarctic were on display a few years later with the opening of discussion on constructing a polar logistics ship to resupply Argentina's research stations based there.¹⁵⁹

Macri and the 'Recalibration' of Argentina-China Relations

Hailed by some as the end of leftist populism in the country, the election of Mauricio Macri in 2015 in fact marked the start of a recalibration of ties with China. Indeed, in his first months in office, Macri seemingly took a hard look at the array of Chinese infrastructure projects signed up to by his predecessor.¹⁶⁰ For instance, Macri reviewed the contract for two nuclear power stations signed by his predecessor as well as the two hydroelectric dams in the provinces. Apparently 'cross default' clauses in loan contracts made it prohibitive to terminate the costly energy projects.¹⁶¹ As a result,

Macri reduced exposure to his predecessor's decision to co-finance the purchase of China's Hualong-1 reactor (with China putting in $8 billion and Argentina $4 billion), although in the end Argentina was not able to fund the project. The purchase of Chinese military hardware was put on hold by Macri as well while the sinking of a Chinese vessel illegally fishing in Argentine waters in March 2016 seemingly signalled the new hard line approach towards China.[162]

Behind these initiatives were not only Buenos Aires' concerns about ties with China but the parlous condition of Argentina's foreign reserves, springing originally from the economic crisis and default in 2001, which continued to haunt successive governments. The restructuring of debt with Western creditors in 2005 and again in 2010 allowed for a return to payments on over 90 per cent of debt, reinforced by the Macri government's decision to agree to pay off remaining creditors in 2016.[163] An IMF loan package worth $57 billion, coupled with an upgrading by rating agencies, set the stage for a full restoration of Argentina to international financial markets.

Indeed, according Lin Hua, though the first year focused on reviewing joint projects, the fundamentals of the relationship remained solid, founded on 'complementary, mutual benefit and interdependence ... and the improvement in ties with Europe and the United States, as well as the rapprochement with the Pacific Alliance, are reflections of pragmatism and diplomatic balance (under Macri)'.[164]

The strength of Argentine-Chinese relations was evident as Macri relaunched the bilateral dialogue process with discussion between the two presidents at the Nuclear Security Summit in Washington in April 2016. Jack Ma's Alibaba Group met with Macri in May 2017, in advance of the Argentine president's official visit to China, and signed an agreement to promote e-commerce between the two countries.[165] The Argentine government simultaneously launched the $33 billion 'Plan Nacional de Transporte e Infraestructura' in July and less than two months later, the minister of transportation travelled to Beijing for discussions with Chinese officials. This reactivation of the bilateral Economic and Trade Committee opened up a host of new areas of cooperation and the eventual signing of thirty-five new agreements.[166] Areas that had generated contest disputes between Buenos Aires and Beijing, such as Argentine farmers' limited access to the processed soyameal market in China, were lifted in 2019 as the US-China trade war reduced soya exports by US agricultural suppliers.[167] According to some estimates at the time, China was expected to import up to 90 per cent of Argentina's soya production by 2020.[168] Macri even advised Chinese officials that the Belt and Road Initiative (BRI) would align well with the Integración de la Infraestructura Regional Sudamericana (IIRSA). For their part, Chinese officials noted with satisfaction that the two presidents had met an unprecedented five times in three years, paving the way for a deepening of bilateral ties.[169]

However, President Macri's credibility as a business-friendly administration aimed at contesting his predecessor's dubious deals with China was challenged by the publication of the Panama Papers in 2016, opening up public scrutiny of his offshore financial holdings.[170] Seven companies with direct or close connections to the Macri Group or the president and his father were uncovered as sheltered by tax havens. Moreover, in spite of actions undertaken by Macri to stabilize the economy, Argentina entered into a national election with an economy in a tailspin, currency devaluation, growing poverty and the threat of another default. The stage was set for the return of the Peronists to power.

Return of the Peronists

With the election of Alberto Fernández to the presidency in December 2019, and Cristina Fernández de Kirchner returning to the vice presidency, the cautious engagement towards Beijing was swept aside in favour of an acceleration of the relationship. Standing in the way, however, was $16.9 billion in borrowing from Beijing between 2007 and 2018 and the inability of the cash-starved Argentine government to provide its promised financial payments to support these infrastructure projects.[171]

At the same time, the public unwillingness of the Peronist government to pay down remaining debt obligations to hedge funds ('vulture funds' as Fernández de Kirchner put it) in New York produced another standoff with Western creditors. In that volatile context, China offered an $18.5 billion currency swap facility to ease financial liquidity problems and meet payments to Chinese firms engaged in infrastructure projects. In spite of this, only $300 million was actually used by the Argentine government. A second sovereign default took place in May 2020, sparking another reversal for the Argentine economy.

In the aftermath, the Fernández government revisited the extension of the currency swap mechanism, securing an additional three years from Chinese officials in August 2020. Buenos Aires joined the Asian Infrastructure Investment Bank (AIIB) the following month and indicated a willingness to sign on to the BRI. Argentina borrowed a further $4.7 billion to fund massive improvements to the Belgrano Cargas network of railroads from the interior to the capital and neighbouring countries.[172] Following in the wake of railway reconstruction was the signing of an MOU to purchase a further 211 electric vehicles from China Railway Construction Company

(CRRC) to replace diesel engines and carriages for $490 million.[173] They also reopened discussions on the purchase of Chinese armaments, with the J-10CE, the country's most advanced fighter jet, being considered. Despite their increasingly close relationship, continuing problems with the Argentine economy remained an obstacle to the ability of both countries to overcome the financial constraints this imposed.

Conclusion: Chile, Peru and Argentina

More than any other Latin American state along the Pacific coast, Chile has been shaped by the broader framework of Asia-Pacific trade agreements and related initiatives in its relationship with China. It has inspired high hopes and real disappointments. On the one hand, the sustained growth in bilateral trade ties since the signing of the FTA, coupled with strategic Chinese investments, demonstrated that real economic gains could accrue to Chile; on the other hand, there were disappointments that Chile was unable to optimise its special position as China's 'gateway' to South American markets.[174] The fact that the much-touted Trans-Oceanic Railway sidesteps Chile altogether came as a shock to Chilean policymakers and upended comfortable assumptions about the relationship. Trade with China did expand into new areas like agricultural products, but over 70 per cent remain in the copper extractive sector. The amended FTA, opening more sectors to Chinese investment, coupled with the government's expansion of infrastructure saw a further surge in China's economic interest in Chile. This was reflected in a seven fold increase in Sino-Chilean two-way trade from $8 billion in 2005 to $57.72 billion by 2021.[175] In this respect, Chile's pioneering role as the first mover remains an important element in the bilateral relationship.

With respect to Peru, reaching out to Beijing and embedding the economic relationship in mechanisms such as the Peru-China Free Trade Agreement 2009 has brought a tide of FDI to its shores, opened up market opportunities in both countries and in the process generated a new cycle of commodity-led growth.[176] Bilateral trade with China has boomed since the first major investment in the mining sector in 1992, rising from $273 million in 1992 to $16 billion in 2016,[177] while projected grand-scale infrastructure projects like the multi-billion dollar Trans-Oceanic Railway are offering unprecedented opportunities to breach the geographic obstacles to economic integration.[178] Moreover, unlike the criticism emanating from Brazil and Mexico, Peru's engagement with China has not prompted discussions of 'reprimarization', but generated positive spillovers which helped grow the Peruvian economy.

It would be fair to say that – in contrast to the Chilean strategy of seeking a 'first mover advantage' – the Peruvians have sought benefit from 'late comer advantage'. This meant that Peru could structure their engagement in ways that, over time, have managed to extract Chinese financial resources for key sectors of the economy. And yet, from the perspective of some Peruvians, the costs of mining ventures remain too high while others have wondered where the state was in the uneven contestation between Chinese multinational firms and local communities.[179]

In the case of Argentina, the political theatre of changing leadership and political parties overshadowed the continuities that have worked to sustain the relationship. From middle-class consumers to strategic resources, opportunities abound and both Macri interests and the Kirchner dynasty recognize the benefits from Chinese investment and loans in the resource and infrastructure sectors, as well as new areas such as e-commerce. Furthermore, China's position as a leading creditor in Argentina put Beijing in a strong position to secure better terms in pursuit of its own interests. Indeed, as the head of the Argentina-China Chamber of Commerce, Ernesto Fernández Taboada, explains:

> When I ask Chinese companies why they come here with such a difficult financial situation, they always say the same thing. They invest abroad always thinking of the long-term, so they are not worried about not being paid.[180]

This Chinese confidence in the long terms opportunities in Argentina, echoed to varying degrees in other parts of the region, signal a willingness to ground bilateral ties in longstanding elite and commercial relationships.

4

Venezuela, Ecuador and Bolivia – Incautious Embrace

Populist governments of the Left in Latin America, spurred on in part by persistent inequalities within their societies and a desire to unshackle their economies from elite and US dominance, have seen in China an alternative source of moral and economic support. What was quickly labelled by the media a 'pink tide' in Latin America spoke the rhetoric of revolution, targeted the chronically neglected poor and raised their expectations while winning their political support. Riding the wave of the commodities boom, these self-declared 'Bolivarian republics' could embark on nationalization policies that redistributed some of these abundant revenues to poorer communities through social programmes and employment creation.[1]

To bolster their regional solidarity, the Alianza Bolivariana para los Pueblos de Nuestra América (ALBA) was founded by Venezuela and Cuba. It has grown to comprise a range of like-minded governments; however, the Bolivarian republics themselves (with the exception of Morales' Bolivia) have largely avoided tackling politically charged issues like land reform and, as a result, have left intact much of the underlying structural sources of inequality.

For Beijing the enthusiasm of Bolivarian republican leaders for China was unexpected, bewildering and welcomed in roughly equal measure. It was bewildering in that their evocations of Maoist ideology were an uncomfortable reminder of China's past misguided policies promulgated by the paramount leader, a period implicitly condemned by Deng Xiaoping and his immediate successors as well as a generation of party members and scholars.[2] Yet such affinity for the founder of the Chinese Communist Party was welcome as it offered inroads into the top circles of power in these republics and, through them, access to much-coveted government licences for extraction and contracts for infrastructure construction.

For the Bolivarian republics the commodity super-cycle – yielding high prices for energy resources in particular and sustained by Chinese demand – offered an unprecedented opportunity for a progressive development agenda. 'Progressive extractivism', a term coined to denote the policy of states to 'regulate the appropriation of resources and their export by nationalising companies and raw materials, revising contracts, and increasing export duties and taxes', became the policy watchword of the three governing parties.[3] The revenues generated by commodity exports, when coupled with statist intervention in the economy, was to be utilized to pursue domestic development agendas that focused on poverty alleviation and expansive social programmes.[4] This reconfiguration of commodity extraction development suited the Chinese well. As a top official at the China Development Bank said of its relationship with Venezuela, 'We [China] have lots of capital and lack resources, they have lots of resources and lack capital, so it's complementary.'[5]

China's influence in these three states, welcomed by governments increasingly under siege for their authoritarianism (Venezuela) or victims of neo-liberalism (Ecuador and Bolivia), has become more pronounced over time. Whether it was resource exploitation, provisions for development finance or support for infrastructure development, the Chinese buoying presence in the local economies – enhanced by its elevated diplomatic standing in the eyes of Bolivarian leaders as a counter to US hegemony – yielded a closer friendship than any other bilateral relationship in Latin America and the Caribbean. In this situation, Beijing found it could gain footholds in vital national resource sectors in these countries and exploit commercial opportunities on a scale that it could not have dreamed of a few short years before. As China's ambitions in the Bolivarian republics expanded, however, its exposure to economic and political risk grew commensurately. Handling these risks, the spectacle of unsustainable debt in particular, and deepening regime dependency on Beijing, proved to be a daunting task for China as once-popular governments began to lose their domestic support base.

Venezuela

If the Chileans' calculated pragmatism underpinned their foreign and economic policy engagement of China, the Venezuelan approach is informed more by ideological considerations that run parallel to its commercial and, increasingly, its domestic partisan political interests. In particular, the desire to pivot away from US dominance was a cardinal point for the government of Hugo Chávez and his successor Nicolás Maduro. Informing his decision to seek out sources of capital, markets and technology alternative to traditional reliance on the US was the firm ideological position that regime survival increasingly depended upon China and other external actors. Venezuela's energy resources, amongst the largest in the world,[6] provided the means for engineering an ambitious social agenda at home and foreign policy agenda abroad.

Building the Bolivarian Republic of Venezuela

Hugo Chávez, a former colonel in the Venezuelan army, came to power in 1998 and was re-elected in 2000 as the leader of the Fifth Republic Movement. His programme of social reforms coupled with the nationalization of key sectors marked a departure from liberal market capitalism in this prosperous but deeply unequal middle-income country. The ratification of a new constitution, which dissolved the bicameral legislature in favour of a unicameral national assembly, featured emergency powers that Chávez could use to implement his ambitious transformative policy agenda known as the 49 Laws. By April 2002, after thwarting a coup attempt (later alleged by Chávez to be inspired by Washington), the government was confronted by a three-month strike led by the opposition and supported by the country's largest union, Confederación de Trabajadores de Venezuela, aimed at forcing another election. Weathering the crisis, Chávez fired eighteen thousand senior and middle-management PDVSA staff and replaced them with lower-level employees and supporters. Chávez then embarked on a more wide-ranging agenda of changes to Venezuela's economy and governing structures in order to further the 'Bolivarian revolution'.

In the new constitution of 1999 lay the institutional basis for a radical departure from the political economy of the previous decades; the Petróleos de Venezuela (PSDVA), the once-autonomous Venezuelan national oil parastatal and the financial centrepiece of the revolution, furnished the means. Initial steps were made to secure 'full oil sovereignty' with the reintroduction of the requirement that all oil companies, private or parastatal, pay royalties to the state based on volume and price.[7] Funds from increasing oil revenues were channelled into national development foundations, enabling Chávez's Misións Bolivarianos programme, starting in 2003, to provide poorer Venezuelans greater access to housing, education and social benefits.[8] And the coup attempt and subsequent strike furnished the rationale for Chávez's increasingly authoritarian measures such as limits on independent media and persecution of opposition parties. Working closely with Cuban advisers and security forces, Chávez's government developed tighter control over key state institutions and sectors of the economy, and reinforced its support through solidarity networks and militias such as Círculos Bolivarianos.[9] The establishment of the ALBA Social Movements Council at local, national and even regional levels of governance further extended and cemented this state of affairs.

With rising oil prices underwriting his expanding ambitions at home and across the region, Chávez turned to the task of realigning Venezuela's foreign and economy policy away from its long-standing dependency on the US.

In 2000, Chávez came out against the Bush administration's gambit to negotiate a Free Trade Area of the Americas (FTAA), adding to the coalition of states led by Brazil which effectively stalled the process. Chávez went on to launch ALBA as an alternative regional organization to the FTAA. Venezuela created the Banco del Sur in 2007 along with Ecuador, Argentina, Brazil, Uruguay and Bolivia, whose aim was to provide a source of development finance for infrastructure projects and social programmes alternative to that of conventional multilateral banks.[10]

The Unión de Naciones Suramericanas (UNASUR), set up in 2008, promoted regional integration by other means than what might be termed the corporatist protectionism of Mercosur,[11] which in effect sought to become South America's answer to the European Union.[12] Moreover, for Caracas, pursuing relations with countries professing an antipathy to the US on the global stage drew them instinctively closer to Russia, Iran and China.

China-Venezuela – Diplomacy, Trade and Development Finance

Formal ties between Venezuela and China had existed since 1974, but it was under Hugo Chávez that a deliberate personal effort was made to expand them. On an official visit to Beijing in 2001 the Venezuelan president effused over the possibilities for closer ties, declaring that Simon Bolivar and Mao Zedong were 'soulmates', and that Venezuelan oil supply and Chinese demand for it presented a solid case for the enduring complementarity of their two economies.[13] Unexpectedly, given that a sustained political and economic relationship would be the usual precursor to such a move, President Hu Jintao designated Venezuela a strategic partner of China, emphasized the opportunities inherent in such a relationship and signed the first in a long series of MOUs and other bilateral agreements.[14] The search for secure supplies of energy had driven China's energy SOEs as far afield as Africa, and the opportunity to tap into the world's largest known oil reserves proved to be irresistible. Nevertheless, China responded to Chávez more cautiously in its public statements – shearing off Chávez's flights of ideological rhetoric – reflecting both its inherent pragmatism and its policy of avoiding conflict with US interests in a country long dominated by them.[15]

Behind Chávez's drive for alternatives to Washington was a broader national agenda to promote 'twenty-first-century Socialism', that is, a state-led market economy with strong distributive policies to undergird national autonomy in a multi-polar international system.[16] The paradox inherent in China's own economic rise to power, fostered by Western FDI and multilateral lending by the World Bank and the Asian Development Bank, and realized under a gradualist embrace of liberal economics, seems to have escaped Chávez's grasp. This uncritical assessment of China as an alternative to the West and the simplistic reading of economic complementarities, characteristic of other leftist-oriented governments in the region, greased the way for an ever-closer relationship. It was a pattern that the other Bolivarian republics, Ecuador and Bolivia, were to follow in the coming years.

Bilateral trade expansion followed warming diplomatic ties under Chávez. The first foray in translating diplomacy into direct economic value came in the aftermath of Premier Li Peng's visit in 1996 and the consequent securing of oil leases for CNOOC, the Chinese SOE, in two disused fields for $358 million, at the time one of China's largest overseas investments.[17] Within a year, eleven Chinese SOEs had opened offices in Venezuela and were exploring commercial opportunities.

In 2001 bilateral trade between Venezuela and China stood at $457 million.[18] This number began rising after Caracas recognized China as a market economy in 2004, and with that exemption from double-taxation, it reached $4.33 billion in 2009, the bulk of which were mostly exports to $4.034 billion.[19] The majority of these Venezuelan exports were oil and petroleum products (64.1 per cent).[20] By 2017, two-way trade between Venezuela and China was valued at $8.02 billion, with $6.42 billion worth of oil exports to China, while Venezuela imported Chinese goods worth $1.6 billion.[21] The structure of Venezuelan exports to China consisted of oil (91 per cent), iron ore (4.1 per cent) and refined petroleum (2.7 per cent), while Venezuela's imports from China included a vast array of machinery, appliances, rolled iron, rubber and other finished, high value-added products. A quarter of Venezuela's oil exports were destined in this period for China, another quarter to India and a whopping 44 per cent continue to be exported to the US. China's overall investment stock, as calculated by the Chinese Ministry of Commerce, had risen from 0.2 per cent in 2006 to 8.3 per cent in 2014. But it was in the area of development finance that Beijing was to leave its mark.[22]

Substantial Chinese investment, be it in the form of loans for existing sectors or actual greenfield investment, was still slow in coming despite the promising rhetoric of cooperation. A key reason was the structural and geographical impediments to effective commercial exploitation, as Chinese Ambassador Ju Yijie made clear in an interview by a leading Venezuelan newspaper in December 2005.[23] In the oil sector, where China's energy needs converged with Venezuela's vast reserves in the Orinoco basin, the viscous quality of the oil required refinery capabilities that China lacked, while its ultra-sized supertankers were too big for the Panama Canal and had to traverse the slower and more costly route across the Atlantic and Indian Oceans. Venezuela's attempt to sell CITGO, its US-based subsidiary of PDVSA, and its established refinery capacity to CNOOC was blocked by the US government. Bureaucratic impediments inside PDVSA were, before Chávez's ousting of top and middle-ranking officials in 2003, an obstacle to closer cooperation, too. Notably, on another official visit to Beijing in December 2004, the Venezuelan leader gave assurances to Chinese investors that the presidency controlled decision making now.[24]

The turning-point in economic relations with China came in 2006. It was a touchstone of the long-term strategic thinking that had shaped the two countries' cooperation, and the beginning of China's loans-for-oil *entente* with Venezuela.[25] Its centrepiece was a series of multi-million-dollar loans from China channelled through a jointly managed investment fund (see below) not only to extract oil in the Orinoco Belt, but also to provide financing to develop Venezuela's capacity in the upstream and downstream oil sectors, to be paid for by the export of a fixed volume of oil per day. Oil production increases through targeted investments would be key to a sustainable cycle of growth, generating revenue for loan repayments. Chávez declared that oil production, which in 2006 stood at 150,000 barrels per day shipped to China, would be able to rise to 500,000 barrels per day by 2010 (whereas Sino-PDVSA JV declared production could be raised only to a more modest 400,000 barrels per day by 2011).[26]

The China-Venezuela Fund, a strategic fund jointly managed by China Development Bank, which provided $4 billion, and Venezuela's National Development Bank (BANDES), which provided $2 billion, was to be an institutional vehicle for collaborative project support. Established in 2007, it was capitalized in three 'tracks', with the first track closing in 2009. A second track opened that same year with $4 billion from the China Development Bank and, when that was expended, a third track consisting of loans totalling $5 billion was made available.[27] According to Rosales, these commodity-backed loans were paid back at the rate of 300,000 barrels a day. Supporting the fund was the China-Venezuela High-Level Joint Commission, which provided policy guidance and bilateral government oversight of the process.

As critics were to point out later, the arrangements were deliberately structured to bypass Venezuela's Comptroller General and conventional legislative budgetary processes, undercutting regulatory oversight functions set up to combat corruption. Like the National Development Foundation (FONDEN), established in 2005 as the vehicle to underwrite social programmes and funded directly out of PDVSA revenues – with the consequent decreased internal investment in production – the China-Venezuela Fund evaded accountability almost totally.[28]

Following on from the setting up of the China-Venezuela Fund was an acceleration of oil-backed loans derivative of these arrangements. In September 2008, for instance, a $16 million loan from China ExIm Bank was arranged to underwrite Sinopec's exploitation of an oil block in the Gulf of Paria.[29] A year later, in September 2009, Venezuela signed up to another $16 million loan from China ExIm Bank for CNPC to extract 450,000 barrels of oil per day from a different oil block.

To address Venezuela's national development aspirations to diversify beyond oil extraction, Chinese ship manufacturers were commissioned to build eighteen ships, including three double-hulled supertankers to be flagged by Venezuela in a major expansion of its fleet.[30] The 2016 widening of the Panama Canal, led in part by Hong Kong's Hutchison-Whampoa and its subsidiaries, who had won the contract to improve capacity at the port of Balboa in 2014, would enable these tankers to cut travel time to China considerably. The Venezuelan government reportedly agreed to build three oil refineries in China to handle the 'heavy' oil it was shipping to the Chinese market.[31] Beyond Venezuela's commitment, China began searching for an oil refinery platform in the region, which led them to negotiate with Costa Rica and later with Trinidad and Tobago (see Chapter 7).

Encouraged by financing from the China-Venezuela Fund, Chinese companies began to take up other positions in the Venezuelan economy; for instance, in October 2007 a joint venture with a Chinese firm set up a mobile phone assembly plant under Estatal Venezolana de Telecomunicaciones, while Hisense opened an appliance assembly facility. By 2018 the former had produced 7.8 million mobile phones, including debuting smart phone technology with its Chinese partners.[32] By contrast, in July 2009 China Railway Engineering Corporation entered into a joint venture with a Venezuelan counterparty to build a $7.5 billion railroad that would feature Venezuelan-produced locomotives, cars and rails using Chinese technology and expertise. The subsequent withdrawal of China Railway and Engineering Corporation in 2015, citing its Venezuelan partner's corruption, left a half-completed infrastructure project and a $400 million debt.[33]

In the meantime, following election to his third term in December 2006, Chávez proceeded with his nationalization of the oil, telecom and electricity-generation sectors, moves that would contribute to expanding the state's management of the strategic heights of the economy.[34] The defeat of his referendum the following year to place the national bank under direct government control dealt the first major setback to his agenda. Chávez's untimely death from cancer in March 2013 and the election of his successor, Nicolás Maduro, five weeks later with a narrow 1.5 per cent victory, set the stage for a renewal of political contestation as the country's economy teetered towards collapse.[35] Maduro tightened the state's grip on the National Assembly, where the opposition had secured a majority in a prior election over his Partido Socialista Unificado de Venezuela (PSUV), and stepped up harassment of opponents.[36]

After Chávez and Oil

With the collapse of oil prices in 2014, the systematic overspending and indebtedness inherited by Maduro began to take their toll on the grand ambitions of the Chávez years. While poverty had been reduced from 44 per cent to 28 per cent of the population by 2006 through massive social spending, two years later Venezuela's unsound public finances had already begun to eat away at these gains.[37] In a sign of the Maduro government's desperate straits, the collapse of commodity prices coupled with a devaluation of Venezuela's currency precipitated a serious payments crisis. Beijing's accommodative financing, which had helped underwrite the expansion of social services through oil revenues channelled through its national foundations, Misións Bolivarianos programmes and a host of infrastructure projects since 2001, became more stringent overnight. Whereas Chinese officials had been content to offer advice on macro-economic policy and infrastructure development in the past, there was 'serious concern from the Chinese part on how the money is spent because it has not been destined to increase oil production, which is ultimately, their main concern'.[38]

Other extractive sectors, however, began to attract more interest and investment, especially in light of the diminishing returns on oil after 2014. Based on a national survey of Venezuela's mining resources jointly conducted by China and Venezuela in 2012, joint ventures delved into what was labelled the Orinoco Mining Arc, which in 2016 had been designated a Special Development Zone by Maduro. Operating in the remote southeast of the country, Chinese mining interests joined up with a collection of artisanal miners, armed militants and state-sanctioned operations, expanding into gold, coltan, diamonds and other extractable minerals.[39] Other ventures included an industrial park modelled in line with China's Special Economic Zones; however, these had only limited success in attracting Chinese FDI.[40]

By 2015, the full effects of the collapse in oil prices had hit the Venezuelan economy. Unable to secure loans to meet its debt obligations from either the IMF or regional banks, Caracas turned once again to Beijing. According to the former Minister of Planning and senior economist at the Inter-American Development Bank, Ricardo Hausmann, the terms offered by Beijing required Venezuela to accept secret clauses that favoured Chinese firms in the automotive and appliances sectors in return for access to credit.⁴¹ To give a sense of the disproportionate position as debtor to China that Venezuela held, according to one study, half of China's total loans for Latin America – over $50 billion – went to Venezuela by 2015.⁴²

In the meantime, President Xi Jinping's visit to Venezuela in 2014 corresponded with the elevation of the country to the status of Comprehensive Strategic Partnership.⁴³ As evidence from Venezuela and other countries demonstrates, far from just a titular honorific, comprehensive strategic partnerships involved commitments to a set of regular consultations at head of state and ministerial level to strategic planning, assessing areas for closer alignment of policy and, where necessary or desirable, addressing problems and challenges in realizing cooperation.⁴⁴ By January 2020 Venezuela and China had signed 'hundreds of agreements' on the basis of sixteen Joint High-Level Commission meetings, according to Foreign Minister Jorge Arreaza.⁴⁵

Indebtedness and the inability of Caracas to manage its declining economic fortunes increasingly came to define ties with China. Desperate for bridging finance, the Venezuelan president embarked on an emergency visit to Beijing in May 2016 (following in the footsteps of Argentina's President Cristina Fernández de Kirchner several months earlier, who had successfully negotiated a big loan package), and was granted a second grace period for repayment.⁴⁶ In addition, the Venezuelans secured a $6 billion loan on much less-favourable terms, reflecting the heightened risk of default. Productivity in the oil sector, however, continued to suffer from a neglect of government investment, with an average drop of 30 per cent in the annual output of barrels of oil which was insufficient to compensate for the natural decline of 24 per cent per annum in deposits.⁴⁷ Whereas PDVSA had been expected to export 300,000 barrels per day in 2018, it was actually only able to export half that amount.⁴⁸ Despite introducing price controls, rampant inflation and budget cuts plagued the five hundred estatals and parastatals and, along with anaemic growth in the private sectors, brought the economy to a standstill.

Opposition Politics, Regime Collapse and Risk Mitigation

Though the Bolivarian Republic had faced down opposition threats before, the deepening economic crisis inspired a renewed effort by a cross-section of society to challenge Maduro's grip on power. The disputed elections in late 2018 saw Juan Guaidó, opposition candidate and leader of the National Assembly, declare victory and assume the mantle of interim president until new elections could be called. Recognized by the US, Brazil and Colombia, he began a domestic protest campaign to oust the Maduro government.

The response of the international community, including the US and China, became crucial to the success of this initiative.

Given Washington's historical involvement in Venezuela's domestic politics, notably backing the dictator Perez Jimenez in the 1950s, and a record of covert action in the region during the Cold War, this assertive US policy towards the government raised alarm bells. As far back as 2015, the Obama administration had declared Maduro's government a 'national security threat' and imposed targeted sanctions on key individuals in his circle, a process renewed annually from that point on. With Trump in office, the opposition was emboldened to act, with Guaidó denouncing the December 2018 elections as fraudulent and declaring himself the rightful president in January 2019. The US Secretary of State, Mike Pompeo, along with key countries like Brazil and Colombia, exerted international pressure to support the sustained demonstrations against Maduro in the weeks that followed. In the end, despite thousands of protesters on the streets, Russian-Cuban active measures apparently played a key role in convincing top officials in the government and the military – and even, it was rumoured, in getting Maduro to keep his nerve – in the final hours.[49]

Throughout this tumultuous period when Russia and Cuba were vocal in their support of Maduro, the Chinese government kept a low profile. The economy was plagued by difficulties stemming from the original loan agreement to use dollar-denominated payments based on transfers of oil directly to CNCP and Sinopec. Falling production at PDVSA, initially spurred by Chávez's purge of thousands of experienced industry experts, but exacerbated by plummeting internal reinvestment, caused extended power outages and a collapsing transport network, compounded all the more by the other horrendous economic problems facing the country. Despite its efforts to impose restrictions on the Venezuelan government's exploitation of the country's oil revenues and shift these to improvements in PDVSA, China was unable to stop the annual slide in productivity. Analysts from China's University of Petroleum succinctly captured the pending failure of Chinese policy in an article in 2016:

> Before 2014, the Sino-Venezuelan deal had been China's high-stakes game. Venezuela has had difficulties in meeting both its repayment and oil obligations since the oil-for-loan deal was implemented, because Venezuela's oil output has steadily declined since Hugo Chávez became president in 1999. After 2014, the falling oil prices have made the Sino-Venezuelan oil-for-loan deal become China's high-stakes gamble. The falling oil prices since June 2014 have heavily weakened the Venezuelan economy and it may trigger social and political unrest, which might lead Venezuela to default on its loan.[50]

With the situation spiralling into economic collapse, Caracas again in 2018 had to turn to Beijing for a bailout. Despite exposure to the dilatory effects of sustained hyperinflation and its impact on asset values, authorities in Beijing continued to loan money to the crisis-ridden country without, however, the conditionalities that could bring about policy changes that might improve the economy, and with repayments still required to be made in scarce US dollars. Far from ameliorating the crisis, or even nudging the government towards a solution, China effectively prolonged and even worsened Venezuela's distress.[51] The tally of loans had reached $60 billion by this time, with no end in sight.

For the Chinese, the continuing downward spiral in the economy and the upsurge in unrest made it appear that risk mitigation was the only strategy left at this point. Censure of the US position on regime change coupled with continued diplomatic support for Maduro demonstrated a measure of public resolve on the part of Beijing. Foreign Minister Wang Yi, for instance, reminded Washington that the Monroe Doctrine was 'outdated' as the unrest increased.[52] Yet, despite announcements by Caracas of new agreements in fisheries, agriculture and industrial parks to be funded by Chinese investment, Beijing could not disguise its growing reluctance to risk further involvement. Its hosting of the annual Inter-American Development Bank meeting in Chengdu, a first for China and another sign that it had 'arrived' as a major player in Latin America, had to be abruptly cancelled in May 2019 to avoid an international dispute over whether to seat a representative of Maduro's or Guaidó's choosing.[53]

In this situation, reducing the risk exposure of Chinese firms involved in the oil business in Venezuela became a major priority to avoid outcomes emanating from US sanctions or worse that might harm China's economic influence; for instance, both CNPC and Sinopec blocked their subsidiaries in Venezuela from having direct involvement in the shipment of oil and ordered them to cut ties with local suppliers.[54] Still more worrying for Beijing was the looming spectre of bilateral default after the opposition began calling all Chinese debt 'odious' and 'null and void' for its lack of transparency.[55]

Quietly, Chinese government officials, along with their Russian counterparts, began contacting the Venezuelan opposition in search of a resolution to the crisis and, concurrently, to establish ties with potentially the next government. For some observers, the fact that these contacts began in May 2020 on the day after China supported Venezuela taking up a seat on the UN Human Rights Council was no accident.[56] Irrespective, Beijing continued to exude confidence in public that it would be able to weather the turmoil in Venezuela, stating their aim to be to facilitate a smooth democratic transition and conserve economic relations.[57]

Ecuador

Chinese involvement in the Ecuadorian economy is, as in Venezuela, by invitation. More than a decade of neo-liberal policies pursued by his predecessors only furthered Rafael Correa's election in November 2006 and his radical turn away from these policies. Inequality between the wealthy elites, a small but significant middle class and the majority of the populace created the political fault lines for Ecuador's embrace of China, and Correa's debt default in 2008 repositioned Beijing as the lender of last resort in Quito. In contrast to Venezuela, where the Chávez government characterized engagement with China in reductionist geopolitical terms, the Ecuadorian government sought to frame its newfound ties with China in terms of the logic of a *buen vivir* ('good living') philosophy and development, without compromising either.

As time went on, however, this rhetorically fuelled stance found itself at odds with elements of leftist populism and indigenous movements, cornerstones of Correa's political support, and their anti-imperialist critique, environmentalism and collectivist sympathies. Local reactions to the conduct of Chinese firms in the extractive sector of oil and mining, coupled with scathing attacks on the rising burden of the debt to China assumed by Correa's government, polarized society. After the 2017 election, Lenin Moreno, the new president, struggled to unwind the debt and contractual obligations assumed over the previous decade.[58]

Ecuador and China Embrace – Rebalancing in the Era of *'Buen Vivir'*

Ecuador's relations with China, albeit rooted in commercial exchanges during the colonial period, and reinforced by a small Cantonese community that migrated from Peru in the nineteenth century, hardly extended beyond the diplomatic representative and commercial offices opened after the restoration of democracy in 1980.[59] US dominance of the economy and intervention in the political life of the country had prevailed for much of the twentieth century. Cycles of instability between military juntas and periods of fledgling democratic rule hampered economic growth and sharpened inequality in Ecuador.

The point of departure for contemporary US economic dominance in Ecuador was the promulgation of neo-liberalism and, through Washington's Andean Trade Preferences Act of 1991, the strengthening of trade relations with the US. The country's oil reserves offered investment opportunities which enticed US oil companies into the Amazonian region; however, a lawsuit lodged by indigenous tribes in 1993 against the destruction of the rainforest by US oil companies stymied further exploitation of this move.[60] The abrupt suspension of the US-Ecuador Free Trade Agreement (FTA) in 2004 by George W. Bush, in retaliation for the cancellation of Occidental Petroleum's oil contract by the Ecuadorian government, triggered the latter's withdrawal from the negotiations on a region-wide FTA with the US. From 2000, Ecuador abandoned its currency in favour of the US dollar, which, despite the surrender of sovereign control of its fiscal policy, ushered in a period of low inflation and macro-economic stability.[61] But the impact of this policy was high and rampant political and social instability, coupled with the rising costs to its economy of debt service, forced two presidents out of office before the election of the Finance Minister, Rafael Correa, in November 2006.

Correa's first major act upon taking office as president was to convene a constituent assembly that would decide whether to give the state greater control of strategic sectors of the economy and recalibrate its share of natural resource revenues, empowering his government to accelerate social spending, including income grants to the poorest. His focus on reforming the constitution strengthened the office of the presidency, allowed for two consecutive terms, and authorized a greater role for the state in the public sector while reducing the statutory position of business in corporatist institutions.[62] The principles of *buen vivir*, environmental protection and indigenous rights were enshrined in the new constitution as well.[63] Following its overwhelming ratification in September 2008, these aspirations were realized in policy terms by a shift away from neo-liberalism, a recalibration of relations with the US and an outreach to China.

Correa sought to shed the debt accumulated by previous governments, and in December 2008 he announced a partial default on $3.2 billion worth of sovereign Ecuadorian bonds.[64] This act landed the government in court and eventually brought it to renegotiate them to 60 per cent of their value, a step towards Correa's pledge to redirect state revenues away from debt-service and towards social programmes.[65] In a parallel step, the government expanded its role in PetroEcuador, enabling it to raise more revenue for social services. Correa's national plan for *buen vivir*, founded on infrastructure development, aimed at moving away from a carbon-based economy to a hydropower-driven economy, and formed the keystone of his economic restructuring programme.[66] New roads and hydroelectric dams were linked to expansion of the mining sector as a source of revenue and employment. Ecuador's economy grew rapidly in the initial years of the Correa government and, concurrently, the poverty rate in cities fell sharply from 49 per cent in 2002 to 32 per cent in 2011, while extreme poverty declined from 19 per cent to 10 per cent in the same period.⁶⁷ Commodity prices, especially oil, provided the bulk of the country's earnings, complemented by the contribution of remittances, and the Ecuadorian economy achieved upper middle-income status.⁶⁸

Meanwhile, relations with the US continued to deteriorate under Correa, with Quito not renewing the licence for the US airbase at Manta in September 2009, which fuelled speculation that the government would turn the facility over to the Chinese or Russians.⁶⁹ The decision to offer asylum to Edward Snowden and Julian Assange, with the latter eventually holed up in the Ecuadorian embassy in London for nearly seven years, was another source of friction.⁷⁰

Ecuador had already signed loan agreements for $40 million with China back in 2002; however, Beijing's actual entry point into Ecuador was its response to the country's debt crisis, where Chinese finance proved crucial to restoring fiscal balance and, with that, investor confidence.⁷¹ By providing credit in the aftermath of the government's partial default in 2008, Beijing's loans played a key role in helping secure capital for the national development plan, as Ecuador's ability to raise funds from other sources had been curtailed.⁷²

Trade, Development Finance and Infrastructure Projects

Chinese trade with Ecuador follows the familiar pattern of other Latin American countries. Starting from a low base in 2000 when commerce between the two economies was negligible ($32 million), China-Ecuador two-way trade had risen to $4.4 billion ($3.68 billion imports from China and $778 million Ecuadorian exports to China) by 2017.⁷³ The structure of trade in 2017 was dominated by Chinese imports of Ecuadorian oil (43.5 per cent), crustaceans (14.4 per cent), metals (8.41 per cent) and bananas (8.6 per cent), while Ecuadorian imports from China consisted of a huge variety of machinery, computers, rolled iron and related manufactured goods.⁷⁴ The trade balance is especially skewed in China's favour when one removes oil imports from the picture.

After the World Bank and Inter-American Development Bank had declined to finance Ecuador due to the talk of debt default (ultimately implemented), Correa turned to Beijing to underwrite a host of infrastructure projects deemed necessary to fulfil his government's promises of ambitious development plans. Ecuadorian officials greeted with enthusiasm China's willingness to finance several high-profile projects, – including a grand infrastructure project linking the Brazilian Amazon with the Ecuadorian coast. But the transcontinental infrastructure project, revised by Chinese officials as they held corresponding discussions in Peru, Brazil, Chile and Bolivia, got bogged down as studies failed to demonstrate the viability of the project. But Beijing's interest in acquiring energy resources in Ecuador proved to be the key to unlocking China's massive financial resources.

In 2007 China's CNPC acquired a lease to exploit oil resources in Ecuador's Amazon region for $1.42 billion from the Canadian firm, EnCana, and launched a joint venture with the national oil parastatal, Petro-Ecuador. The arrangements involved a $2 billion loan at 7 per cent interest in exchange for guaranteed exports of 62,000 barrels a day to Chinese oil firms at a fixed dollar-denominated price.[75] In common with other deals struck by Chinese oil firms, the latter preferred to sell the oil on to the spot market to capture the higher prices, as the Chinese state required oil to be sold at a lower fixed price to Chinese consumers at the time. By 2013 Chinese loans were providing 61 per cent of Ecuador's general public expenditures, while Ecuador was exporting nearly 90 per cent of its oil to the Chinese. The collapse in commodity prices forced Quito in 2015 to seek another $7.53 billion loan from the China Development Bank in combination with the Bank of China and China ExIm Bank to assist in bridging payments to Beijing. By 2016 the Ecuadorian government owed 32.2 per cent of its GDP, most of it to China.[76]

In 2007 the Ecuadorian government announced a radical programme to combat climate change. Yasuni-ITT National Park plan would leave portions of its known oil resources – 900 million barrels – unexploited with the expectation that the international community would recognize and monetize this contribution to the environment in the form of a national trust fund.[77] Unfortunately, the concurrent pursuit of a 'Plan B' that did involve leasing and drilling, under environmental and social mitigation measures, sent mixed messages to potential green investors (especially Germany), and together with the effects of the global financial crisis forced Quito to drop the innovative initiative by 2013.[78]

Chinese interests in Ecuador extended beyond oil. Two Chinese SOEs, Tongling Non-Ferrous Metals Group and China Railway Construction Corporation, purchased a Canadian mining company's lease and set up a joint venture with an Ecuadorian enterprise, EcuaCorriente. The Mirador open-pit copper mine, a $1.4 million project covering 10,000 hectares in the middle of a pristine part of the eastern Andes and Amazon region of Ecuador, is expected to produce 3.18 million tonnes of copper and lesser amounts of silver and gold.[79] It was launched with much fanfare by the government in 2012, but its environmental destructiveness and the forced relocation of communities stirred protests, eventually causing the government to declare a state of emergency and send in the riot police in 2017.[80] The unexplained murder of one of the mine's critics in 2015 only fuelled local suspicions. The gap between EcuaCorriente's declared policies of abiding by legal requirements, its hiring and safety practices and its numerous outreach programmes for local communities, and how those communities actually experienced it all, is considerable. Xu Ying's contention is that Chinese firms have a weak understanding of corporate social responsibility, and this explained their poor conduct towards Ecuadorian communities.[81] The courts brought the project to a standstill in 2018 due to the environmental damage wrought to the area.

One of the most damaging outcomes of involvement with China was the controversial Coca Codo Sinclair hydroelectric dam project. Funded with a portion of a $6 billion loan from the China Ex-Im Bank in 2009, it was part of an initiative to build seven dams across the country to reduce Ecuador's reliance on coal. After several years' delay, the 1,500-megawatt dam's operations were commenced in November 2016 by President Xi Jinping during a state visit.[82] However, the cost of the dam far surpassed the amount borrowed from Chinese sources, as Ecuador was to discover. Sinohydro, contracted to replace another Chinese firm, completed the dam in record time but only by deliberately using sub-standard materials according to the Comptroller's Office.[83] The joint decision to locate the dam near a live volcano, prone to periodic eruptions and earthquakes – wilfully ignoring environmental impact reports produced by independent consultants, and China ExIm Bank's negligent conditionality on that prerequisite – proved to be a dreadful mistake when cracks appeared in the dam wall and the entire project had to be overhauled.[84] CELEC (Electric Corporation of Ecuador) then reviewed the work of and terminated the contract with China National Electrical Engineering Company (CNEEC) for non-compliance with technical standards in its ongoing construction of three other dams.[85] Crucially, however, its debt obligations to China forced the government to continue to pay off the $6 billion loan through sales of Ecuadorian oil at fixed rates.

Other resources came under threat from Chinese interests: for instance, Ecuador's maritime interests extend beyond its coast to the Galapagos Islands in the Pacific Ocean. Chinese fishing vessels operating illegally in Ecuadorian waters using unsustainable techniques significantly impacted fisheries, the iconic Galapagos marine park in particular. In 2017, ten thousand shark fins were discovered by the Ecuadorian navy on a Chinese 'reefer' ship transiting through the waters around the Galapagos.[86] According to former President Moreno, this transhipment storage vessel was part of a two-hundred-strong Chinese fishing fleet operating seasonally and illegally within Ecuador's maritime Exclusive Economic Zone.[87]

Chinese immigration to Ecuador increased as well during this period. An estimated thirty thousand Chinese now reside in the country.[88] Complaints from local retailers about Chinese competition and allegations of under-pricing of consumer goods grew proportionately with the opening of Chinese shops.[89] By 2020 nearly a hundred Chinese firms were operating in Ecuador, and, after Beijing designated Ecuador an approved tourist destination, annual visits by Chinese tourists jumped to over 26,231, while 14,300 Ecuadorians visited China.[90] The boost to the Ecuadorian economy was an important component in expanding its tourist outreach beyond North America and Europe. Chinese migration to Ecuador even featured in the Latin American film *Vacio*, which won an award at a national film festival in 2020.

Chinese Development Models and *Buen Vivir*

Underpinning Quito's embrace of China was a reading of the logic of economic complementary and, increasingly, a perception of growing ideological affinity. Correa himself described the rationale behind his turn away from close economic relations with the US and towards China in stark terms: 'In 2006, 75 percent of our oil was going to the United States […] this year, 50 percent has been committed to China, in exchange for billions of dollars.'[91] Beyond the desirability of reducing dependency on the US, Correa saw in China's model of state-led development the possibility of an alternative development path, one that would be realized through the benign influence of South-South solidarity. Correa's assumption that state-dominated market systems were superior echoed claims regarding the efficacy and the moral authority of the Chinese socialist market system.[92] Aligning this position with the 2008 constitution's ideal of *buen vivir*, which encapsulated a set of principles for fostering a harmonious plurinational society infused with an environmentalist ethos, was becoming increasingly problematic to say the least.[93]

Correa's populist credentials were dented by his own conduct towards social movements and even media critics.[94] Dismissive of the 'infantile left' and its unwillingness to sanction the exploitation of natural resources for economic growth's sake, Correa became increasingly alienated from his support base in the Alianza Pais party;[95] moreover, unlike his cohorts in Venezuela and Bolivia, he seemed resolved to avoid creating structures that would empower social movements to participate in policy-making.[96] CONIE (Confederación de Nacionalidades Indígenas del Ecuador), which had harboured suspicions about Correa as far back as 2006, became increasingly disenchanted with his ambiguous stance on indigenous cultural rights and his single-minded push for mining and infrastructure projects without involving indigenous communities in decision-making.

Correa's harsh reaction to criticism, whether in the form of public sector strikes or attacks by the local media – a media which, interestingly, the US ambassador even characterized as biased in favour of business elites – ultimately led Ecuador to expand state participation in the media.[97] Security had never featured highly in bilateral relations; however, in 2012 the Chinese government loaned Correa's government $240 million for electronic surveillance equipment to expand its security and surveillance reach across the country.[98] ECU 911, aimed at improving emergency responses and cutting crime, consists of a network of 4,300 surveillance cameras, sixteen regional centres and over three thousand employees dedicated to effecting responses and analysing data. Real commercial possibilities are hinted at by the impressive Chinese-Ecuadorian research and production centre in Quito (engineered by China National Electronics Import and Export Corporation and Huawei) and by the accolades that the ECU 911 surveillance system has received from governments across the region, which inspired the Venezuelan government to adopt it and the Bolivian government to set up its own BOL 110.[99] According to Xinhua News Agency, Ecuador was able to use facial recognition technology to reduce crime in its cities significantly.[100]

Though analysts are divided as to the significance of 'dual-use' surveillance technology – with seemingly robust democracies such as Britain having the dubious honour of running the highest number of surveillance cameras per capita in the West – there were other indicators of intent. Correa's publicly stated aversion to the media and NGOs, which he viewed as self-serving and subject to foreign influence, suggested uses beyond conventional regulatory functions.[101] Another indication of intent was his government's battery of Executive Decrees that tightened registration requirements on and restricted the conduct of the media and NGOs. Moreover, Quito joined fellow ALBA members' initiative to water down the media and human rights commissions at the Organization of American States (OAS) in 2013, which were seen as hostile to the Bolivarian Republics.[102]

Future Imperfect

The election of Correa's protégé, Lenin Moreno, in May 2017 was seen as a continuation of his legacy which, however mixed, had made substantive reductions in poverty alongside the now notorious debt burden and the hosting of controversial Chinese-led infrastructure projects. Within a few months Moreno unexpectedly distanced himself from Correa's policies, a reversal that seems to have been linked to disclosures of the direness of the debt situation and to corruption charges subsequently levelled at the former president. As one economist said,

Correa thought he was a genius and he has escaped accountability by giving the problem to someone else. Moreno knew he was inheriting a country in bad shape but wasn't fully aware of the things he has to do to correct the problem.[103]

Correa fled into exile in Europe as Moreno desperately sought to renegotiate the debt terms during a visit to China in December 2018 and, again, in 2019. In the meantime, the Ecuadorian economy became virtually stagnant, saddled with debt payments amounting to 40.9 per cent of GDP by 2018, a consequent inability to borrow on international capital markets and a resultant growth rate of less than 1 per cent from 2015–2019.[104] Moreno sought to be less confrontational with local business organizations, while his domestic policies reintroduced neo-liberal strictures in an effort to restore economic stability.[105] Even so, his government did not dismantle the state surveillance system, which was in use during the protests in 2019. ECU 911's production and marketing appeal was such that it was declared a 'regional benchmark'.[106] Rapprochement with the US was not long in the making, and the US presence at the airbase in Manta returned in 2018. Moreno abandoned Julian Assange to the UK authorities in 2020.[107]

Ecuadorian agency was evident while the Correa government had sought to carve out an alternative to Ecuador's historical dependency on the US. The rationale of strategic rebalancing by utilizing Chinese development finance was arguably a sound means of achieving that aim, but in light of the outcomes – a government locked into unsustainable debt directly payable by 90 per cent of its oil exports, in exchange for sub-standard, costly, even dangerous infrastructure projects – it proved a deeply debilitating one.[108] Notably, upon announcing austerity measures and public spending cuts in an effort to secure IMF loans and issuing bonds to meet existing debt obligations, Moreno tried to put a brave face on the situation: 'Thanks to the firm decisions I have made, we are not what Venezuela is today...we have recovered democracy.'[109] In effect, Ecuador's oil-backed Chinese loans, like Venezuela's, had not liberated the country, but had become the backbone of a new dependency on another external actor.

Bolivia

Despite the opening of official diplomatic ties between Bolivia and China in 1985, a bilateral economic relationship did not blossom until Evo Morales's election in 2005. The complexity of domestic politics and the partial nationalization of the country's resources sector made the rapid economic engagement by China seen in other Latin American countries advance more slowly in Bolivia. Two-way trade did improve from a paltry $75.3 million in 2000 to $2.46 billion in 2017, with Bolivian exports valued at $463 million (zinc ore [38 per cent], precious metal ore [32 per cent] and bovine meat [13 per cent]) – making China Bolivia's fifth-largest export destination – while China's $2.06 billion worth of exports to Bolivia were concentrated in machinery, vehicles, flat rolled iron and pesticides.[110] While the Bolivian government's acts caused some foreign companies to view it as a risk and to shy away from investing in new projects, the Chinese approached Bolivia with a measure of openness to opportunities in the resource sector and in infrastructure development. Behind China's cautious optimism was a risk mitigation strategy to limit the uncertainty caused by Bolivia's new political leadership and its nationalization agenda by sticking to loans tied to the engagement of Chinese firms in any projects.

The election of indigenous leader Evo Morales and his Movimiento al Socialismo-Instrumento Político por la Soberanía de los Pueblos (MAS) in December 2005 was hailed as a revolution against the elites and the ushering-in of a new era of transformative politics.[111] Morales sought to address the historic neglect of the majority indigenous population, whose standard of living was marred by poverty, unemployment and lack of education. His background as an activist for coca growers from Chapare helped him build up a national profile as a leader of a succession of loose coalitions of social movements forged into a Unity Pact. Under the new constitution of the Plurinational State of Bolivia and the Framework Law on Autonomous Regions passed in 2009, the Morales government could profess a strong commitment to economic justice, anti-corruption and job creation for its grassroots supporters, with *buen vivir* guiding its approach to negotiating the exploitation of the country's abundance of natural resources.[112] Consultation with indigenous groups on national policies was guaranteed by the constitution and identified with the years of activism by social and environmental movements, including MAS, which was rooted in local communities.[113] The relatively benign macroeconomic conditions inherited by Morales, including a budget surplus of 4.6 per cent of GDP and healthy foreign reserves derived from the commodity boom, meant that his government had the resources and policy flexibility to achieve his national aims.[114]

Following the announcement of the renationalization of the hydrocarbon sector on 1 May 2006, foreign parastatals like Petrobras and Repsol scrambled to assess the impact on their business.[115] The Morales government undertook a radical review of existing contracts starting in late 2006, which instigated a round of legal suits, stoppages by foreign companies and in some cases violent clashes with protesters. Endeavouring to reach out beyond Western conglomerates, the Bolivian government negotiated a $2 billion agreement with India's Jindal Corporation to develop an iron ore mine and natural gas plant, but lack of contractual clarity and continuing disputes over power generation finally scuppered the deal.[116] By 2014, $1.9 billion in payments had accrued to the Bolivian government through the nationalization process, contributing a whopping 6.7 per cent to overall GDP.[117] The sharp decline in commodity prices after 2014, however, put renewed pressure on Morales to secure deals that would produce not only mining revenues, but also develop the sector to benefit local communities through bigger income streams, training and employment.

If there was widespread support for Morales and MAS in the Andean highlands, the reaction of communities in the lowland region of eastern Bolivia, dominated by the commercial agricultural sector in Santa Cruz, was to claim greater regional autonomy from La Paz, initially through a referendum held in July 2006.[118] Racial violence and separatist sentiment gripped the region for the two years that followed, with indigenous protesters and farm labourers killed, and was only quelled after Morales overcame a recall referendum in 2008. The key to Morales's success in avoiding the cycle of coups and counter-coups, which too often had marred Bolivian history, lay in maintaining close ties with the military, traditionally a bastion of the right, but who were implacably against any separatist movement that could break up the country.[119] Wider-spread agrarian reforms followed the ratification of the 2009 constitution, and within four years over 134 million acres of land had been formally demarcated and titled, though far less would be actually distributed to local communities.[120]

Trade and Investment

Into this uncertain context China entered to forge new economic relations with Bolivia. As one of the least-developed countries in South America, it was not the domestic market that caught the attention of Chinese business interests, but rather Bolivia's natural resources first and foremost.

A country divided by the rugged Andean mountains, criss-crossed by rivers and lowland savannah, needed roads and railways to carry on the commercial life of the nation. Ambitious plans for electrification and rural development, as enumerated in Bolivia's national development plans, afforded opportunities for Chinese banks and construction firms alike. A $60 million loan from the China ExIm Bank to purchase oil drilling equipment in 2009, followed by an undisclosed loan for military aircraft and a $251 million loan from China Development Bank to build and launch Bolivia's first communications satellite, Túpac Katari 1, transpired in 2013. Already, however, there were troubling signs: in 2013 China's Yunnan Chinhong purchased a controlling stake in three Bolivian firms that stood accused by over eighty Andean communities of polluting local water supplies.[121] By 2015 the Bolivian government had awarded over $2 billion in contracts to Chinese firms, the majority of them tied directly to Chinese loans totalling more than $600 million (6.2 per cent of the national debt), most of them at non-concessional interest rates (over the Libor base line rate).[122]

For Bolivian farmers in the agricultural lowland basin east of the Andes, the advent of China presented a commercial opportunity to access new markets for soyabeans and other crops. Like Brazilian farmers across the border in the state of Mato Grosso, Bolivia's farmers were deeply invested in growing soyabeans and exporting them via Brazilian ports to China.[123] Chinese construction of roads to ease access for exports abroad was a long-sought improvement to make the local economy more competitive. At the same time, while new incomes through expanding markets were welcome in the lowland areas, there were concerns about the high volumes of low-cost Chinese consumer goods flowing into the towns and villages, especially in that they displaced traditional suppliers.

Chinese loan conditionalities have fared no better. Their loans are no less conditional than Western loans, merely of a different kind; i.e. compelling the use of Chinese labour and management. This has generated as much controversy as the seemingly inveterate habit of Chinese firms to ignore local labour laws, neglect community relations and dismiss environmental concerns.[124] One study by a leading Bolivian think tank noted over four hundred negative reports in the Bolivian media and complaints from other sources about Chinese businesses and their practices.[125] Cases of labour abuses were aggravated by incidents of poor execution of projects, such as pipelines bursting a few hours after CAMC's Misicuni Dam began operating or Shenzhen Vicstar's newly built bridge collapsing.[126] The economic activities of Chinese working for their construction firms went beyond the expected building of roads and bridges. An upsurge in the illegal wildlife trade – especially in jaguar teeth and skins – escalated in areas where the Chinese were operating. Radio advertisements were even broadcast in the northern region encouraging locals to bring jaguar parts to Chinese middlemen for onward sale in Chinese domestic markets and Bolivian police seized shipments of teeth and skulls from Chinese involved in the illicit trade.[127]

After discussions in Beijing in October 2015, Morales announced that China's policy banks would underwrite eleven of the capstone projects outlined in Bolivia's National Development Plan 2016–2020 with a $7.5 billion loan, later extended to $10 billion.[128] This included Chinese firms building nine roads, Sinohydro constructing the Rositas hydroelectric dam, the Santa Cruz airport expansion project and resuming modernization of the El Mutún iron and steel works abandoned by Jindal. This battery of loans made China Bolivia's largest bilateral creditor with 84 per cent of its debt, according to the National Bank of Bolivia.[129] Tucked in to this package was a $105 million loan announced two months later by the Chinese government to facilitate Bolivia's purchase of a security and disaster emergency surveillance system engineered by CEIEC and Huawei, including provisions for six hundred surveillance cameras, 120 employees and a command centre in La Paz.[130] An additional phase would introduce 840 cameras to read licence plates on transport networks.[131]

As the revolutionary fervour excited by Morales diminished over time, the once unwavering support for the president and his party began to fade. Charges of corruption inside MAS and in the conduct of public officials were brought to light by investigative journalists and impacted the government's popularity amongst all but Morales's staunchest followers; in particular, the awarding of 84 per cent of all government-funded contracts to Chinese firms without tenders came under intense scrutiny.[132] The catalogue of complaints about Chinese violations of labour and environmental codes expanded to include low project completion rates and sub-standard materials.[133] By 2016 even Morales's personal conduct was implicated by the press, with rumours of a Chinese mistress and child hidden from the public eye. The reality was more troubling, his affair seemingly tied to her position as manager in the China Agriculture and Machinery Corporation (CAMC) firm and a government contract being awarded to it.[134] Morales's attempt to secure a fourth term as president through another national referendum was narrowly defeated that same year.

Playing the China Card

China's interests in Bolivia's natural resources, still in play but largely unrealized, were to converge with the Bolivian government's need to re-energize its development agenda. The focus shifted to the country's massive reserves of lithium – found in abundance in the mountainous regions south of La Paz (near the historic silver mountain of Potosí) – which offered Chinese mining firms the opportunity to cement their lead in the booming market for batteries needed for high-technology industries, especially electric vehicles. The remoteness of the deposits at Salar del Uyuni, located at altitudes of 3,600 metres and by some estimates the largest in the world, had defeated the Bolivian government's past attempts to attract investors.[135] The world's newfound interest in lithium changed the situation completely, as foreign mining companies looked more closely at the country as a potential supplier to this fast-developing market. For Morales, who saw lithium as an opportunity for Bolivia to become a 'global powerhouse' in a resource deemed crucial for the twenty-first-century economy, the stakes were high.[136]

Many mining conglomerates had chosen to invest in neighbouring Argentina and Chile (not to mention Australia and Russia), each with their own sizable and more easily extracted lithium deposits, but more marginal companies began exploratory discussions with La Paz. The cancellation of a deal in November 2018 with a small German firm which had no track record in mining lithium, over terms that would have left Bolivia's local communities with only a small percentage of the profit share, allowed Chinese firms to step in.

The agreement of a Strategic Partnership on Morales's state visit to China on 19 June 2018 was an important signal that the Bolivian government would look to China to fulfil its development goals. It featured agreements to boost Bolivian agricultural exports to China and to donate $30 million to build a highway through Bombeo Villa Tunari.[137] This revival of Morales' controversial infrastructure project linking the Cochabamba region to San Ignacio de Moxos – and running through the Isiboro Sécure National Park and Indigenous Territory (TIPNIS) – risked renewed dissent amongst lowland indigenous communities, and ignored the history of this project which had sparked a protest march by indigenous groups, suppressed by police violence, and the Morales government's own promise in October 2011 that the TIPNIS area should thenceforth be 'untouchable'.[138] By throwing the gauntlet down again with once-key allies in the MAS-led Unity Pact, Morales seemed to be gambling that he could shore up his weakening political support with the majority of Bolivians by inaugurating a set of dramatic mega-projects.

By December 2018 the Chinese SOE Xinjiang TBEA Group was holding preliminary discussions with the Bolivian government, and in February 2019 it was announced that a deal had been secured with the Bolivian parastatals Yacimientos de Litio Bolivianos (YLB) and Comibol to divide the profits – 51 per cent for YLB and 49 per cent for Xinjiang TBEA Group.[139] An investment of over $2.3 billion was promised for the initial phase of the project, which was expected to expand to include a sizeable battery manufacturing plant employing thousands of local Bolivians. Bolivia's launch of a locally manufactured electric car, Quantum, signalled the importance of lithium to its national development.[140] Morales justified his selection of a Chinese firm in a public broadcast: 'Why China? There's a guaranteed market in China for battery production.'[141] Debate within the mining sector as to the quality and commercial viability of Bolivia's lithium deposits raised questions about whether companies were engaged in speculation or taking a longer-term position in securing licences to mine these assets.[142] Morales's sudden resignation a few days after the Chinese-Bolivian announcement of the deal raised his supporters' suspicions of a US-backed 'coup'.[143]

The return of MAS to power in national elections in October 2020 under the leadership of Luis Arce came with a pledge to reopen discussions with potential investors in the lithium sector.[144] The struggle over power and legitimacy between urban elites, racist hierarchies and indigenous rural communities was set to continue to shape political dynamics in Bolivia and its response to China.

Conclusion: Venezuela, Ecuador and Bolivia

The Bolivarian republics, intent on breaking their historical dependency on the US, found in China a willing if cautious accomplice. China's development finance and technical resources in petroleum, construction and others were brought to bear precisely on replacing losses in these sectors and even on expanding long-term development opportunities. The sustained rise in commodity prices enabled these governments to seek rents from export tax revenues and redirect them to development and social programmes targeting their historically neglected constituencies – 'neo-extractivism'. Beijing's explicit commitment to non-interference in domestic affairs promised that deepening economic engagement would not devolve into the interventionism that follows reliance on the US.

The anti-imperialist rhetoric stoked by the Bolivarian republics disguised their continuing dependency on the US, despite the expanding Chinese presence, and it also obscured the commercial intent and practices pursued by Chinese firms. This dependency and the centrality of Chinese commercial drivers was epitomized by the export of Venezuelan and Ecuadorian oil to US refiners by China's SOEs which captured windfall profits from the fixed prices in their contracts with these governments. The onset of a debilitating debt cycle with China, coupled with many Chinese firms' wilful neglect of the concerns of local communities, environmentalists and labour activists, were echoes of the worst conduct of North American and European governments and firms. And, contrary to the repetitive official disclaimers of non-interference by Beijing, Chinese involvement in domestic politics now looms large in the story of China's relations with Venezuela, even if there is little evidence of it in Ecuador and Bolivia. In all three cases the local leadership's development plans and concurrent political fortunes increasingly must rely on China to offset waning popular support. It underscores how China has gone from a very marginal presence in Latin America to a 'grey eminence' widely perceived to be in league with particular governments.

This situation, exemplified by the Bolivarian republics, is generating unease in Beijing. Such is the fear of disappointment that the soaring rhetoric employed by Latin American governments and scholars has alarmed Chinese experts on the region, who protest, 'Latin America has too high expectations of China'.[145] The costs of entanglement with sitting regimes and their policies, alongside the complexities of sustaining Chinese interests in the face of rising local discontent and electoral (or more violent) change, continue to mount.[146] It is a problem China also faced with its largest trading partner and most important diplomatic partner in the region, Brazil.

5

Brazil – Partnership to Populism

Brazil's engagement with China reflected its lofty ambitions, from propelling transformative development at home to assuming global leadership on the world stage, and became a national priority with the election of Lula Da Silva in 2002.[1] Latin America's largest economy and biggest population presided over an abundance of natural resources, a dynamic agro-industry and technological prowess in key sectors as well as a substantive market that attracted Chinese firms and financial resources. Moreover, Brazil's recognized standing as an emerging power paved the way for its founding role in BRICS (Brazil, Russia, India, China and South Africa) in 2009.[2] In short, Brazilians were mesmerized by Beijing's multi-billion financial proposals for development, the boundless trade opportunities and the prospects of sharing global leadership of a world in transition.

Unfettered ambitions, however, soon turned to unmitigated concern as Brazilian businesses grappled with the impact of competition from Chinese imports while Chinese companies faced unanticipated regulatory obstacles to their trade and investment. Economists worried that China's role in extracting resources constituted 'reprimarization' that would undermine the country's development gains.

The Brazilian government, battered by the collapse in commodity prices in 2013–2014 as a lagging aftershock of the global financial crisis that 'ended' in 2009, was struggling to raise capital to reignite growth and fund its mounting debt burden, exacerbated by the unfolding Petrobras scandal.[3] The result was that the mergers and acquisitions by SOEs that typically led Chinese investment in LAC underwent an unprecedented surge that made Brazil the third-largest recipient of Chinese FDI by 2016.[4] The sharpening divergence in global diplomacy and national politics had an impact on relations with China, which moved from embrace by Lula da Silva to Jair Bolsonaro's populist rhetoric. But in the end the economic entanglement of the two countries only seemed to pause, its inexorability undiminished.

Brazil and China – From Imperial Relations to Emerging Powers

Brazil's relations with China began in the Imperial period, when Emperor João VI imported three hundred Macanese labourers in 1814 to work in the National Botanical Gardens to aid his government's plans to expand into agricultural export crops like tea and coffee.[5] Although Brazil did not abolish slavery until 1888, its plantation owners felt the international and domestic pressure, and, like their counterparts in the West Indies, from the 1850s began to look to Chinese labour to address the prospect of manumission. Cantonese were contracted to work on plantations and on the seminal Central Brazil railroad project that was to link Rio de Janeiro, São Paulo and the mineral-rich territory of Minas Gerais. In 1880 the Brazilian Imperial government negotiated a treaty with Imperial China to facilitate the large-scale import of Chinese contract labour. Over time, twenty thousand Chinese from the Canton area migrated to Brazil, settling in the towns that sprung up along *Trem de Prata* ('Silver Train') railroad junctions like Japeri in the southeast of Rio de Janeiro State.

The global outlook stemming from its Imperial past solidified its foreign policy in the aftermath of the First World War. Brazilian involvement in the League of Nations set it apart from the more inward-looking countries of Latin America. A member of the Allies in the Second World War and a founding member of the United Nations, Brazil's ties with China's Nationalist government were close enough to warrant a state visit to Rio de Janeiro by Chiang Kai-shek's influential wife, Soong Mei-ling, in 1944.[6] Despite this, Brazilian diplomacy sought to carve out a position of autonomy for itself at the height of the Cold War, when then Vice-President João Goulart paid a formal visit to the People's Republic of China in August 1961, resulting in the mutual exchange of trade representatives.[7] This 'normalization' was cut short by a military coup, which overthrew Goulart in 1964 and saw the arrest of nine Chinese officials working in the trade liaison office, accused of espionage by the junta.[8]

Diplomatic relations with China were not established until 1974, following the rapprochement between Beijing and Washington, but concrete measures were stalled until 1982 by hardliners in the military junta.[9] With Chinese exports of industrial products and imports of Brazilian oil dominating the exchange in the mid-1980s, two-way trade began to increase, up from $65 million in 1973 to the modest figure of $817 million in bilateral trade in 1985, before declining again.[10] During President José Sarney's visit to China in 1988, the cornerstone of scientific cooperation was laid with the launching of the China-Brazil Earth Resources Satellite programme and, in the aftermath of the Tiananmen Square massacre, Brazil became one of the first countries to host a state visit by China's President Yang Shangkun (Aylwin's Chile did as well on that trip). By 1993 Beijing had designated the relationship as a Strategic Partnership, one of the first to be named as such in China's constellation of formalized diplomatic arrangements. The intervening period did not yield the expected commercial opportunities in China for Brazilian construction multinationals, who failed to secure a leading role in the construction of the Three Gorges Dam project – though a Brazilian subsidiarity was contracted to manufacture some of the power generation equipment – while agribusiness found itself unable to access the Chinese domestic market.[11] A Brazilian vote censuring China at the UN Human Rights Commission in 1997 (alleged by Brazilian diplomats to have been a mistake), inspired the creation of the China-Brazil Human Rights Commission which, however, had fallen into desuetude by 2004.[12]

Lula and the Era of Expansive Cooperation – Trade, Investment and Competition

The visit by Hu Jintao to Brasilia in November 2004, following on from Lula da Silva's official trip to Beijing earlier in the year, proved to be another milestone in the relationship. Lula (as he is universally known) had campaigned on a platform of internationalizing Brazil and had identified China as likely to cooperate. Once in office, his administration operationalized this by diplomatic missions and broadened bilateral, institutionalized cooperation.[13] Hu and Lula agreed to raise the dialogue to a China-Brazil High Level Coordination and Cooperation Commission involving senior officials. The China-Brazil Business Council was inaugurated, chaired by the heads of Vale (then known as CVRD) and Minmetals. Partnerships were formed between Brazilian multinationals and Chinese SOEs aspiring to internationalization, including joint exploration for oil by Petrobras and Sinopec in Ecuador and Iran, and the opening of a Baosteel and Vale steel production site in the State of Maranhão, amongst others. When Lula signed an MOU during Hu Jintao's visit he committed Brazil – against the express advice of his ministers and the leading business interests – to acknowledge China as a 'market economy',[14] it may have been because the Chinese government had indicated it would invest up to $10 billion in Brazil over the next three years.[15] Reportedly, Lula overrode the objections of the ministers of development, trade and industry, and external affairs in granting market economy status after twenty hours of single-minded negotiations on the part of the Chinese.[16]

Notably, a key demand of the Brazilian government during Lula's state visit to China six months earlier had been Beijing's public endorsement of a Brazilian permanent seat on the UN Security Council. A long-standing ambition of Brazilian diplomacy, under Lula and his deputy Celso Amorim, the push for a seat came to the forefront of foreign policy. While officials in Beijing gave Lula private assurances of support, China officially stuck to a less-than-resounding formulation in public: 'the UNSC should be expanded, the developing world needs representation on the UNSC, and Brazil is a developing nation'.[17] Negotiations over an FTA with Mercosur, initially voiced on the Lula state visit, were eventually shelved in talks in Brasilia due to resistance from the business community.[18]

Brazilian commercial concerns notwithstanding, the momentum generated by the visit produced an elevation of government-to-government ties, with the formation of the Comissão Sino-Brasileira de Alto Nível de Concertação e Cooperação (COSBAN, or High-Level Coordination and Cooperation Commission) following on from successive state visits by Lula in May and Hu Jintao in November of 2004. The first meeting of COSBAN and its eleven ministerial-level sub-committees, ranging from economic cooperation to scientific and research collaboration, was held in Beijing in 2006.[19] Led by both countries' vice-presidents, its role was to develop and follow up on the five-year action plans as part of a bilateral strategic dialogue process. According to one Brazilian analyst involved in COSBAN, it was significant as a mechanism for raising specific problems in bilateral relations and mobilizing political will to resolve them:

> Cosban is instrumental in addressing business issues because it is the moment when leaders from both countries sit down and negotiate their interests. Business executives deal with different levels of the government on a regular basis, but it is during Cosban that regulatory issues are decided. Examples of success include the opening of the [Chinese] poultry and beef markets (in which Brazilian exports last year amounted to US$3.5 billion), agreements between oil companies and agreements to integrate financial markets, with banks being able to open in both countries.[20]

The second COSBAN meeting was held in Brasilia in February 2012, while in November 2013, the third COSBAN meeting was held in Guangzhou, again with the same eleven ministerial-level sub-committees.[21] This process was repeated in 2015, where the fourth COSBAN meeting authorized the action plan of 2015–2021, but as the Brazilian government was later to admit, the process stagnated under the weight of Brazil's unfolding domestic political scandals.

The Lula administration's enthusiasm for expanding trade with China was remarkable: after Hu Jintao's visit in 2004, over the next seven years there were twenty-five Brazilian trade missions to China, reciprocated by twenty-seven Chinese trade missions to Brazil.[22] Two-way trade had slowly been edging up before 2000, to $36.91 billion in 2009, but this happened after the signing of the MOU in 2004, when commercial exports grew much faster, reaching $21 billion in 2009, making China Brazil's leading trade partner.[23] From 2000 onward, Brazil maintained a trade surplus with China, reflecting the high price and weighting of commodities in bilateral commercial exchanges; at the same time, however, the trade structure started shifting increasingly in favour of China's export of manufactured products, including those with higher technological inputs, in exchange for Brazil's basic agricultural, energy and ore products.[24] Vale alone doubled its total worldwide iron ore exports to China from 28 per cent of all exports in 2004 to 42 per cent in 2008. In fact, the high concentration of Brazil's exports in just a few commodities replicated China's exchanges with other trading partners within Latin America.[25]

The outcome of expanding Chinese trade in commodities coupled with its competitiveness over local producers in manufactured goods, led economists to talk about Brazil's de-industrialization or, in local parlance, 'reprimarization'.[26] Moreover, Chinese firms' market penetration in textiles, toys and electronics – goods produced locally in Brazil – was to crater Brazilian company revenues and employment.[27] Equally bad, competition between Brazil and China in third-country markets in Latin America exhibited worrying trends as well;[28] for instance, Chinese market penetration in neighbouring Argentina accelerated from 5.6 per cent of the country's total imports in 2002 to 12.5 per cent 2010. Meanwhile, Brazil's share of Argentina's imports only grew from 25.6 per cent in 2002 to 31.4 per cent in 2010.[29] The competition introduced by Chinese imports rattled Brazilian business confidence, and calls were heard for revoking China's market economy status. These were troubling developments for Lula's Partido dos Trabalhadores (PT) government, which had pegged its fate on reinvigorating industrialization strategy through state planning. The uproar signalled the importance of traditional manufacturing and, concurrently, a recognition of the necessity of innovation to next-generation production.[30] Even Brazilian diplomats, once a stronghold of support for closer ties, were no longer as sanguine about the economic impact of China on their country's interests.[31]

In 2005 Congressman Antonio Carlos Pannunzio tabled a bill, PDC1630/2005, calling for the repeal of the 'market economy' MOU. Though an MOU does not have the force of law, the validity of this MOU was challenged in Brazilian federal court, and this set the stage for Brazil's charges of Chinese 'dumping' at the WTO. At this point, the Brazilian government was responding cautiously to the trade tensions with local industry, so as to allow the ambivalent legal position of the MOU to provide potential leverage in bilateral negotiations.[32] However, as Chinese imports moved into higher-end knowledge- and technology-intensive sectors, Lula's administration finally disregarded its MOU and began to pressure China by applying the full range of measures allowed by WTO in bringing anti-dumping cases, such as imports of Chinese pharmaceuticals in April 2012.[33] Beijing took Brazil's newfound assertiveness in its stride, declaring that 'trade friction and disputes are inevitable' as bilateral ties become closer.[34]

For some observers, Brazil's slowness to utilize the WTO dispute settlement mechanism came down to an unwillingness to harm the larger emerging power agenda embodied in closer economic and political cooperation at the global level. It increasingly pitted ministries against each other, especially Itamaraty (as Brazil's Ministry of External Affairs is commonly known) versus other interests in government, the business community and trade unions, putting the Lula administration in an increasingly defensive position with the Brazilian public as to the benefits of China.[35]

The public veneer espoused by Lula's Brazil of being an emerging-power peer with China notwithstanding, evidence was periodically surfacing that Brazil occupied the subordinate position. For instance, when Celso Amorim, Brazil's Foreign Minister, sought out high-level meetings in Beijing in advance of Lula's visit in May 2009, he was overlooked in favour of US Secretary of State Hillary Clinton, despite his counterpart having met with the Brazilian president earlier that year. Subsequently, Itamaraty downgraded the proposed five-day visit and scaled back its expectations of achieving any major economic breakthroughs.[36]

Trade and Investment in the Building of a Comprehensive Strategic Partnership

After fourteen years (1995–2009) of trading, Chinese investment in Brazil stood at the relatively low figure of $255 million;[37] however, from 2010 onward, Chinese investment grew phenomenally, reaching $102.5 billion in 2018 according to official data out of Beijing.[38] Studies demonstrated nonetheless that only half of the 199 projects ever announced were actually realized, so a more realistic figure would be about $58 billion.[39] An estimated 145 Chinese firms were working on projects in Brazil (though the overall number of private SMEs was believed to be far greater). According to the Brazil-China Business Council, investment initially was focused on resources (oil, soyabeans, minerals), but by 2010 this resource-seeking approach was being supplemented by a move to diversify into Brazil's 200-million-strong consumer market with a focus on high-end products such as automotive, electronics and communication devices.[40] Following the steep downturn in the Brazilian economy in 2013, investment moved into the financial services sector, while more recently the emphasis has been on infrastructure investments in the national electricity grid and innovation-seeking through M&A of leading Brazilian technology firms.[41]

Interestingly, Chinese investment flowing into Brazil after 2010 was rather 'statistically hidden' inasmuch as it entered overwhelmingly via Caribbean tax havens like the Cayman Islands and, even more so, the British Virgin Islands, and was not immediately identifiable as Chinese.[42] According to a 2018 Banco Central do Brasil study, between 83 per cent and 98 per cent of Chinese investment was attributed to intermediary sources in the period from 2010 to 2017;[43] indeed, this trend accelerated after 2015 with China becoming the third-largest investor in Brazil after the US and the Netherlands, so that the global significance of Brazil as a destination for Chinese investment grew as it became the fifth target destination for FDI and the only developing economy (the others being Australia, US, UK and Switzerland). Between 2010 and 2018 Brazil came to account for 51 per cent of total Chinese FDI in South America at $59.4 billion.[44] However, the election of Bolsonaro in October 2018 corresponded with a 41 per cent fall in Chinese FDI in Brazil, suggesting to some that his high-profile use of anti-Chinese rhetoric during the campaign had raised concerns in China.

The agricultural sector has been a consistent interest, but increasingly Chinese FDI has targeted the whole value chain, with investments in production, transport, distribution networks and port infrastructure.[45] The State of Mato Grosso, which produces the bulk of soyabean exports that end up in China, became a particular locus of Chinese commercial agricultural interests, which expanded to beef exports and infrastructure provisions over time.[46] The media's emphasis on Chinese FDI in manufacturing was tantalizing in the context of losses to Chinese competition in other sectors; however, the touted investment fell far short of expectations.[47] From 2013 on, the Chinese financial sector expanded operations by opening branches in cities around the country and buying up shares in Brazilian banks, which furnished critical insights into market opportunities, risk assessment and how to join up Chinese interests to local-regional networks.[48]

Holding together the economic relationship was a renewed push to diversify Chinese investment in Brazil while simultaneously sounding a cautionary note. Succeeding President Dilma Rousseff, a member of Lula's inner circle, voiced a measure of concern about bilateral ties. Speaking at the Brazil-China Business Council in Beijing in 2011, she said 'the prosperity of a nation cannot be at the expense of others', arguably a comment on the collapse of a joint venture in the aviation sector; and that deepening bilateral ties would have to be based on 'reciprocity'.[49] Her decision to impose import taxes to protect local industries like automobiles was indicative of Brazil's new and tougher approach.

The deals signed during the new President Rousseff's six-day visit – opening a $300 million soyabean processing plant in Bahia, authorizing Brazilian exports of pork, a new automobile assembly factory and a new $300 million Huawei research facility in São Paulo – signalled China's receptivity to Brazilian concerns. A year later Brazil and China upgraded their relationship to a 'Comprehensive Strategic Partnership' during Premier Wen Jiabao's state visit. As with other Latin American countries designated under this appellation, certain pre-conditions regarding existing bilateral ties as well as aspirations held by officials in Beijing about the potential of closer ties are expected. In Brazil's case, the progression of economic interdependence and the potential to extend that through greater cooperation at ministerial level was reflected in the decision to create a special investment fund to accelerate this development.

Additional to these conditions, which feature in many other comprehensive strategic partnerships such as Peru's and Chile's, was the larger global position that Brazil occupies as regional power and its diplomatic cooperation through BRICS. As the five-year plan for joint cooperation came to an end in 2013, the third meeting of COSBAN was held in Guangzhou and featured agreements in agriculture and aerospace.[50] Even while domestic scandals were engulfing Brazilian politics, the fourth COSBAN event met in Brasilia in June 2015 and secured the final agreement on a specialized vehicle to coordinate Chinese investment in the Brazilian economy. As in the past, the Brazilian representatives pressed for greater access to the Chinese market for Brazilian exports, with specific mention of value-added manufactured goods.[51]

The China-Brazil Fund for Expansion of Production Capacity, known as the China-Brazil Fund, capitalized by the China Investment Cooperation Fund in Latin America at $15 billion and by the Banco Nacional de Desenvolvimento Econômico e Social (BNDES) and the Caixa Economical Federal at $5 billion, is the mechanism established in 2015 for aligning development policy and development finance for infrastructure projects. The aim, according to the Brazilian ambassador, 'is to finance priority projects in logistics and industry through Chinese companies with Brazilian partners'.[52]

Like its counterpart in Venezuela, funding is provided on a project basis and managed by a steering committee consisting of officials from the Chinese Ministry of Commerce and the Brazilian Ministry of Planning, Development and Management. Brazilian officials have pointed out that decision-making on projects is joint – a feature believed to be unique amongst China's bilateral investment funds – and that projects need not involve Chinese companies or purchase materials from China.[53] The Chinese ambassador, speaking at the launch, declared:

> With our comprehensive strategic partnership, Brazil is a priority country for China's strategy of expanding productive capacity. The China-Brazil Fund guarantees the financial mechanism to expand cooperation.[54]

China officials made a point of urging Chinese firms to participate and invest in Brazilian infrastructure, agribusiness, electricity, telecommunications and industrial parks.[55] In May 2018 four infrastructure projects and one industrial project were selected from twenty-nine proposals by a Technical Working Group and then analysed by financial institutions to determine their economic viability.[56] Concessional loans were to be provided in Brazilian currency to avoid the risks of exchange rate fluctuation, and private banks were encouraged to engage.

The China-Brazil Fund seemed to be tailor-made for the kind of visionary infrastructure projects which had long featured in the Brazilian imagination. The Trans-Oceanic Railway (sometimes referred to as the Bi-Oceanic Corridor), linking Brazilian Atlantic coastal cities to the Pacific coastal ports of Andean countries, had been mooted by officials from China Railway Engineering Corporation (CREC) at meetings in South America as early as 2010.[57] It would cut the costs of transporting agricultural products from Brazil to China by $30 per ton.[58] During Li Keqiang's 2015 state visit, Brazil and China agreed to thirty-five trade and investment accords, amongst which is exploring this megaproject, it being suggested that up to $50 billion could be made available to build it.[59] Preliminary surveys by Chinese engineers plotted the railway's path through the Brazilian state of Acre, across the Andes and to the northern Peruvian coast.[60] Deemed uneconomical by the Brazilian Ministry of Planning and Development, a second survey was produced which also proved to be problematic, as it ran through a national park, while a third route cut through Bolivia before reaching Peru (see Chapter 3).

Environmentalists and civil society groups remained wary of the proposal, citing studies of its impact on pristine Amazonian rainforest and indigenous communities.[61] Such environmentally sensitive regulatory regimes were seen as perplexing if not incomprehensible by Chinese managers, according to their Brazilian counterparts, and as a result Brazilian officials preferred to hire local consultancies to handle such issues.[62] Despite these obstacles, initiatives such as the announced plans to build forty dams in the São Luiz do Tapajós river basin continued to incentivize Chinese construction firms to maintain a foothold in the Brazilian market.

Environmentalists who had hoped that China would play a more robust role in support of the preservation of the Amazon as the top importer of Brazilian soyabeans and beef were to be disappointed. Yet one cannot simply accuse the Chinese of destroying the Amazon while so many other industrialized countries have contributed to the situation as well. As one environmental activist put it,

> We've done some work with COFCO and found they are far more into the details and committed to understanding what their supply chain actually is. Cargill, on the other hand, makes a lot of noise and does nothing.[63]

The role of Chinese timber firms, also much apprehended by critics, remained very limited.[64]

The embattled government became increasingly distracted after corruption investigations by federal police began in March 2014. *Operação Lava Jato* yielded at least a thousand warrants implicating employees of Petrobras, politicians of the main parties, presidents of the Republic, members of the Chamber of Deputies and the Federal Senate, State Governors and executives of some of Brazil's biggest businesses.[65] It led to the impeachment of President Rousseff, and by May 2016 she was forced to step down. Vice-President Michel Temer took over. Temer's 'caretaker presidency' was diffident toward China when it came to the kinds of foreign policy initiatives that had been so central to the Lula administration; for example, he was conspicuously absent from the Belt and Road Summit in Beijing in 2017. With the Brazilian economy still faltering, Temer began a massive privatization of state-owned assets in the oil sector, power generation and distribution, airports, roads and refineries, which it was hoped would attract local and foreign capital.[66] Both the China-Brazil Fund and capital-rich Chinese firms were expected to snap up many of these assets.[67] This strategy did give a boost to the Brazilian economy, reflected in turn by a 27 per cent burst of growth in two-way trade to $75 billion in 2017, after four consecutive years of decline.[68]

Temer's inclusion of agroindustry representatives in his Cabinet, and the promotion of legislation to fast-track infrastructure projects that served those as well as construction firms' interests, drew criticism from some of the PT's traditional constituencies.[69] Corruption charges were soon levelled at Temer and, following the election of Jair Bolsonaro in late 2018, he was prosecuted and jailed. He left prison in mid-2019 and it is reported that he now works as a consultant to Huawei to provide legal advice on Huawei's development of 5G business in Brazil.[70]

Focus on the Agricultural Sector

Chinese demand for soyabeans, a key livestock feed and a human foodstuff, shapes China's approach to Brazil. An exporter of soyabeans until 2000, Beijing's decision to open up soyabeans to foreign imports saw domestic production plummet and agroindustry multinationals like ADM, Cargill and Louis Dreyfus step in to refinance local actors. The multinationals came to dominate 70 per cent of China's soya processing capacity by 2010.[71] According to an official of the China Soybean Industry Association, this followed from the government decision to 'abandon soybeans and protect grains', an experiment in allowing the international market integration of this key crop.[72] As White Papers on food security made clear in 1996 and reiterated in 2013, the government was aiming to guarantee food security in grains (non-soyabeans) by a combination of maintaining high levels of fixed targets for domestic commercial production of soyabeans, supplemented by foreign imports.[73] The goal was to achieve 100 per cent self-sufficiency in rice and grains and 80 per cent self-sufficiency in other foodstuffs (like soyabeans). The US-China trade dispute prompted the Chinese to halt its soyabean purchases from the United States and in July 2018 China slapped a 25 per cent retaliatory tariff on US soyabeans. It moved to shift their sourcing to other regions of the world, including LAC, importing fourteen million tons of soyabeans from Brazil.[74] Domestic sceptics of China's heavy reliance on imports of US soyabeans 'perceive South American producers as sharing a similar marginal position in the global soybean complex', while, concurrently, Brazil's production costs in particular are far lower than China's.[75] The inability of China to influence the price of soyabeans, despite the massive volume of its imports, is frustrating for policymakers and the public alike. This helps explain China's diversification into Brazilian and Argentine soyabean imports and away from reliance on the US as well as Beijing's efforts to capture a significant position in South American production and distribution networks.

Chinese interest in Brazilian farmland commenced in earnest with a series of modest purchases by Zhejiang Fudi Agriculture Company and its SOE partner, Beidahuang-Heilongjiang State Farm in Rio Grande do Sul and Tocantins States in late 2007 and 2008. These farms, 600 hectares and 1,600 hectares in size, were sold on to the Chongqing Grain Group in 2011, which was already involved in purchasing a 200,000-hectare soyabean farm in Bahia.[76] Calls to block a 'Chinese land grab' rose with growing frequency in the Brazilian press, citing these examples, and stoked the enactment of bill PL4059/12 in 2010 to tighten regulations on foreign land purchases.[77] For instance, prominent economist and former Minister of Finance Antonio Delfim Netto, interviewed in *O Estado do São Paulo* in August 2010, said in a much-cited statement that 'the Chinese have bought Africa and now they are trying to buy Brazil'.[78] Brazil's ambassador to China echoed this sentiment, claiming that Brazilian agroindustry and mining sectors did not need foreign investments. Newly elected President Rousseff's support for this restrictive legislation aimed ostensibly at foreigners but focused on the Chinese was, according to analysts, a concession by her to the PT traditional agrarian and labour support base, but was also driven by a policy of cultivating agribusiness elites on the part of the politically weak successor to Lula.[79]

This coincided with a re-emphasis on the strategy of foreign investment via mergers and acquisitions, part of a generalized Chinese response to localized nationalism and 'sinophobia'. This proved to be a more successful means of investing in the sector; for instance, in 2016 a subsidiary of the Shanghai Pengxin Group purchased a majority stake in two medium-sized Brazilian firms, Fiagril and Belagricola, involved in soya trading and processing. While the company has ambitious plans to triple its annual exports of Brazilian soyabeans to thirty million tonnes, persistent losses shifted its focus to supplying fertilizers to the market.[80] At a global scale, the decisions of China National Cereals, Oils and Foodstuffs (COFCO) to buy up major stakes in Dutch and Hong Kong agricultural multinationals gave it significant positions in the seeds, processing and trading interests that these firms hold in Brazil.[81] On the other hand, efforts by Chinese agroindustrial firms such as Shanghai Rainbow Group and Huapont-Nutrichem to break into the local chemical fertilizer users' markets proved unsuccessful and lacking the scale needed to achieve serious market penetration.[82] The overall trend was enforced on a global scale by the SOE ChemChina's $43 billion purchase of one of the world's largest seed and pesticide companies, Syngenta, completed in 2018.

Focus on the Manufacturing and Technology Sector: Aviation and Automobiles

Aerospace cooperation included the joint launching of satellites in October 1999 and three subsequent launches from northern China. But it was collaboration between Brazil's prized aircraft maker and a new Chinese aviation firm that caught global attention. Embraer, the leading designer and manufacturer of regional commercial aircraft, and China Aviation Industry Corporation (AVIC II), a leading SOE at the cutting edge of China's efforts to develop its own production capacity in aviation, started a joint venture in the northern city of Harbin in 2002. Aiming to produce the ERJ-145, the signature Embraer commercial airplane to serve expanding Chinese domestic demand, the first jointly produced airplane rolled off the assembly lines in December 2003. However, orders for the ERJ-145 proved to be very slow, partly due to the plane's cost, which was saddled with a 3 per cent duty on imported parts and 17 per cent value-added tax, making it more expensive than its equivalent produced in Brazil.[83] The additional production of the Legacy 650 business jet did not generate local interest and, beyond one order of an E-190 by Hebei Airlines, Embraer failed to secure a single commercial contract in China from its manufacturing base in that country (though, tellingly, Embraer successfully sold forty-four E-jets built in Brazil directly to a Chinese airline).[84] Disputes over the Chinese insistence on technology transfer, a common feature of its joint venture agreements, raised concerns from Embraer officials.[85]

The decision to close the production facility in Harbin in 2011 and the subsequent announcement that AVIC II would be producing aircraft in direct competition with Embraer sent shockwaves through Brazilian business and government circles.[86] For many, this initiative came to embody the deep concerns inherent in the relationship.[87] A subsequent agreement to partner with Boeing was marred by the US manufacturer's series of troubles from the systemic failures of its 737 Max and subsequent cancellation of orders, leading to speculation – fuelled by reports Embraer featured in discussions at the May 2019 COSBAN – that Embraer would look to China once again.[88]

One of China's most successful automobile manufacturers, Chery Automotive Company (CAC), began exploring the Brazilian market in 2006 and exporting the Chery Tiggo into Brazil in July 2009. In a domestic market where first-time buyers should welcome a price-competitive vehicle, the arrival of the SUV made an immediate impact.[89] Cutting into local Brazilian-manufactured cars' business, owners and unions pressurized the Brazilian government until in 2011 Rousseff imposed an industrial products tax surcharge of nearly 30 per cent on the Chinese cars.[90] Faced with a prohibitive tax on imported automobiles, CAC decided to shift production to Brazil.

In 2013 CAC announced it would establish a $130 million automobile assembly plant in Jacareí, in the Brazilian State of São Paulo, with a production capacity of 150,000 vehicles per year. Starting a year later, the Chery car was expected to continue to sell well; unfortunately, the Brazilian economy sank into a long recession that same year, with consumer spending all but drying up. By 2016 as few as two thousand vehicles were being produced annually at the factory where production capacity was set at fifty thousand.[91] After investing over $400 million through 2017 and posting significant losses, the Chinese owners elected to sell a 50 per cent share in the enterprise to the Brazilian firm Grupo Caoa.

Far from being a retreat from the Brazilian market, however, CAC presented this as a strategic move. The General Manager, Chen Anning, commented:

> The partnership between Caoa and Chery is complementary with each other's qualities. Chery can develop, produce and manufacture a quality product, and Caoa has ample knowledge and experience in commercial marketing and services in the Brazilian market.[92]

By 2019 the Caoa-Chery joint venture had launched, to great fanfare, new lines of production, including a newly branded SUV and an electric car, and declared its ambition to capture 5 per cent of Brazil's domestic market.

Focus on the Energy Sector

Petrobras, the national oil company upheld as the flagship of Brazil's global reach in this sector, launched an aggressive programme to expand production and exploration around the world under the Lula Administration. In 2009, faced with the sudden fall in oil prices, the Rousseff Administration turned to China Development Bank (CDB) for a $10 billion loan whose terms included provisions to supply Unipec (a Sinopec subsidiary) with up to 200,000 barrels of oil a day.[93] The Chinese publicly stated their expectation that some of Petrobras' stakes in offshore oil leases would be sold to Chinese firms, which national legislation precluded from making available.[94] In addition, cost cutting required Petrobras to shut down some of its international operations and even sell assets acquired during its previous buying spree.

For Chinese national oil companies, the attraction of Petrobras was as much its technical expertise in deep-water drilling as any shares in oil blocks. Brazil's newly discovered pre-salt oil deposits (mirrored across the Atlantic in offshore Angola, where Sinopec operated), which doubled its proven offshore reserves to twenty-five billion barrels, were only accessible through the highly specialized, costly technologies mastered by a small number of Western firms. CDB's role in Brazil's oil sector reflected its strategic agenda of building a global portfolio in the energy, agriculture and infrastructure sectors.[95] Following an initial $750 million loan agreement with Petrobras in 2007 for Sinopec to build an oil pipeline, negotiations began with the Brazilian government for a much bigger credit line in the wake of the global financial crisis in 2008, which was taken up to the State Council for approval. According to Chen Yuan, the head of CDB, the fact that the leaders of both countries planned state visits in the coming year proved to be influential:

> [O]nce the Ministry of Foreign Affairs, the Ministry of Commerce, the National Development and Reform Commission and the State Council realized this coincidence, they provided their active support. As a result, this project became a national project.[96]

This new agreement lay the foundation for the CNOOC purchase in 2013 of a 10 per cent share of the Libra pre-salts oil field as part of a consortium of foreign oil firms. Six years later it expanded its role in pre-salts oil fields through a contested joint bid with Petrobras.[97]

By 2015 the combination of continuing lower oil prices and mushrooming corruption scandals involving price-fixing and political kickbacks had forced executives out and put Petrobras into deep debt. CDB extended $10 billion more credit to Petrobras in December of the next year in exchange for a guarantee of Unipec's access to at least 100,000 barrels of oil per day (replacing the 2009 agreement for 200,000 barrels per day).[98] Disbursement of the funds was contingent on paying off the existing $2.8 billion loan stemming from the 2009 agreement.[99] In early 2017 Petrobras and CDB signed a further agreement aimed at unlocking the second tranche of the $10 billion credit line to underwrite the costs of leasing oil platforms and joint exploration.

Beyond the upstream investments in Petrobras, Chinese interests extended to other aspects of downstream processing and distribution. In 2018 CNPC subsidiary PetroChina bought shares in petrol distributor TT, while CNPC purchased a 20 per cent stake in Comperj refinery in Rio de Janeiro State, infusing new cash into the company, which enabled it to return to production after a three-year standstill due to corruption scandals and Brazil's economic crisis.[100] Chinese construction firms, working with Brazilian partners, were building refineries in the northeast as well as assessing the possibilities of expanding Brazil's refinery capacity in other parts of the country.[101]

The opportunities inherent in the privatization programme proposed by Temer and carried forward by Bolsonaro, which includes Petrobras, in particular its downstream operations such as refineries, are certainly attractive to Chinese national oil companies.[102] At the same time, the Bolsonaro administration's decision to pay off a $2.8 billion loan to CDB due in 2024, and the $5 billion loan due in 2027, nullifying the condition that Chinese companies are given preferential access to 100,000 barrels of oil per day, suggests that Brazil is looking to diversify beyond China.[103]

One of the key initiatives emerging from the China-Brazil Fund was the support it provided to China's State Grid Corporation to make a $4.1 billion bid for a controlling stake in Companhia Paulista Força e Luz (CPFL) in 2016.[104] According to industry analysts, the Chinese SOE paid well above market value for its shares in CPFL, an indication of longer-term positioning in a strategic sector by the world's largest utility company. State Grid went on to purchase shares in CPFL Energia in 2017, giving it a 94 per cent stake, and reinforcing its position in the Brazilian renewables energy market.[105] It had already secured a $2.2 billion contract the previous year to lay 2,500 kilometres' worth of transmission lines – the world's longest – from the giant Belo Monte hydroelectric dam to Rio de Janeiro, adding to the seven electricity companies bought in its initial foray into Brazil back in 2010.[106]

State Grid's focus on delivery of electricity over ultra-high voltage transmission lines with low losses in power, and its promotion of linkages with renewables like solar and wind power, chimes with the needs of a greening economy.[107] Indeed, State Grid publicizes its environmental credentials in planning and construction of power transmission lines in regions like the northeast of Brazil; however, the cutting down of forests to put in power lines has provoked criticism from environmentalists.[108] The proposed network of forty dams in the São Luiz do Tapajós river basin is of considerable interest to the Chinese SOE and, like the Chinese oil giants, the prospect of the privatization of Eletrobras, Brazil's national electricity and power generating parastatal, has opened up another avenue of opportunity.[109]

Brazilian Companies in China, Chinese Companies in Brazil

While the focus in Brazil-China relations is overwhelmingly on China's engagement in Brazil, there is a modest but telling investment by Brazilian firms in China. Overall, between 2000 and 2010 China represented a tiny proportion of Brazilian outward investment (0.06 per cent).[110] According to Fischtak and Soares, as of 2012 only fifty-seven Brazilian firms were operating in China and of these 51 per cent were service providers (financial institutions), 28 per cent were manufacturers and 21 per cent in the natural resources sector.¹¹¹ Sales and procurement dominated the activities of the manufacturing firms, while natural resources firms were involved in the sales and distribution of their products. Amongst the obstacles faced by Brazilian firms were regulatory barriers, non-recognition of intellectual property rights, misalignment of priorities with Chinese partners and cultural gaps.

As for Chinese businesses in Brazil, around two hundred are operating as of 2019, most of them SOEs and big private firms like Huawei. But this tally fails to account for retail shops and other SMEs operating at local community levels. According to one study, Chinese firms primarily complain about the 'difficulties in dealing with the intricacies of Brazilian tax legislation as well as the application of labour law'.¹¹² Beyond these complications, high-profile announcements of mega-projects by Chinese firms often seem to lack the requisite due diligence; for instance, the joint venture announced with much fanfare in 2009 between Wuhan Iron and Steel Company and EBX to build a $3.29 billion steel factory at the port of Açu, Rio Grande do Norte, were broken off three years later after feasibility studies challenged the project's economic viability.¹¹³ A senior official of the China Communications Construction Company warned the Brazilian government in 2011 that it should encourage better-structured projects and not expect Chinese firms to invest if these were deemed to be unprofitable.¹¹⁴

Global and Regional Diplomatic Dimension of Brazil-China Ties

It was on the international front that China-Brazil cooperation was most visible and reflected the long-standing global aspirations of the two emerging powers. The APEC Conference had become the point of contact with China for Pacific-facing countries in Latin America, but for Brazil – besides the growing bilateral exchanges – the expanding role accorded it in the G7 Plus 5 initiative became the key vehicle for collective cooperation amongst leading emerging powers. Discussions held in that setting helped set the stage for the founding of the India, Brazil and South Africa Forum (IBSA) in 2004 by the foreign ministers of India, Brazil and South Africa, bringing together the leading democracies and market economies in South Asia, South America and Africa.¹¹⁵ Brazil's global aspirations for a permanent seat on the UN Security Council and the prospects of Beijing's support loomed large in Lula's foreign policy agenda, and though Chinese opposition to the G4 initiative to reform the UN Security Council in 2005 contributed to its failure, Brasilia continued to press for Chinese support and received Beijing's private assurances.¹¹⁶ At the same time, analysts were critical of Lula – and to a lesser extent Rousseff – who expended much political capital without achieving their aims:

> Brazilian foreign policy insisted on an unrealistic campaign to obtain a permanent seat at the UNSC (United Nations Security Council). This insistence alienated Argentina and China, Brazil's two most important international partners.[117]

As already indicated above, Brazilian cooperation with China was enhanced through its involvement in BRICS since 2009. While the annual summits afforded an opportunity to discuss areas of mutual interest and even coordinate policy at settings like the G20, within a few years more institutionalized forms of global cooperation began to take shape. Although the New Development Bank (NDB) was an original idea put forward by India (with strong Chinese support) at the fourth BRICS Summit in New Delhi in 2012, Brazil became a pivotal actor in crafting the original structure of the new multilateral institution by arguing vigorously that it should be modelled after the Development Bank of Latin America (CAF), an institution of which Brazil had been a member since 2009. The NDB architects favoured the Brazilian idea enthusiastically and enlisted CAF's President Enrique Garcia to provide crucial advice on how to model the new financial institution.[118] Thereafter at the sixth BRICS Summit in Brazil (Fortaleza in 2014), the leaders signed the agreement establishing the NDB.[119]

In that evolving context, the establishment of the G20 in September 2009 as a more broad-based multilateral setting for global collective action, and the desire to create a forum for emerging powers alternative to G7, further strengthened the resolve of Brazilian foreign policy. The launching of the BRIC (Brazil, Russia, India and China) grouping that same year, expanded to include South Africa in late 2010, provided a basis for closer cooperation in areas such as reform of the International Monetary Fund.[120] BRICS activism extended to the founding of the NDB and other financial initiatives such as the Contingency Reserve Fund and promotion of the renminbi as an international currency. Climate change cooperation at the Copenhagen Conference, followed up by the Rio+20 Summit in 2012, produced a strong stance on 'common but differentiated responsibilities' between industrialized and developing countries, enhancing BRICS's reputation as a diplomatic broker in an emerging world order.[121] A dialogue forum at the 2014 BRICS summit in Fortaleza with Latin American countries, a feature of the BRICS summit in South Africa the previous year, provided a venue for discussions about formally launching a China-plus regional forum, the China-Latin America Cooperation Forum (see Chapter 7). Interestingly, Chinese scholars believed cooperation with Brazil enhanced their overall global influence in key areas, citing consultations at the vice-ministerial level on African affairs and the coordinated efforts to reform the global financial system through the G20.[122]

In the defence area, incremental steps in fostering bilateral cooperation, initiated as far back as the 1990s, had been limited in scope and ambition. BRICS, in this regard, proved to be a platform for preliminary engagement. The Brazilian military, however, was wary of growing Chinese influence in the South Atlantic and African littoral, which encroached upon their own naval projection into that region. And after cultivating closer military cooperation with Namibia over many years through training programmes, the Brazilians were put out by that country's unexpected purchase of Chinese naval ships and by being sidelined by Chinese training programmes.

Bolsonaro – From Rejection to Rebooting the Relationship

The election of Jair Bolsonaro in 2019, a former military captain with a strong support base amongst Brazil's evangelical community, overturned nearly two decades of PT rule. Speaking to audiences across the country, he argued for a strong stance on resource nationalism and for restricting China's role in the Brazilian economy, declaring 'We can't let China come in here and buy up land, buy niobium [a strategic mineral], as if it were just another mineral! No!'[123] Bolsonaro himself had visited Taiwan while campaigning for the presidency in February 2018, stirring much anxiety in Beijing about the future direction of his presidency.[124]

Once in office, Bolsonaro showed a measure of diplomatic disregard for China, occasionally ladling on vitriolic commentary. At the BRICS Summit in Brasilia in 2019, the new president summarily dispensed with the BRICS Plus 5 meetings over a dispute with other members regarding Venezuela, while initiatives such as his predecessor's call for a BRICS intelligence forum were ignored.[125] His consultations with Trump's one-time advisor Steve Bannon added fuel to the fire, while vocal antipathy towards China featured in many statements by Ernesto Araújo, the new foreign minister. The most evident break with the past was Bolsonaro's public support for regime change in Venezuela, putting the Brazilian government at odds with Chinese and Russian policies opposed to US-backed intervention.[126]

It was not long, however, before the Brazilian government found that there were costs to its hostile stance towards its biggest trading partner and a leading investor. Chinese FDI to Brazil plummeted from $11.3 billion in 2017 to $2.8 billion in 2018.[127] Bolsonaro's constituents in mining and agriculture decried the anti-China bias and its impact on their export-led revenues. And the onset of the US-China trade war in 2018 brought about a shift in China's sourcing of key agricultural products like soyabeans away from the US to Brazil, reinforcing the impetus for repairing relations. Chinese diplomatic support for Bolsonaro, who came under withering Western criticism in August 2019 for his lax policies regarding the Amazon, and the concurrent spread of wildfires and logging, sounded just the right notes.

The reset of the COSBAN process, which had stagnated under the Rousseff and Temer governments as their tenure in office became mired in impeachment hearings and successive scandals, was an important signal of the government's intentions. As Brazil's Vice-President Hamilton Mourão explained, the Bolsonaro Administration wanted to:

> ... (f)ind a new way of seeing Cosban – which had been brought to a standstill – and to conduct this meeting in less than six months of government. We showed the Chinese government the Brazilian government's willingness to maintain the commission as a high-level connection mechanism between the two countries.[128]

At the fifth COSBAN meeting in Beijing in May 2019, the first signs of a thaw were evident. While the joint statement lamented the continuing problematic 'concentration of Brazilian exports to China in a limited group of primary goods', it reiterated the Chinese government's commitment to 'create the conditions for diversification into valued-added products sold by Brazil in China'.[129] Under the shadow of the growing US-China trade war, clear opportunities were transpiring to take a larger share of the trade in key agricultural commodities like soyabeans and beef and to unlock obstacles to market access. The surge in Brazilian soyabean exports to China from $20.9 billion to $28.8 billion in 2018, coming off the back of a $6.9 billion drop in soyabean imports from the US, boded well for these opportunities.[130]

During Bolsonaro's state visit to China in November 2019, Chinese officials suggested that $100 billion could be made available for investment in Brazil.[131] The Brazilian president's reaction signalled his willingness to reconcile with his Chinese hosts, saying 'China is more and more part of Brazil's future'.[132] The continuation of Temer's policy to offer national assets to foreign capital via private-public partnerships gave Chinese investors, already in a strong position through the China-Brazil Fund and in domestic banking, a chance to take a more direct role in energy, power, telecommunications and even the financial sector.[133] Bolsonaro's desire to expand the financial ambit of the New Development Bank (NDB) to include other Latin American states marked another change in attitude.[134]

In a step indicative of a new seriousness in its engagement with Beijing, Bolsonaro created a special Department of China with two designated divisions within the Ministry of External Affairs in January 2019.[135] Itamaraty hoped to develop closer working relations with other Brazilian ministries to produce a 'strategic vision' to manage relations with the Asian giant. Brazilian researchers believed China's rise was accelerating into a new phase as the US declined, in evidence in transnational production chains, expanding infrastructure in South America, and institutionalization of intellectual property controls through a Chinese domestic patenting process.[136] They advocated a strengthening of scientific research cooperation through a joint national research centre and equivalent bodies at local level to promote technological innovation and to learn from China's experience.[137]

Controversy nevertheless continued to dog bilateral relations; for instance, the Chinese embassy sent diplomatic notes to all Brazilian members of the Chamber of Deputies to cease and desist from offering any congratulations following the election of Tsai Ing-wen to the presidency in Taiwan. Leaked to the press, the move was roundly criticized by Brazilian politicians and in the press.[138] Heated exchanges between Bolsonaro's son, a member of the Chamber of Deputies, and Chinese officials about the origins of the Covid-19 virus caused controversy.[139]

Conclusion

Brazilian ambitions have converged with Chinese expectations to produce a relationship of greater economic depth, more focused technical cooperation and international significance beyond any other in Latin America. With Lula da Silva and his successor Dilma Rousseff, Beijing was able to forge a partnership that reflected many of the economic complementarities that both countries could capitalize on in pursuit of development, and which contributed to a more authoritative voice on developing country issues on the global stage. The mutual push to institutionalize cooperation through COSBAN and other mechanisms like the China-Brazil Fund for Expansion of Production Capacity as well as BRICS at the international level demonstrated how these opportunities could be translated into concrete initiatives at both the state-to-state level and through private investment. The steady growth in Chinese loans, mergers and acquisitions and greenfield investments reflected improved confidence in the relationship, which contributed to a gradual expansion of cooperation into new sectors outside of natural resources. That 71 per cent of China's investment stock still remained in the resource sector, despite signs of diversification in recent years, indicated the limits of expanding the portfolio.[140] It also highlighted continuing fears that Brazil would become 'another Africa' in local parlance, that is, a resource pot for China rather than an equal development partner.

The two-way partnership also revealed the difficulties of implementing closer cooperation. Irrespective of shared aspirations, Brazil's pervasive regulatory regimes, powerful business associations, the trade union movement, NGOs in consumer rights and indigenous rights groups all served as constraints on deepening economic engagement Chinese-style. Even at the international level, where analyses of the venal, self-serving conduct of Western powers abounded, Brazilian officials and civil society found themselves to be uncomfortable with shameless endorsement of authoritarian policies on exhibit. And it was these same disparities in perspectives and expectations which gave rise, in part, to the election of Bolsonaro on an anti-China ticket.

The gap between the harsh rhetoric of Bolsonaro's populist election campaign and his selective accommodation with Beijing upon taking office illustrates the sometimes contrary structural constraints that the ongoing global economic shift imposes on Latin American countries. With Trump's 'America First' policies providing an unprecedented economic opportunity to expand new agricultural markets in China, the Brazilian president sought to secure the backing of the powerful agricultural lobby. Concurrently, his government sought to reconcile these policies with the 'nativist' impulses of his coalition of small businesses, anti-elites and evangelical supporters. For China, navigating that uncertain terrain of domestic politics and regime change introduces new challenges to its most important diplomatic relationship and a key economic partner in the region.

6

Mexico – Competition and Cooperation

Mexico's relations with China stand out for their simultaneous competitive and cooperative character. As the most dynamic economy in Latin America and partner in a comprehensive FTA with the US and Canada, Mexico's fortunes are primarily shaped by the logic of competition for markets, investments and innovation. While bilateral trade and investment with China has expanded over the last two decades, Mexico's concern about the impact of Chinese competition on its economic interests has qualified episodes of enthusiasm for closer cooperation. In particular, escalating losses of export share to Chinese firms in the all-important US market – even when later that was reversed in some sectors as production costs in China rose – continue to weigh on the Mexican mind. Its overall cautious approach manifests in restrictive policies in key sectors and abiding nationalist sentiment on issues of trade and development, periodically putting the brake on Chinese aspirations for closer engagement.

Underneath these dynamics are long-term, sometimes countervailing, global trends which impact and influence Mexican interests. This is seen in the growing integration of global supply chains – exacerbated by NAFTA's renegotiation and the tightening of rules of origin in particular – between Mexico and the Asia-Pacific, especially Japan, South Korea and Taiwan, which is underpinned by complementary and competitive advantages propelling greater economic collaboration.[1] This is even evident in the fallout of the US-China trade war; e.g. Chinese investment in multinational agricultural firms and the opening of the Chinese market to Mexican produce. Finally, these megatrends are reflected in Mexico's pragmatic pursuit of regional trade agreements, whether with the North American economies by replacing NAFTA with the USMCA or US-Mexico-Canada trade agreement,[2] or with the Asia-Pacific economies, after President Trump irrationally withdrew from the TPP in 2017, by revitalizing it as the Comprehensive and Progressive Agreement for Trans-Pacific Partnership (CPTTP).[3] All of these developments and initiatives offer glimpses into the potential scope and depth of Mexican cooperation with China, too.

Mexican-Chinese Diplomatic Relations

The historical roots of Chinese ties with colonial Mexico during the Manila Galleon epoch were explored in Chapter 1, as was the role of Chinese migrants in the development of infrastructure in the nineteenth century, and the proliferation of Chinese communities in the capital, the coastal cities and the small towns of Mexico's northern states.

Formal diplomatic ties between the Republic of Mexico and Imperial China commenced on 14 December 1899, with the signing of a treaty of friendship and the sending of a legation in Peking in 1902.[4] Like its US counterpart, the Mexican government recognized Sun Yat-sen's Republic in 1912 and subsequently found itself obliged to evacuate its legation from Nanjing to Chongqing as the Nationalist government retreated from the Japanese onslaught and, eventually, Mao's guerrillas.[5]

During the Cold War, President López Mateos sought to 'globalize' Mexican foreign policy beyond its dependency on the US and pursue a distinctive internationalist path, as witnessed in its recognition of Castro's Cuba and to a lesser degree its ties with the Soviet Union.[6] Respecting China, Mexico maintained its embassy in Taipei, but Mexican officials sought to extricate themselves from Washington's position on Asia, especially after López Mateos began to engage with Nehru in India and endorsed the Non-Aligned Movement.[7] When student protests erupted in 1968, the Mexican Left, which had embraced Castro and Che Guevara, deployed symbolic affinities with Maoist Communism the way student movements in Europe and North America did at the time.[8] The surprise announcement of talks between the US and China in 1971 allowed the Mexican government to support the General Assembly resolution calling for the People's Republic of China to take China's permanent seat on the UN Security Council and to open diplomatic relations in February 1972.

Thereafter, every single Mexican president has paid a state visit to China. In 2004 Mexico City approached Beijing about setting up a Binational Commission. Meeting sporadically thereafter, the joint commission served as a platform for discussing common areas of cooperation, including the formation of working groups and a possible FTA, though little concrete action materialized at that stage.[9] A strategic dialogue was set up in 2008 and a parliamentary forum in 2010.[10] Joint participation in the G20 played an important part in convincing Mexican officials of the central role China was assuming in the emerging structures of global economic governance. Following on from that was the decision to upgrade bilateral relations to a Comprehensive Strategic Partnership in 2013, introducing a more intensely cooperative phase into the relationship.

Evolving Economic Ties – Between Competition and Collaboration

Mexico's ambivalence towards China was behind its hostility to its application for membership to the WTO in the early 1990s and its unwillingness after China acceded – unlike most other Latin American countries – to recognize it as a market economy.[11] Behind these policy positions was the Mexican business community's deep concerns, fortified by labour unions, that Chinese competition would undercut the US-Mexico trade links forged by NAFTA in 1994. The Mexican economy had high tariff barriers in the early 1980s but, after joining GATT in 1986, embraced the export-led growth development model and underwent a surge in annual GDP growth. This accelerated policy liberalization at home, which under NAFTA caused a boom as non-maquiladora tariffs on goods were lowered to 4.1 per cent.[12] However, within less than a decade after NAFTA was signed, and only two years after formally acceding to the WTO, China by 2003 had displaced Mexico as the largest US trading partner.[13] This initially manifested as falling two-way trade between Mexico and the US in sectors like textiles, apparel and appliances, and commensurate increases in US imports from China in the same sectors.[14] A study commissioned in 2005 to assess the impact of China went so far as to say Mexico would be a net 'loser' in its economic relationship with the Asian giant.[15]

These worries only deepened over time as Mexican exports to the US continued to erode, sinking from a high of $9.3 billion or 91.3 per cent of Mexico's total exports in 1999 to 77.7 per cent of total exports in 2012.[16] This became especially pronounced in sectors wherein until recently Mexico had achieved hard-fought value-added gains, such as production of televisions and electronic components.[17] Though rising steadily from 2001 to 2010, Chinese wages still undercut maquiladora wages, and increasingly it was the proximity of Mexico to the US market that was its outstanding manufacturing advantage.[18] Mexico–China trade actually grew during the same period: imports from China amounted to $2.5 billion in 2001 and rose to $83.5 billion by 2018;[19] however, despite minor successes in breaking into Chinese markets, exports to China only amounted to $7.2 billion in 2018. Notably, Mexico's exports were generally more diverse than other Latin American trade with China, consisting of copper ores, auto parts, cathodes, other ores and concentrates.[20]

Over and above this unequal trade balance, it was Chinese competition in third-country markets, the US being the most important by far, that raised alarms in Mexico City. To the dismay of Mexican economists, China's proportion of global trade based on its manufacturing prowess expanded from 2.8 per cent in 1993 to 15.4 per cent in 2011, outpacing Mexico's proportional expansion from 0.6 per cent in 1993 to 2 per cent in 2011.[21] President Vincente Fox echoed the views of many Mexicans in business, labour and academia when he declared 'China is a real threat' to the country's current economic position and global aspirations.[22]

These downward trends in bilateral trade, however, did not tell the whole story; for instance, the liberalization encoded in the NAFTA Treaty – from falling producer prices to access to FDI – put some Mexican firms in a better position to internationalize.[23] For them the imperative of breaking out of traditional markets meant looking for new low-cost suppliers of goods produced in Mexico and consumed locally or exported abroad. As Dussel-Peters and Gallagher have demonstrated, Chinese firms were able to gain market share through integrating into Mexican production chains which themselves were displacing higher-cost US suppliers of parts and components.[24] It was the structure of the *bilateral* Mexico-China trade that highlighted the problems of their economic relations in stark terms. Both economies were highly trade-dependent as well as dependent on foreign inputs and foreign capital (though for the Chinese this became less significant over time); for instance, electronics and auto parts were 36.1 per cent of Mexico's export portfolio in 2010, while these products were 44.3 per cent of China's export portfolio that same year.[25]

During this period, Mexico experienced a fall in investment in key sectors and its redirection to China. Investment fluctuated over that time. Between 2000 and 2009, 563 Chinese companies opened offices in Mexico.[26] The Mexican energy sector in particular attracted Chinese interest, with CNPC picking up licences to explore oil fields which PEMEX had abandoned. Peña Nieto's proposal to open the once-sacred energy sector to foreign investment excited a flurry of interest amongst Chinese energy SOEs. The China-Mexico Fund, capitalized and managed under the International Financial Center of the World Bank, was launched in anticipation of a surge of Chinese capital.[27] As in other parts of Latin America, Chinese investment underwent a change after 2013, from direct partnership through mergers and acquisitions to taking up equity positions in Mexican firms.

The global financial crisis marked, in Mexico as in other parts of Latin America (and the world more generally), a turning-point not only in the content of trade and investment, but, just as importantly, in Mexican perceptions of China's rise and US decline as well as the commensurate necessity of diversifying. President Felipe Calderón endeavoured to situate the Mexican economy more firmly in the high-growth Asia-Pacific region, as reflected in his Plan Nacional de Desarrollo (National Development Plan) 2013–2018 and its specific commitments to expanding relations with China and India.[28] Accompanying this was a whole series of diplomatic initiatives, most notably the Pacific Alliance with Chile, Peru and Colombia in 2011, and the invitation to China to join as an observer in 2012. Concurrently, the government began to think more deeply about China, sponsoring development of a Mexico-China Strategy Agenda involving seventy experts in a variety of fields, which laid out a comprehensive roadmap to dealing with China.[29]

Calderón's successor, President Enrique Peña Nieto, took the process further in 2013 by forming an institutional cooperation framework with China. In September that same year, President Xi Jinping paid an official visit to Mexico, during which a bilateral Comprehensive Strategic Partnership was agreed. Most notable was that, unlike other Comprehensive Strategic Partnerships across Latin America and the Caribbean (and notwithstanding the governmental dissembling and public uproar that ensued in Brazil on this matter), it was not conditional on Mexican acceptance of China as a market economy. For Beijing, the opportunities were too good not only in Mexico but, more importantly, to secure China's position in the incipient triangular economic relationship between China, Mexico and the United States.[30] The commercial opportunities in developing closer ties through Mexico were reflected in Chinese calls for an FTA with the Pacific Alliance, modelled on the ASEAN-China FTA.[31]

Mexico's outward-looking approach to the Asia-Pacific region was driven by a broader endeavour to inspire renewed interest in foreign investors in sectors like infrastructure, industrial production and, through privatization, Mexico's natural resources sector.[32] Part of the changing rationale for investment in Mexican manufacturing was rising labour costs in coastal China, which was making Mexican industry gradually more competitive again.[33] It was hoped that the net result of these initiatives would be a diversification of Mexico's foreign trade away from sole reliance on North American partners toward the Asia-Pacific, inspired in part by the trickle of US companies moving from China to Mexico after 2013.[34] Mexico just might have been able to capture a fraction of the US market share in the Chinese auto parts market given real incentives and a functional industrial policy, but Mexican politicians did not have the interest to bring it about.[35]

Trade and Investment: Spotlight on Infrastructure

Mexican ambitions for major transport infrastructure projects linking disparate regions caught the attention of Beijing and fit in with its agenda to promote its own high-speed railways. Discussions began in 1994 about constructing a rail link between Mexico City and the industrial cluster in the El Bajío region, but these plans were shelved. The project was relaunched in

2014 under the new, expansive economic policies of President Peña Nieto and the China Railway Construction Corporation won the bid. However, it was abruptly cancelled a few short days after the announcement, coming on the eve of the president's official visit to China to attend the APEC Summit in November 2014 and amidst disclosures of corruption involving the president's immediate family. After China Railway Construction Corporation sued, the Mexican government was obliged to pay them a $1.31 million fine in May 2015.[36]

The appetite for 'big ticket' region-wide infrastructure, often tied to electoral promises by politicians, continued unabated. As a presidential candidate, Andrés Manuel López Obrador campaigned on building a 227-kilometre railway project in the neglected southern states of the Yucatán peninsula. The '*Tren Maya*', launched in December 2018 by the newly elected president, stopped at cities and tourist sites dotting the peninsula. This public-private partnership, underwritten by the National Tourism Fund, issued a series of tenders for sections of the rail network, with a Mexican, Portuguese and Chinese consortium securing one such bid.[37]

Trade and Investment: Spotlight on Special Economic Zones

Inspired by the Chinese experience, the Peña Nieto government sought to promote FDI in the neglected southern region of the country by setting up seven Special Economic Zones (SEZs) in the States of Chiapas, Oaxaca, Veracruz, Campeche and Tabasco. Announced with much fanfare in September 2015, the project had about $53 million set aside for it a year later in the national budget, to support infrastructure development and attract investors – including US and Chinese – with tax incentives, 'flexibility' in regulation, and specific customs regimes to finance 'anchor' projects that might attract industrial clusters.[38] A special agency within the Treasury was to oversee the development of a 'master plan' and coordinate cross-ministerially to facilitate cooperation and compliance. The plan envisaged the eventual creation of an 'integral administrator', a private entity or parastatal attached to each SEZ that would provide policy guidance and oversight, and manage the process.

Throughout 2016 and 2017, as master plans were devised and approved, a series of presidential decrees were issued establishing the SEZs in Puerto Chiapas, Chiapas; Salina Cruz, Oaxaca; Lázaro Cárdenas-La Union, Michoacán-Guerrero; Coatzacoalcos, Veracruz; Seybaplaya, Campeche; Dos Bocas, Tabasco; and Progreso, Yucatán. Key provisions were ten-year tax exemptions for investors and facilitation of imports and exports. Welcomed by local business associations, there were nonetheless concerns over the sheer number of SEZs being rolled out in the region, over the uncritical assessment of the proposed 'anchor' firms and their capacity to deliver good employment opportunities as well as attract other investors, and over the avoidance of the mixed record of the Chinese SEZs themselves.[39]

After Peña Nieto's PRI party was defeated in 2018, the new Congresso signalled that they would review the SEZ initiative.[40] Despite a reported $3 billion in investments already committed to the SEZs, and the additional eighty-six businesses considering participation, Obrador was determined to undo what he viewed as the excessive liberalization of the economy under his predecessor. By the end of March 2019, Mexico's four-year experiment with Chinese-inspired special economic zones had been closed down.[41]

Trade and Investment: Spotlight on the Retail Sector

In May 2014 the Mexican Department for the Environment closed down a much-vaunted Dragon Mart mega-mall situated two miles south of the resort of Cancún, and, at 1,400 acres, set to be the largest retail venue in Latin America. The $200 million mart, modelled on a similar mega-mall built in Dubai in 2004, was expected to import $2 billion worth of Chinese merchandise into the country annually. Moreover, it would position Chinese retailers to access not only Mexican consumers but, as is the case in Dubai, serve as a regional entrepôt to the Caribbean, Central America and even the US.

Fearing its impact on local manufacturers and retailers, the Mexican Chamber of Commerce joined the city of Cancún in opposing this modern equivalent to the trade emporiums of the Manila Galleon epoch, like the Parian. A federal court had nevertheless overruled the opposition and construction had begun in 2013. But a few months into the project, the developers were found to have razed over 370 acres of pristine coastline and were fined an unprecedented $1.5 million in January 2015.[42] This proved to be the last straw and investors moved on to examine the possibilities of setting up further afield in Panama.[43]

Mexican Companies in China, Chinese Companies in Mexico

Penetrating the Chinese market has proven difficult for many Latin American firms, but in the Mexican case the focus on the Asian giant has been limited. Simple tariff rates in China were higher than in Mexico and non-tariff barriers added to the burden, with one study of the Mexican footwear industry noting that the 'cost of compliance with the documentation requirements is 70 per cent higher for imports into China than for imports into Mexico'.[44] Grupo

Modelo's Corona beer experienced difficulties with its Chinese partner as well as copyright infringement and illegal production of its brand in the first years of its export into the Chinese market, before securing a position in local markets.[45] By 2019 the global conglomerate Anheuser-Busch, which had purchased Grupo Modelo six years before, decided to open a production plant in China to better expand its market share there.[46]

Nevertheless, niche markets in China have been successfully targeted by FEMSA (Fomento Económico Mexicano), and television producers have subtitled Mexican soap operas for Chinese audiences.[47] Aside from Grupo Modelo, leading multinationals in the food sector succeeded with a long-term strategy for penetrating the Chinese market; Grupo Bimbo, for instance (known as *Bin Bao* in China), initially acquired a small Spanish bakery operation in China in 2006, then opened eleven bakeries across the country in rapid succession after taking over local bakery Mankattan in 2018.[48] A major manufacturer of catalytic converters, Katcon, opened a factory in Shanghai in 2013 and within a few years had expanded to six facilities in cities around China.[49] Grupo Alfa, forming a joint venture with Hong Kong-based Noble Group (partly owned by the Chinese sovereign wealth fund CITIC), acquired Latin America's largest independent oil company in 2015.[50] Gruma, an agricultural multinational, exported maize (corn) to China, while another Mexican agricultural multinational, Sigma (affiliated with Grupo Alfa), eventually bought out Shuanghui's joint ownership of meat industry firm Campofrio in 2015, which Shuanghui – later renamed WH Group – had acquired during its takeover of US pork industry producer Smithfield.[51]

In the case of Chinese companies, recognized Chinese firms like Huawei, ZTE, Lenovo, Hutchinson-Whampoa as well as a host of smaller retail companies made up the core of China's businesses involved in Mexico directly or through subsidiaries.[52] Chinese imports of Mexican agricultural products remained relatively low through 2017. The big Chinese energy SOEs have expressed an interest in Mexican oil reserves, but they have yet to secure a substantial position in that sector. By far the most compelling aspect of Chinese business involvement in the Mexican economy was, as mentioned above, possible evidence that Mexican firms were inside Chinese supply chains. This trend, still modest in scale, was to receive a boost from the assertion of economic nationalism in US politics.

One Chinese market for Mexican products was, however, particularly troubling. The decimation of wildlife in Mexican territory, a process which integrates the existing illegal and legal trade in animals and animal products for destinations like the US and Europe, is accelerating alongside conventional economic activities. The remote Baja California region, for instance, is suffering from the use of gillnets to catch totoaba fish for their bladders, a process inadvertently reducing the once plentiful vaquita dolphin population down to twenty-two individuals.⁵³ Local fishing communities are selling the totoaba bladders to a Chinese-Mexican cartel, who processes them in Ensenada and ships them on to China, where consumers consider them a prize delicacy.⁵⁴

Trump, NAFTA 2.0 and Trade Wars

The election of Donald Trump in November 2016 sent shockwaves through Mexico. Having framed his campaign around racist-tinged attacks on Mexican migrants and a spurious effort to build a wall along the US-Mexican border, the Trump administration embarked on a renegotiation of NAFTA – the centrepiece of the Mexican economy since 1994 and the primary driver of its deepening integration into production chains and markets in the US, Mexican and Canadian economies. With just under 80 per cent of Mexican exports bound for the US and 46 per cent of Mexico's imports from the US in 2017, NAFTA was indispensable as renegotiations opened.⁵⁵ This followed the summary decision to pull the US out of the Trans-Pacific Partnership, another pillar of Mexican economic strategy aimed at expanding trade with the dynamic Asia-Pacific region, which preceded the US-China trade war in 2018. In the end, after much debate and haranguing in Washington, Mexico City and Ottawa, the US-Mexico-Canada Agreement (USMCA) was signed off by all three leaders in November 2018. The key features of the renegotiated agreement offered an update on labour wages and environmental standards, coupled with a reworking of cross-border trade content rules regarding automobiles, dairy and timber.⁵⁶

These measures, some admittedly more couched in the rhetoric of 'America First' than the substance of policy, had a dramatic impact on the Mexicans and their relationship with the US. The Mexican government and business community began a process of re-examination of its one-sided reliance on North American markets and its neglect of export opportunities in other parts of its own region. The expectation was that this friction would result in a second look at the potential of economic ties with China. Indeed, Beijing had already revived the idea of an FTA in 2017 in an address its ambassador, Qiu Xiaoqi, gave at National Autonomous University.⁵⁷ In talks between Peña Nieto and Xi Jinping a few months later, the Chinese president urged Mexico to forge supply chains that would bind the two economies more closely and put Mexico in a better position to be the region's 'economic pivot'.⁵⁸ These arguments, against the backdrop of Trump's blatant racism against Mexicans during his campaign and in office, received a new hearing in Mexico.

While improving economic ties was welcomed, there was little evidence of Mexican interest in pursuing alternative trading arrangements with China, despite the disruptions caused by renegotiating NAFTA. The bare facts of trade (in terms of exports from Mexico) – $290 billion with the US, $23 billion with Canada and $7 billion with China – spoke to Mexico's priorities. And the details of clause 32.10 in USMCA, once made public, were seen to preclude any scope for a China-Mexico FTA, as they restricted any of the three signatories, without the formal endorsement of the other two, from inking a trade agreement with a country not recognized as having a free market. Moreover, the inclusion of stronger local-condition provisions in USMCA induced new thinking on the part of China-reliant supply chains; for instance, one outcome was that leading Taiwanese manufacturing companies Foxconn and Pegatron announced a possible shift of production to sites in Mexico, which would provide a major boost for the domestic economy.[59] Another example was the reorientation away from the US market, exemplified by the decision of Chinese SOE JAC Motors and Mexican billionaire Carlos Slim's Giant Motors to shift production towards supplying SUVs to the Latin American markets to sidestep incoming content restrictions under USMCA.[60] In fact, according to some reports, Chinese firms were relocating or setting up offices in Mexico at a rate of ten a month in early 2020.[61] Even the energy sector, which had undergone a dramatic reform under Peña Nieto that opened the sector up to FDI under new regulatory bodies, was impacted by USMCA, with critics pointing out that it gave Washington a veto over Chinese investment in energy.[62]

Aside from Chinese and other foreign firms anxious to better their position in response to USMCA and the ongoing trade war, opportunities were developing in new areas which pointed to the future direction of Mexico-China trade relations. The discovery of massive lithium deposits in northern Mexico brought in the global conglomerate Ganfeng Lithium to develop the site. The open pit mine generated concerns about the impact on the environment and the health of workers, prompting the governing party to call for nationalization. Declaring that that had failed in Bolivia, Ganfeng Lithium's CEO Wang Xiaoshen proposed the joint venture of a battery production and recycling plant with Tesla to take advantage of the electric vehicle market in the US and Latin America.[63] Concurrently, the opening of Chinese markets to more Mexican agricultural products, including avocados, bananas, pork and sorghum, offered concrete opportunities to widen the basket of primary goods exported to China. Tough negotiations on phytosanitary standards were the principal obstacle, holding up trade in some items for over eight years, but once overcome, Mexican exports to China took off.[64]

Plans to improve integration of Chinese and Mexican firms, and to develop a virtual platform for SMEs to sell Mexican goods and services directly to the Chinese market, were behind the outreach to China's media and trading giant, Alibaba, which generated both interest and concerns over high entry costs.[65] Teaming up with Mexico's GINgroup, Alibaba also committed itself to roll out 'digital villages' in all thirty-two Mexican states and enrol one thousand Mexican students in its business school.[66]

On the broader stage of the global economy, Mexico's pursuit of diversification of counterparties and multilateralism in trading arrangements indicated its ongoing alignment with the liberal international economic order. Like other countries involved in the TPP, and despite the US pull-out, the Mexican government supported a marginally revised version with stricter standards on labour, environment protection and dispute resolution. This posed a challenge to China, one left unaddressed for Latin American members of the Comprehensive and Progressive Agreement for Trans-Pacific Partnership (CPTPP). China riposted in the form of the all-Asia Regional Comprehensive Economic Partnership (RCEP). The tension between the rules under USMCA and the CPTPP, and the aspirations to further enhance economic links with China, suggest that Mexico intends to pursue a range of economic agendas within the framework of multilateralism.

Conclusion

In many ways, Mexico's engagement with China demonstrates the difficulties Beijing experiences in translating its economic power into real gains on the ground. The problems Chinese firms have faced in breaking into sectors in the Mexican economy traditionally open to them in other parts of the region, such as railway infrastructure and energy, have as much to do with the Mexicans' orientation towards NAFTA as any other factors.[67] This tepid response to Chinese overtures is compounded by a concern that Chinese competition fundamentally threatens Mexico's economic position with its primary market, the US. As a result, where the Chinese have penetrated the Mexican economy, distinctive features are seen that more resemble the patterns in industrialized and regulated economies in Europe and Southeast Asia than the resource economies of other parts of Latin America and the Caribbean. The changes in Mexico's policy towards China since 2017 reflect the deteriorating diplomatic relationship with the US under Trump, the disruptions of the US-China trade war, and a belated recognition that the country needs to do more to reach out to new markets and sources of investment and technical innovation if Mexico is to continue to prosper.

7

Central America and the Caribbean – Dollar Diplomacy and Development

Any examination of Central America and the Caribbean, a sub-region comprising twenty states – without Mexico – with a total population of just under 100 million and less than 2 per cent of combined GDP of the whole region, offers up a particularly complex picture of Chinese involvement in Latin America. Here the lingering shadows of Cold War diplomacy jostle with chronic underdevelopment, limited resources, dependency on migrant remittances, and twenty-first century financial centres, all giving an eclectic character to relations with China. Small domestic markets and low levels of regional integration, especially pronounced in the Caribbean islands due to geographic isolation, largely constrain the kind of economic appeal that China has for South America and Mexico. This is notwithstanding the statistical anomaly produced by large Chinese financial flows into offshore accounts in the Cayman Islands. Weak state institutions, fragile democracies and authoritarian regimes, overlain at times by drug-fuelled violence and social unrest, contribute an inward-looking character to the region. Above all, the overarching presence of the United States as the largest economic actor and self-appointed policeman of Central America and the Caribbean has traditionally dominated commercial activity and politics everywhere.

However, within the confines of these historically defined conditions, some key features of Chinese engagement stand out: the preponderance of economic interests as drivers, the competitive diplomacy between China and Taiwan, and – until the advent of the US-China trade war – the cautious approach adopted by Beijing towards the sub-region. All of these factors have influenced the shape and direction of China's policy in an area of overwhelming US power.

Economic Engagement: Development Financing for Infrastructure, Resources and Tourism

Chinese interests in Central America and the Caribbean, mirroring those motivating China in other parts of Latin America, are economic too, if not to the same degree. To date, these are smaller in scale and scope compared to the rest of the region, reflecting the distribution of resources, and the size of local economies and markets. The construction of public buildings, the building of port facilities, and the expansion of tourist infrastructure are all to be found amongst Chinese initiatives in this sub-region. That said, some major undertakings in the area of infrastructure are underway or mooted in countries as different as Jamaica, Costa Rica, Nicaragua and Panama which speak to the development possibilities of China's ambitious expansion. As will become apparent in the next section, the contestation between China and Taiwan over diplomatic representation has shaped some of the options and the timing of Beijing's engagement of particular countries.

It is worth noting as well that China's engagement with both Central American states and the island nations of the Caribbean seems to follow a general pattern. Diplomatic recognition, if an obstacle, is achieved and then followed by a grant aid project, usually a stadium built by Chinese firms or a public building of one kind or another, often accompanied by the establishment of a Confucius Centre at a local university. Concessional loans for a small infrastructure project such as a national highway or a new airport terminal are negotiated and, once completed, serve as the basis for Chinese firms to secure more contracted business through larger Chinese infrastructure loans. These are aimed at building or modernizing, on a grand scale, local ports, roads and railways, productive facilities like refineries, and even tourist resorts. With more substantive ties the money seems to move into digital infrastructure, including underwater cables and other ICT facilities built by firms like Huawei or ZTE, and the management of port logistics by China Merchant Holdings or its affiliates.

Nevertheless, the lack of transparency between Beijing and host governments in negotiating the terms of large loans for infrastructure projects tends to provoke unease and pushback from local firms, trade unions, and environmental and social activists. Chinese SOEs do publish bids for public sector tenders, often touting their low cost and rapid construction in contrast with native firms. Debt-financed projects escalate in quantity and as often in cost, to alarming proportions in some cases like Jamaica, while in other cases like Costa Rica, they are contested by activist civil society for their detriments through legal instruments and public protest.

China's support for development in Central America and the Caribbean is carried on through provision of development finance and is an important component of Beijing's outreach to the sub-region. This is particularly so as many of the governments there have struggled for decades to attract FDI and large-scale lending – especially for infrastructure – to support development of services, industry, and the agricultural sector.[1] As in other parts of Latin America, China provides grant aid, non-concessional and concessional loans, and technical assistance as part of the menu of financial options available to countries. China ExIm Bank and China Development Bank are both active in debt financing in the sub-region, while the battery of Chinese SOEs – China Harbour Engineering Company, China Construction Communication Company, China National Petroleum Company – are all involved in commercial ventures tied to these loans. Concerns over rising indebtedness in the sub-region have prompted calls at the China-Caribbean Trade and Economic Cooperation Forum meeting in Santiago, Chile, in 2018 for China to facilitate a new, sustainable form of development finance.[2]

Since 2005 there has been a sharp rise in investment in this sub-region in particular. Like other multinational firms and global funds, the Chinese use the Cayman Islands and British Virgin Islands as tax havens. This skews readings of Chinese FDI in the region and, once removed, a much lower level is exhibited than the official figures suggest.[3] Further complicating the picture here, as elsewhere in the world, is the conflation of loans with FDI coupled with the overall lack of transparency. Between 2005 and 2013, according to Bernal, Chinese FDI stock in the Caribbean alone rose from $81.2 million to $604.45 million, with Guyana, Cuba and Jamaica being the top recipients.[4] But during the same period, the Chinese government regularly reported providing $1 billion in investment to projects in the Bahamas.

Commending the role of development finance is a newfound alignment between China's interests and the development aspirations of the sub-region. Upgrading and expanding port facilities, building new airports and connecting cities with modern infrastructure all featured in the national development plans of these governments. China's orientation and proven capabilities in financing physical infrastructure, even introducing leading-edge digital technology, appeals enormously to many locals, and is perceived as a solution to achieving their ambitions. In the shipping and port logistics sector, Hong Kong's Hutchinson-Whampoa, backed by private capital and the Chinese sovereign fund CITIC, has assumed an increasingly important role in Panama and the Bahamas. In the latter, the steady stream of investment tallying up to $1 billion in 2009, as reported by Chinese officials at the time, started with a deal by Hutchinson-Whampoa to acquire a 50 per cent stake in harbour and container companies in Freeport in 2004, the construction of a new international airport, and the offer of an initial $99 million China ExIm bank loan for, as well as 2.7 per cent equity stake in the Baha Mar resort and casino complex.[5]

Where there was particularly strong convergence between local development aspirations and Chinese interests, a comprehensive approach was merited. In Grenada, for instance, a team of researchers from the China Development Bank began working directly with the government to draw up a national development plan in 2017, and it is revealing as to the proposed trajectory of a collaborative partnership with China.[6] According to a confidential report on the planning process, the island was to be divided into seven zones, with the capital serving as the administrative, business and industrial centre as well as the cargo and cruise ship transport hub. Five districts would be devoted to renewable energy projects like wind farms, commercial agriculture, fisheries and tourism, including medical tourism, while one mountainous region would serve as a national park and educational centre.[7] The recommendations further suggested that Grenada should adopt the legislative framework necessary to position itself, like other Caribbean islands, as an offshore tax haven for companies and individuals. The significance of the project, the status of which is enhanced by its designation as part of the Belt and Road Initiative,[8] is that it demonstrates to the countries of the sub-region that Chinese designed, financed and constructed development can produce positive sustainable growth.[9]

Turning to the specifics of China's involvement in the sub-region, extractive resources play a modest – if significant, in specific bilateral cases – part in the trade and investment profile. Amongst the more consequential resources to have captured the interest of Chinese SOEs are energy in Trinidad and Tobago, bauxite in Jamaica, and nickel in the Dominican Republic, where SOEs hold or have sought concessions. In Trinidad and Tobago the Chinese sovereign wealth fund CITIC purchased a 10 per cent stake in the national oil and gas company in 2011.[10] Agricultural production in Central America and the Caribbean, especially sugar cane, coffee and bananas, have also caught Chinese attention. In Jamaica, a Chinese investment SOE, Complant, has bought out three of the country's largest sugar plantations.[11]

As is evident throughout the sub-region, infrastructure development plays a vital part in China's engagement in local economies, some of which have been struggling for years to attract support for modernization of their colonial-era facilities. Pride of place goes to the China Harbour Engineering Company (CHEC), a subsidiary of China Construction and Communication Company, as a leader in the construction of ports, container holds, and facilities in Panama, the Bahamas, Jamaica, and Trinidad and Tobago. A proposed high-speed railway running across Panama and Costa Rica has the potential to cut further along Central America's spine to link up with its equivalent railway in Baja California in Mexico. Bernal reported that twenty-three Chinese companies were operating in the Caribbean back in 2010, with the number now substantially higher, but difficult to calculate as many of these firms establish operations via third countries.[12] Chinese construction of government office buildings including the Ministry of Foreign Affairs in nearby Surinam was financed by grant aid authorized by Beijing. Productive infrastructure such as the $400 million aluminium smelting plant in Trinidad and Tobago, built in 2008, was never put to use after the host government abandoned the project.[13] By way of contrast, in 2018 the same government welcomed CHEC's decision to build a dry dock in La Brea, partly, according to Ellis, to help absorb local workers laid off after the closure of the national refinery.[14] From the swampy Caribbean coastline in Nicaragua the Hong Kong tycoon Wang Jin proposed to build a canal that would surpass the nearby Panama Canal. Launched with much fanfare in December 2014, the $40 billion project became mired in controversy under local protests and litigation by environmentalists.[15] The expiration of the contract in 2019 signalled the end of that project.

Controversy surrounding the importation of Chinese labour to build these projects continues to simmer across the sub-region. In Trinidad and Tobago, for instance, public protests greeted the nearly three thousand Chinese workers granted work permits in the country to do construction.[16] In Barbados and Jamaica, trade unions protested the employment of Chinese workers to build road projects.[17] In the Bahamas the state was leading a rescue of the beleaguered $3.5 billion Baha Mar, the Caribbean's largest resort and casino complex, which had collapsed because of the 2008 global financial crisis. After it went into receivership in 2015, Hong Kong magnate Chow Tai Fook took over a stake in the assets with a China ExIm Bank $2.8 billion loan, which was conditioned on China State Construction Engineering Company using Chinese labour.[18] Numbers vary, but in the midst of the Covid-19 crisis in October 2020, 278 Chinese workers and former workers were repatriated back to China, a Chinese embassy official admitting there were 'several hundred' working in the project and outside as well.[19] At the same time, proponents argued that the expansion of the hospitality industry by Chinese investment and labour would be offset by long-term employment opportunities in these new tourist facilities.[20]

For the island nations of the Caribbean, especially, where tourism is the mainstay of the economy, deepening economic engagement with China focuses on expanding opportunities in this sector. The local tourism industry looked forward with eagerness to taking advantage of the flood of Chinese tourists into world travel, which exceeded US tourists in numbers in 2014, and were noticeably identifiable as big spenders.[21] Exploiting the potential of large-scale Chinese tourism is dependent in the first instance upon gaining Beijing's recognition of the country as an approved destination. This status licenses official group tourism, which remains under the auspices of the China National Tourism Administration, in the participating country, and typically increases the numbers of Chinese tourists.[22] But as the Caribbean Council on Tourism observed in 2014, the absence of direct long-haul flights other than to Havana (and even that involves a stopover in Montreal), as well as the variety of similar opportunities closer to home, has limited the prospects of gaining much from this boon.[23] The report moreover concluded that to capitalize on China's potential, the tourism infrastructure would have to develop gambling, horseracing and other related pursuits that appeal to Chinese tourists. Interestingly, Chinese tourist infrastructure requires installation of Chinese social media platforms like WeChat and payment platforms like Alipay, as has been done in parts of Southeast Asia.[24]

Scholars have identified tourism as an instrument of Chinese economic statecraft, which has put restrictions on tour group travel to signal displeasure over host government policies in cases as varied as Turkey, Israel and South Korea.[25] The patent vulnerability of the small island economies to boycotts of the kind organized against South Korea would presumably be balanced by the absence of high-stake strategic issues of the kind found in East Asia, although the evidence from other examples suggests that pressure could be deployed for lesser issues. Granting preferred visa status to Chinese citizens is also an important step in encouraging tourism as well as facilitating investment but, as the differing cases of Jamaica and Costa Rica suggest, it has been treated with caution by local officials.[26] For Bahamian officials, discussions with Beijing over visa-free access and direct flights reportedly took place in late 2019 to pave the way for the influx of large package groups to the Baha Mar resort and casino facilities then under reconstruction.[27]

If resources, infrastructure and tourism are of inherent economic interest to Chinese firms, other important dimensions of the sub-region also matter to Beijing. One of the strongest attractions of Central America and the Caribbean for Chinese commercial interests is precisely the formal and preferred access to US markets enjoyed through arrangements such as the Central American Free Trade Area plus the Dominican Republic (CAFTA-DR), to Canada through the Caribbean-Canadian Trade Agreement, and to a lesser extent, to EU markets through the Caribbean Community and Common Market (CARICOM). CAFTA, concluded in 2005, built upon the export access to the US market achieved through the Caribbean Basin Initiative back in the mid-1980s, allowing the products of the five member states plus the Dominican Republic to enter the US market virtually tariff-free. In the case of CARICOM, created after the failure of Anglophone local initiatives like the West Indies Federation, the 2008 European Economic Partnership Agreements with CARICOM countries plus the Dominican Republic allowed for preferential access to European markets as well.[28]

At Beijing's initiative, the China-Caribbean Trade and Economic Cooperation Forum (sometimes called the China-Caribbean Forum or CCF) and the China-Caribbean Business Council were created in 2004.

These are key nodes for mini-lateral economic diplomacy with CARICOM but excludes those countries that recognize Taiwan.[29] Commitments made at CCF meetings and accompanying actions included the successive promotion of $1 billion or more in aid, mostly in the form of loans made available for infrastructure projects, $1 billion in commercial loans for infrastructure by China Development Bank, and wide-ranging education scholarships and training programmes for the Caribbean. The anomaly that Surinam and Guyana are part of CARICOM and the China-Caribbean Trade and Economic Cooperation Forum has meant that a large part of these loans and education programmes can fund development in these countries on the northern margin of South America as well. Meetings of the CCF were often held as sideline events in conjunction with CELAC ministerials or summits.

Reflecting these opportunities, the boom in textiles and apparel in countries like the Dominican Republic and El Salvador was partly funded by Chinese investors in that sector, who were seeking a third-country platform for export into the US market. In some cases, they were merely entering in the wake of Taiwanese disinvestment in places like the Dominican Republic, following the elimination of import quotas by Washington in 2005.[30] The overall impact of Chinese competition in third-country markets has had a deleterious effect on Central American exports to the US and Mexico in particular (see Chapter 5). This is exacerbated by the lack of suitable resources for export to China, a key factor in the worsening sub-regional development prospects caused by China's increasingly competitive economic profile.[31]

Finally, consumer markets are small especially in the Caribbean, but in the aggregate they are buoyed by the purchasing power in some of the lower-middle- and middle-income countries in the sub-region. The low-priced goods available from China compare favourably with higher-priced goods from the US, Mexico and elsewhere, and have captured consumer markets in some products.[32] One impact of imports into Central America (barring the anomalous case of Costa Rica) and the Caribbean from China – and the limited volume and value of their exports back to China – is the sharp rise in their trade deficits.[33]

Dollar Diplomacy

The Cold War's many legacies are still felt across the sub-region, not least in Cuba and Nicaragua, but one in particular continues to hold significance, that of official diplomatic recognition of the PRC. Since the founding of the People's Republic of China under the Communist Party of China (CPC) in

1949, and the flight of the Nationalist Party (or KMT) to the island redoubt of Taiwan, the CPC and the KMT regimes have been in competition to secure formal recognition of their status as the sole government of China. Until 1971, when US President Richard Nixon arranged secret talks with mainland China that paved the way for Beijing to replace Taipei on the UN Security Council, culminating with Washington's de-recognition of the Republic of China (Taiwan) in 1979, most states in the sub-region still recognized Taiwan. Even with the gradual diminution of that recognition, with only thirty countries still left, the countries of Central America and the Caribbean remain a stronghold of diplomacy favouring Taiwan.

The impact of this contest on the sub-region has been limited but not without detriment; for instance, in 1997 China exercised its veto in the UN Security Council to block a UN peacekeeping observer mission to Guatemala, on the grounds that this would tend to legitimize Guatemala's formal recognition of Taiwan.[34] The chorus of censure across the UN of Beijing's first exercise of the veto in twenty-five years brought about a softening of its policy on peacekeeping operations. Central America and the Caribbean have stood firm as one of the last bastions of diplomatic support for Taipei on the global stage. For Central American governments, the politics of anti-communism espoused by local rightist regimes weighed heavily in the choice to hold fast to Taiwan; for instance, when the US Congress shut down military training programmes with Guatemala in 1982 due to egregious human rights violations, Taipei took over the programme.[35] For other countries, especially in the Caribbean, politics was often secondary to opportunistic responses to financial enticements by Taiwan versus China.

Over the years, formal relations with Taiwan have produced some tangible economic benefits in the form of trade and investment as well as development assistance; for instance, by the new millennium – and in response to Beijing's promotion of FTAs with other developing countries in Latin America and the Caribbean – Taipei agreed a battery of FTAs starting with Panama in 2003, then Guatemala in 2005, Nicaragua in 2006, and El Salvador and Honduras in 2007.[36] These FTAs should be viewed not only as bilateral trade initiatives but also within the larger context of Taipei's ambitions to access US markets through the CAFTA-DR trade deal with the US.[37] These FTAs produced modest investment flows from Taiwanese businesses to Central America, focused principally on the textile, apparel and footwear sectors, with some support from its own ExIm Bank.[38] Behind all this commercial interest in Central America was a policy to take advantage of these countries' privileged access to North American markets in general.

Concurrently, a series of regional and bilateral concessional loans to the sub-region were made to support larger development projects. Taiwan's role as an observer in the System of Central American Integration (SIECA) and the Central American Bank of Economic Integration positioned it to promote regional integration, as in the rehabilitation of Nicaragua's port facilities.[39] Technical cooperation, especially in the area of agricultural development and SME training, also featured in bilateral aid packages. Finally, the Taiwanese provided grant allocations to certain projects such as building the Presidential Palace and remodelling the National Assembly building in Nicaragua.[40] There was also a $100 million loan in February 2019 to the embattled Ortega government following a violent crackdown that left over three hundred people dead.[41]

Despite this history of engagement, however, the bald facts of trade were that a large imbalance exists between Taiwan and the countries of Central America and the Caribbean, and, while trade with China replicated some features of trade with Taiwan, its overall value was estimated even as far back as 2006 to be five times that of the Taiwan trade.[42]

On the diplomatic front, Taipei has gradually moved away from its dogmatic approach to the 'one China policy' to more flexibility.[43] After 1991, when Taiwan's then president Lee Tsinghua launched the 'pragmatic diplomacy' of promoting 'dual recognition' as a stepping-stone to a solution to Taiwan's growing diplomatic isolation, the competition became more heated. Taipei's efforts to hold off any diplomatic switch by countries included lavish events for Central American and Caribbean leaders, the expansion of technical assistance, and the promise of further investment in local economies. For its own part, Beijing offered a similar package of inducements to countries considering recognition of China.

Called 'dollar diplomacy', in its heyday small states of the region (and around the world) were able to extract resources and commitments from the two Chinese governments to further their own national (or at times the leader's personal) agenda. Ministries in the sub-region have received funds in the past marked for internal projects and, at least in the case of Costa Rica's Foreign Ministry, as a kind of 'slush fund' allegedly to disburse as the Minister saw fit.[44] Funds for political campaigning channelled through the KMT to presidents' coffers helped keep key allies in office. The media disclosure that Guatemalan President Alfonso Portilla received $1.5 million from Taiwan in 2005 created a scandal that ultimately brought him down.[45] Several cases ended up in lawsuits by defeated opposition candidates, bringing the illicit funding to light and as a result tarnishing Taiwan's image as a democratic paragon.[46] Interestingly, during the 2000 Taiwanese election the Democratic People's Party expressly renounced this policy (although it went on to selectively use it through a system of 'brokers').[47]

An almost comedy of changing diplomatic ties transpired, with some states shifting their allegiances back and forth in apparent response to financial and ideological exigencies. St Lucia shifted between China and Taiwan several times, initially recognizing Taiwan at its independence, switching to China in 1972, switching back to Taiwan in 1984, then changing again in 1996 and then again back to Taiwan in 2007. Dominica also switched recognition from Taiwan to China in 2004, earning a commitment of $112 million in economic aid – an unprecedented step for Beijing – including provisions for an annual multi-million dollar budget package for the subsequent five years.[48] Nicaragua itself had changed from recognizing Beijing in 1985 to Taipei and back again when opposition leader Violeta Chamorro was elected in 1990.[49] Nicaragua's attempt to promote 'dual recognition' of Taipei and Beijing – a strategy promoted by the South African government before it formally switched to Beijing in 1998 – was short lived. Costa Rica's surprise switch of diplomatic recognition to China in 2007 inspired other Central American and Caribbean states to explore switching ties.

By 2008, however, the election of KMT's Ma Ying-jeou yielded an informal truce in the diplomatic competition (which Beijing feared would only inspire Taiwanese nationalist sentiment for independence), and a concomitant increase of direct links between Taiwan and mainland China.[50] In this new environment, urgency was replaced by complacency, and Taipei's promised assistance and investment either languished, was withdrawn or – in most cases – never materialized. For some leaders, such as Leonel Fernándes, the then president of the Dominican Republic, this made clear that his country's preference should be Beijing but, under the de facto moratorium against ousting Taiwan's official recognition, this had been blocked by China.[51] When in 2014 a Hong Kongese businessman proposed building the canal through Nicaragua, which would have fulfilled the country's long-standing dream to compete with Panama, the recognition debate in that country was once again reignited.

The diplomatic standstill held until the election of Democratic People's Party leader Tsai Ing-wen to the presidency in 2016 and her subsequent failure to acknowledge the 1992 consensus, by which both sides had affirmed their shared belief in one China, but disagreed on who was the rightful government. After condemning Tsai at the CCP's nineteenth Party Congress in October 2017, China started a concerted campaign to pick off some of the last states that still officially recognized Taiwan.

The results of this renewed offensive were not long in coming. On 13 June 2017 Panama announced it was breaking ties with Taipei in favour of Beijing. President Juan Carlos Varela's decision stunned the US into issuing a warning to Panamanians to beware of Chinese intentions. In less than a year, on 1 May 2018, the Dominican Republic announced it too would recognize the People's Republic of China as China's sole representative. Taiwanese officials were dazed, especially as this came in the wake of diplomatic losses in Africa and the Pacific as well.

Not to be outdone by his fellow presidents, in August 2018 El Salvador's Salvador Sánchez Cerén issued a statement indicating that the country would be switching its diplomatic recognition to China. Following so quickly upon Panama's announcement, this brought public censure from Washington and a veiled threat that the Trump administration would review its own bilateral ties with El Salvador. While at the time this seemed to have been the end of the story, in fact, the election in March 2019 of a new president, Nayib Bukele and his Nuevo Ideas party, signalled a review of the recognition decision. The expected termination of El Salvador's FTA with Taiwan was suspended by the Supreme Court because of a lawsuit by the Salvador Sugar Association for whom exports to Taiwan were worth $40 million.[52] On 27 June 2019, however, Bukele affirmed his predecessor's decision and El Salvador became the latest country to ditch Taiwan for China.

Focus on Costa Rica

Costa Rica stands out as one of the few countries in the sub-region to engage in a comprehensive strategic approach towards China, and to reap substantial economic rewards as a result.[53] From the point when Costa Rica decided on diplomatic recognition for Beijing, a process begun in 2005 and concluded in 2007, to the onset of negotiations that culminated in a Free Trade Agreement in 2011, the government in San José has exhibited a calculated understanding of the challenges and opportunities represented by China.

Part of the source of Costa Rican ambition lay in its economic diversification plan and, in particular, its early embrace of high-tech industries. For some, Costa Rica's unique position in high-tech production chains made it 'el Silicon Valley Latino Americano' and as such offered salutary lessons to the sub-region's other countries.[54] Fostered by Costa Rican and US interests as far back as the 1950s, the creation of the export-processing zone in Belén, where Intel had set up a manufacturing and testing plant for microchips, enabled the country to heighten its profile in global production chains, exporting high-end technology to China for assembly in personal computers.[55] However, the closure of the manufacturing side of the business in 2014 – shifting production to Vietnam and Malaysia where wages and labour standards were lower – marked a setback for Costa Rican development.[56]

The motive for switching diplomatic recognition was embedded in the strategic calculus of Costa Rican President Óscar Arias, recipient of the Nobel Peace Prize for his mediation role in the Central American peace process in the 1980s, who was by now on to his second term in office. His dramatic elevation to international stature had encouraged him to think about Costa Rica's position in the wider international system. Appreciating the global economic shift to Asia, and recognizing that Costa Rica's Pacific orientation was a growing component of trade in his own region, Arias sought to enhance its position. In the longer term, however, joining the Asia-Pacific Economic Forum (APEC) was a priority which, so long as Costa Rica recognized Taiwan, was out of reach.[57] A web of FTAs with key Asia-Pacific countries, it was felt, would be necessary to secure APEC membership and meet the competition from other, bigger economies in that region.[58] Against these grand strategic considerations stood the diplomatic conferences organized by Taiwan, in which, as then-Foreign Minister Bruno Stagno put it, 'We [the Costa Rican government] found ourselves still attending supposedly international meetings with countries like Burkina Faso and Vanuatu'.[59] The fault lines of ambition and diplomatic circumstances galvanized the Costa Rican government's next move.

Secret talks about diplomatic relations with Chinese officials began in New York in 2005. Taiwanese officials got wind of these talks and, according to the former Foreign Minister, alternatively suggested economic incentives to stave off the switch or, when that didn't work, applying pressure.[60] Costa Rica's 'no' vote on Taiwanese membership of the World Health Organization in May 2007 was the death knell indicating Costa Rica's willingness to break with Taiwan.[61] Notably, in that same month Arias himself penned a newspaper article decrying Taiwan's 'stinginess' and suggesting it might lose allies as a result.[62] The local Costa Rican media, however, challenged the rumours of a pending switch and appeared to rally support for Taiwan, carrying on a campaign critical of Chinese goods.[63] Countering that were corruption charges levelled against the Costa Rican Health Minister through misappropriation of Taiwanese funds channelled into the Ministry, and a Taiwanese businessman's illegal $500,000 donation to Abel Pacheco in his successful presidential election bid in 2002.[64] Despite all of these manoeuvres, on 1 June 2007 the Costa Rican government formally cut ties with Taiwan and recognized the People's Republic of China.

The benefits of the country's new relations with China were not long in coming. The two governments signed eleven agreements in the month after the changeover, while Chinese President Hu Jintao visited Costa Rica in 2008, followed by President Arias's official visit to Beijing a few months later, all of which clarified what the advantages for Costa Rica were in recognizing

China. Beijing agreed to build a new sports stadium in San José priced at $100 million, to engage in a joint venture exploration in the oil and gas sector with leading national parastatals, to upgrade and expand the Moín oil refinery, to build and improve road infrastructure in the country as well as to provide $20 million in humanitarian relief.[65] Most importantly – and this was only disclosed accidently via the Costa Rican Foreign Ministry website – Costa Rica secured a $300 million bond buy from Beijing to shore up its finances.[66] On the diplomatic side, with China's support Costa Rica was elected a non-permanent member of the UN Security Council in September 2007.[67] An invitation to be an observer at APEC in 2008, while falling short of full membership, nonetheless brought Costa Rica closer to its coveted strategic aims.

That same year, Costa Rica opened negotiations with China on an FTA.[68] Concluded in May 2008, the Minister for Foreign Trade, Anabel González, underscored its significance to the country's wider strategic goals: 'The negotiation over the FTA with China fits into Costa Rica's strategy to position itself in the Asian continent.'[69]

Costa Rica's trade profile with China started to change, with its traditional commodity base in decline, while its export of manufactured goods in computers and electronics increased significantly along with its services sector.[70] The FTA provided for 60 per cent of Costa Rican and Chinese products to enter their respective export markets duty-free immediately, and a further 30 per cent to be phased in over five to ten years. This translated into an immediate boost in trade, from $195 million in 2011 to $371 million in 2013.[71] Within Central America, Costa Rica would capture over 50 per cent of all the sub-region's trade with China by 2014, a remarkable achievement in such a short time.

Investment, however, was not forthcoming, and despite the unprecedented one-hundred-person business delegation that accompanied Hu Jintao's state visit in 2008, very little of this translated into the expected FDI flows.[72] When the Costa Rican Foreign Minister Stagno periodically raised the issue with Beijing, Chinese officials continually pressed to have Costa Rica lift visa restrictions, saying that this would encourage more interest and possible investment in the country. Unwilling to offer such unrestricted access – especially as it has an important ecotourism image to protect – the retort was that the Foreign Ministry would be 'happy to grant visas to any Chinese business man who demonstrated a serious financial interest in Costa Rica.'[73] Neither tourists nor investment did in fact arrive in any significant numbers.

All of these developments nevertheless set the stage for deepening Chinese involvement in Costa Rica. The significance of Costa Rica's positive economic relations with China went beyond the bilateral relationship itself.

For some scholars, the Costa Rican example is proof that positive trade-based relations can be developed by savvy local officials who preside over a well-regulated market economy such that it does not disadvantage their country.⁷⁴ Xi Jinping himself declared on a state visit in June 2013 that their relations could serve as 'a model of cooperation between countries of different sizes and national conditions'.⁷⁵ The Costa Rican government's own confidence in the success of its FTA with China played into their decision to follow on with an FTA with Singapore in 2013.⁷⁶

The case of the promised upgrading of the Moín oil refinery off the Caribbean coast is emblematic of the limits of Chinese economic inducements, however, even when there is host government support for such ventures. Talks on the refinery began immediately after recognition in 2007 and just as quickly ran into a host of obstacles. Costa Rican democracy is notable for its strong local constituent roots, whereby local government and its representatives are active and constitutionally capable of asserting their local prerogatives.⁷⁷ Equally, the Costa Ricans are known to be vocal environmentalists with a strong civil society opposed to oil refineries. President Xi Jinping's visit in early June 2013 seemed to suggest new momentum for the project; however, hopes were dashed a few weeks later. A lawsuit demanded a review of the joint venture's original environmental impact assessment, on the grounds that, unbeknownst to the Costa Ricans, it had been conducted by a subsidiary of CNPC, Huanqiu Contracting and Engineering Corporation (HCEC), entailing a conflict of interest. An independent consultancy firm produced a critical report that resulted in the Comptroller General blocking the refinery on 20 June 2013.⁷⁸ Amongst the disclosures were an overstated profit margin and the commitment by Costa Rica's state oil firm, Recope, to pay for half the wages of Chinese workers and all bonuses as well as any environmental damages.⁷⁹ The $1.5 billion project, underwritten by a $900 million loan from China Development Bank with undisclosed interest and repayment terms, was finally abandoned with significant financial losses for Recope.

In light of the above, some observers suggest that the characterization of the relationship as a success is an exaggeration. China maintains an upbeat story of FTA engagement in the region to demonstrate that there are gains from pursuing this course.⁸⁰ Thus, exports of Intel microchips accounted for 90 per cent of Costa Rican overall exports to China in 2009 but, in fact, were not a result at that stage of expanding economic relations.⁸¹ To keep up the aura of mutual benefit, it was necessary to downplay the role that 'tied aid' played in the building of the national stadium, in which Anhui Foreign Economic Construction Company used 750 Chinese labourers and no Costa Ricans.⁸² The repayment rates on the $300 million in bonds were not even concessionary, but rather market terms of 2 per cent.[83] This is consistent with the analysis of experts on Chinese development finance who argue that Beijing's lending is 'a coordinated credit space model that blends non-concessional and concessional lending, aid and commercial lending'[84] in 'every corner of the world'.[85]

In all of this, there remained a strong protectionist impulse exerted through the Chinese embassy in San José to preserve Costa Rica's advantages and not allow the runaway effect that Chinese companies would bring on local businesses. Costa Rican officials made clear their discontent with the quantity and quality of Chinese imports, and their supplanting of local wares.[86] In balancing this narrative with a concomitant imperative to demonstrate positive bilateral gains, Costa Rican President Luis Guillermo Solís announced, at the CELAC summit in January 2015, talks aimed at setting up a Costa Rican SEZ that would host Chinese businesses such as automotive assembly plants and a solar panel production factory.[87]

Finally, beyond economic considerations from some inside and outside Costa Rica, engagement with China had a deleterious effect on Costa Rica's image as a bastion of human rights and democracy. In particular, the abrupt cancellation of the Dalai Lama's visas to visit Costa Rica on two separate occasions was greeted with indignation by human rights activists.[88] In one case, it was excused by the fact that his visit would come too close to a visit by China's Premier Li Keqiang, and would cause offence. Irrespective, there was a negative impact on Óscar Arias in particular as a member of the select group of Nobel Peace Prize recipients and the country's image at large was tainted in the minds of many who had held both Arias and Costa Rica in high moral esteem.

Focus on Panama

In a country whose lifeblood is derived from the ribbon of waterways and canal locks cutting across the hilly jungle terrain, linking the Atlantic and the Pacific Oceans, Panama's relationship with China is bound up in roads, railways and canals. Panama's formal relations with Imperial China stretch back to the dawn of Panamanian statehood after secession from Colombia in 1903, and before that the recruitment of Chinese labour to help construct the trans-Isthmus railway in the 1850s and again the Panama Canal itself in 1914. The collapse of Imperial China and the rise of the Republic coupled with the ensuing civil war in China brought Chinese (in effect) refugees to Panama, sowing the seeds for one of Latin America's largest Chinese communities. Panama's unique status – the ten-mile-wide Canal Zone being financed, built, owned and administered by the US government and occupied by a contingent of US marines – has caused historian Richard Koster to declare that 'The Panama Canal was the great work of the industrial age, as symbolic to the US as the Great Wall is to China.'[89]

An agreement struck between US President Jimmy Carter and Panamanian strongman Omar Torrijos in 1977 fixed a period of joint US-Panamanian administration of the Canal Zone to end on 31 December 1999 with a handover of formal control to Panama. Key to the US Congress's ratification of the Carter-Torrijos agreement was a concomitant agreement providing that the US retained a permanent right to defend the Canal from any threat that might interfere with the neutrality of its operation.

China's ascendency as an economic power could be measured by the growing volume of shipping originating from China that used the canal to reach ports in the Atlantic in the 1990s. In 1997, Hutchison-Whampoa, the Hong Kong-based firm owned by billionaire Li Ka-Shing, was awarded the concession by Panama to refurbish and manage the ports of Cristobal and Balboa – outside of the Canal Zone itself – for an annual rent of $22.2 million a year over a fifty-year period.[90] Li Ka-Shing, a close ally of Chinese paramount leader Deng Xiaoping, had played a crucial role in the handover of Hong Kong from British rule to Chinese sovereignty that same year. In a measure of Beijing's pragmatism, the commercial involvement of a Hong Kong company with links to CITI, the premier Chinese sovereign wealth fund, in the rehabilitation of the Atlantic and Pacific ports on either end of the Panama Canal was not (as one would have expected) hampered by Panama's official recognition of the Taiwanese government. Rumours circulated amongst US critics of these canal deals that Hutchinson-Whampoa was granted privileges, including the right to take over the US Rodman Naval Station, which in fact violated provisions of the treaties negotiated between Carter and Torrijos.[91]

Things began to change in 2007. Panama demurred when asked to host the president of Taiwan, and at the December 2007 World Health Organization meeting abstained from supporting Taiwan's bid to achieve membership (as contrasted with Costa Rica, which took a stronger position by voting against Taiwan's bid).[92] The CCP-KMT moratorium on diplomatic contestation of 2008, however, stalled a process seemingly on the cusp of claiming another country breaking off with Taiwan. Meanwhile, the Panamanian government of Martin Torrijos, son of Omar who died under suspicious circumstances in 1981, let a tender won by a consortium of European firms cut a third, wider canal, built between 2007 and 2016 and running parallel, to accommodate the larger Panamax supertankers about to dominate the market.

The revival of diplomatic contestation between Beijing and Taipei in 2017, following the election of a Taiwanese nationalist leader that year, reignited the possibilities for change. President Juan Carlos Varela, intent on recognizing the People's Republic, held secret talks with Chinese authorities which, as events seemed to suggest, involved a wide range of diplomatic and commercial topics.[93] China's expanding investment in the country played an important part in building confidence in the process; for instance, early on in Varela's Presidency, in October 2015 Huawei decided to relocate its operations away from Mexico, where it was experiencing regulatory difficulties, to its Latin American corporate headquarters in the Colón Free Trade Zone, bringing with it five hundred jobs and the prospect of managing its entire distribution to the region.[94] Working with the Panamanian Ministry of Education, Huawei donated laptops to schools in remote regions and offered scholarships for short training courses in its world headquarters in Shenzhen.[95]

The formal launching in early June 2017 of China Landbridge Group's $1 billion investment in a deep-water container port and logistics complex on Margarita island off of Colón paved the way for it to become the thirteenth-largest container port in the world. A week later, on 12 June 2017, President Varela made the official announcement of the country's switch to Beijing, declaring it represented 'the correct path for our country'.[96] In an unprecedented affront, the US ambassador was informed only an hour before the formal declaration, provoking consternation in Washington.[97]

Crucially, and a sign of Varela's striking while the iron was hot to place Panama at the centre of China's Belt and Road strategy for the whole Latin America and Caribbean region, Panama became the first country in the region to endorse the BRI in November 2017.[98] As a gateway of international trade between the Atlantic and Pacific, Panama's position was always going to be strategic to the fulfilment of the BRI's expanding global vision. Reflecting Panama's elevated standing in Beijing, the threat of a rival Nicaraguan canal, which had produced so much anxiety in Panama since ground was broken in 2014, was declared by China's *The Global Times* to be dead within a few days of Panama's recognition of China.[99]

Thereafter the pace of bilateral engagement and locking-in agreements was unrelenting. By July 2018 the Panamanian government and China had signed an astonishing battery of twenty-eight agreements covering everything from free trade and infrastructure development to tourism and cultural exchanges. President Xi Jinping's visit to Panama in December 2018, following on from Varela's earlier trip to China's capital the previous year, resulted in a further nineteen new agreements that covered extradition, infrastructure, banking and tourism.[100] The day after Xi's departure from Panama, a Chinese consortium led by China Communications Construction Company (CCCC) was awarded a $1.4 billion contract to build a fourth bridge over the canal.

Meanwhile, bilateral talks on a Free Trade Agreement begun in June 2018 were deliberately fast-tracked by both governments for completion before the end of Varela's term and the onset of Panamanian elections (initially set for March, but delayed until May 2019).[101]

Amongst the initiatives derived from this flurry of diplomacy was the possible construction of a $4.1 billion high-speed railway between Panama City and the northern city of David on the border with Costa Rica (potentially extending to San José) which would reportedly generate six thousand jobs.[102] There ensued discussions on constructing another port on the Amador peninsula exclusively for cruise ships. Other sectors besides infrastructure included investment in Panama's agricultural sector in the neglected rural areas, which offered a potential means of solving the perennial problem of unemployment there.[103] Interestingly, China made some efforts to relocate projects experiencing difficulties in Mexico, including the controversial Dragon Mart mega-mall, to a more conducive setting in Panama (see Chapter 5).[104]

The tempo of negotiations with China, all conducted through the Office of the President and with no legislative or public scrutiny, drew increasingly negative reactions from the National Assembly and the public at large as time went on.[105] Problems with tendering procedures, for instance in the contracts given to some Chinese companies in the power transmission sector, generated alarm, while others questioned the economic viability of the high-speed train.[106] While Panama's reputation as a fast-growing economy had won plaudits from economists over the last decade, its high income inequality and poor record of transparency risked tarnishing that newly acquired reputation. Indeed, Panama's status as a global financial centre, already damaged by the disclosures of the 'Panama Papers' in 2016, had forced it to impose restrictions on the capital flows which had made it an attractive site for laundering money from around the region and beyond.[107]

With the election of political veteran Laurentino Cortizo in May 2019, the new government began a process of reviewing the battery of commitments made under Varela.[108] The Cortizo government shelved the high-speed train to Costa Rica and a grand electric transmission network, awarded the construction of an extension to Panama City's metro to a South Korean firm as well as trimming back the costly bridge over the canal.[109] Most significantly, it undertook a review of the terms of Panama Ports Company, suggesting that Hutchison-Whampoa's concession might not be renewed in 2022.[110] According to one analyst, behind these reversals was the threat of withholding US visas and inscription on the US Treasury's 'Clinton list', which would have resulted in sanctions against certain individuals and companies (and real financial ruin).[111]

Focus on Jamaica

China's relations with Jamaica date back to the end of the slave trade in the early nineteenth century when colonial officials sought alternative terms of labour. The first major importation of Chinese contract labourers began in 1854, when Jamaican plantation owners employed 'coolies' to take up work in the sugar fields.[112] After their contracts had come to an end, they began to move into the retail trade and, by the early twentieth century, had come to dominate it across the island.[113] Intermarriage brought integration into society but also led to racist incidents fuelled by discrimination and fears of competition, which sparked anti-Chinese riots in 1918, 1938 and 1965.[114] Despite these setbacks, the small Chinese community in Jamaica grew and prospered, assuming an importance not only in the economy but in political and cultural life. Like its counterparts in the Caribbean and Central America, the Jamaican government wrestled with the question of diplomatic recognition but, showing a more astute reading of trends in international politics than some states in the sub-region, recognized Beijing in 1972.

After independence in 1962, the Jamaican economy grew rapidly, achieving middle-income status through increasing diversification, but retaining problems of poverty in parts of the country. With an economy reliant on exports like bauxite, sugar, fish and coffee, the government promoted manufacturing and international tourism to broaden its economic base. By the 1990s, however, Jamaica began to undergo a cycle of debt-fuelled crises that hampered further growth and forced the government to make severe cuts in public spending.[115] In 2013, with its debt-to-GDP ratio at 147 per cent – amongst the highest in the world at the time – the government found itself unable to borrow on the international capital markets. Punitive policies promoted by the IMF aimed at stabilizing the economy forced the government to hold a 7 per cent budget surplus compared to GDP, achieved by capping public expenditure at a great political cost.[116] It was at this point that China moved from the margins to assume a central position in the economic life of the country.

Jamaica's actual economic engagement with China was limited until 2006 when Beijing authorized a $30 million concessional loan. Thereafter two-way trade rose rapidly from a low baseline of $52 million in 2000 to $383 million in 2017.[117] Over 60 per cent of Jamaican exports to China consisted of scrap copper, scrap iron and scrap aluminium in 2010, and imports from China consisted of textiles, telephones, tyres and other consumer goods, while eight years later, Chinese imports from Jamaica consisted of 78 per cent copper and exports were an even wider variety of products from electronics to refrigerators.[118] In some initial forays into investment, the China National

Complete Plant Import and Export Company (Complant) purchased three sugar plantations for $9 million in 2010 as part of the Jamaican government's privatization of state assets. In addition to refurbishing the processing plant and hiring hundreds of local contractors, Complant went on to move into construction, building a stadium and 3,500 housing units on the back of a China ExIm Bank loan.[119] Taking these into account along with CHEC's projects, the Chinese ambassador declared in 2015:

> At peak time, as many as 4,000 Jamaicans are employed by CHEC and Pan-Caribbean Sugar [the Complant subsidiary]. According to incomplete statistics, 150 local contractors are harvesting and transporting sugar canes from more than 1,650 sugar farming families, creating direct or indirect employment opportunities to more than 80,000 Jamaicans.[120]

In the course of furthering economic engagement, Jamaica had become not only the largest site for investment in the Caribbean but also China's largest loan recipient in the sub-region by 2016.

In June 2012, facing a stagnant economy, the new prime minister, Portia Simpson Miller, declared in a parliamentary session that her government would be looking for development partners to construct the North-South link of Highway 2000, refurbish the Kingston container terminal and develop a new container terminal at Fort Augusta to take advantage of the proposed Free Trade Zone in the neighbouring Cayman Islands.[121] Significantly, it was the prospect of Chinese loans that enabled realization of the government's plans for infrastructure development and employment creation for the embattled Jamaican economy.[122] Following an official visit to China in August 2013, Prime Minister Miller announced a number of new projects financed by the China Exim Bank, including a $720 million loan to the Jamaican government for the North-South Highway 2000 linking Kingston with the town of Ochos Rios, to be built by China Harbour Engineering Company (CHEC).[123] The choice of CHEC, as noted previously, was controversial, as it was under a ban by multilateral lenders due to corruption and fraud. In return, the Chinese SOE was granted 1,200 acres alongside the highway on which they could build luxury hotels to serve incoming Chinese tourists. An additional upgrade of the coastal highway along the southern coast was authorized, while, as part of the grant aid, China would provide a scholarship and training programme for Jamaicans and a two-hundred-bed children's hospital.[124]

What caught the imagination of Jamaican officials and businesses, however, was the prospect of Chinese development of an enormous port and logistical complex at Fort Augusta. The proposed $1.5 billion deep-water port facility at Fort Augusta, which aligned with Jamaica's long-term national development plan 'Vision 2030', and which CHEC had agreed to lead, would involve dredging and land reclamation on two ecologically protected islands off the coast. Studies had previously found that Jamaica's physical port limitations had constrained its insertion into the modernizing trends in shipping, and thus it was missing out on national revenue on the order of 2.3 per cent of GDP as well as large employment gains.[125] Appreciation of Panama's and, potentially, Cuba's competition drove Jamaica after 2011 to closed-door bilateral discussions with China and other interested parties, ultimately leading to the announcement of a formal project in 2014.[126]

Complications, however, followed. Outrage at the surprise announcement sparked protests and concerns over transparency, as Diana McCauley of Jamaica Environment Trust explained:

> The details of the port project have never been released, no plans have been put forward publicly, we have had to use the access to information laws to get what details we have … Our concern is that this is an environmentally protected area, its environmental importance was protected by law internationally and by the Government of Jamaica, so to turn around and announce while in Beijing that this port was being planned, before any discussions were held with anyone in the region, makes a mockery of their environmental protection. They are just selling off our islands not even perhaps to the highest bidder.[127]

After closer scrutiny of the proposed site, CHEC decided to withdraw from the project, citing that it was insufficient in size for their planned scale of development.[128] The Jamaican government extended the MoU with CHEC as it searched for an alternate site, reminding the public that the Chinese investors had promised to include transhipment facilities, a logistics hub, industrial plants, a cement factory and a prospective power plant as well as employing two thousand workers over a five-year period.[129] By 2016 the government declared that the environmental impact would be too grievous, and agreed to relocate the transhipment facility to another, undetermined site.[130]

More trouble followed. The acquisition of the Alpart aluminium plant by the Chinese SOE Jiuquan Iron and Steel Company (JISCO) from its Russian owners, Rusal, for $299 million in 2016 was accompanied by extravagant promises of employment growth in the thousands for members of the local community in Nain.[131] Despite the fact that two hundred work permits were to be issued for Chinese technicians, the Minister for Transport and Mining assured the population at the time of the acquisition that 'No Jamaican who is qualified for these [jobs] ... is left out.'¹³² The use of Chinese construction workers angered the trade unions, who disputed their technical qualifications and claimed they were in fact doing manual labour.¹³³ Two years later, JISCO shut down the Alpart plant outright and hundreds of Jamaicans were laid off.¹³⁴ Opposition parties railed against the Chinese presence in all sectors of the Jamaican economy, with People's National Party's MP Peter Bunting declaring that 'there is a form of economic colonialism by Chinese businesses operating in Jamaica'.¹³⁵

In an interesting twist, a framework agreement between the Jamaican government and the government of Gansu Province, where JISCO is based, committed the latter to invest $6 billion to develop an industrial park that would include a second refinery as well as a Special Economic Zone in Nain.¹³⁶ China's ambassador to Jamaica, Niu Qingbao, declared that the project would ensure 'hundreds of industrial jobs, decent incomes for thousands of farmers, better trade terms and better supplies of vegetables, beef and dairy', while COSCO's participation signalled the project's importance.¹³⁷ The Alpart plant was reopened a year later, but continued to be a subject of controversy for its numerous pollution offences cited by the National Environmental and Planning Agency, causing China's newly appointed ambassador to publicly rebuke JISCO for failing to adhere to local environmental standards.¹³⁸

In the meantime, the debt burden taken on by Jamaica in this period continued to rise, reaching approximately $2 billion by 2019.¹³⁹ Although China's share represented only 3.9 per cent of its total debt portfolio, it seemed to have generated the bulk of the domestic criticism, to say nothing of complaints from the US government.¹⁴⁰ In July 2019 the incoming Prime Minister Andrew Holness announced that Jamaica was taking out a $384 million loan from China ExIm Bank to underwrite highway construction in the southeast, with his government raising $57 million from other sources; however, on a state visit to China in November 2019, Holness was obliged to publicly disavow any further debt from Chinese sources, saying Jamaica 'would not negotiate any new loan programmes with our Chinese partners', and that future economic arrangements would take the form of joint ventures.¹⁴¹

The ramifications of Jamaica's financial woes, exacerbated by the Covid-19 pandemic, continued to impact its economic ties with China. Chief amongst them was CHEC's $12.9 billion contract to upgrade the Southern Coastal Highway as well as a new international airport, and a $9.5 billion contract to build 1,650 housing units in St Catherine.¹⁴² By June 2020 the budget for the Southern Coastal Highway had had to be slashed by half due to the impact of Covid-19 on tourism, forcing further delays to a project already behind due to tussles over the siting of the road and the trade-offs between the environment, existing land use, and cost implications.¹⁴³ Hurried negotiations ensued between Jamaican officials and the Chinese company in hopes of arranging a *modus vivendi*.

Conclusion

As Jamaica struggled with sustaining its economy through debt-financed infrastructure development, the Chinese 'juggernaut' continued to move forward in other parts of Central America and the Caribbean. In Grenada, grandiose development plans were beginning to be realized with the construction of a six-hundred-unit housing development, the upgrade of the international airport underwritten by Chinese loans, and visa-free travel for Chinese citizens by 2020.¹⁴⁴ Back in El Salvador, President Nayib Bukele's ambivalent approach to China in his first days in office in 2019 turned into enthusiastic embrace a year later, courtesy of what he called 'gigantic, non-refundable cooperation', including a new stadium, water treatment plant and library.¹⁴⁵ Meanwhile, in the Bahamas, the Freeport Container Port in Abaco, completed in 2019 after unanticipated repairs to faulty construction by CHEC, remains unused, while the $2.7 billion Baha Mar resort and casino, now co-owned by Hong Kong magnate Chow Tai Fook, had to be shut down in 2020 due to the Covid-19 pandemic.

Clearly from the perspective of most governments in Central America and the Caribbean, prospective Chinese development finance, access to its market, and the arrival of its tourists were seen to be a net gain for their economies.¹⁴⁶ Despite this appeal, the experience of economic engagement was mixed and in some cases provoked outright dissent from local businesses and communities; for instance, public protests in the Bahamas against a leaked MOU promising to give fishing rights to Chinese vessels in November 2016 were followed by disclosures in July 2019 that the $39 million port facility at Abaco lacked means to recoup its costs to repay the loan.¹⁴⁷ Panama's reneging of permission for Chinese construction firms to build major infrastructure demonstrated how the vagaries of electoral politics have exposed China's vulnerability to changes in the governments of its clients. All of that said, Chinese officials, when confronted by protests or confounded by changes in government, always seemed able, their financial wherewithal and market power evident to all, to find a government interested in participating in a project or in considering an investment.

Bernal diagnosed the sources of China's appeal as far back as 2010, saying that 'CARICOM countries and the region as a whole have become less important to the United States since the end of the Cold War … and are understandably receptive to increased economic relations with China.'[148] Other analysts have suggested that the sub-region is 'too democratic and too poor' to garner much attention from Washington.[149] This was despite the fact that, as one US scholar of the region pointed out, 'No area of the world is more tightly integrated into the United States political-economy system and none ... is more vital to North American security than Central America.'[150]

Following the election of Trump in 2016, the scattered voices in US circles raising concerns about China's growing presence found an administration that shared their anxieties. The subsequent dismantling of Taiwanese diplomatic recognition in Central America which had served as a de facto bulwark of US interests, coupled with the escalating (if still modest) surge in Chinese finance in other countries in the area, was enough to warrant a hard look at its impact on US strategic interests. If the Trump Administration signalled the change of heart towards Chinese involvement in Central America and the Caribbean, it was politicians like Marco Rubio, the powerful Senator from Florida, who were articulating the concerns about China's economic competition and its strategic purpose.[151] The warning bells sounding in Central America and the Caribbean told of a new Cold War in the making.[152]

8

Global China, the United States and the New Geopolitics of Latin America

There is no din from the noise of clattering pots, blaring horns or shouting through megaphones, but it is just as effective. Positioned in front of the home of a debtor, a man dressed in an absurdly large top hat with a black coattail and a black briefcase stands day after day proclaiming through his silent presence to all that the family inside owes money and was refusing to pay it back. The *cobrador del frac* is a very old tradition of shaming, one which was brought over by nineteenth-century immigrants from Spain and Portugal with antecedents in the Middle Ages, and is still in practice in cities and small towns across Latin America and the Caribbean as well as in the 'old country'.[1] US Secretary of State Mike Pompeo, stuffed and suited though he was on his whirlwind tour of Latin America in 2018, cannot have epitomized the typically silent *cobrador del frac*, yet his persistently decrying the dangers of Latin American debt owed to China smacked of that role.

The conversation about China and development in Latin America and the Caribbean, so long the point of departure for assessing Beijing's presence in the region, was beginning to change. Debt burdens and risk management were replacing recitations of win-win formulas and calculations of market share in regional capitals as well as in Beijing. But it was more than just a reconsideration of the perils of debt-funded development, there was a recasting of a relationship once seen exclusively in economic terms to one of geo-strategic significance. Xi Jinping's Belt and Road Initiative (BRI) set in motion, by its economic aspirations and geopolitical ambitions, a process that sought to institutionalize cooperation with Latin America in a more comprehensive manner through CELAC. For important regional politicians like Bolsonaro in Brazil, this exceeded the bounds of strategic autonomy and was enough to give pause to an unfettered embrace of all things Chinese. Compounding these doubts was the alarm in Washington at the rapid expansion of Chinese diplomacy and economic statecraft in its proverbial backyard. With the US stirring into action to counter Beijing in the region, the seeds of a new geopolitics of Latin America and the Caribbean were sown.

Institutionalizing China and Latin America's Common Destiny: From Strategic Partnerships to Regional Forums

From the outset of their drive for economic engagement in Latin America and the Caribbean, Chinese officials had mooted the idea of formalizing cooperation through a regional network of strategic partnerships. Building on diplomatic arrangements with regional powerhouse Brazil, the strategic partnership formula entailed a binational commission and, in keeping with China's own evolving sense of its global diplomatic outreach at the time, a set of bilateral ministerial sub-commissions tasked with regular consultations on areas of mutual interest. Some of this initial institutional structure owed its origins to US diplomatic practices – for instance, the binational commissions and public diplomacy initiatives – and provided a basis for Chinese engagement with relatively unknown countries. However, as Chinese diplomacy became more exposed to the depth of institutionalized cooperation between the US and the Latin American and Caribbean states, its own ambitions seemed to rise accordingly.

These bilateral initiatives paralleled regional and multilateral outreach efforts; for instance, Beijing actively sought out participation in existing regional bodies like the OAS and the IDB. China petitioned successfully for a seat as observer at the OAS in May 2004 and at the IDB in 2008, while providing $350 million to public and private sector infrastructure development.[2] As an observer at the OAS, Beijing could challenge the efforts of Taiwan, supported then by twelve OAS member states that recognized it, to acquire observer status a year later.

Multilateral involvement in the Western Hemisphere was not all economic. In September 2004, with the diplomatic row over China vetoing a UN peacekeeping mission to Guatemala that provoked an outcry in the UN General Assembly fresh in mind, China sent a police contingent to participate in a UN peacekeeping mission to Haiti.[3] This demonstrated a new flexibility towards states like Haiti that still recognized Taiwan. Eight Chinese peacekeepers died in the course of that mission, making it not only the first Chinese UN military deployment in the Western Hemisphere but also its most costly.

CELAC and 1+3+6

In 2012, during a visit to Chile, Premier Wen Jiabao called for a China-Latin America Forum similar to the arrangements Beijing has with Africa, the European Union, and the Arab League.[4] The Comunidad de Estados Latinoamericanos y Caribeños, or CELAC, was the channel for this forum and it became a reality when it was announced in July 2014 by President Xi Jinping at the first Summit of Leaders of China and Latin America and the Caribbean, held in Brasilia. This is where China broached the '1+3+6' programme, a large-scale cooperation framework for 2015–2019 where '1' means 'one plan', the China-Latin American Countries and Caribbean States Cooperation Plan (2015–2019); '3' means 'three engines', the development of China-Latin America practical cooperation on trade, investment and finance, which aims to scale up China-Latin America trade to $500 billion and investment stock in Latin America up to $250 billion within ten years with local currency settlement and currency swaps in bilateral trade; and '6' means the 'six fields' of industry: energy and resources, infrastructure construction, agriculture, manufacturing, scientific and technological innovation, and information technologies.[5]

Next Steps: White Paper on China and Latin America and the Caribbean 2016

China's first ever White Paper on Latin America and the Caribbean, published in 2008 on the eve of the global financial crisis, displayed a cautious tone and studious economic focus, but the second White Paper issued in 2016 reflected the confidence and assertiveness of Xi Jinping's global expansion.[6] This second paper was launched to coincide with Xi Jinping's visit to the region in November 2016. It laid out a plan for the years up to 2020, based on the China-CELAC Forum's China-Latin American and Caribbean Countries Cooperation Plan (2015–2019) – which featured 'a continued concentration on natural resources and energy, but supplemented with upstream and downstream investments to create supply chains in related industries'.[7]

These regional White Papers have been crucial for Beijing to gain trust in the region and also for Chinese diplomats to develop specialist knowledge of the various LAC countries that recognize the PRC diplomatically (as of 2021, twenty-four countries do so). These Papers also fit into the wider context of the BRI, Xi Jinping's hugely ambitious plan to lead transcontinental infrastructure development and expansion across Asia, Europe, and parts of East Africa. Evolving over time, the inclusion of Latin America in the BRI and, concurrently, the opening of the Asian Infrastructure Investment Bank (AIIB) to Latin American membership placed the region within an overarching strategic framework linking up their economies with China.[8] The promise of a Sino-Latin American future beckoned.

Autumn of the Patriarch? US Response to China in Latin America and the Caribbean

The hallmarks of the US reaction to China's expanding presence in Latin America and the Caribbean were ignorance and indifference. Even as late as 2014, a former Obama administration Assistant Secretary of State for Western Hemispheric Affairs casually dismiss strategic concerns over Beijing's growing influence by declaring, 'I think this is great – the more money comes from China to the region, the more funds Latin Americans will have in their pockets to spend in the United States.'[9] There were a few US diplomats on the ground in the Caribbean who voiced concerns as far back as 2005 about China's penetration of the region and, notably, its strategic implications, especially as China took up significant economic initiatives in the Caribbean. One such diplomat observed in a secret cable:

> The China-Bahamas relationship fits within the broader regional pattern of expanding Chinese activity and success in its effort to supplant previous ties with Taiwan in much of the Caribbean. *However, the substantial Chinese shipping and port presence gives the Bahamas relationship an added strategic and economic importance* ... Closer ties to the Bahamas will provide the PRC a dominant shipping and cargo foothold close to the U.S. and international support in a region of growing Chinese influence. [italics added][10]

Dan Burton, Chairman of the House Sub-Committee on the Western Hemisphere in hearings held in 2005 warned of the dangers to US interests if China became a 'dominant force' in the region.[11]

Academics, in particular Evan Ellis, also raised concerns about issues such as the satellite tracking capabilities of a Chinese military base in Argentina's Patagonia region, established in 2014, or the significance of CELAC's deliberate exclusion of US representatives that same year.[12] But at least for the US defence establishment, the imperatives of carrying out the so-called 'forever wars' in the Middle East proved to be sufficient distraction from events nearer to home in the Western Hemisphere. Even the rising tempo of territorial disputes in East Asia and the South China Sea seemed to have no discernible effect on US policy towards China in Latin America. The Obama administration's supreme confidence that it could manage Beijing on both sides of the Pacific through economic containment in the form of the Trans-Pacific Partnership guided its approach to Latin America and the Caribbean.

Latin Americans, habituated for generations to US dominance and its wilful exercise of its interests through hard power, expressed astonishment at the absence of a reaction to China by Washington; for example, Leonel Fernández, the former president of the Dominican Republic, wondered if the US had forgotten about the Monroe Doctrine, while former ministers in Peru and Chile marvelled at the US lack of interest in developments in their region.[13] And while a few academics in Argentina and Chile spoke darkly of Chinese intentions in setting up the military base in Patagonia, and Argentine civil society raised questions about the lack of transparency, it was a *New York Times* investigation that brought the issue to the attention of the American public.[14] But it was Chinese actions in Central America and the Caribbean – in particular Panama with its iconic canal – combined with the arrival of Trump's 'America First' that made Washington receptive to misgivings about Chinese intentions, and ultimately caused a change in US policy.

Strategic Competitor

The designation of China as a 'strategic competitor' in the US National Defense Strategy Summary in January 2018 marked a turning point in its approach.[15] Availing itself of its considerable power in the region, the US introduced measures designed to countervail growing Chinese influence.

Chief amongst these was a public campaign by US Secretary of State Mike Pompeo to tour the region and pressurize countries to review their foreign policies towards Beijing. And the US Department of Treasury became a leading tool in raising the costs of closer engagement with China. Legislation such as Countering America's Adversaries through Sanctions Act (CAATSA), enacted in December 2020, penalized with real sanctions foreign governments as well as individuals seen to be operating against US interests. Crucial to the success of this policy was the instrumentalization of institutions, such as 'lawfare', the mobilization of law to pursue national security aims.[16] Concurrently, the securitization of telecommunications, long debated within defence and security communities in the US, came to the forefront as a critical part of the Pompeo public campaign to resist the extension of Huawei's 5G into foreign markets (see below). The activities of Chinese companies like CHEC, CCCC and CRBC – which the World Bank had blacklisted in the past from participating in procurement bids due to fraud, bribery and other irregularities – received continual scrutiny. Those caught in corruption in association with Chinese firms who held US bank accounts or interests in the US were potentially liable for punitive sanctions, including denial of visas to visit relatives in the US.[17] Even US enforcement of transparency in the global fishing industry, enshrined in the 2016 UN-brokered Agreement on Port State Matters, held implications for China's subsidized fishing fleet's unreported catches in the waters off of the Pacific coast of Latin America.[18] Pompeo's 'naming and shaming' of Chinese fishing practices in August 2020 called out Beijing both for its failure to promote sustainability and for its fishing fleet's systematic violation of sovereignty.[19]

The onset of the US-China trade war in 2018, as noted elsewhere in this book, produced a variety of contrary impacts on Latin American economies. On the one hand were countries like Mexico that exported goods of which some components depended on the Chinese supply chain and were thus potentially affected by tightening rules of origin or security prohibitions. On the other were those like Brazil and Argentina, which stood to benefit from the end of US agricultural trade with China to expand their own market share in soyabeans and other agricultural products.

The destabilizing effect of the Trump administration's trade war on the global economy and its single-minded attacks on China's contribution to Latin America's debt-financed development inspired criticism within the US foreign policy establishment. Amongst them were former US Assistant Secretary of State for East Asian and Pacific Affairs, Kurt Campbell and academician Ely Ratner, who pointed out that 'Washington is at risk of adopting an approach that is confrontational without being competitive; Beijing, meanwhile, has managed to be increasingly competitive without being confrontational.'[20]

The New Geopolitics of Latin America

The reassertion of geopolitics had an immediate effect on China's ties with Latin America and the Caribbean. Recasting China's development agenda in terms that ruptured a core appeal of Chinese power – that of an alternative to the dominant hegemon – took direct aim at the celebrated binary of 'win-win' development. This transformed the modalities of agency by Latin Americans reacting to Chinese 'entreaties' into ones that assumed a patriotic veneer of resisting possible infringements on sovereignty. On their side, Chinese worries about the rising costs of debt and related complications of involvement in the region produced its own recalibration of risk exposure.

Development Reframed

The most obvious reframing is the one that interpreted development finance, that lodestar of China's strength on the global stage, as 'debt-trap diplomacy'.

After acquiring a ninety-nine-year lease for a port facility in Sri Lanka in 2017 to meet outstanding debts owed to China, China's asset recovery strategy came under closer international scrutiny. The apparent pattern of employing assets seizures to offset inability to meet scheduled debt payments was denounced by Washington as part of a campaign warning of the dangers of borrowing from China. While concerns about Chinese lending practices have been raised before, most were addressed to countries outside Latin America and focused on issues like the budgetary implications of non-repayment or the lack of proper environmental impact assessments for given projects.[21] What was different now was that Chinese loans were construed to be deliberate policies to entrap recipients into a spiralling cycle of debt that would ultimately result in China taking over key national assets. As these assets were, as represented by critics, key infrastructure projects like ports, railways and airports constructed by Chinese firms and financed by Chinese loans, this discourse naturally inspired wariness about engaging economically with China.

Alongside development finance was a concern amongst Latin American policymakers that China's overall economic effect on the regional economy would combine deindustrialization with reprimarization. Certain US economists like Dani Rodrik ascribed 'premature deindustrialization' to globalization and trade liberalization; that is, labour was being pushed out of manufacturing into services before the per capita incomes befitting upper-middle income emerging economies were being hit. This meant the services added too little value. Self-inflicted conformity to the Washington Consensus had quickened the trend.[22] Other Latin American economists like Paul Cooney noted another regional trend towards reprimarization, or expansion of economic activity in the primary sector (*viz.*, mining, oil, beef, soya), which correlates with the growth of the commodities markets and in the wake of expanding trade with China.[23]

This matter was not politicized as much (so far, at least) as were features in the development finance contest, but public debate – partly inspired by Bolsonaro's incendiary rhetoric and experiences in countries with significant Chinese involvement like Venezuela – now goes well beyond the uncritical embrace of 'China as the alternative'. The irony that Brazil, which as late as the early 1990s had dominated bilateral trade with its exports of industrial products and imports of Chinese oil, and whose multinationals had been exemplars for Chinese SOEs seeking to penetrate developing markets across all regions, was now beholden to China. This was a shock.[24] The unenviable position of countries like Venezuela, which had courted China and absorbed more than half of all Chinese investments and loans in its region, gave further pause. Recent sectoral gains in agricultural trade notwithstanding, it was becoming increasingly clear that the new political economy of South-South cooperation being forged between China and Latin America would produce its own set of risks to the region's development aspirations.

Agency Reconsidered

Agency in cases of Latin American and Caribbean relations with China is demonstrated through one key tendency above all: namely, seeking out an alternative to the US, whether it manifests as a search for new sources of development finance and markets or for an ideological ally. In the parlance of Russell and Tokatlian's work on relational autonomy, it includes strategic alignment with great powers ('coupling'), balancing and hedging against great powers ('accommodation' or 'limited opposition') and collective action ('challenging').[25] However, in the context of settled US dominance in the Western Hemisphere, agency is primarily pursued to create policy conditions for relational autonomy within the framework of an international political economy whose power, rules and logic are determined by US hegemony. The pursuit of an alternative path to development which would break this dependency, and allow Latin American governments to choose 'neo-extractivist' domestic policies over neo-liberal ones, for instance, was the driving force behind their manoeuvres towards China.

Besides new sources of development finance and new markets as different as Brazil and Jamaica, a related dimension is the ideological motive behind such actions. Alignment with China by the Bolivarian republics was framed in terms that foregrounded the affinity of Latin American leftist ideologies with China's formal stance as the last major bastion of communism in the world. Parties of the left recognized that, in reorienting their political economy towards 'South-South' trade and investment, they would be contributing towards systematically realigning the international order as a whole. Bolivia's key economic adviser, Carlos Villegas, spelled out the rationale for engaging with China in geo-political terms in 2006:

> (The) United States is no longer the only axis of economic and military hegemony. Now, a triad dominates the world – the United States, the European Union and Asia – and the only thing we're doing is looking at reality and making contact with the different countries.[26]

But the anti-imperialist rhetoric stoked by the Bolivarians merely disguised their continuing dependency on the US in the teeth of the expanding Chinese presence, and it glamorized China's overwhelmingly commercial motives and practices, captured in the marketing jingle 'win-win'. The Venezuelan government's inability to make basic interest payments forced Beijing to 'bring in advisors, they suggest changes in Venezuelan economic structure … they start to impose conditions that they didn't include when Venezuela had a budgetary surplus and political and economic stability'.[27] Yet in a country with the region's most expansive Chinese debt and investment profile, this is a wearily familiar feature of the traditional creditor-debtor relationship, and one supposedly escaped by stepping outside of Western strictures. That China is an alternative for Latin America is still held to be true, but what the longer-term implications of dependency on China mean is only now beginning to be recognized by the countries of the region.

China Re-evaluates Risk in Latin America and the Caribbean

For Beijing, the outreach to Latin America and the Caribbean, which began in earnest in 2004, has become an exercise in tempering expectations and recalibrating risk assessments. In particular, Latin American populism, with its dizzying array of putative ideological expressions, came as a shock – Chávez on the left and Bolsonaro on the right – either of which might enhance or distress Chinese interests. Resource nationalism introduced uncertainty in contractual arrangements as much as militant trade unionism scuppered infrastructure projects. And volatility in commodity prices coupled with collapses in demand in key Western markets for Chinese-produced goods held serious implications for repayment of dollar-denominated debt. The region's election cycles that so often alternate friendly governments, such as Correa's in Ecuador or Kirchner's in Argentina, with opposition figures introduced the possibility of hostile turns in policy or even debt defaults.

All of this has taken place in a worsening global economic context, which saw a dramatic decrease in lending by Chinese policy banks. In 2019 the amount lent to the region was the lowest in a decade (only $1.1 billion).[28] Yang Chengxu, a former ambassador and head of the influential China Institute of International Studies (CIIS), spelled out the problems facing China in Latin America in an op-ed for a Chinese newspaper in January 2020:

> The disorder in Latin America is expected to continue to spread this year. Maduro proposed holding parliamentary elections, which seemed to be intended to defeat the opposition. Latin America is full of turmoil. The root cause is the widening gap between the rich and the poor and the sluggish economy. Even if the regime changes, the basic problems of people's livelihoods are difficult to solve.[29]

For China, this shapeshifting terrain of domestic politics and regime change clouds relationships and exposes the vulnerability of seemingly secure economic ties.

Geopolitics Ascendant – Huawei and Covid Diplomacy

Determined to reduce Chinese penetration in key technology sectors in the global economy, the US initiated a global campaign targeting China's telecom giant Huawei. Once a small operator in Shenzhen, it grew into a multi-billion dollar global business producing routers, switches and smartphones. It entered the Latin American market in the early 2000s. Its price-competitive technology and hardware communication systems gained a foothold in these developing markets, and within a few years it had secured important stakes in improving the telecommunications infrastructure in countries like Chile.[30] The Chinese government's ambitious strategy to transform its own economy from a manufacturing hub to a (if not 'the') leading technological innovator and driver of the Fourth Industrial Revolution – epitomized by its widely publicized 'Made in China 2025' strategy – caused alarm in Western business and industry circles and spurred the Trump Administration into action. For instance, Huawei and ZTE were designated threats to US national security in a series of steps starting in May 2019 that forbade US companies to engage in business with them, and, after legislation was tightened in May 2020, effectively blocked or at least discouraged non-US firms and governments from working with them as well.[31]

The impact of this on Chinese interests in Latin America was not long in coming. Sino-Chilean plans to build a submarine fibre-optic cable from Chile directly to Shanghai, announced in 2017, became a target of public and private pressure from the US, including a lightning visit to Chile by Pompeo in advance of the Chilean president's visit to Beijing. Subsequently, the Sino-Chilean project was dropped by Piñera's government. Santiago then announced that a submarine cable from Chile to Australia would be built by Japan.[32] In Brazil, US pressure contributed further to divisions within the Bolsonaro Administration over allowing Huawei to play a role in the development of 5G networks in the country.[33] Others like Argentina and Mexico carried forward their existing arrangements with Huawei. The Pompeo-led campaign did have one additional impact: Huawei smartphone sales to the region plummeted in 2020; however, a host of smaller Chinese brands stepped in to take its place, partnering with local firms in Mexico, Peru, Brazil and Chile.[34]

The outbreak of Covid-19 in October 2019 in Wuhan shook the international system as few things had in the new century. Raging across the world and settling in Latin America by early 2020, the virus brought millions of deaths, social isolation and economic dislocation to societies already burdened by the weight of inequality. In Brazil, Ecuador and elsewhere in the region, censure of Beijing for not handling the contagion was coupled with a spike in anti-Chinese xenophobia, leading to everything from discrimination to stoppage of ongoing infrastructure projects.[35] The Bolsonaro government in particular deliberately fanned popular anger at China with a series of tweets that claimed the virus was 'part of a plan of world domination', inspiring Chinese officials to retort on social media.[36]

After initially struggling to contain the spread of the virus in late 2019, a more confident Chinese government sought to turn its success into a public outreach campaign aimed at Latin America and other parts of the world. In June 2020 Beijing mobilized state and private resources, including billionaire entrepreneur Jack Ma's Alibaba Foundation, to distribute millions of masks, PPE equipment, and testing kits to countries in Latin America and the Caribbean as part of a 'health silk road'; for instance, Venezuela was the largest recipient of Chinese medical aid ($41 million), while Chile received $12.6 million, Brazil $9.7 million[37] and Peru $7.5 million, as well as grants, donations and loans for health infrastructure.[38] As Chinese scientists worked on devising a vaccine, arrangements were made to test and distribute inoculations in partner countries. Interestingly, in Brazil this meant that Chinese officials worked together with more than one federal state in defiance of the national government, to jointly administer trials of Sinovac. The death of one of the Brazilian participants inspired yet another anti-Chinese outburst by Bolsonaro, but this did not slow the process of rolling out the programme.[39] With the US reeling from its own failed response to Covid-19 and the lack of any coordinated outreach to Latin American countries, China's soft-power 'vaccine diplomacy' scored considerable successes for its contributions across the region.[40]

In this geopolitically charged climate, it was not always just the US that exerted pressure on Latin American and Caribbean states. When El Salvador's President Bukele announced that his country would receive an unprecedented $150 million grant from Beijing, critics were quick to remind the public that this was a much-diminished level of support compared to what had been promised to his predecessor for breaking with Taiwan. It transpired that Japan had blocked China's funded proposal of a mega-port by indicating it would withdraw its own multi-million dollar aid to the country if Bukele authorized the project.[41]

For Beijing, these unwelcome and, in its view, egregious attacks merited public pushback by a more forthright engagement with the Latin American public via social media; for instance, in response to Pompeo's efforts to drum up support around the region, Chinese embassy officials noted with sarcasm:

It seems that some U.S. politicians cannot go anywhere without attacking China, tarnishing China's reputation, starting fires and fanning the flames and sowing discords ... They can go on talking the talk if they so wish, but we will continue walking the walk. The world will tell plainly who is stirring up trouble and who is trying to make a difference.[42]

As troubling for the CPC was the disquietude of some Latin American partners on matters such as Xinjiang and Hong Kong. That former Chilean President Michelle Bachelet, one of the two Latin American leaders who participated in the seminal BRI summit in 2017, and had received China's support to head up the UN Human Rights Council, could become a major critic was unexpected. She called for UN observers to be allowed into the Uighur detention camps and offered carefully worded criticisms of the suppression of demonstrations in Hong Kong.[43]

Resources, Railroads and Migrants Redux – Global China's New Silk Road and the Remaking of Latin America

In examining China-Latin America relations, one cannot resist reading the present through the shadows of the past. The restoration of China's pre-eminent role in Latin American economies marks a return to the primordial forces and relations that forged the modern world. Historical globalization began with the countries of the Iberian Peninsula scrambling to develop new trade routes with Asia and China discovering new sources of precious metals and markets through exchanges with Europeans in the Western Hemisphere. This triangular trade relationship of China, Latin America and Europe thrived for two hundred years, fed by the appetite for resources and finished goods on the back of exploitation of indigenous peoples and African slaves. By the nineteenth century, Spanish state monopolies had given way to nascent Anglo-American multinational firms like W. R. Grace and Company, who traded in guano, cotton and Chinese indentured labour with representative offices in London, New York, Lima and Canton.

When scholars say China isn't rising but is being restored to its historical stature on the international stage, then surely Latin America's position within that historical political economy occupies a critical place in China's return to global power. Latin American resources – silver in particular – were the beating heart of Imperial China's financial system for nearly three hundred years and fanned out across Asia from the sixteenth to the eighteenth centuries. Latin American consumption of Chinese products – the refined silks for dresses worn from Mexico City to Buenos Aires, ivory statues of the Virgin Mary found in churches and homes, ubiquitous *qianban* plates, cups and vases used by elite families in Lima and Havana, the sophisticated cannons in Veracruz produced by *Sangley* smiths imported from Manila – were all a crucial part of the colonial economy. Moreover, efforts by Europeans and Latin Americans to produce copies of silks, porcelain and other products for the local market – an ironic twist on the contemporary debates on intellectual property that point an accusing finger at China – failed to meet the demand for high-quality Chinese goods and, ultimately, were overwhelmed by Chinese imports. As we demonstrate in this book, the contours of independent nation states and their role within the emerging industrial international economy owes much to this past.

In the contemporary twenty-first century, of course, the European world occupies a different position – and by extension, so does contemporary North America – in relation to China: no longer merely a consumer of Chinese merchandise but today also a recipient of its capital and technology. For Latin America, China's return represents a new market for resources and some products as well as a steady flow of Chinese consumer goods, financial investment, technology and even labour (albeit not in its nineteenth-century form!). US, Canadian and European multinationals operate alongside Chinese SOEs and Latin American *multilatinas*, raise capital in New York, London and Hong Kong as well as in local Latin American stock exchanges and find they are even edged out of markets by joint Sino-Latin American ventures. No longer passive, Chinese diplomacy now looms large in the capitals and boardrooms across the region, leaving the once-unassailable US dominance scrambling to regain its standing.

While the putative 'Cold War' between the US and China hots up around the world, this global competition as played out in Latin America and the Caribbean may in fact obscure the future determinants of China-Latin America relations. Consider that it took less than ten years from China's joining the WTO in 2001 to becoming the second largest trading partner with behemoth Brazil in 2010. From there Beijing has gone on to become a leading investor in key resource sectors such as copper, iron and lithium in the region. China's role as creditor in Venezuela, Ecuador, Jamaica and Surinam is assuming alarming proportions and, contrary to the thrust of the debt trap diplomacy narrative, poses significant risks for China.

And yet there is little evidence that China is prepared for the depth of complexities arising from closer economic ties with the region. Heeding the lessons of Latin American economists like Carlos Díaz Alejandro, whose work reflected on historical patterns of conduct in Latin America in order to ascertain the dangers of a systemic crisis, becomes an imperative under these circumstances.[44] Moral hazards associated with debt have intertwined with domestic and foreign expectations, producing, according to Díaz Alejandro, a volatile cocktail that has tipped the region into economic depression before.

Moreover, evident amongst the Chinese was a growing nervousness about meeting Latin Americans' soaring hopes for the relationship. As one Chinese scholar-turned-businessman bluntly put it to his Latin American colleagues: 'It is not realistic to go beyond complementary economies.' If this assessment proves true, the 'complementarity' of a relationship principally defined by the exchange of Chinese finished products for Latin American resources is deeply troubling for those who anticipated that engagement with China would spur development advances. Already, as indicated in our book, there is scepticism of Chinese intentions in official circles across the region, which seems impervious to efforts to dispel it. To cite but one example, the Consul General of the Brazilian Consulate in Shanghai, Marcos Caramuru de Paiva, declared back in 2011 that 'China's strategy is very clear: it is doing everything possible to control the supply of commodities.'[45] This perspective is bolstered by a growing recognition that more comprehensive integration into global value chains with China may offer an array of financial, policy and even political ties alternative to the US, but it doesn't reduce Latin Americans' exposure to the vagaries of outside influence. In the end, the vulnerability is self-inflicted. The inability of Latin Americans to integrate into global value chains with China is the rub in China-LAC trade relations. Mercosur keeps Argentina and Brazil in their own little box, and Mexico with but a toe in the door lacks the domestic industrial policy needed to wedge into a stable niche in China's value chains.

Even the process of policy formulation and alignment envisaged in bilateral comprehensive strategic partnerships and reinforced through high-level strategic dialogue and inter-ministerial cooperation may not be enough to reconcile such fundamental differences. In their seminal study, Dezalay and Garth identified a transformation of Latin American elites from 'heritiers' of European legal culture to technocrats of US neo-liberalism in conjunction with shifts in global economic power away from Europe to the US.[46] Is China's global ascendancy going to produce another 'retooling' of the Latin American elite towards one that finds its ideological lodestar in Beijing? There is arguably preliminary evidence of that process in the Bolivarian Republics' promotion of 'neo-extractivism', the embrace of China's state-led development paradigm and the corroding effect all of this is having on human rights.

As important as elite orientation is the response of local communities and society as a whole to the increasingly prominent role of China in the economic and political life of their countries. Here, the conduct of managers of Chinese SOEs in the mining community, the role of Chinese competitors operating in the same sector as locals, and the views of myriad retail business owners will all shape how Latin Americans understand and experience this burgeoning relationship. As the many examples in our book show, the record to date is mixed, with the ease of cultural familiarity in urban society in Peru and Brazil contrasting with the clashes with indigenous communities and labour activists in Bolivia and Jamaica. Chinese frustrations with the delays and the costs encountered in the region may yet bring about a recalibration of their exposure to risk with implications for future investment.

At the international level, Latin American responses to global transformation indicate that 'China as an alternative to the US' is a powerful message that comports well with its continual drive for strategic autonomy. One wonders, however, at what point does this impulse manifest as Latin Americans seeking out alternatives to China's dominant position in their country's economic and political life? Would the US, Japan or European countries – perhaps even Brazil or Mexico – be approached to offset Chinese influence? The role of Pacific Alliance countries in supporting the reworking of the TPP process in the aftermath of Trump's withdrawal suggests that this thinking is already beginning to take hold. So, too, the fact that the Lima Group adopted a position at odds with China (and Russia) on Venezuela was another indication of this trend.

In the end, China's relationship with Latin America and the Caribbean is evolving with a rapidity that both sets it apart from other traditional external powers and is also beginning to point to longer-term developments. Beijing's ability to adapt to changing circumstances, be it new domestic political conditions or the impact of the US-China fallout on trade, remains the signature feature of its approach to the region. At the same time, Latin Americans' understanding of China and the internal dynamics which drive policy is improving and, through that, the possibility of better policy outcomes that support development aspirations. In a world experiencing profound transformation, they are forging a future that will surely help define the international political economy in the twenty-first century.

Appendices

The following appendices are provided to illustrate trade figures, foreign direct investment (FDI) and other important political and strategic ties between LAC and China.

Appendix A: Trade Figures – China and Latin America

Bilateral trade volumes with most countries of the region have steadily mounted to now reach vast quantities. According to the latest figures available from the World Bank, the total volume of Chinese-LAC trade is now at least twenty times larger than it was in 2001. The PRC is now the main trading partner of a number of LAC countries, including Brazil which is the largest economy in the region.

Table A.1 Imports, Exports and Total Trade between Latin America and China

Year	Imports (US$ bn)	Exports (US$ bn)	Total trade (US$ bn)
2000	8.31	3.86	12.17
2001	10.29	5.28	15.57
2002	12.40	6.51	18.91
2003	17.95	11.25	29.20
2004	27.72	14.33	42.05
2005	36.34	19.13	55.47
2006	54.40	23.14	77.54
2007	71.79	33.82	105.61
2008	96.00	39.55	135.55
2009	81.62	46.84	128.46
2010	120.34	67.81	188.15
2011	152.25	86.34	238.59
2012	165.27	83.80	249.07
2013	175.68	92.91	268.59
2014	175.59	85.06	260.65
2015	170.64	74.49	245.13
2016	157.20	74.38	231.58
2017	173.88	94.22	268.10
2018	193.11	122.52	315.63
2019	184.20	123.74	307.94

Source: Adapted by authors from World Bank Data (https://wits.worldbank.org/)

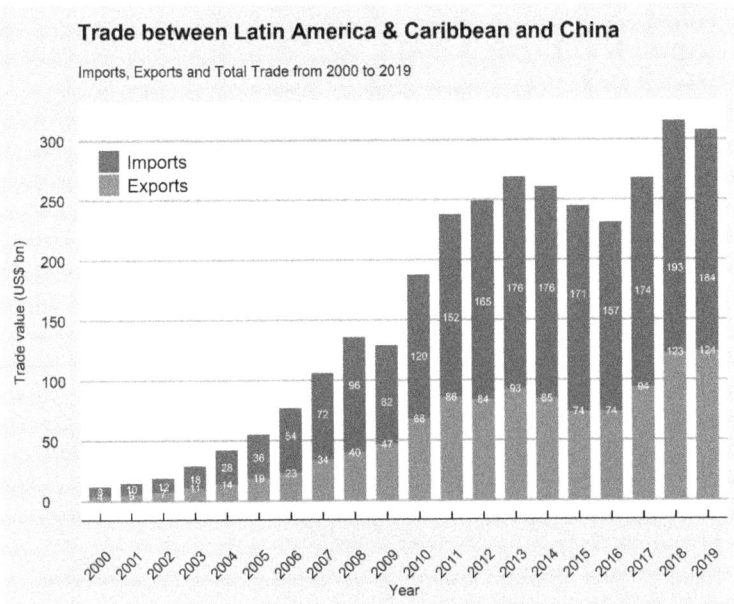

Figure A.1 Bar Chart – Trade between Latin America and China 2000–2019
Source: Adapted by authors from World Bank Data (https://wits.worldbank.org/)

Appendix B: Foreign Direct Investment Figures

Chinese FDI in Latin America and the Caribbean might seem insignificant next to inflows from other great economic powers, rarely amounting to more than 2 per cent of the whole, officially; it was 1.6 per cent in 2018 compared to 50 per cent from the EU and 22 per cent from the USA. Even this modest share has been attained only since 2010. Before then, the Chinese had invested less than $400 million per annum. This figure spiked to $3 billion in 2011 but has trended downwards to just 0.6 per cent in 2019 (including Hong Kong), which only mirrors Chinese performance everywhere of late. The future of Chinese FDI remains shrouded.[1]

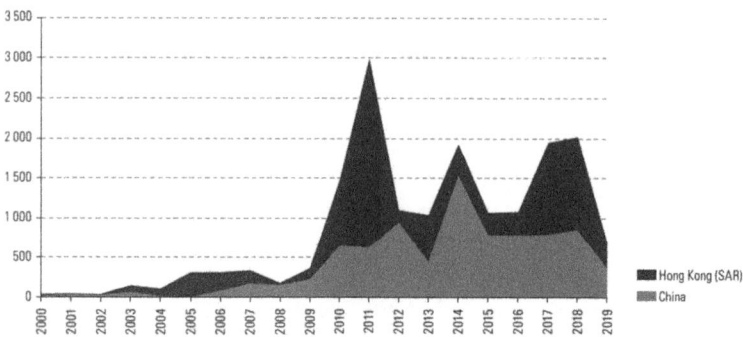

Figure B.1 LAC: FDI Inflows from China and Hong Kong 2000–2019 *(amounts in millions of dollars)*
Source: ECLAC (2021, 90)

Appendix C: Diplomatic and Geopolitical Matters

The importance of the PRC to the thirty-three countries of LAC is increasingly visible and evident among politicians, academics, entrepreneurs and civil society of the region. In the seven decades since its founding in 1949, the PRC has become one of the actors with the most economic and political influence in the continent as a whole. It is acknowledged that current Chinese policy in LAC may be driven mostly by economic, diplomatic and cultural motives, but in a region historically considered Washington's backyard, geopolitics must not be discounted as a motive. It does not follow that the PRC has a 'secret plan to take over the region'; rather, that, as an emerging great power in world politics, Beijing sees LAC as fertile ground for consolidating its own geostrategic position and to assert its national interest. The centrality of the region for China is evidenced in three interrelated aspects: 1) *diplomatic ties* – at the time of writing, a total of twenty-five out of the thirty-three countries in LAC recognize the PRC diplomatically (see Table C.1); 2) *enshrining the One-China policy* – Taiwan still enjoys the diplomatic recognition of eight countries in LAC, but has lost the monopoly it once had. The rapid pace at which LAC countries are cutting diplomatic ties with Taiwan in favour of the PRC gives rise to a presumptive expectation that the holdouts will follow suit in the foreseeable future (see Table C.2); and 3) *endorsement of the Belt and Road Initiative (BRI)* – the BRI is President's Xi Jinping's co-prosperity plan, an ambitious initiative in development diplomacy consisting of two forks, an overland route and a maritime route launched in 2013. As of July 2022, the

BRI has been endorsed by twenty-one countries in the region (see Table C.3). This number is likely to increase in the near future.

Table C.1 PRC – Diplomatic Relations with LAC (1960–2022)

Country	Country's leader	China's leader	Date established
1. Cuba	Fidel Castro	Mao Zedong	28 September 1960
2. Chile	Salvador Allende	Mao Zedong	15 December 1970
3. Peru	Juan Velasco	Mao Zedong	02 November 1971
4. Mexico	Luis Echeverría	Mao Zedong	14 February 1972
5. Argentina	Alejandro Agustín-Lanusse	Mao Zedong	19 February 1972
6. Guyana	Linden Forbes Burnham	Mao Zedong	27 June 1972
7. Jamaica	Michael Manley	Mao Zedong	21 November 1972
8. Trinidad and Tobago	Eric Eustace Williams	Mao Zedong	20 June 1974
9. Venezuela	Carlos Andrés Pérez	Mao Zedong	28 June 1974
10. Brazil	Ernesto Geisel	Mao Zedong	15 August 1974
11. Suriname	Johan Ferrier	Mao Zedong	28 May 1976
12. Barbados	Jon Michael Geoffrey	Hua Guofeng	30 May 1977
13. Ecuador	Jaime Roldós Aguilera	Hua Guofeng	02 January 1980
14. Colombia	Julio César Turbay Ayala	Hua Guofeng	07 February 1980
15. Antigua and Barbuda	Vere Bird	Hu Yaobang	01 January 1983
16. Bolivia	Hernán Siles Zuazo	Hu Yaobang	09 July 1985
17. Grenada†	Herbert Bleize	Hu Yaobang	01 October 1985
18. Uruguay	Julio María Sanguinetti	Zhao Ziyang	03 February 1988
19. Bahamas	Hubert Ingraham	Jiang Zemin	23 May 1997
20. Dominica	Roosevelt Skerrit	Hu Jintao	23 March 2004
21. Costa Rica	Óscar Arias	Hu Jintao	01 June 2007
22. Panama	Juan Carlos Varela	Xi Jinping	12 June 2017
23. Dominican Republic	Danilo Medina	Xi Jinping	01 May 2018

| 24. El Salvador | Salvador Sánchez Cerén | Xi Jinping | 21 August 2018 |
| 25. Nicaragua †† | Daniel Ortega | Xi Jinping | 10 December 2021 |

Source: Authors' from multiple sources

† Grenada first established diplomatic relations with the PRC on 1 October 1985, but because Grenada also reached out to Taiwan in 1989, the PRC severed relations with it on 7 August 1989. Both sides resumed relations much later, on 20 January 2005.

†† Nicaragua first established diplomatic ties with the PRC in 1985 under the Sandinistas after they rose to power in 1979, but Managua moved to re-recognize Taiwan on 6 November 1990, a move that prompted the PRC to suspend diplomatic ties with Nicaragua the next day.

Table C.2 Diplomatic Allies of Taiwan in LAC as of July 2022

Country	Date diplomatic ties established
1. Belize	13 October 1989
2. Guatemala	15 June 1933
3. Haiti	25 April 1956
4. Honduras	6 November 1944
5. Paraguay	8 July 1957
6. Saint Lucia	30 April 2007
7. St. Kitts and Nevis	9 October 1983
8. St. Vincent & the Grenadines	15 August 1981

Source: Authors' from multiple sources

Table C.3 LAC Countries that have endorsed the BRI as of July 2022

LAC country	Endorsement date
1. Panama	17 November 2017
2. Trinidad & Tobago	15 May 2018
3. Antigua & Barbuda	6 June 2018
4. Bolivia	19 June 2018
5. Dominica	13 July 2018
6. Guyana	27 July 2018
7. Uruguay	20 August 2018
8. Costa Rica	3 September 2018
9. Venezuela	14 September 2018

10. Grenada	21 September 2018
11. Suriname	23 September 2018
12. El Salvador	01 November 2018
13. Chile	02 November 2018
14. Dominican Republic	02 November 2018
15. Cuba	09 November 2018
16. Ecuador	14 December 2018
17. Barbados	26 February 2019
18. Jamaica	15 April 2019
19. Peru	26 April 2019
20. Nicaragua	12 January 2022
21. Argentina	6 February 2022

Source: Authors' from multiple sources

Notes

Introduction

1. The authors were present at this event. The Maritime Agreement was signed in Beijing on 17 November 2017 and came into force on 17 May 2018. One of the key elements of the comprehensive Agreement is contained in Article 5, which states that 'Each Contracting Party should grant the vessels of the other Contracting Party the *Most Favored Nation* treatment with regard to access to ports, the use of infrastructure and auxiliary services of those ports, the collection of port fees and dues and tonnage tax, the boarding and disembarking of passengers, the customs formalities and assignment of berths and facilities for loading and uploading', see 'ACUERDO ENTRE EL GOBIERNO DE LA REPÚBLICA DE PANAMÁ Y EL GOBIERNO DE LA REPÚBLICA POPULAR CHINA SOBRE TRANSPORTE MARÍTIMO.' ACUERDOS PANAMÁ-CHINA (2017), published online on 17 November, https://mire.gob.pa/images/PDF/documentos%20y%20formularios/Acuerdoschina/ACUERDO%20TRANS%20MARITIMO.pdf.
2. Zhang Yujing, Director of China Chamber of Commerce for Import and Export of Machinery and Electronic Products, China-Panama Expo, Panama City, 9 May 2018.
3. Lok C. D. Sui (2005) *Memoirs of a Future Home: diasporic citizenship of Chinese in Panama*. Stanford, CA: Stanford University Press; Matthew Parker (2007) *Hell's Gorge: The battle to build the Panama Canal*. London: Arrow Books, 29.
4. The authors use the term Latin America to refer to Latin America and the Caribbean (LAC). In some instances, the authors simply use 'LAC' when referring to the region.
5. Matthew Parker (2007) *Hell's Gorge: the battle to build the Panama Canal*. London: Arrow Books, xix.
6. Ricardo J. Sánchez, Daniel E. Perrotti and Alejandra Gomez Paz Fort (2021) 'Looking Into the Future Ten Years Later: big full containerships and their arrival to South American ports', *Journal of Shipping and Trade* 6 (2).
7. INEC, 'Panamá en Cifras: Años 2012–16' (Ciudad de Panamá: Instituto Nacional de Estadistica y Censo, 2017), https://www.contraloria.gob.pa/inec/archivos/P8551PanamaCifrasCompleto.pdf.
8. Offshore Energy (2017) 'Construction of Panama Colón Container Port Kicks Off', press release, 14 June, https://www.offshore-energy.biz/construction-of-panama-colon-container-port-kicks-off/.
9. Álvaro Méndez and Chris Alden (2021) 'China in Panama: from peripheral diplomacy to grand strategy', *Geopolitics* 26 (3): 838–60.

10 Daniel McDowell (2019) 'The (Ineffective) Financial Statecraft of China's Bilateral Swap Agreements', *Development and Change* 50(1): 122–43, https://doi.org/10.1111/dech.12474
11 Leonardo Stanley (2018) 'Argentina's Infrastructure Gap and Financial Needs: the role of China', in E. Dussel-Peters, A. Armony and Sh.-J. Cui (eds), *Building Development for a New Era: China's infrastructure projects in Latin America and the Caribbean*, 77–101. Pittsburgh, PA: University of Pittsburgh.
12 According to some authors funds from China are given as a "combination of traditional grants and concessional or interest free loans", see Carol Wise (2020) *Dragonomics: how Latin America is Maximizing (or Missing Out On) China's International Development Strategy*. New Haven, CT: Yale University Press, 9. Other authors maintain that China's lending to the region also includes non-concessional loans, see Bernabé Malacalza (2019) 'What Led to the Boom? Unpacking China's Development Cooperation in Latin America', *World Affairs* 182 (4): 378. See also Kevin Gallagher (2020) 'Chinese Development Finance in the Americas', in *Southern-Led Development Finance: solutions from the Global South*, ed. Diana Barrowclough, Kevin P. Gallagher and Richard Kozul-Wright. Abingdon, UK: Routledge, 143.
13 Currently there are eight countries in Latin America that still recognize Taiwan diplomatically. This is more than 50 per cent of all countries that recognize Taipei globally. The list of countries includes: Belize, Guatemala, Haiti, Honduras, Paraguay, Saint Lucia, St. Kitts and Nevis, and St. Vincent and the Grenadines; see Álvaro Méndez (2021) 'Geopolitics in Central America: China and El Salvador in the 21st century', in *China-Latin America and the Caribbean: assessment and outlook*, ed. Thierry Kellner and Sophie Wintgens, 207–21. Abingdon, UK: Routledge. See also: Mendez, A. and Forcadell, F. J. (2022) 'China y America Latina. Diplomacia, comercio y geopolítica', in Estrada, G. (ed.) *América Latina Hoy*. Madrid, Spain: Fundación Felipe Gonzales., pp. 174–191.
14 Mexico is one of the key countries in the region, but its economy has not performed very well over the last two decades. With an annual GDP growth of 2 per cent, it has been the worst performer among other key countries like Argentina, Brazil, Chile and Costa Rica; see Carol Wise (2020) *Dragonomics: how Latin America is Maximizing (or Missing Out On) China's International Development Strategy*. New Haven, CT: Yale University Press, 101.
15 H. Niu (2018) 'A Strategic Analysis of Chinese Infrastructure Projects in Latin America and the Caribbean', in E. Dussel-Peters, A. Armony and Sh.-J. Cui (eds), *Building Development for a New Era: China's infrastructure projects in Latin America and the Caribbean*, 180180–94. Pittsburgh, PA: University of Pittsburgh; J. Blazquez-Lidoy, J. Rodriguez and J Santiso (2006) 'Angel or Devil? China's Trade Impact on Latin American Emerging Markets', OECD Development Centre Working Papers, No. 252, OECD Publishing, Paris, https://doi.org/10.1787/422232033888.
16 Interview by the authors with former Foreign Minister and Defence Minister of Brazil, Celso Amorim, London, 12 February 2017.

17 World Bank (2021) 'Brazilian Product Exports and Imports to China', *World Integrated Trade Solution (WITS)*, https://wits.worldbank.org/CountryProfile/en/Country/BRA/Year/2009/TradeFlow/EXPIMP/Partner/CHN/Product/all-groups.
18 South Africa was invited to join BRICs in December 2010; see Chris Alden and Yu-Chan Wu, eds (2021) *South Africa–China Relations: a partnership of paradoxes*. Cham, Switzerland: Springer, 43.
19 C. Hiratuka (2018) 'Chinese infrastructure projects in Brazil: two case studies', in E. Dussel-Peters, A. Armony and Sh.-J. Cui (eds), *Building Development for a New Era: China's infrastructure projects in Latin America and the Caribbean*, 122–43. Pittsburgh, PA: University of Pittsburgh.
20 *Reuters* (2016) 'China Loan to Petrobras May Help Pay 2016 Debt', 27 February, https://www.reuters.com/article/us-brazil-petrobras-china-idUSKCN0W001T.
21 Lucianan Dyniewicz (2018) 'Declaração de Bolsonaro derruba ações da Eletrobrás', *Estadão*, 11 October, http://economia.estadao.com.br/noticias/geraldclaracao-de-bolsonaro-derruba-acoes-da-electrobras,70002542992.
22 Dennis O. Flynn and Arturo Giráldez (1995) 'Born with a "Silver Spoon": the origin of World Trade in 1571', *Journal of World History* 6 (2): 201–21, 204.
23 Ibid., 214.
24 Luis Corrochano-Garcia and Ruben Tang (2011) *Las Relaciones entre el Perú y China*. Lima, Perú: Pontificia Universidad Católica del Perú, 156–7.
25 Philip Dennis (1979) 'The Anti-Chinese Campaigns in Sonora, Mexico', *Ethnohistory* 26 (1): 65–80.
26 Lok C. D. Sui (2005) *Memoirs of a Future Home: diasporic citizenship of Chinese in Panama*. Stanford, CA: Stanford University Press, xv.
27 Weinong Gao (2017) 'New Chinese Migrants in Latin America: Trends and Patterns of Adaptation', in *Contemporary Chinese Diasporas*, ed. Min Zhou. Singapore: Springer, 339.
28 Song Xiaoping (2015) 'China and Latin America in a World in Transition: a Chinese perspective', in Adrian Bonilla and Paz Milet, *Latin America, the Caribbean and China: sub-regional scenarios*, 59. San José, Costa Rica: FLASCO/CAF.
29 Gaston Fornes and Álvaro Méndez (2018) *The China-Latin America Axis: emerging markets and their role in an increasingly globalised world*, 2nd edn. London: Palgrave Macmillan, 46.
30 World Bank (2021) 'Latin America & Caribbean Product Exports and Imports to China 2017', *World Integrated Trade Solution (WITS)*, https://wits.worldbank.org/CountryProfile/en/Country/LCN/Year/2017/TradeFlow/EXPIMP/Partner/CHN/Product/all-groups.
31 Gaston Fornes and Álvaro Méndez (2018) *The China-Latin America Axis: emerging markets and their role in an increasingly globalised world*, 2nd edn. New York, NY: Palgrave Macmillan, 66. See also China–CELAC Forum

(2015) 'Cooperation Plan (2015–2019)', http://www.chinacelacforum.org/eng/zywj_3/201501/t20150123_6475954.htm.
32 See Jaime Ortiz (2012) 'Déjà Vu: Latin America and Its New Trade Dependency This Time with China', *Latin American Research Review* 47 (3): 175–90; Rhys Jenkins (2012) 'Latin America and China—a new dependency?', *Third World Quarterly* 33(7): 1337–58.
33 Bilde Ertin and Jose Antonio Ocampo (2012) 'Super Cycles of Commodity Prices Since the 19th Century', Desa Working Paper No. 110, UN Department of Economic and Social Affairs, New York, 1–27.
34 Krishnadev Calamur (2018) 'Tillerson to Latin America: beware of China', *The Atlantic*, https://www.theatlantic.com/international/archive/2018/02/rex-in-latam/552197/; also see Kevin Gallagher and Roberto Porzecanski (2008) 'China Matters: China's Economic Impact in Latin America', *Latin American Research Review*, 43(1): 185–200, 195; S. T. Silva (2015), 'Los patrones de internacionalización china en once años del proyecto Going Global', in E. Dussel-Peters, *América Latina y el Caribe-China. Economía, comercio e inversión*, 399–413. México: Unión de Universidades de América Latina y Caribe.
35 Pedro da Motta Veiga and Sandra Poilonia Rios (2019) 'China's FDI in Brazil: recent trends and policy debate', *Policy Brief* 19/20, Policy Center for the New South, June.
36 *Reuters* (2021) 'China's Nov forex reserves unexpectedly rise to $3.222 trln', https://www.reuters.com/markets/currencies/chinas-nov-forex-reserves-unexpectedly-rise-3222-trln-2021-12-07/.
37 Kevin Gallagher and Amos Irwin (2016) 'China's Economic Statecraft in Latin America: evidence from China's Policy Banks', in C. Wise and M. Myers (eds), *The Political Economy of China-Latin American Relations in the New Millennium: brave new world*, 50–68. London: Routledge. According to Gallagher and Irwin, 87 per cent of China's loans to Latin America are in the infrastructure sector while traditional multilateral development financiers provide 30 per cent; Mark Wenner and Dillon Clarke (2016) 'China's Rise in the Caribbean: what does it mean for Caribbean stakeholders?', Inter-American Development Bank, Technical Note No. IDB-TN 1073, Washington, DC, July, 6.
38 Roberto Russell and Juan Gabriel Tokatlian (2011) 'Beyond Orthodoxy: asserting Latin America's new strategic options toward the United States', *Latin American Politics and Society* 53(4): 127–46.
39 Álvaro Méndez (2017) *Colombian Agency and the Making of US Foreign Policy: Intervention by Invitation*. London: Routledge.
40 Chris Alden and Álvaro Méndez (2019) 'Perú, China y la nueva multipolaridad – navegar en la política internacional en tiempos inciertos', in J. Alcalde, C. Alden, A. Guerra-Baron and A. Méndez (eds), *La Conexión China en la Política Exterior del Perú en el siglo XXI*, 278–307. Lima: Pontificia Universidad Católica del Perú.

41 Cobus van Staden, Chris Alden and Yu-Shan Wu (2020) 'Outlining African Agency Against the Background of the Belt and Road Initiative', *African Studies Quarterly* 19 (3–4): 115–34.
42 Denisa Kostovicova and Marlies Glasius, eds (2011) *Bottom Up Politics: an agency-centred approach to globalization*. Basingstoke: Palgrave.
43 Russell Crandall (2008) *The United States and Latin America after the Cold War*. Cambridge: Cambridge University Press.
44 June Beittel (2013) 'Political and Economic Relations and US Relations', Congressional Research Service, Washington, DC, 1–9.
45 Adrián Bonilla and Paz Milet (2015) 'China's Impact on the International Relations of Latin America and the Caribbean', in Adrian Bonilla and Paz Milet (eds), *Latin America, the Caribbean and China: sub-regional scenarios*, 9–10. San José, Costa Rica: FLASCO/CAF.
46 State Council, PRC (2008) 'China's Policy Paper on Latin America and the Caribbean', https://china.usc.edu/chinas-policy-paper-latin-america-and-caribbean.
47 The TPP was a large trade agreement which was one of the key strategic cornerstones of President Obama's Pivot to Asia, see Carol Wise (2020) *Dragonomics: How Latin America is Maximizing (or Missing Out On) China's International Development Strategy*. New Haven, CT: Yale University Press, 131. The TPP was signed by twelve Pacific Rim countries, including three from Latin America (Chile, Peru and Mexico); for additional information, see Council of Foreign Relations (2021) 'What's Next for the Trans-Pacific Partnership (TPP)?', https://www.cfr.org/backgrounder/what-trans-pacific-partnership-tpp.
48 John A. Agnew (2003) *Geopolitics: Re-visioning World Politics*, 2nd edn. London: Routledge. Also see Saul Bernard Cohen (2015) *Geopolitics: The Geography of International Relations*, 3rd edn. Lanham, MD: Rowman & Littlefield; Colin Flint (2017) *Introduction to Geopolitics*, 3rd edn. London: Routledge.
49 Some analysts argue that debt-trap diplomacy is a misconception because China is not organized enough to pursue coherent geopolitical aims, see L. Jones, S. Hameiri and Royal Institute of International Affairs (2020) *Debunking the Myth of 'Debt-Trap Diplomacy': how recipient countries shape China's belt and road initiative*. Royal Institute of International Affairs. The case of Venezuela may substantiate that thesis as Beijing was willing to restructure its loans to Venezuela; see Francisco Monaldi (2019) 'China Can Help Save Venezuela. Here's How', *Americas Quarterly*, https://www.americasquarterly.org/article/china-can-help-save-venezuela-heres-how/.
50 *The Guardian* (2020) 'China outraged as Brazilian minister suggests COVID 19 is part of "plan of world domination"', 7 April, https://www.theguardian.com/world/2020/apr/07/china-outraged-after-brazil-minister-suggests-covid-19-is-part-of-plan-for-world-domination.

51 Ted Piccone (2016) 'China's Policy Paper on Latin America and the Caribbean', Washington, DC: Brookings Institute.
52 State Council, PRC (2008) 'China's Policy Paper on Latin America and the Caribbean', https://china.usc.edu/chinas-policy-paper-latin-america-and-caribbean; State Council, PRC (2016) 'China's Policy Paper on Latin America and the Caribbean', http://english.www.gov.cn/archive/white_paper/2016/11/24/content_281475499069158.htm.
53 R. Evan Ellis (2014) 'China's Growing Relationship with Latin America and the Caribbean: in the context of US policy towards the region', *Air and Space Power Journal* (2nd Semester): 79; also Frank Mora (1997) 'The People's Republic of China: from indifference to engagement', *Asian Affairs: an American Review* 24 (1): 53–4.Frank Mora went on to become Deputy Assistant Secretary of Defence for Western Hemispheric Affairs from 2009–2013.
54 For example, see Carol Wise (2016) 'Playing Both Sides of the Pacific: Latin America's Free Trade Agreements with China', *Pacific Affairs* 89(1): 75–101.
55 J. Peter Pham (2010) 'China's Strategic Penetration of Latin America: what it means for US interests', *American Foreign Policy Interests*, 32 (10), https://www.tandfonline.com/doi/abs/10.1080/10803920.2010.535762; also see R. Evan Ellis (2005) *U.S. National Security Implications of Chinese Involvement in Latin America*, U.S. Army War College Strategic Studies Institute Monograph. Carlisle, PA: Strategic Studies Institute.
56 Lei Yu (2015) 'China's Strategic Partnership with Latin America: a fulcrum in China's rise', *International Affairs* 91 (5): 1050. According to Lei Yu, Chinese IR scholars like Baojun Yang (2012) and Jianfei Lin (2013) argue that in response to the US pivot to Asia, China should embed itself into America's backyard.
57 Xiaoyu Pu and Margaret Myers (2021) 'Overstretching or Overreaction? China's Rise in Latin America and the US Response', *Journal of Current Chinese Affairs* 186810262110282, 4.
58 US Department of Defence (2018) 'Summary of the 2018 National Defense Strategy of the United States', Washington, DC. Also see remarks by top US general in charge of South Command, 'Commander alarmed as China makes inroads in Americas', *National Defense Magazine* 12 February 2020, https://www.nationaldefensemagazine.org/articles/2020/12/2/commander-alarmed-as-china-makes-inroads-in-americas.
59 Lindsay Gabow (2020) 'The Strategic Competition We've Neglected: Confronting China in Mexico', *Real Clear Defense*, 14 May, https://www.realcleardefense.com/articles/2020/05/14/the_strategic_competition_weve_neglected_confronting_china_in_mexico_115287.html.
60 Álvaro Méndez and Mariano Turzi (2020) *The Political Economy of China–Latin America Relations: the AIIB Membership*. New York, NY: Palgrave Pivot, doi: 10.1007/978-3-030-33451-2.

61 We are not implying that the US has stopped being an important economic player in Latin America as the numbers are still significantly higher. In 2019, for instance, total trade between China and LAC was $307 billion. During the same year, that between the US and Latin America was $761 billion. Foreign direct investment (FDI) figures paint a similar picture. In 2018, China's FDI influx to the region was $129.8 billion, see Carol Wise (2020) *Dragonomics: How Latin America is Maximizing (or Missing Out On) China's International Development Strategy*. New Haven, CT: Yale University Press, ix. Figures from 2005 to 2019 also indicate that most of the FDI to the region still comes from traditional investors such as the USA and Europe (Spain in particular), see Victoria Chonn Ching (2021) 'Butting in or Rounding Out? China's Role in Latin America's Investment Diversification', Global Development Policy Center, https://www.bu.edu/gdp/files/2021/06/GCI_WP_016_FIN.pdf.

62 R. Evan Ellis (2018) 'China's Strategy in Latin America and the Caribbean', in *China Steps Out: Beijing's Major Power Engagement with the Developing World*, ed. Joshua Eisenman and Eric Heginbotham, 123–52. Abingdon, UK: Routledge; Enrique Dussel Peters, ed. (2019) *China's Foreign Direct Investment in Latin America and the Caribbean: conditions and challenges*. Mexico, DF: Universidad Autonoma de Mexico, see Section II (chapters 5 to 15). ECLAC (2021) *Foreign Direct Investment in Latin America and the Caribbean 2021*. Santiago, Chile: Economic Commission for Latin America and the Caribbean, 75–122, see Chapter II, 'Chinese investment in a changing world: repercussions for the region'; Margaret Myers and Kevin Gallagher (2020) 'Scaling Back: Chinese Development Finance in LAC, 2019', *China-Latin America Report*, March, https://www.bu.edu/gdp/files/2020/03/Chinese-Finance-to-LAC-2019.pdf; Ding Ding et al. (2021) 'Chinese Investment in Latin America: Sectoral Complementarity and the Impact of China's Rebalancing', IMF Working Paper, https://www.imf.org/en/Publications/WP/Issues/2021/06/07/Chinese-Investment-in-Latin-America-Sectoral-Complementarity-and-the-Impact-of-Chinas-50217.

63 Ana Cristina Alves (2013) 'Chinese Economic Statecraft: a comparative study of China's oil-backed loans in Angola and Brazil', *Journal of Current Chinese Affairs* 1: 99–130; William Norris (2016) *Chinese Economic Statecraft: Commercial actors, grand strategy and state control*. Syracuse, NY: Cornell University Press. Kevin Gallagher (2020) 'Chinese Development Finance in the Americas', in *Southern-Led Development Finance: solutions from the Global South*, ed. Diana Barrowclough, Kevin P. Gallagher and Richard Kozul-Wright, 125–52. Abingdon, UK: Routledge.

64 R. Evan Ellis (2014) *China on the Ground in Latin America*. Basingstoke: Pagrave; Álvaro Méndez and Chris Alden (2021) 'China in Panama: from peripheral diplomacy to grand strategy', *Geopolitics* 26 (3): 838–60.

Chapter 1

1. Evelyn Hu-DeHart and Kathleen Lopez (2008) 'Introduction: Asian Diasporas in Latin America and the Caribbean – an historical overview', *Afro-Hispanic Review* 27 (1): 10.
2. Stanley Payne (1973) *A History of Spain and Portugal*, vol. 1. Madison, WI: University of Wisconsin Press, 188–9.
3. They were not the first. In 1291 two Genoese ships sailed out of the Mediterranean Sea and into the Atlantic in an effort to circumvent their Venetian rivals by finding another route to India. They were never heard from again. Roger Crowley (2011) *City of Fortune: how Venice won and lost an empire*. London: Faber and Faber, 153.
4. Stanley Payne (1973) *A History of Spain and Portugal*, vol. 1. Madison, WI: University of Wisconsin Press, 198.
5. Roderich Ptak (2006) 'Trade Between Macau and South East Asia in Ming Times: a survey', *Monumenta Serica* 54: 470–1; Timothy Brook (2013) 'Trade and Conflict in the South China Sea, 1514–1523', in Lucia Coppolaro and Francine Mackenzie (eds), *A Global History of Trade and Conflict Since 1500*, 20–37. Basingstoke: Palgrave.
6. Dennis Flynn and Artur Giráldez (1996) 'Silk for Silver: Manila-Macao trade in the 17th century', *Philippine Studies* 44 (1): 470–1.
7. A misnomer as these 'factories' were more like bonded warehouses.
8. Dennis Flynn and Arturo Giráldez (1995) 'Born with a Silver Spoon: the origin of world trade in 1571', *Journal of World History* 6 (2): 206.
9. John Fisher (1997) *The Economic Aspects of Spanish Imperialism in America, 1492–1810*. Liverpool: Liverpool University Press, 26–7; also see Shi Mingxiong (1976) *The Silk Industry in Ching China*. Ann Arbor, MI: University of Michigan Press.
10. Dennis Flynn and Artur Giráldez (1996) 'Silk for Silver: Manila-Macao trade in the 17th century', *Philippine Studies* 44 (1): 55.
11. Ibid., 53.
12. Ibid., 58.
13. Luis Francia (2014) *A History of the Philippines: from Indios bravos to Filipinos*. New York, NY: Overlook Press, 56.
14. Katharine Bjork (1998) 'The Link that Kept the Philippines Spanish: Mexican merchant interests and the Manila trade', *Journal of World History* 9 (1): 25–50.
15. Ibid.; Luis Francia (2014) *A History of the Philippines: from Indios bravos to Filipinos*. New York, NY: Overlook Press, 63.
16. Ibid., 56.
17. Edward Slack (2010) 'Sinifying New Spain: Cathay's influence on colonial Mexico via the *Nao de China*', in Walton Look Lai and Tan Chee-Beng (eds), *The Chinese in Latin America and the Caribbean*, 5–27. Leiden: Brill.

18 Thomas Gage (1625) cited in Robert Buffington and Lila Baimari (eds), *Keen's Latin American Civilization: history and society, 1492 to the present*, 8th edn. Boulder, CO: Westview 2004, 159; also see William Schurz (1918) 'Mexico, Peru and the Manila Galleon', *The Hispanic American Historical Review* 1 (4): 389–90. It is possible that they were actually part of a Japanese contingent sent through there to Spain that elected to stay on in Mexico City.
19 Edward Slack (2010) 'Sinifying New Spain: Cathay's influence on colonial Mexico via the *Nao de China*', in Walton Look Lai and Tan Chee-Beng (eds), *The Chinese in Latin America and the Caribbean*, 20–1. Leiden: Brill.
20 Stanley Payne (1973) *A History of Spain and Portugal*, vol. 1. Madison, WI: University of Wisconsin Press, 274, 282–4.
21 Katharine Bjork (1998) 'The Link that Kept the Philippines Spanish: Mexican merchant interests and the Manila trade', *Journal of World History* 9 (1): 31.
22 Roderich Ptak (2006) 'Trade between Macau and South East Asia in Ming Times: a survey', *Monumenta Serica* 54: 470–1.
23 Kris Lane (2019) *Potosí: the Silver City that changed the world*. Berkley, CA: University of California Press, 1.
24 John Fisher (1997) *The Economic Aspects of Spanish Imperialism in America, 1492–1810*. Liverpool: Liverpool University Press, 98–9.
25 Recent research confirms the Spanish galleons carried enormous cargoes of mercury; Sam Jones (2019) 'Spain logs hundreds of shipwrecks that tell story of maritime past', *The Guardian*, 1 March, https://www.theguardian.com/science/2019/mar/01/spain-logs-shipwrecks-maritime-past-weather-pirates.
26 John Fisher (1997) *The Economic Aspects of Spanish Imperialism in America, 1492–1810*. Liverpool: Liverpool University Press, 98–9; M. F. Lang (1968) 'New Spain's Mining Depression and the Supply of Quicksilver from Peru, 1600–1700', *Hispanic American Historical Review* 48 (3): 640.
27 John Fisher (1997) *The Economic Aspects of Spanish Imperialism in America, 1492–1810*. Liverpool: Liverpool University Press, 98–9.
28 Dennis Flynn and Arturo Giráldez (1995) 'Born with a Silver Spoon: the origin of world trade in 1571', *Journal of World History* 6 (2): 204. Also see Kris Lane (2019) *Potosí: the Silver City that changed the world*. Berkley, CA: University of California Press, 8.
29 W. J. Streeter (1984) *The Silver Mania: an exposé of the causes of the high price volatility of silver*. Boston, MA: D. Reidel Publishing, 12.
30 Noel Maurer and Carlos Yu (2011) *The Big Ditch: how America took, built, ran and ultimately gave away the Panama Canal*. Princeton, NJ: Princeton University Press, 28.
31 Dennis Flynn and Artur Giráldez (1996) 'Silk for Silver: Manila-Macao trade in the 17th century', *Philippine Studies* 44 (1): 61–2.
32 Alan Peyrefitte (1993) *The Collision of Two Civilizations: the British expedition to China 1792–94*. London: Harville, 451.

33 John Fisher (1997) *The Economic Aspects of Spanish Imperialism in America, 1492–1810*. Liverpool: Liverpool University Press, 106–7.
34 Edward Slack (2010) 'Sinifying New Spain: Cathay's influence on colonial Mexico via the *Nao de China*', in Walton Look Lai and Tan Chee-Beng (eds), *The Chinese in Latin America and the Caribbean*, 21. Leiden: Brill.
35 Ibid., 20.
36 William Schurz (1918) 'Mexico, Peru and the Manila Galleon', *The Hispanic American Historical Review* 1 (4): 394.
37 Chuck Meide (2002) 'A Plague of Ships: Spanish ships and shipbuilding in the Atlantic colonies, sixteenth and seventeenth centuries', College of William and Mary, December, 5.
38 See Lawrence Clayton (1980) *Caulkers and Carpenters in the New World: the shipyards of colonial Guanyaquil*. Athens, OH: Ohio University Press.
39 Cited in Chuck Meide (2002) 'A Plague of Ships: Spanish ships and shipbuilding in the Atlantic colonies, sixteenth and seventeenth centuries', College of William and Mary, December, 11–15.
40 Ibid., 7; also see Hugh Thomas's belief that Cortez from the outset saw the ship construction as a precursor to navel conquest of China. Hugh Thomas (2010) *The Golden Age: the Spanish Empire of Charles V*. London: Penguin, 68.
41 Edward Slack (2010) 'Sinifying New Spain: Cathay's influence on colonial Mexico via the *Nao de China*', in Walton Look Lai and Tan Chee-Beng (eds), *The Chinese in Latin America and the Caribbean*, 24. Leiden: Brill.
42 Ibid., 12.
43 Ibid., 17–19.
44 W. Borah, cited in Dennis Flynn and Artur Giráldez (1996) 'Silk for Silver: Manila-Macao trade in the 17th century', *Philippine Studies* 44 (1): 62.
45 William Schurz (1918) 'Mexico, Peru and the Manila Galleon', *The Hispanic American Historical Review* 1 (4): 395–6.
46 Cited in ibid., 401.
47 John Fisher (1997) *The Economic Aspects of Spanish Imperialism in America, 1492–1810*. Liverpool: Liverpool University Press, 152.
48 M. F. Lang (1968) 'New Spain's Mining Depression and the Supply of Quicksilver from Peru, 1600–1700', *Hispanic American Historical Review* 48 (3): 638–9.
49 John Fisher (1997) *The Economic Aspects of Spanish Imperialism in America, 1492–1810*. Liverpool: Liverpool University Press, 139–40.
50 Ibid., 151–2.
51 Alan Peyrefitte (1993) *The Collision of Two Civilizations: the British expedition to China 1792–94*. London: Harville, 310.
52 Jonathan Fenby (2008) *A History of Modern China: The fall and rise of a great power*. London: Penguin, 14.
53 According to some accounts, Heshen's personal fortune of 900 million silver taels was equivalent to a decade of annual budget surpluses of the Qing imperial Treasury.

54 W. J. Streeter (1984) *The Silver Mania: an exposé of the causes of the high price volatility of silver*. Boston, MA: D. Reidel Publishing, 17–19.
55 Jonathan Spence (1996) *God's Chinese Son: the Taiping heavenly kingdom of Hong Xiuquan*. New York, NY: Norton.
56 Michale Gonzales (1989) 'Chinese Plantation Workers and Social Conflict in Peru in the Late Nineteenth Century', *Journal of Latin American Studies* 21 (3): 385. See also Lomarsh Roopnarine (2021) 'Chinese Indentured Servitude in the Atlantic World', *Oxford Bibliographies*, doi: 10.1093/OBO/9780199730414-0294.
57 James Ferguson King (1944) 'The Latin American Republics and the Suppression of the Slave Trade', *The Hispanic American Historical Review* 21 (3): 387–411. Also see Anthony Sullivan (2020) *Britain's War Against the Slave Trade: the operations of the Royal Navy's West Africa Squadron, 1807–1867*. Yorkshire: Frontline Books.
58 Stanley Engerman (1984) 'Economic Change and Contract Labor in the British Caribbean: The end of slavery and the adjustment to emancipation', *Explorations in Economic History* 21: 145–8.
59 B. G. Higman (1972) 'The Chinese in Trinidad, 1806 –1838', *Caribbean Studies* 12 (3): 21–4. Also see Elliot Young (2014) *Alien Nation: Chinese migration in the Americas from the coolie era through World War II*. Chapel Hill, NC: University of North Carolina.
60 Walton suggests that this region was a source of outward migration to Southeast Asia for hundreds of years. Walton Look Lai (2010) 'Asian Diasporas and Tropical Migration in the Age of Empire: a comparative overview', in Walton Look Lai and Tan Chee-Beng (eds), *The Chinese in Latin America and the Caribbean*, 45. Leiden: Brill.
61 B. G. Higman (1972) 'The Chinese in Trinidad, 1806 –1838', *Caribbean Studies* 12 (3): 27–30.
62 Mary Turner (1974) 'Chinese Contract Labour in Cuba, 1847–1874', *Caribbean Studies* 14 (2): pp. 66–81.
63 Ei Murakami (2016) 'The End of the Coolie Trade in Southern China: Focus on the Treaty Port of Amoy', in Hideaki Suzuki (ed.), *Abolitions as a Global Experience*, 141–3. Singapore: National University of Singapore Press.
64 Alexander de Secada (1985) 'Arms, Guano and Shipping: the W.R. Grace interests in Peru, 1865–1885', *The Business History Review* 59 (4): 608.
65 Evelyn Hu-DeHart (2010) 'Indispensable Enemy or Convenient Scapegoat? A critical examination of Sinophobia in Latin America and the Caribbean, 1870s–1930s', in Walton Look Lai and Tan Chee-Beng (eds), *The Chinese in Latin America and the Caribbean*, 72. Leiden: Brill.
66 St. John Robinson (2010) 'The Chinese of Central America: diverse beginnings, common achievements', in Walton Look Lai and Tan Chee-Beng (eds), *The Chinese in Latin America and the Caribbean*, 104–6. Leiden: Brill.

67 Alan Adamson (1972) *Sugar without Slaves: The political economy of British Guiana 1832–1904*. New Haven, CT: Yale University Press; J. Ankum-Houwink (1974) 'Chinese Contract Migrants in Surinam between 1853 and 1870', *Boletín de Estudios Latinoamericanos y del Caribe* 17: 42–68.

68 Ei Murakami (2016) 'The End of the Coolie Trade in Southern China: Focus on the Treaty Port of Amoy', in Hideaki Suzuki (ed.), *Abolitions as a Global Experience*, 130–48. Singapore: National University of Singapore Press.

69 Charles Dickens (1860) 'The Coolie Trade in China', *All the Year Round*, 28 July. London: Chapman and Hall, 365.

70 Cited in Walton Look Lai (2010) 'Asian Diasporas and Tropical Migration in the Age of Empire: a comparative overview', in Walton Look Lai and Tan Chee-Beng (eds), *The Chinese in Latin America and the Caribbean*, 52. Leiden: Brill.

71 Alexander de Secada (1985) 'Arms, Guano and Shipping: the W.R. Grace interests in Peru, 1865–1885', *The Business History Review* 59 (4).

72 According to Robinson, there was an earlier effort to recruit Chinese labourers, about which little is known. St. John Robinson (2010) 'The Chinese of Central America: diverse beginnings, common achievements', in Walton Look Lai and Tan Chee-Beng (eds), *The Chinese in Latin America and the Caribbean*, 105–6. Leiden: Brill.

73 Lucy M. Cohen (1971) 'The Chinese of the Panama Railroad: preliminary notes on the migrants of 1854 who "failed"', *Ethnohistory* 18(4): 309–20.

74 St. John Robinson (2010) 'The Chinese of Central America: diverse beginnings, common achievements', in Walton Look Lai and Tan Chee-Beng (eds), *The Chinese in Latin America and the Caribbean*, 118. Leiden: Brill.

75 Walton Look Lai (2010) 'Asian Diasporas and Tropical Migration in the Age of Empire: a comparative overview', in Walton Look Lai and Tan Chee-Beng (eds), *The Chinese in Latin America and the Caribbean*, 71. Leiden: Brill.

76 Evelyn Hu-DeHart (1995) 'The Chinese of Peru, Cuba and Mexico', in Robert Cohen (ed.), *The Cambridge Survey of World Migration*, 220–3. Cambridge: Cambridge University Press.

77 Evelyn Hu-DeHart and Kathleen Lopez (2008) 'Introduction: Asian Diasporas in Latin America and the Caribbean – an historical overview', *Afro-Hispanic Review* 27 (1); also see Dobyns and Doughty (1976) *Peru: a cultural history*. Oxford: Oxford University Press. Some of the one hundred and eighty Japanese converts to Christianity, sent by their lord to Spain in 1613 via Acapulco, stayed on in Mexico and became successful businessmen in New Spain.

78 Evelyn Hu-DeHart and Kathleen Lopez (2008) 'Introduction: Asian Diasporas in Latin America and the Caribbean – an historical overview', *Afro-Hispanic Review* 27 (1): 14.

79 Marcello Carmagnani (2011) *The Other West: Latin America from invasion to globalization*. Berkley, CA: University of California Press, 43. Another scholar put the rate of migration from the Iberian peninsula to be between one thousand and two thousand annually from 1526 to 1538. Hugh Thomas (2010) *The Golden Age: The Spanish Empire of Charles V*. London: Penguin, 81.
80 Luis Corrochano-Garcia and Ruben Tang (2011) *Las Relaciones entre el Perú y China*. Lima, Perú: Pontificia Universidad Católica del Perú, 156–7.
81 Isabel Lausent-Herrera (2009) 'Tuscans (tusheng) and the Changing Chinese Community in Peru', *Journal of Chinese Overseas* 5: 116.
82 Philip Dennis (1979) 'The Anti-Chinese Campaigns in Sonora, Mexico', *Ethnohistory* 26 (1): 65–80.
83 Howard Johnson (1982) 'The Anti-Chinese Riots in Jamaica in 1918', *Caribbean Quarterly* 28 (3): 19–32.
84 Isabelle Lausent-Herrera (2009) 'Tusans (tusheng) and the Changing Chinese Community in Peru', *Journal of Chinese Overseas* 5 (1): 115–52.
85 Arthur Chung was the first president of Guyana from 1970 to 1980; and George Richards was president of Trinidad and Tobago from 2003 to 2013.
86 Evelyn Hu-DeHart and Kathleen López (2008) 'Asian Diasporas in Latin America and the Caribbean: an historical overview', *Afro-Hispanic Review* 27 (1): 9–21.
87 Ruben Carillo (2015) 'Mexique: La Chine Poblana ou le construction d'un mythe national', *Raison Presente* (193): 33–41.
88 Lok C. D. Sui (2005) *Memoirs of a Future Home: Diasporic citizenship of Chinese in Panama*. Stanford, CA: Stanford University Press, xv.
89 W. Gao (2017) 'New Chinese Migrants in Latin America: Trends and Patterns of Adaptation', in M. Zhou (ed.), *Contemporary Chinese Diasporas*, 333–48. Singapore: Palgrave Macmillan, 339. For a summary of other estimates in selected countries, see Jacquelin Mazza (2016) 'Chinese Migration to Latin America and the Caribbean', *Inter-American Dialogue*, October: 1-13, https://www.thedialogue.org/wp-content/uploads/2016/10/Chinese_Migration_to_LAC_Mazza-1.pdf.
90 Jesús Hermoso and María Victoria Fermín (2019) 'The Venezuela-China Relationship, Explained', SupChina, 7 January, https://supchina.com/2019/01/07/venezuela-china-explained/.

Chapter 2

1 For instance, Thomas Robinson and David Shambaugh's edited definitive study of China's foreign policy has no separate chapter for China-Latin America relations, though there are chapters on all the other regions. Thomas Robinson and David Shambaugh, eds (1994) *Chinese Foreign Policy: theory and practice*. Oxford: Clarendon Press. Shambaugh's latest

edited book *China and the World* (2020) includes a section on Latin America, but it is merged with Africa and the Middle East in one single chapter. More generally, the influential Cambridge Series on the Cold War, which has published numerous regional studies of that period, has not produced a specific study on Latin America. Matthew Rothwell, examining the question of Maoism influence in Latin America, posits reasons including North American-Eurocentrism in scholarship, Latin Americanists' limited knowledge of Chinese history and the general revulsion towards Shining Path atrocities. Matthew Rothwell (2013) *Transpacific Revolutionaries: the Chinese revolution in Latin America*. London: Routledge, 93–5.
2. Rendered as the *Guomindong* in pinyin.
3. Marie-Claire Bergère (2000) *Sun Yat-Sen*. Palo Alto, CA: Stanford University Press, 69–173.
4. Kerry Brown (2017) *CEO, China: the rise of Xi Jinping*. London and New York, NY: I.B. Tauris & Co. Ltd.
5. Álvaro Méndez (2021) 'Geopolitics in Central America: China and El Salvador in the 21st Century', in Thierry Kellner and Sophie Wintgens (eds), *China-Latin America and the Caribbean: assessment and outlook*, 207–21. London: Routledge.
6. William E. Ratliff (1969) 'Chinese Communist Cultural Diplomacy toward Latin America, 1949–1960', *The Hispanic American Historical Review* 49 (1): 53–79.
7. Matthew Rothwell (2013) *Transpacific Revolutionaries: the Chinese revolution in Latin America*. London: Routledge, 19–20.
8. Interview by one of the authors with Fernando Reyes Matta (Chilean Ambassador to China 2006–2010', Santiago, Chile, 16 December 2015. In 1954, Allende was a Senator. Reyes Matta was part of this initial trip.
9. Chile was a key target by the PRC to obtain diplomatic recognition at this early stage. Scholars also document visits of Chilean actors, acrobats and journalists from 1956 to 1959; see William A. Joseph (1985) 'China's Relations With Chile under Allende: a case study of Chinese foreign policy in transition', *Studies in Comparative Communism* 18 (2).
10. Robert G. Sutter (2011) *Historical Dictionary of Chinese Foreign Policy*. Lanham, ND: Scarecrow Press, 70.
11. Luis Gonzales (2011) 'Foros de amistad de China, AL y el Carib, *Listin Diario*, https://listindiario.com/las-mundiales/2011/11/20/211565/foros-de-amistad-de-china-al-y-el-caribe.
12. Carol Wise (2020) *Dragonomics: How Latin America is Maximizing (or Missing Out On) China's International Development Strategy*. New Haven, CT: Yale University Press, 67.
13. Álvaro Méndez (2021) 'Geopolitics in Central America: China and El Salvador in the 21st Century', in Thierry Kellner and Sophie Wintgens (eds), *China-Latin America and the Caribbean: assessment and outlook*, 207–21. London: Routledge.

14 Matthew Rothwell (2013) *Transpacific Revolutionaries: the Chinese revolution in Latin America*. London: Routledge, 20.
15 Sergey Radchenko (2010) 'The Sino-Soviet Split', in Melvyn Leffler and Odd Arne Westad (eds), *The Cambridge History of the Cold War*, vol. II: *Crises and Détente*, 394–72. Cambridge: Cambridge University Press.
16 David Shambaugh (2014) *China Goes Global: the partial power*. Oxford: Oxford University Press.
17 Yinghong Cheng (2007) 'Sino-Cuban Relations During the Early Years of the Castro Regime, 1959–1966', *Journal of Cold War Studies* 9 (3): 78–9, 100.
18 Ibid., 95.
19 Ibid., 109–10.
20 Jeremy Friedman (2018) *Shadow Cold War: the Sino-Soviet competition for the Third World*. Chapel Hill, NC: University of North Carolina Press, 112.
21 Ibid., 205–6.
22 According to Friedman, Soviet officials were nervous about the radical declarations made by Castro at the Tricontinental Conference in Havana in 1966. Jeremy Friedman (2018) *Shadow Cold War: The Sino-Soviet competition for the Third World*. Chapel Hill, NC: University of North Carolina Press, 156–7.
23 Wang Jisi (1994) 'International Relations Theory and the Study of Chinese Foreign Policy: a Chinese perspective', in Thomas Robinson and David Shambaugh, *Chinese Foreign Policy: theory and practice*. Oxford: Clarendon Press, 485.
24 William E. Ratliff (1969) 'Chinese Communist Cultural Diplomacy toward Latin America, 1949-1960', *The Hispanic American Historical Review* 49 (1): 57–8.
25 Jeremy Friedman (2018) *Shadow Cold War: the Sino-Soviet competition for the Third World*. Chapel Hill, NC: University of North Carolina Press, 156.
26 Matthew Rothwell (2013) *Transpacific Revolutionaries: the Chinese revolution in Latin America*. London: Routledge, 17.
27 Jeremy Friedman (2018) *Shadow Cold War: the Sino-Soviet competition for the Third World*. Chapel Hill, NC: University of North Carolina Press.
28 Matthew Rothwell (2013) *Transpacific Revolutionaries: the Chinese revolution in Latin America*. London: Routledge, 6.
29 Ibid., 43–6.
30 Ibid., 49–50.
31 Ibid., 57.
32 Ibid., 59–64.
33 Michael Gerson (2010) 'The Sino-Soviet Border Conflict: deterrence, escalation, and the threat of nuclear war in 1969', Report Number ASCO 2010 07, Center for Naval Analysis, US Department of Defense, November.

34 Jeremy Friedman (2018) *Shadow Cold War: the Sino-Soviet competition for the Third World*. Chapel Hill, NC: University of North Carolina Press, 151, 195–9, 210–11.
35 Debra Soled, ed. (1995) 'Deng's China (1979–1989)'. Washington, DC: Congressional Research Service, 89–108. Also see Jude Howell (1993) *China Opens its Doors: the politics of economic transition*. Boulder, CO: Lynne Rienner; Jonathan Spence (1990) *The Search for Modern China*. New York, NY: Norton, 653–9.
36 For insights into intra-politburo views, see Willy Wo-Lap Lam (1999) *The Era of Jian Zemin*. New Jersey, NJ: Prentice-Hall, 44–6.
37 Penelope Prime (2002) 'China Joins the WTO: how, why and what now?', *Business Economics* XXXVI April: 26–32; Doug Guthrie (2006) *China and Globalization: the social, economic and political transformation of Chinese society*. London: Routledge, 323–9.
38 Gaston Fornes and Álvaro Méndez (2018) *The China-Latin America Axis: Emerging Markets and their Role in an Increasingly Globalised World*, 2nd edn. New York, NY: Palgrave Macmillan.
39 Justin Yifu Lin, Fang Cai and Zhou Li (2002) *State-Owned Enterprise Reform in China*. Hong Kong: Chinese University Press, 49–76; also see Gary Jefferson and Thomas G. Rawski (1994) 'Enterprise Reform in Chinese Industry', *Journal of Economic Perspectives* 8 (2): 47–70.
40 C. Fred Bersten, Bates Gill, Nicholas Lardy and Derek Mitchell (2006) *China: the balance sheet: what the world needs to know now about the emerging superpower*. New York, NY: Public Affairs, 23–4.
41 For insight into that migration, see Tom Miller (2012) *China's Urban Billion: the story behind the biggest migration in human history*. London: Zed.
42 Bo Kong and Kevin Gallagher (2017) 'Globalizing Chinese Energy Finance: the role of policy banks', *Journal of Contemporary China* 26 (108): 834–51.
43 Linda Jakobson and Ryan Manuel (2016) 'How are Foreign Policy Decisions Made in China?', *Asia and the Pacific Policy Studies* 3 (1): 101–10.
44 Oscar Ugarteche and Caros De Leon (n.d.) 'China's Financing of Latin America'. http://www.obela.org/system/files/china%20financing%20latin%20america.pdf.
45 Chris Alden and Martyn Davies (2006) 'A Profile of the Operations of Chinese Multinationals in Africa', *South African Journal of International Affairs* 13 (1): 83–96.
46 Government of the PRC (2008) '中国的能源状况与政' 白皮书 'zhongguo de nengyuan zhuangkuan yusheng' baipishu [China's Energy Situation and Politics' White Paper], foreword, paragraph 3, https://www.mfa.gov.cn/ce/cebr//chn/ztzl/bpsh/t476161.htm.

47 Government of the PRC (2012) 中国的能源政策 (2012) *Zhongguo de nengyuan zhangce (2012)* [China's Energy Policy], Section 1, paragraph 11, http://www.scio.gov.cn/zfbps/ndhf/2012/Document/1233790/1233790.htm.

48 Ministry of Natural Resources (2008) 全国矿产资源规划(2008~2015年) *Quanguo kuangchan ziyuan guihua* (2008–2015 *nian*) [National Mineral Resource Plan 2008–2015], Section 4.3. http://www.shanxi.gov.cn/zw/zfgkzl/fdzdgknr/ghxx/202005/t20200520_801655.shtml.

49 Ministry of Land and Resources (2016) 全国矿产资源规划 (2016–2020年) *Quanguo kuangchan ziyuan guihua* (2016–2020 *nian*) [National Mineral Resource Plan 2016–2020], 4, http://extwprlegs1.fao.org/docs/pdf/chn189649.pdf.

50 Reference: Communist Party of China (2000) 中共中央、国务院关于做好二〇〇〇年农业和农村工作的意见(二〇〇〇年一月十六日) *zhonggong Zhongyang, guowuyuan guanyu zuo hao er ling ling ling nian nongye he nongcun gongzuo de yijian (er ling ling ling nian yi yue shiliu ri)* [Opinions of the Central Committee of the Communist Party of China and the State Council on Progress in Agriculture and Rural Work in 2000 (16 January 2000)], http://www.gov.cn/gongbao/content/2000/content_60664.htm.

51 Central Government of the PRC (2003) 2004年中央一号文件 *2004 nian zhongying yi hao wenjian* [2004 Document Number 1 of the Central Committee], Section XIII, http://www.gov.cn/test/2006-02/22/content_207415.htm.

52 Jose León-Manríquez and Luis F. Alvarez (2014) 'Mao's Steps in Monroe's Backyard: towards a United States-China hegemonic struggle in Latin America?', *Revista Brasileira Politica Internacional* 57: 15–16; Guoli Liu (2017) *China Rising: Chinese foreign policy in a changing world*. Basingstoke: Palgrave, 166–7.

53 Jeffrey Telep and Richard Lutz (2018) 'China's Long Road to Market Economy Status', *Georgetown Journal of International Law* 49: 695–9.

54 Ibid., 1–12. Also see Francois Godement (2016) 'China Market Economy Status and the European Interest', *ECFR* 180: 1–12.

55 R. Evan Ellis (2014) *China on the Ground in Latin America: challenges for the Chinese and impacts on the region*. New York: Palgrave Macmillan; see also Rebecca Ray and Adam Chimenti (2015) 'A Line in the Equatorial Forests: Chinese Investment and the Environmental and Social Impacts of Extractive Industries in Ecuador', *Global Economic Governance Initiative*, Discussion Paper 2015-6, https://media.business-humanrights.org/media/documents/files/documents/Ecuador1.pdf.

56 See Margaret Myers and Jie Guo (2015) 'China's Agricultural Investment in Latin America: a Critical Assessment', *China and Latin America Report*, https://www.thedialogue.org/wp-content/uploads/2015/06/Chinas-Agricultural-Investment-in-Latin-America.pdf. The authors provide an excellent overview of Chinese land-related investments in Latin America.

They emphasize that not all these investments have been utilized to produce agricultural exports to China.
57 IDB (2010) *Ten Years After the Take-off: taking stock of China-Latin America and the Caribbean economic relations*. Inter-American Development Bank.
58 Margaret Myers and Jie Guo (2015) 'China's Agricultural Investment in Latin America: a critical assessment', *China and Latin America Report*, https://www.thedialogue.org/wp-content/uploads/2015/06/Chinas-Agricultural-Investment-in-Latin-America.pdf.
59 Jose León-Manríquez and Luis F. Alvarez (2014) 'Mao's Steps in Monroe's Backyard: towards a United States-China hegemonic struggle in Latin America?', *Revista Brasileira Politica Internacional* 57: 15.

Chapter 3

1 Neatro Saavedra-Rivano (1993) 'Chile and Japan: opening doors through trade', in Barbara Stallings and Gabriel Szekely, *Japan, the United States and Latin America*, 191–209. Basingstoke: Macmillan.
2 Oddly enough, it is frequently Chinese sources that mistakenly identify Chile as the first Latin American country to recognize China: the Cuban government in fact did so in 1960. For analysis of Allende's predecessor and the role of the CIA in overthrowing Allende, see Sebastian Hurtado-Torres (2020) *The Gathering Storm: Eduardo Frei's Revolution in Liberty and Chile's Cold War*. Ithaca, NY: Cornell University Press.
3 William Joseph (1985) 'China's Relations With Chile Under Allende: a case study of Chinese foreign policy in transition', *Studies in Comparative Communism* XVIII 2/3: 126–7.
4 Ibid., 135–6.
5 H. Zhou and H. Xiong, eds (2017) *China's Foreign Aid: 60 years in retrospect*. Singapore: Springer.
6 William A. Joseph (1985) 'China's Relations with Chile under Allende: a case study of Chinese foreign policy in transition', *Studies in Comparative Communism* 18 n (2): 140.
7 Ibid., 136.
8 Ibid., 144–5.
9 Juan Carlos Gachuz (2012) 'Chile's Economic and Political Relationship with China', *Journal of Current Chinese Affairs* 41 (1): 134.
10 Rachel Schurman (1996) 'Chile's New Entrepreneurs and the "Economic Miracle": the invisible hand or a hand from the state?', *Studies in Comparative International Development*, Summer: 83–109.
11 Juan Carlos Gachuz (2012) 'Chile's Economic and Political Relationship with China', *Journal of Current Chinese Affairs* 41 (1): 147.
12 Zhiqun Zhu (2013) *China's New Diplomacy: rationale, strategies and significance*, 2nd edn. Farnham, UK: Ashgate Publishing Limited.

13 Carol Wise (2016) 'Playing Both Sides of the Pacific: Latin America's free trade agreements with China', *Pacific Affairs* 89 (1).
14 Interview by the authors with Alejandro Foxley (15 May 2016), former Chilean Minister of Foreign Affairs 2006–2009. Santiago, Chile.
15 Juan Carlos Gachuz (2012) 'Chile's Economic and Political Relationship with China', *Journal of Current Chinese Affairs* 41 (1): 148.
16 R. Evan Ellis (2011) 'China-Latin America Military Engagement: good will, good business and strategic position', Strategic Studies Institute, US Army War College, Carlyle, PA, August, 18–19; Jorge Dominguez (2006) 'China's Relations with Latin America: shared gains, asymmetric hopes', Weatherhead Center for International Affairs, 7.
17 R. Evan Ellis (2016) 'Cooperation and Mistrust between China and the U.S. in Latin America', in C. Wise and M. Myers (eds), *The Political Economy of China-Latin America Relations in the New Millennium: brave new world*, 31–49. London: Routledge.
18 Interview by the authors with Jose Miguel Insulza (9 May 2016), former Secretary General of the Organization of American States OAS 2005–2015. Santiago, Chile.
19 R. Evan Ellis (2011) 'China-Latin America Military Engagement: good will, good business and strategic position', Strategic Studies Institute, US Army War College, Carlyle, PA, August, 30.
20 Hanban News (2018) 'Confucius Institute Latin America Regional Center Holds China-Latin America Forum on "Bond across the Ocean"', 29 January. http://english.hanban.org/article/2018-01/29/content_716734.htm.
21 R. Evan Ellis (2017) 'China's Relationship with Chile: struggle for the future regime of the Pacific', *China Brief*, 17 (15), Jamestown Foundation, Washington, DC, 16, 19.
22 William Joseph (1985) 'China's Relations With Chile Under Allende: a case study of Chinese foreign policy in transition', *Studies in Comparative Communism* XVIII 2/3: 141.
23 Interview with Peter Draper (November 2006), ex-Department of Trade and Industry, South Africa. Also see anonymous quotation in Juan Carlos Gachuz (2012) 'Chile's Economic and Political Relationship with China', *Journal of Current Chinese Affairs* 4 (1): 143.
24 Juan Carlos Gachuz (2012) 'Chile's Economic and Political Relationship with China', *Journal of Current Chinese Affairs* 4 (1): 142. This builds on earlier foreign-local elite accounts; see also Claes Brundenius (1972) 'The Anatomy of Imperialism: the case of the multinational mining corporations in Peru', *Journal of Peace Research* 9 (3): 189–207.
25 World Bank (2021) 'Chile Product Exports and Imports to China 2008', World Integrated Trade Solution (WITS), https://wits.worldbank.org/CountryProfile/en/Country/CHL/Year/2005/TradeFlow/EXPIMP/Partner/CHN/Product/all-groups.

26 World Bank (2021) 'Chile Product Exports and Imports to China 2010', World Integrated Trade Solution (WITS), https://wits.worldbank.org/CountryProfile/en/Country/CHL/Year/2012/TradeFlow/EXPIMP/Partner/CHN/Product/all-groups.
27 World Bank (2021) 'Chile Product Exports and Imports to China 2019', World Integrated Trade Solution (WITS), https://wits.worldbank.org/CountryProfile/en/Country/CHL/Year/2019/TradeFlow/EXPIMP/Partner/CHN/Product/all-groups.
28 World Bank (2021) 'Chile Product Exports, Imports, Tariff by Country and Region 2009', World Integrated Trade Solution (WITS), https://wits.worldbank.org/CountryProfile/en/Country/CHL/Year/2009/TradeFlow/EXPIMP/Partner/all/Product/Total.
29 World Bank (2021) 'Chile-China Trade Exports (2005–2019)', World Integrated Trade Solution (WITS), https://wits.worldbank.org/CountryProfile/en/Country/CHL/StartYear/2005/EndYear/2019/TradeFlow/Export/Indicator/XPRT-TRD-VL/Partner/CHN/Product/Total#.
30 Andrew Muhammad, Amanda Leister, Lihong McPhail and Wei Chin (2013) 'The Evolution of Foreign Wine Demand in China', *The Australian Journal of Agricultural and Resource Economics* 58: 397; Rachel Arthur (2019) 'China's wine market: the latest data is starting to show us what China will look like as a mature market', *Beverage Daily*, https://www.beveragedaily.com/Article/2019/06/14/China-s-wine-market-The-latest-data-is-starting-to-show-us-what-China-will-look-like-as-a-mature-market; Cathy Huyghe (2019) 'Reinventing what wine is supposed to be: Wine from Chile in China', *Forbes*, 28 January, https://www.forbes.com/sites/cathyhuyghe/2019/01/28/reinventing-what-wine-is-supposed-to-be-wine-from-chile-in-china/#4523ac494983.
31 Carol Wise (2020) *Dragonomics: How Latin America is Maximizing (or Missing Out On) China's International Development Strategy*. New Haven, CT: Yale University Press, 149.
32 *Global Times* (2019) 'Chile's cherry exports to China market offer growth opportunity for producers', 11 August, http://www.globaltimes.cn/content/1161036.shtml.
33 Jorge Heine (2021) 'Still Trailblazing? The Chile-China relationship at fifty', China Foresight at LSE IDEAS, https://blogs.lse.ac.uk/cff/2021/08/23/still-trailblazing-the-chile-china-relationship-at-fifty/.
34 Interview by the authors with Ignacio Walker (16 December 2015), former Chilean Minister of Foreign Affairs 2004–2006. Santiago, Chile.
35 OECD/ECLAC/CAF (2015) *Latin American Economic Outlook 2016: towards a new partnership with China*. Paris: OECD, 100.
36 Yanying Zhang, Gaiyan Zhang and Hung-Gay Fung (2007) 'The Prospects for China's Free Trade Agreements', *Chinese Economy* 40 (2): 17.

37 OECD/ECLAC/CAF (2015) *Latin American Economic Outlook 2016: towards a new partnership with China*. Paris: OECD, 118.
38 Interview by the authors with Ignacio Walker (10 May 2016), former Secretary General of the Organization of American States OAS 2005–2015. Santiago, Chile.
39 Juan Carlos Gachuz (2012) 'Chile's Economic and Political Relationship with China', *Journal of Current Chinese Affairs* 41 (1): 137–40, 143.
40 Atlantic Council and OECD (2019) *Chinese FDI in Latin America: new trends with global implications*; Juan Carlos Gachuz, 'Chile's Economic and Political Relationship with China' (2012) *Journal of Current Chinese Affairs* 41 (1): 145.
41 OEC World, Chile-China trade, https://oec.world/en/profile/bilateral-country/chl/partner/chn.
42 R. Evan Ellis (2014) *China on the Ground in Latin America: challenges for the Chinese and impact on the region*. Basingstoke: Palgrave, 23–4; also see 'Chile and China make huge investments to increase copper production', https://en.mercopress.com/2010/01/20/chile-and-china-make-huge-investments-to-increase-copper-production.
43 R. Evan Ellis (2017) 'China's Relationship with Chile: struggle for the future regime of the Pacific', *China Brief* 17 (15), Jamestown Foundation, Washington, DC, 16. See also Geological Survey (2012) *Minerals Yearbook*. US Department of the Interior: United States Bureau of Mines.
44 Chilean businessman, private conversation, Santiago.
45 Interview by the authors with Ignacio Walker (16 December 2015), former Chilean Minister of Foreign Affairs 2004–2006. Santiago, Chile.
46 Interview by the authors with Luis Schmidt (10 May 2015), Chilean Ambassador to the People's Republic of China (PRC) 2010–2014 and 2018 to present. Santiago, Chile.
47 *China Daily* (2018) 'More Chilean wines pour into Chinese market', 18 November http://www.chinadaily.com.cn/a/201811/02/WS5bdb9680a310eff30328611d.html.
48 Ministry of Commerce, PRC (2017) 'China-Chile FTA upgrading negotiations concluded, agreement signed', 13 November, http://fta.mofcom.gov.cn/enarticle/enchile/enchilenews/201712/36339_1.html.
49 Jeppe Sarinene (2019) 'China-Chile FTA upgraded, new market opportunities for investors', *China Briefing*, 4 March, https://www.china-briefing.com/news/china-chile-fta-upgraded-market-opportunities-investors/.
50 *Reuters* (2017) 'Codelco in talks to sell copper to China's Minmetals in three year deal', 8 October, https://www.reuters.com/article/us-metals-lmeweek-codelco-usa-exclusive/exclusive-codelco-in-talks-to-sell-copper-to-chinas-minmetals-in-three-year-deals-idUKKCN1MI10H.
51 *Financial Times* (2019) 'China's mining M&A spree driven by fossil fuel transition', 25 January.

52 *Reuters* (2019) 'China's Tianqi agrees truce in battle over Chilean lithium miner SQM', 11 April, https://www.reuters.com/article/us-sqm-tianqi-lithium/chinas-tianqi-agrees-truce-in-battle-over-chilean-lithium-miner-sqm-idUSKCN1RN2B0.
53 Juan Enrique Serrano Moreno, Alejandra Perez Ceballos and Maria Gabriela De Abreu Negron (2020) 'Beyond Copper: China and Chile Relations', *Asian Education and Development Studies* February, https://www.emerald.com/insight/content/doi/10.1108/AEDS-08-2019-0132/full/html; *Santiago Times* (2017) 'Chile joins lithium manufacturers club – with world's most productive deposits', 31 March, https://santiagotimes.cl/tag/lithium-production/.
54 *DCD* (2019) 'Huawei opens Chile data center, pitches to join Asia-Latam cable', 10 September, https://www.datacenterdynamics.com/news/huawei-opens-chile-data-center-pitches-join-asia-latam-cable/.
55 Yohei Hirose and Naouyuki Toyama (2020) 'Chile picks Japan's trans-Pacific cable route in snub to China', *Financial Times*, https://www.ft.com/content/674557bc-13c7-4010-a7f8-7b8c06b3a32e.
56 Juan Enrique Serrano Moreno, Alejandra Perez Ceballos and Maria Gabriela De Abreu Negron (2020) 'Beyond Copper: China and Chile Relations', *Asian Education and Development Studies* February, https://www.emerald.com/insight/content/doi/10.1108/AEDS-08-2019-0132/full/html.
57 Ibid.
58 This Trans-Oceanic Railway never came to fruition, but Latin American policymakers still talk about the possibility that this project could become a reality. Anonymous interviews with various policymakers in the region 2018–2019.
59 Barbara Fraser (2003) 'Peru: Hanging up on the public sector', *NACLA Report on the Americas* 36 (4): 39–42. See also Ruben Gonzalez-Vicente (2012) 'Mapping Chinese Mining Investment in Latin America: politics or market?', *The China Quarterly* 209: 35–58.
60 Luis Corrochano-Garcia and Ruben Tang (2011) *Las Relaciones entre el Perú y China*. Lima: Pontificia Universidad Católica del Perú, 37–49.
61 Ibid.
62 For more detailed discussion, see ibid., 76–89.
63 Cited in W. A. C. Adie (1962) 'China, Russia and the Third World', *China Quarterly* 11, July–September: 201, fn 6.
64 Luis Corrochano-Garcia and Ruben Tang (2011) *Las Relaciones entre el Perú y China*. Lima: Pontificia Universidad Católica del Perú, 118–19.
65 Ibid.
66 Shange Hunt (1975) 'Direct Foreign Investment in Peru: new rules for an old game', in Abraham F. Lowenthal (ed.), *The Peruvian Experiment: continuity and change under military rule*. Princeton, NJ: Princeton University Press.

67 David Scott Palmer (2006) 'The Often Surprising Outcomes of Asymmetry in International Affairs: United States–Peru Relations in the 1990s', in J. Carrion (ed.), *The Fujimori Legacy: the rise of electoral authoritarianism in Peru*, 227–41. Pennsylvania: Pennsylvania State University Press.
68 C. M. Conaghan (2005) *Fujimori's Peru: Deception in the Public Sphere*. Pittsburgh, PA: University of Pittsburgh Press.
69 David Scott Palmer (2006) 'The Often Surprising Outcomes of Asymmetry in International Affairs: United States–Peru Relations in the 1990s', in J. Carrion (ed.), *The Fujimori Legacy: the rise of electoral authoritarianism in Peru*, 227–41. Pennsylvania: Pennsylvania State University Press.
70 Orin Starn (1995) 'Maoism in the Andes: the Shining Path', *Journal of Latin American Studies* 27 (2): 399–421.
71 Stefanie Mann (2006) *Peru's Relations with Pacific Asia: democracy and foreign policy under Alan García, Alberto Fujimori, and Alejandro Toledo*. Berlin: LIT Verlag.
72 Ronald Bruce St. John (2017) 'Peruvian Foreign Policy in the New Millennium: continuity and Change', *Revista del Instituto Riva-Agüero (PUCP)* 2(2): 65–119.
73 Chris Alden and Álvaro Méndez (2019) 'Perú, China y la nueva multipolaridad – navegar en la política internacional en tiempos inciertos', in Javier Alcade, Chris Alden, Angelica Guerra-Barron and Álvaro Méndez (eds), *La Conexion China en la Politica Exterior del Peru en el Seculo XXI*, 278–93. Lima: Pontifica Universidade Catolica del Peru.
74 Interview by authors with Alan Wagner (9 March 2016), Peruvian Minister of Foreign Affairs 1985–1988; 2002–2003. Lima, Peru.
75 Olaf Jacob (2010) 'Peru and Chile: the challenge of playing a determinant role in multilateral Pacific fora', in J. Dosch and O. Jacob (eds), *Asia and Latin America: political, economic and multilateral relations*, 139–54. London: Routledge.
76 Gaston Fornes and Álvaro Méndez (2018) *The China-Latin America Axis: emerging markets and their role in an increasingly globalised world*, 2nd edn. London: Palgrave Macmillan.
77 'China and Peru' Ministry of Foreign Affairs, Beijing (n.d.), https://www.fmprc.gov.cn/mfa_eng/wjb_663304/zzjg_663340/ldmzs_664952/gjlb_664956/3513_665118/.
78 *El Comercio* (2016) 'PPK e Xi Jinping acuerdan mejorar TLC entre el Peru e China', 21 November, https://elcomercio.pe/politica/gobierno/ppk-xi-jinping-acuerdan-mejorar-tlc-peru-china-149535-noticia/.
79 Interview by authors with Alan Wagner (9 March 2016), Peruvian Minister of Foreign Affairs 1985–1988; 2002–2003. Lima, Peru.
80 Interview by authors with Jose Garcia Belaunde (11 March 2016), Peruvian Minister of Foreign Affairs 2006–2011. Lima, Peru.
81 *Diálogo Chino* (2019) 'How to really "optimize" free trade between Peru and China', 29 January, https://dialogochino.net/29018-how-to-really-optimise-free-trade-between-peru-and-china/.

82 Interview by authors with Gonzalo Gutierrez (8 March 2016), Peruvian Ambassador to the People's Republic of China 2011–2014, Peruvian Minister of Foreign Affairs 2014–2015. Lima, Peru.
83 Carol Wise (2016) 'Playing Both Sides of the Pacific: Latin America's free trade agreements with China', *Pacific Affairs* 89 (1): 80.
84 Ibid., 80–1.
85 SICE (Foreign Trade Information System) Organization of American States, http://www.sice.oas.org/TPD/PER_CHN/PER_CHN_e.ASP.
86 Ruben Gonzalez-Vicente (2012) 'The Political Economy of Sino-Peruvian Relations: a new dependency?', *Journal of Current Chinese Affairs* 41 (1): 108.
87 World Bank (2021) 'Peru Product Exports and Imports from China 2010 & 2014', World Integrated Trade Solution (WITS). This link shows the latest trade data from 2019. Readers can select data all the way from 1992, see: https://wits.worldbank.org/CountryProfile/en/Country/PER/Year/2019/TradeFlow/EXPIMP/Partner/CHN/Product/all-groups.
88 A quasi-symbolic recognition because the actual recognition of China as a market economy can not happen until all the WTO Members agree on granting this recognition. See James Nedumpara and Weihuan Zhou, eds (2018) *Non-market Economies in the Global Trading System: the special case of China*. Singapore: Springer.
89 World Bank (2021) 'Peru Product Exports and Imports from China 2004–2019', World Integrated Trade Solution (WITS). This links shows data from 2019. For comparison purposes, readers can choose other years all the way back to 1992, see: https://wits.worldbank.org/CountryProfile/en/Country/PER/Year/2019/TradeFlow/EXPIMP/Partner/CHN/Product/all-groups.
90 Cited in BizLatinHub (2019) 'How will the Peru-China Free Trade Agreement Boost Investment?', 5 March, https://www.bizlatinhub.com/peru-china-free-trade-agreement/.
91 *Andina* (2019) 'Peru announces entry of quinoa into Chinese market', 6 December, https://andina.pe/ingles/noticia-peru-announces-entry-of-quinoa-into-chinese-market-777515.aspx; *Andina* (2019) 'Peru: blueberry exports likely to exceed $700 million in 2019', 25 November, https://andina.pe/ingles/noticia-peru-blueberry-exports-likely-to-exceed-700-million-in-2019-776201.aspx.
92 OEC World, 'What does Peru export to China 2018'. https://oec.world/en/visualize/line/hs92/export/per/chn/show/2018.
93 Ruben Gonzalez-Vicente (2012) 'The Political Economy of Sino-Peruvian Relations: a new dependency?', *Journal of Current Chinese Affairs* 41 (1): 109.
94 Yvonne Lee (2013) 'CNPC buys Petrobras Peru business in $2.6 billion deal', *Wall Street Journal*, 13 November, https://www.wsj.com/articles/SB10001424052702303289904579195341085131708.
95 *The Guardian* (2017) '$1billion to clean up the oil in Peru's northern Amazon' 3 August, https://www.theguardian.com/environment/andes-to-the-amazon/2017/aug/03/us1-billion-oil-perus-amazon.

96 Ruben Gonzalez-Vicente (2012) 'The Political Economy of Sino-Peruvian Relations: a new dependency?', *Journal of Current Chinese Affairs* 41 (1): 111.
97 *Diálogo Chino* (2019) 'How to really "optimize" free trade between Peru and China', 29 January, https://dialogochino.net/29018-how-to-really-optimise-free-trade-between-peru-and-china/.
98 Cynthia Sanborn and Victoria Chonn Ching (2017) 'Chinese Investment in Peru's Mining Industry: blessing or curse?', in Rebecca Ray, Kevin Gallagher, Andrés López and Cynthia Sanborn (eds), *China and Sustainable Development in Latin America: The Social and Environmental Dimension*, 183–226. London: Anthem Press.
99 Ibid.; Peter Noland and Godrey Yeung (2001) 'Big Business with Chinese Characteristics: two paths to growth of the firm in China under reform', *Cambridge Journal of Economics* 25 (4): 443–65; Peter Nolan and Godfrey Yeung (2001) 'Large firms and catch-up in a transitional economy: the case of Shougang Group in China', *Economics of Planning* 34 (01–02): 159–78.
100 Yongjin Zhang (2003) *China's Emerging Global Businesses: Political economy and institutional investigations*. Basingstoke: Palgrave, 213–14.
101 Barbara Kotschwar, Theodore Moran and Julia Muir (2011) 'Do Chinese Mining Companies Exploit More?', *Americas Quarterly*, Fall, https://www.americasquarterly.org/do-chinese-mining-companies-exploit-more.
102 (2017) 'Chinese Investment in Peru's Mining Industry: blessing or curse?', in Rebecca Ray, Kevin Gallagher, Andrés López and Cynthia Sanborn (eds), *China and Sustainable Development in Latin America: The Social and Environmental Dimension*, 183–226. London: Anthem Press, 22–3. Other research suggests that they have been delinquent in paying taxes.
103 Business and Human Rights Resource Center (2019) 'Peru: Shougang mining activities suspended by the OEFA to prevent pollution in San Nicolas Bay', 16 January, https://www.business-humanrights.org/en/peru-shougang-mining-activities-suspended-by-the-oefa-to-prevent-pollution-in-san-nicolas-bay.
104 Barbara Kotschwar, Theodore Moran and Julia Muir (2011) 'Do Chinese Mining Companies Exploit More?', *Americas Quarterly*, Fall, https://www.americasquarterly.org/do-chinese-mining-companies-exploit-more.
105 *Diálogo Chino* (2018) 'The Chinese mining giant and the ghost town', 5 December, https://dialogochino.net/15576-the-chinese-mining-giant-and-the-ghost-town/.
106 *Diálogo Chino* (2016) 'Las Bambas conflict presents PPK with a huge opportunity', 22 July, https://dialogochino.net/6870-las-bambas-conflict-presents-ppk-with-a-huge-opportunity/.
107 Mitra Taj (2019) 'Peru declares state of emergency near China-owned mine as protests mount', *Reuters*, 29 March, https://www.reuters.com/article/peru-copper-mmg-ltd-idINL1N21G1IT.
108 Peru signed up to the Extractive Industries Transparency Initiative (EITI) in 2007. Peru was the first country to sign to EITI, see: https://eiti.org/blog-post/look-future-eiti-latin-america.

109 BNAmericas (2019) 'Cosco see 2020 start for US$3 bn Chancay port', 26 June, https://www.bnamericas.com/en/news/cosco-sees-2020-construction-start-for-us3bn-chancay-port.
110 Luis Corrochano-Garcia and Ruben Tang (2011) *Las Relaciones entre el Perú y China*. Lima: Pontificia Universidad Católica del Perú, 76–81, 152–4.
111 Interview by authors with Gonzalo Gutierrez (8 March 2016), Peruvian Ambassador to the People's Republic of China 2011–2014, Peruvian Minister of Foreign Affairs 2014–2015. Lima, Peru.
112 Luis Corrochano-Garcia and Ruben Tang (2011) *Las Relaciones entre el Perú y China*. Lima: Pontificia Universidad Católica del Perú, 155.
113 R. Evan Ellis (2018) 'China's Strategy in Latin America and the Caribbean', in J. Eisenman and E. Heginbotham (eds), *China Steps Out: Beijing's major power engagement with the developing world*, 193–222. London: Routledge.
114 Juan Pablo Cardenal (2018) 'Reframing Relations in Peru', in J. P. Cardenal, J. Kucharczyk, G. Mesežnikov and G. Pleschová (eds), *Sharp Power: rising authoritarian influence*, 68–9. Washington, DC: National Endowment for Democracy.
115 See noted expert on Tuscan community, Isabelle Lausant-Herrara, 'China has great draw, and the sense of identity for the Tuscan is diminishing in the process of globalization', cited in ibid., 69.
116 J. P. Cardenal (2017) 'Sharp Power: rising authoritarian influence', in J. P. Cardenal, J. Kucharczyk, G. Mesežnikov and G. Pleschová (eds), *Sharp Power: rising authoritarian influence*, 67–93. Washington, DC: National Endowment for Democracy. International Forum for Democratic Studies, https://www.ned.org/sharp-power-rising-authoritarian-influence-forum-report/.
117 Ibid.
118 Dragontail interactive (2018) 'How NTOs can encourage Chinese tourism in the case of Peru', 23 May, https://dragontrail.com/resources/blog/how-ntos-can-encourage-chinese-tourism-the-case-of-peru; *Andina* (2018) 'Peru looks to lure more Chinese visitors' 17 June, https://andina.pe/ingles/noticia-peru-looks-to-lure-more-chinese-visitors-713696.aspx.
119 Darren Lim, Victor Ferguson and Rosa Bishop (2020) 'Chinese Outbound Tourism as an Instrument of Chinese Statecraft', *Journal of Contemporary China* 29 (126): 916–33.
120 For a detailed study of this early period in Argentina-China relations, see Eduardo Daniel Oviedo (2010) *Historia de las Relaciones Interncionales entre Argentina y China, 1945–2010*. Buenos Aires: Dunken, 81–354.
121 Noam Lupu (2016) 'The End of the Kirchner Era', *Journal of Democracy* 27 (2): 39.
122 *La Nacion* (2004) 'China invertiría en el país 20.000 millones de dólares', 7 November; Ruben Laufer (2013) 'Argentina-China: new courses for an old dependency', *Latin American Policy* 4 (1): 123–43.

123 Eduardo Daniel Oviedo (2010) *Historia de las Relaciones Interncionales entre Argentina y China, 1945–2010*. Buenos Aires: Dunken, 457–60.
124 Ibid., 451–3.
125 Ibid., 461–3. Oviedo says that, like Brazilian Foreign Minister Celso Amorin, Bielsa claimed the Chinese had deceived him.
126 Raul Bernal-Meza and Juan Manuel Zanabria (2020) 'A Goat's Cycle: the relations between Argentina and the People's Republic of China during the Kirchner and Macri administrations', in Raul Bernal-Meza and Li Xing (eds), *China-Latin America Relations in the 21st Century: the dual complexities of opportunities and challenges*. Basingstoke: Palgrave, 139.
127 Bernadett Lehockzi (2015) 'Relations between China and Latin America: inter-regionalism beyond the triad', *Society and Economy* 37 (3): 396.
128 World Bank (2021) 'Argentina Soya Beans; Whether or Not Broken Exports to China in 1998', World Integrated Trade Solution (WITS), https://wits.worldbank.org/trade/comtrade/en/country/ARG/year/1998/tradeflow/Exports/partner/CHN/product/120100; see also World Bank (2021) 'Argentina Soya Beans; Whether or Not Broken Exports to China in 2010', World Integrated Trade Solution (WITS), https://wits.worldbank.org/trade/comtrade/en/country/ARG/year/2010/tradeflow/Exports/partner/CHN/product/120100.
129 Julian Donaubauer, Andrés López and Daniela Ramos (2015) 'FDI and Trade: is China relevant for the future of our environment? The case of Argentina', Discussion Paper 1, Global Economic Governance Initiative, Boston University, 6. Also see Sol Mora (2021) 'Land Grabbing, Power Configurations and Trajectories of China's Investment in Argentina', *Globalizations*, 7, doi: 10.1080/14747731.2021.1920197.
130 COFCO purchased Noble Group and Dutch grain trader Nidera BV in 2014.
131 Rodrigo Orelihuela (2011) 'Beidahuang will invest £1.5 billion on Patagonian farms that it won't own', Farmlandgrab.org, 9 June, https://www.farmlandgrab.org/post/view/18764-beidahuang-will-invest-1-5-billion-on-patagonian-farms-that-it-wont-own; Felicity Lawrence (2011) 'Global Food Crisis: China land deal causes unease in Argentina', *The Guardian*, 1 June.
132 Environmental Justice Atlas (2018) 'Heilongian-beidhuang in Rio Negro Argentina', https://ejatlas.org/conflict/heilongian-beidahuang-in-rio-negro-argentina.
133 Sol Mora (2021) 'Land Grabbing, Power Configurations and Trajectories of China's Investment in Argentina', *Globalizations*. doi: 10.1080/14747731.2021.1920197.
134 Hugh Bronstein (2021) 'Argentina extends key Parana river dredging contract ensuring grain exports', NASDAQ, 28 April, https://www.nasdaq.com/articles/argentina-extends-key-parana-river-dredging-contract-ensuring-grains-exports-2021-04-28.

135 Ibid.; *Buenos Aires Times* (2021) 'Soy shipping turmoil deepens with transport minister's death', 29 April, https://www.batimes.com.ar/news/economy/soy-shipping-turmoil-deepens-with-transport-ministers-death.phtml.
136 Juan Pedro Tomas (2021) 'Argentine government hands river control to port administrator AGP', Agricensus, 1 July, https://www.agricensus.com/Article/Argentine-gov-hands-river-control-to-port-administrator-AGP-17292.html; *Buenos Aires Times* (2021) 'Soy shipping turmoil deepens with transport minister's death', 29 April, https://www.batimes.com.ar/news/economy/soy-shipping-turmoil-deepens-with-transport-ministers-death.phtml.
137 Margaret Myers, cited in Hugh Bronstein (2019), 'China set to deepen Argentine trade ties with bid for "grains superhighway"', *Reuters*, 16 August, https://www.reuters.com/article/us-argentina-china-grains-cccc-exclusive-idUSKCN1V60AW.
138 *Xinhua* (2010) 'CNOOC buys 50% of Bridas Energy subsidiary', 6 March, https://www.chinadaily.com.cn/bizchina/2010-05/06/content_9815831.htm.
139 R. Evan Ellis (2021) 'New Directions in the deepening Chinese-Argentine Engagement', *Global Americans*, 11 February, https://theglobalamericans.org/2021/02/new-directions-in-the-deepening-chinese-argentine-engagement/.
140 R. Evan Ellis (2014) *China on the Ground in Latin America: challenges for the Chinese and impacts for the region.* Basingstoke: Palgrave, 165. Also see rionegro.com.ar (2011) 'La Justicia confirmó suspensión de actividad minera en Campana Mahuida', 5 April, https://web.archive.org/web/20151117023354/http://www.rionegro.com.ar/diario/la-justicia-confirmo-suspension-de-actividad-minera-en-campana-mahuida-595714-9701-nota.aspx.
141 Las empresas de China y Japón que invierten en activos mineros de Chile y Argentina – BNamericas, see: https://www.bnamericas.com/es/reportajes/las-empresas-de-china-y-japon-que-invierten-en-activos-mineros-de-chile-y-argentina.
142 *Reuters* (2017) 'China's Shandong Gold in $960 million deal for half of Barrick's Veladero Mine', 6 April, https://www.reuters.com/article/us-barrick-gold-mine-shandong-gold-idUSKBN1780KW.
143 Ganfeng Lithium, 'Walk into Ganfeng: Argentina's Cauchari-Olaroz Project', 20 August, http://www.ganfenglithium.com/new_detail_en/id/41.html.
144 *La Nacion* (2013) 'Estatizan el Ferrocarril Belgrano Cargas', 23 May, https://www.lanacion.com.ar/economia/estatizan-el-ferrocarril-belgrano-cargas-nid1584612/.
145 Oliver Cuenca (2020) 'Argentina Selects Chinese Companies to Restore Freight Lines and Supply Trains', *International Railway Journal*, 27 December, https://www.railjournal.com/financial/argentina-selects-chinese-companies-to-restore-freight-lines-and-supply-trains/.

146 Ibid.
147 Joaquim Gonzalez (2019) 'Argentina's Belgrano Cargas undergoes a major revamp with help from China', *DatamarNews*, 22 January.
148 Andres Napoli and Maria Marta de Paola (2017) 'Aprovechamientos hidroeléctricos del río Santa Cruz – IEASA ['Argentina suspends Patagonia dams'], *Diálogo Chino*, 23 January, https://dialogochino.net/en/climate-energy/8356-argentina-suspends-patagonia-dams/.
149 Ibid.
150 Ruben Laufer (2013) 'Argentina-China: new courses for an old dependency', *Latin American Policy* 4 (1): 138.
151 Ibid.; also see Eduardo Daniel Oviedo (2010) *Historia de las Relaciones Interncionales entre Argentina y China, 1945–2010*. Buenos Aires: Dunken, 465.
152 Fermin Koop (2019) 'Argentina Crisis Prompts Shift in Chinese Investment', *Diálogo Chino*, 25 October, https://chinadialogue.net/en/energy/11606-argentina-crisis-prompts-shift-in-chinese-investment-2/.
153 *TeleSur* (2020) 'Macri and father linked to more Panama Papers firms', 20 April.
154 Eduardo Daniel Oviedo (2015) 'Argentina and China: an analysis of the actors in the soybean trade and the migratory flow', *Journal of Chinese Political Science* 20: 250, cf 6. Also see Eduardo Daniel Oviedo (2010) *Historia de las Relaciones Interncionales entre Argentina y China, 1945–2010*. Buenos Aires: Dunken, 479–80.
155 Natasha Niebieskikwiat (2018) 'Un G20 con blindados y motos de China, helicópteros de Francia e Italia, lanchas israelíes y aviones de Estados Unidos', 16 November, https://www.clarin.com/politica/g20-blindados-motos-china-helicopteros-francia-italia-lanchas-israelies-aviones-unidos_0_q8Q0UPRqT.html.
156 R. Evan Ellis (2021) 'New Directions in the deepening Chinese-Argentine Engagement', *Global Americans*, 11 February, https://theglobalamericans.org/2021/02/new-directions-in-the-deepening-chinese-argentine-engagement/.
157 Fermin Koop (2019) 'Argentina Crisis Prompts Shift in Chinese Investment', *Diálogo Chino*, 25 October, https://chinadialogue.net/en/energy/11606-argentina-crisis-prompts-shift-in-chinese-investment-2/.
158 Erin Watson-Lynn (2020) 'The Gravity of China's Space Base in Argentina', Lowry Institute, 9 June, https://www.lowyinstitute.org/the-interpreter/gravity-china-s-space-base-argentina.
159 R. Evan Ellis (2021) 'New Directions in the Deepening Chinese–Argentine Engagement', *Global Americans*, 11 February, https://theglobalamericans.org/2021/02/new-directions-in-the-deepening-chinese-argentine-engagement/.

160 See Lin Hua (2017) 'Las relaciones económicas y comerciales entre China y Argentina en la era de Mauricio Macri', *Relaciones Internacionales* 26 (53): 230.
161 A. Gelpern, S. Horn, S. Morris, B. B. Parks and C. Trebesch (2021) *How China Lends: a rare look into 100 debt contracts with foreign governments*. Peterson Institute for International Economics, Kiel Institute for the World Economy, Center for Global Development, and AidData at William & Mary, 7.
162 BBC (2016) 'Argentina sinks Chinese fishing boat Lu Yuan Yan Lu 010', 16 March.
163 A court ruling in 2014 put the Argentine government in the invidious position of having in effect to pay all creditors or none at all, which stymied efforts by Buenos Aires to restructure payments to prioritize some creditors over others.
164 Lin Hua (2017) 'Las relaciones económicas y comerciales entre China y Argentina en la era de Mauricio Macri', *Relaciones Internacionales* 26 (53): 232.
165 Ibid., 233–4.
166 Ministry of Foreign Affairs, Argentina (n.d.) 'New boost to strategic relations with China', https://www.cancilleria.gob.ar/en/news/newsletter/new-boost-strategic-relations-china.
167 Hugh Bronstein and Tom Polanska (2019) 'Crushing It: Argentine farmers cheer China soymeal deal while US growers fret', *Reuters*, 11 September, https://www.reuters.com/article/us-argentina-soyproducts-china-idUSKCN1VW21E.
168 Juan Pedro Tomas (2019) 'China to account for 90% of Argentina's soybean exports this year', *Fast Markets Agricensus*, 18 September, https://www.agricensus.com/Article/China-to-account-for-90-of-Argentina-s-soybean-exports-this-year-Zeni-13520.html.
169 Consul-General of the People's Republic of China in Kolkata (2018) 'China, Argentina eye new era of partnership', 3 December, https://www.mfa.gov.cn/ce/cgkolkata/eng/zgbd/t1618246.htm.
170 *TeleSur* (2020) 'Macri and father linked to more Panama Papers firms', 20 April.
171 Fermin Koop (2019) 'Argentina Crisis Prompts Shift in Chinese Investment', *Diálogo Chino*, 25 October, https://chinadialogue.net/en/energy/11606-argentina-crisis-prompts-shift-in-chinese-investment-2/.
172 R. Evan Ellis (2021) 'New Directions in the Deepening Chinese-Argentine Engagement', *Global Americans*, 11 February, https://theglobalamericans.org/2021/02/new-directions-in-the-deepening-chinese-argentine-engagement/.
173 Oliver Cuenca (2020) 'Argentina Selects Chinese Companies to Restore Freight Lines and Supply Trains', *International Railway Journal*, 27

December, https://www.railjournal.com/financial/argentina-selects-chinese-companies-to-restore-freight-lines-and-supply-trains/.
174   Interview by the authors with Ignacio Walker (10 May 2016), former Chilean Minister of Foreign Affairs 2004–2006. Santiago, Chile.
175   https://merics.org/en/chiles-once-pioneering-relationship-china-turning-dependency#:~:text=In%202021%2C%20Chile's%20bilateral%20trade,percent%20year%2Don%2Dyear.
176   Cynthia Sanborn and Victoria Chonn Ching (2015) 'Chinese Investment in Peru's Mining Industry: Blessing or Curse?' Working Group on Development and Environment in the Americas, 8.
177   WITS (2018) *Peru Trade Flow (1992–2016)*, https://wits.worldbank.org/CountryProfile/en/Country/PER/StartYear/1992/EndYear/2016/TradeFlow/Import/Indicator/MPRT-TRD-VL/Partner/BY-COUNTRY/Product/Total.
178   Enid Lopez Camacho (2016) 'Tren bioceánico: tras firmar con Perú, Bolivia mira a Brasil', *Los Tiempos*, 16 November, https://www.lostiempos.com/actualidad/economia/20161116/tren-bioceanico-firmar-peru-bolivia-mira-brasil.
179   Cynthia Sanborn and Victoria Chonn Ching (2015) 'Chinese Investment in Peru's Mining Industry: blessing or curse?', Working Group on Development and Environment in the Americas, 8.
180   Fermin Koop (2019) 'Argentina Crisis Prompts Shift in Chinese Investment', *Diálogo Chino*, 25 October, https://chinadialogue.net/en/energy/11606-argentina-crisis-prompts-shift-in-chinese-investment-2/.

Chapter 4

1   Analysts refer to the commodity boom as the period between 2000 and 2014 when the prices of commodities, like metals and oil, increased massively thanks to great demand from countries like India and China; see Ravi Balakrishnan and Frederik Toscani (2018) 'How the Commodity Boom Helped Tackle Poverty and Inequality in Latin America', IMF BLOG, published online 18 June, https://blogs.imf.org/2018/06/21/how-the-commodity-boom-helped-tackle-poverty-and-inequality-in-latin-america/.
2   William Ratliff (2006) 'Beijing's Pragmatism Meets Hugo Chávez', *The Brown Journal of World Affairs* 12 (2): 77–8; Jiang Shixue (2006) 'A New Look at the Chinese Relations With Latin America', *Nueva Sociedad* (203), https://static.nuso.org/media/articles/downloads/3351_2.pdf.
3   Hans-Jürgen Burchardt and Kristina Dietz (2014) '(Neo-)extractivism – a New Challenge for Development Theory from Latin America', *Third World Quarterly* 35 (3): 470; also see Eduardo Gudynas (2009) 'Diez tesis urgentes sobre el nuevo extractivismo', in *Extractivismo, Política y Sociedad*, 187–225. Ecuador: CAAP y CLAES.
4   Maristella Svampa (2019) 'Neo-extractivism in Latin America: socio-environmental conflicts, the territorial turn and new political narratives', in Maria Victoria Murillo, Juan Pablo Luna, Tulia Falleti and Andrew

Schrank (eds), *Elements in Politics and Society in Latin America*, 1–65. Cambridge: Cambridge University Press.

5   Cited in Yanran Xu (2017) *China's Strategic Partnerships in Latin America: case studies of Chinese oil diplomacy in Argentina, Brazil, Mexico and Venezuela, 1991–2015*. Lanham, MD: Lexington Books, 67.

6   Venezuela has the fifth-largest recoverable petroleum reserves in the world. Chávez sought to reclassify 'bitumen' or heavy oil reserves, of which the country holds an estimated 270 billion, which would push Venezuela up the list to the top of proven reserves. For a discussion on Venezuela as a Petrostate, see: https://www.cfr.org/backgrounder/venezuela-crisis.

7   Antulio Rosales (2016) 'Deepening Extractivism and Rentierism: China's role in Venezuela's Bolivarian Developmental Model', *Canadian Journal of Development Studies* 37 (4): 563.

8   Mike Gonzalez (2014) *Hugo Chávez: Socialist for the 21st Century*. London: Pluto Press, 100–7; also see the official Venezuelan government website, https://www.misionesbolivarianas.com/.

9   In 2000, Caracas and Havana signed a deal to provide 53,000 barrels of oil a day at a discount, increased to 90,000 b/d allegedly in response for its support in putting down internal dissent in 2004 and 2005. Mike Gonzalez (2014) *Hugo Chávez: Socialist for the 21st Century*. London: Pluto Press, 91, 116–117.

10 Óscar García Agustín (2016) 'Venezuela and China: independency and dependency in the context of interdependent hegemony', *Journal of Contemporary International Relations* 108.

11 Nahuel Arenas-Garcia (2012) '21st Century Regionalism in South America: UNASUR and the search for development alternatives', *eSharp* 188, 64–85, https://www.gla.ac.uk/media/Media_228378_smxx.pdf.

12 Shannon K. O'Neil (2018) 'Latin America Needs More Home-Grown Supply Chains', *Council on Foreign Relations*, published online 23 May, https://www.cfr.org/blog/latin-america-needs-more-home-grown-supply-chains.

13 Jorge Dominguez (2006) 'China's Relations with Latin America: shared gains, asymmetric hopes', Weatherhead Center for International Affairs, 42.

14 Yanran Xu (2017) *China's Strategic Partnerships in Latin America: case studies of Chinese oil diplomacy in Argentina, Brazil, Mexico and Venezuela, 1991–2015*. Lanham, MD: Lexington Books, 63.

15 V. Shanshima (2016) 'China-Venezuela Strategic Partnership: problems and prospects', *World Economy and International Relations* 60 (8): 96–102, https://www.imemo.ru/en/jour/meimo/index.php?page_id=685&id=7573&jid=7555&jj=49.

16 Antulio Rosales (2016) 'Deepening Extractivism and Rentierism: China's role in Venezuela's Bolivarian Developmental Model', *Canadian Journal of Development Studies* 37 (4): 563–5; also see Mike Gonzalez (2014) *Hugo Chávez: Socialist for the 21st Century*. London: Pluto Press, 100–7.

17 Xulio Rios (2013) 'China and Venezuela: Ambitions and complexities in an improving relationship', *East Asia* 30 (1): 56.
18 World Bank (2021) 'Venezuelan Product Exports and Imports to China 2001', World Integrated Trade Solution (WITS), https://wits.worldbank.org/CountryProfile/en/Country/VEN/Year/2001/TradeFlow/EXPIMP/Partner/CHN/Product/all-groups.
19 World Bank (2021) 'Venezuelan Product Exports and Imports to China 2009', World Integrated Trade Solution (WITS), https://wits.worldbank.org/CountryProfile/en/Country/VEN/Year/2009/TradeFlow/EXPIMP/Partner/CHN/Product/all-groups.
20 OEC World (2009) 'What does China import from Venezuela?', https://oec.world/en/visualize/tree_map/hs92/import/chn/ven/show/2009/.
21 OEC World (2017) 'What does China import from Venezuela?', https://oec.world/en/visualize/tree_map/hs92/import/chn/ven/show/2017/.
22 Harold Trinkunas (2016) 'Reminbi Diplomacy? The limits of China's Influence on Latin America's Domestic Politics', *Geoeconomics and Global Issues*, Paper 3, Brookings Institution, Washington, DC, 6.
23 Cited in William Ratliff (2006) 'Beijing's Pragmatism meets Hugo Chávez', *The Brown Journal of World Affairs* 12 (2): 79–80.
24 Jorge Dominguez (2006) 'China's Relations with Latin America: shared gains, asymmetric hopes', Weatherhead Center for International Affairs, 42.
25 Rita Giacalone and José Briceño Ruiz (2013), 'The Chinese–Venezuelan Oil Agreements: Material and Nonmaterial Goals'. *Latin American Policy*, Vol. 4, No. 1, 76–92; see also: Ana Cristina Alves (2013), 'Chinese Economic Statecraft: A Comparative Study of China's Oil-backed Loans in Angola and Brazil'. *Journal of Current Chinese Affairs* 1/2013: 99–130.
26 Jens Erik Gould, 'Venezuela-China team sets Orinoco target; expects to be producing 200,000 b/d heavy oil by 2010', *Platts Oilgram News* 84:163, 25 August 2006.
27 Antulio Rosales (2016) 'Deepening Extractivism and Rentierism: China's role in Venezuela's Bolivarian Developmental Model', *Canadian Journal of Development Studies* 37 (4): 566–7.
28 Ibid., 564.
29 Even figures for projected outputs were unclear due to contradictory statements by government officials at the time. Jens Erik Gould (2006) 'Venezuela-China team sets Orinoco target; expects to be producing 200,000 b/d heavy oil by 2010', *Platts Oilgram News*, August, 84: 163, 25.
30 William Ratliff (2006) 'Beijing's Pragmatism meets Hugo Chávez', *The Brown Journal of World Affairs* 12 (2): 79; Jens Erik Gould (2006) 'Venezuela-China team sets Orinoco target; expects to be producing 200,000 b/d heavy oil by 2010', *Platts Oilgram News*, August, 84: 163, 25.
31 Xulio Rios (2013) 'China and Venezuela: Ambitions and complexities in an improving relationship', *East Asia* 30 (1): 56.

32 Jesús Hermoso and María Victoria Fermín (2019) 'The China Venezuela Relationship Explained', SupChina, 7 January, https://supchina.com/2019/01/07/venezuela-china-explained/.
33 Ibid.
34 Economic Intelligence Unit (2009) '*Venezuela: country profile 2009*', London: EIU, 19.
35 Benigno Alarcón, Ángel E. Álvarez and Manuel Hildago (2016) 'Latin America's New Turbulence: can democracy win in Venezuela?', *Journal of Democracy* 27 (2): 20–34.
36 Mia Armstrong (2018) 'Venezuela Shows us How China is Starting to Export its Authoritarian Surveillance Tech', 15 November, https://slate.com/technology/2018/11/venezuela-china-zte-authoritarian-surveillance-social-control-tech.html.
37 Marc Weisbrot and Luis Sandoval (2008) 'Update: The Venezuelan Economy in the Chávez Years', Center for Economic and Policy Research, Washington, DC.
38 Barbara Hogenboom (2014) 'Latin America and China's Transnationalizing Oil Industry: A Political Economy Assessment of New Relations', *Perspectives on Global Development and Technology* 13: 635–6; Nagel, cited in Antulio Rosales (2016) 'Deepening Extractivism and Rentierism: China's role in Venezuela's Bolivarian Developmental Model', *Canadian Journal of Development Studies* 37 (4): 571.
39 Antulio Rosales (2019) 'Radical Rentierism: gold mining, crypto currency and commodity collateralization in Venezuela', *Review of International Political Economy* 26 (6): 1319–23.
40 *China.Org* (2014) 'China, Venezuela lift ties to comprehensive strategic partnership', 21 July, http://www.china.org.cn/china/2014-07/21/content_33009951.htm.
41 Harvard Kennedy School (n.d.) 'Understanding the Venezuelan Crisis with Ricardo Hausmann', Wiener Conference Calls, https://www.hks.harvard.edu/wiener-conference-calls/ricardo-hausmann.
42 Harold Trinkunas (2016) 'Reminbi Diplomacy? The limits of China's Influence on Latin America's Domestic Politics', *Geoeconomics and Global Issues*, Paper 3, Brookings Institution, Washington, DC, 6.
43 *China.Org* (2014) 'China, Venezuela lift ties to comprehensive strategic partnership', 21 July, http://www.china.org.cn/china/2014-07/21/content_33009951.htm.
44 Also see Chris Alden and Yu-Shan Wu (2020) 'Leadership, Global Agendas and Domestic Determinant of South Africa's Foreign Policy towards China: the Zuma and Ramaphosa years', in Chris Alden and Yu-Shan Wu (eds), *South Africa and China: a partnership of paradoxes*. Basingstoke: Palgrave.
45 Simon Garcia (2020) 'Venezuela and China deepen unbreakable comprehensive strategic partnership of cooperation', *Ministerio del Poder*

Popular para Relaciones Exteriores de Venezuela, 17 January, http://mppre. gob.ve/en/2020/01/17/venezuela-china-partnership-cooperation.
46. *Diálogo Chino* (2015) 'Will Venezuela pull through for China?', 29 April, https://dialogochino.net/en/trade-investment/2235-will-venezuela-pull-through-for-china/.
47. According to a study by Venezuela's Centre for Energy and Environment of the Institute of Advanced Administrative Studies; *Diálogo Chino* (2018) 'Maduro's disputed re-election jeopardises repayment of China debt', 23 May, https://dialogochino.net/en/extractive-industries/11187-maduros-disputed-re-election-jeopardises-repayment-of-china-debt/.
48. Jesús Hermoso and María Victoria Fermín (2019) 'The China–Venezuela Relationship Explained', SupChina, 7 January, https://supchina.com/2019/01/07/venezuela-china-explained/.
49. Uri Friedman (2019) 'How an Elaborate Plan to Topple Venezuela's President went Wrong', *The Atlantic*, 1 May, https://www.theatlantic.com/politics/archive/2019/05/white-house-venezuela-maduro-failed/588454/.
50. Qiang Wang and Rongrong Li (2016) 'Sino-Venezuela Oil-for-Loan Deal – the Chinese Strategic Gamble', *Renewable and Sustainable Energy Reviews* 65: 817.
51. Harvard Kennedy School (n.d.) 'Understanding the Venezuelan Crisis with Ricardo Hausmann', Wiener Conference Calls, https://www.hks.harvard.edu/wiener-conference-calls/ricardo-hausmann.
52. Foreign Ministry of People's Republic of China (2019) 'Wang Yi: Reviving Monroe Doctrine is to reverse the course of history', 29 May https://www.fmprc.gov.cn/mfa_eng/wjb_663304/zzjg_663340/ldmzs_664952/xwlb_664954/t1668322.shtml.
53. Andrés Bermúdez Liévano (2019) 'Venezuela crisis touches down in China', *Diálogo Chino*, 25 March, https://dialogochino.net/en/trade-investment/25282-venezuela-crisis-touches-down-in-china/.
54. Alicia Hernandez (2020) 'China remains quiet and pragmatic on Venezuela crisis', *Diálogo Chino*, 20 January, https://dialogochino.net/en/trade-investment/32971-china-remains-quiet-and-pragmatic-on-venezuela-crisis/.
55. Anders Corr (2017) 'Remove Maduro, and China, send 80 billion in emergency aid to Venezuela', *Forbes*, 21 April, https://www.forbes.com/sites/anderscorr/2017/04/21/remove-maduro-and-china-send-80-billion-in-emergency-aid-to-venezuela/#574193262a2f.
56. Alicia Hernandez (2020) 'China remains quiet and pragmatic on Venezuela crisis', *Diálogo Chino*, 20 January, https://dialogochino.net/en/trade-investment/32971-china-remains-quiet-and-pragmatic-on-venezuela-crisis/.
57. Gideon Long, Henry Foy and Sam Fleming (2019) 'Venezuela's opposition reaches out to Russia and China', *Financial Times*, https://www.ft.com/content/a74930e2-3180-11e9-8744-e7016697f225.

58 Lorna Herrera-Vinelli and Mateo Bonilla (2019) 'Ecuador-China Relations: the growing effect of Chinese investment on Ecuadorian domestic politics, 2007–2016', *Journal of Chinese Political Science* 24: 623–41.
59 Ibid., 627–8.
60 June Beittel (2013) 'Political and Economic Relations and US Relations', Congressional Research Service, Washington, DC, 1–9.
61 Arturo Porzecanski (2010) 'When Bad Things Happen to Sovereign Debt Contracts: the case of Ecuador', *Law and Contemporary Problems*: 251–71.
62 Marc Beker (2011) 'Correa, Indigenous Movements and the Writing of a New Constitution in Ecuador', *Latin American Perspectives* 38 (1): 47–62; Thomas Chiasson-Lebel (2019) 'Neoliberalism in Ecuador after Correa', *European Review of Latin American and Caribbean Studies* 108: 158–60.
63 Philipp Altmann (2013) 'Good Life as Social Movement Proposal for Natural Resource Use: the indigenous movement in Ecuador', *Consilience: the Journal of Sustainable Development* 10 (1): 59–71.
64 Jonas Wolf (2011) 'Reengaging Latin America's Left? US relations with Bolivia and Ecuador from Bush to Obama', Report, Peace Research Institute, Frankfurt.
65 Nikolas Kozloff (2008) *Revolution! South America and the Rise of the New Left*. Basingstoke: Palgrave.
66 Unia Villalba (2013) '*Buen Vivir vs Development:* a paradigm shift in the Andes?', *Third World Quarterly* 34 (8): 1434–6.
67 June Beittel (2013) 'Political and Economic Relations and US Relations', Congressional Research Service, Washington, DC, 1–9.
68 The World Bank (n.d.) 'Ecuador', https://data.worldbank.org/?locations=EC-XT.
69 R. Evan Ellis (2017) 'Ecuador under President Moreno: rethinking the US relationship', *Global Americans*, 26 May, https://theglobalamericans.org/2017/05/ecuador-president-moreno-rethinking-u-s-relationship-latin-americas-left/.
70 June Beittel (2013) 'Political and Economic Relations and US Relations', Congressional Research Service, Washington, DC, 1–9.
71 Lorna Herrera-Vinelli and Mateo Bonilla (2019) 'Ecuador-China Relations: the growing effect of Chinese investment on Ecuadorian domestic politics, 2007–2016', *Journal of Chinese Political Science* 24: 627.
72 Arturo Porzecanski (2010) 'When Bad Things Happen to Sovereign Debt Contracts: the case of Ecuador', *Law and Contemporary Problems*: 267; also see Kevin Gallagher and Amos Irwin (2015) 'China's Economic Statecraft in Latin America: Evidence from China's Policy Banks', *Pacific Affairs* 88 (1): 64.
73 World Bank (2021) 'Ecuador Product Exports and Import to China 2017', World Integrated Trade Solution (WITS), https://wits.worldbank.org/CountryProfile/en/Country/ECU/Year/2017/TradeFlow/EXPIMP/Partner/CHN/Product/all-groups. The latest figures are from 2019 and show that

oil is no longer the main import from China; for the latest figures, see World Bank (2021) 'Ecuador Product Exports and Imports to China 2019', World Integrated Trade Solution (WITS), https://wits.worldbank.org/CountryProfile/en/Country/ECU/Year/2019/TradeFlow/EXPIMP/Partner/CHN/Product/all-groups.

74 OEC World (2017) 'What does China import from Venezuela?', https://oec.world/en/visualize/tree_map/hs92/import/chn/ecu/show/2017/.
75 Rebecca Ray and Adam Chimenti (2015) 'A Line in the Equatorial Forests: Chinese investment and the environmental and social impacts of extractive industries in Ecuador', *Global Economic Governance Initiative* (Discussion Paper 2015–16).
76 Focus Economics (2020) 'Ecuador Economic Outlook', 10 November, https://www.focus-economics.com/countries/ecuador.
77 Rafael Correa (2012) Interview, *New Left Review* 77, September–October: 97.
78 Pamela Martin (2014) 'Ecuador's Yasuni-ITT Initiative: why did it fail?', *International Development Policy, Articles and Debates* 5.2, Graduate Institute: Geneva, https://journals.openedition.org/poldev/1705.
79 Rebecca Carvalho (2019) 'How Chinese projects are tearing communities in Ecuador apart', *South China Morning Post*, 25 May, https://multimedia.scmp.com/week-asia/article/3011618/beijing-conquest-latin-america/chapter02.html.
80 Marc Beker (2013) 'The Stormy Relations Between Rafael Correa and Social Movements in Ecuador', *Latin American Perspectives* 190 (40): 43–62; Jonathan Watts (2017) 'Amazon land battle pits indigenous villagers against the might of the Ecuadorian state', *The Guardian*, 19 March, https://www.theguardian.com/world/2017/mar/19/ecuador-indigenous-shuar-el-tink-mining-land-dispute.
81 Xu Ying (2016) 'The Interaction Between Ecuadorian NGOs and Chinese Enterprises in Ecuador: toward better Corporate Social Responsibility', in Shuijun Cui and Manuel Perez (eds), *China and Latin America in Transition: policy dynamics, economic commitments and social impacts*, 243–56. Basingstoke: Palgrave.
82 Nicholas Casey and Clifford Krauss (2018) 'It Doesn't Matter if Ecuador Can Afford This Dam. China Still Gets Paid', *The New York Times*, https://www.nytimes.com/2018/12/24/world/americas/ecuador-china-dam.html.
83 Chris Kraul (2018) 'Ecuador faces a huge budget deficit because of loans it received from China', *LA Times*, 10 December, https://www.latimes.com/world/la-fg-ecuador-loans-china-20181210-story.html.
84 DAR (2014) *Altas y bajas en las salvaguardas ¿Cómo actúan BNDES, China ExIm Bank, CAF y BID?* Lima: DAR, 140; Max Nathanson (2017) 'Damming or Damning the Amazon? Assessing Ecuador-China cooperation', *Mongabay*, 22 November.

85 Genesis Lozano (2019) 'Ecuador's China-backed hydropower revolution', *China Dialogue*, 21 August, https://www.chinadialogue.net/article/show/single/en/11464-Ecuador-s-China-backed-hydropower-revolution.
86 Charlotte Middlehurst (2017) 'Ecuador shark seizure exposes illegal fishing network', *Diálogo Chino*, 25 August, https://dialogochino.net/en/agriculture/9523-ecuador-shark-seizure-exposes-illegal-fishing-network/; Rachel Bale (2017) 'Thousands of sharks found in boat on huge illegal haul', *National Geographic*, 15 August, https://www.nationalgeographic.com/news/2017/08/wildlife-watch-galapagos-illegal-shark-fishing/.
87 *The Guardian* (2020) 'They Just Pull Up Everything! Chinese fleet raises fears for Galapagos sea life', 6 August, https://www.theguardian.com/environment/2020/aug/06/chinese-fleet-fishing-galapagos-islands-environment.
88 Hsiao-Ping Biehl and Luisa Ossa (2015) 'More Than Fried Rice and Plantains: Chinese Populations in Latin America?', Explorer Café 41, http://digitalcommons.lasalle.edu/explorercafe/41.
89 Ana Lucia Salinas de Dosch and Jorn Dosch (2012) 'China's Rise in Latin America', *Journal of International Studies (JIS)* 8: 1–3, https://e-journal.uum.edu.my/index.php/jis/article/view/7923/969, 7.
90 *Ecuador Times* (2020) 'China is the third product destination of Ecuador', 2 January, https://www.ecuadortimes.net/china-is-the-third-product-destination-of-ecuador/.
91 Cited in Rebecca Ray and Adam Chimienti (2017) 'A Line in the Equatorial Forests: Chinese investment and the environmental and social impacts of extractive industries in Ecuador', in Rebecca Ray, Kevin Gallagher, Andres Lopez and Cynthia Sanborn (eds), *China and Sustainable Development in Latin America*, 114. London: Anthem Press.
92 Rafael Correa (2013) 'Busquemos sociedades con mercado, no de Mercado', TeleSur TV, https://www.youtube.com/watch?v=HZi8yZS80F4.
93 Marc Beker (2011) 'Correa, Indigenous Movements and the Writing of a New Constitution in Ecuador', *Latin American Perspectives* 38 (1): 47–62.
94 Marc Beker (2013) 'The Stormy Relations Between Rafael Correa and Social Movements in Ecuador', *Latin American Perspectives* 190 (40): 43–62.
95 Rafael Correa (2012) Interview, *New Left Review* 77, September–October, 89–104 (plus postscript).
96 Marc Beker (2013) 'The Stormy Relations Between Rafael Correa and Social Movements in Ecuador', *Latin American Perspectives* 190 (40): 51.
97 See Catherine Cohaghan (2015) 'Surveil and Sanction: the return of the state and societal regulation in Ecuador', *European Review of Latin America and the Caribbean Studies* 98: 7–27.
98 Charles Rollet (2018) 'Ecuador's all seeing eye is made in China', *Foreign Policy*, 9 August, https://foreignpolicy.com/2018/08/09/ecuadors-all-seeing-eye-is-made-in-china/.

99 Gobierndo de Ecuador (2016) 'ECU 911 fortalece su contingente tecnológico con apoyo de cooperación del gobierno chino', press release, https://www.ecu911.gob.ec/ecu-911-fortalece-su-contingente-tecnologico-con-apoyo-de-cooperacion-del-gobierno-chino/, https://www.ecu911.gob.ec/reconocimientos-2/; Xinhuanet (2019) 'Cutting edge Chinese tech backs Ecuador's emergency hotline', 17 July, http://www.xinhuanet.com/english/2019-07/17/c_138233603.htm; Paul Mozur, Jonah Kessel and Melissa Chan (2019) 'Made in China, Exported to the World: the surveillance state', *New York Times*, 24 April, https://www.nytimes.com/2019/04/24/technology/ecuador-surveillance-cameras-police-government.html.

100 Chris Burt (2018) 'Ecuador tackles crime with Chinese facial recognition technology', *Biometric Update*, 22 January, https://www.biometricupdate.com/201801/ecuador-tackles-crime-with-chinese-facial-recognition-technology.

101 Catherine Cohaghan (2015) 'Surveil and Sanction: the return of the state and societal regulation in Ecuador', *European Review of Latin America and the Caribbean Studies* 98: 13–17.

102 Marc Beker (2013) 'The Stormy Relations Between Rafael Correa and Social Movements in Ecuador', *Latin American Perspectives* 190 (40): 43–62. Also see Rafael Correa (2012) Interview, *New Left Review* 77, September–October: 103–4.

103 Chris Kraul (2018) 'Ecuador faces a huge budget deficit because of loans it received from China', *LA Times*, 10 December https://www.latimes.com/world/la-fg-ecuador-loans-china-20181210-story.html.

104 Forecast Economics (2020) Ecuador Economic Outlook, 21 April https://www.focus-economics.com/countries/ecuador.

105 Thomas Chiasson-Lebel (2019) 'Neoliberalism in Ecuador after Correa', *European Review of Latin American and Caribbean Studies* 108: 162–3.

106 Gobierndo de Ecuador (2016) 'ECU 911 fortalece su contingente tecnológico con apoyo de cooperación del gobierno chino', press release, https://www.ecu911.gob.ec/ecu-911-fortalece-su-contingente-tecnologico-con-apoyo-de-cooperacion-del-gobierno-chino/; https://www.ecu911.gob.ec/reconocimientos-2/.

107 Pablo Vivenco (2018) 'US returns to exert "influence" in Ecuador and the region', *The Progressive*, 5 October, https://progressive.org/dispatches/us-military-returns-to-exert-influence-in-ecuador-and-region-181005/.

108 Rebecca Ray and Kehan Wang (2019) 'China-Latin America Economic Bulletin 2019', *Global Development Policy Center*, Boston University, 13.

109 John Paul Rathbone and Colby Smith (2019) 'IMF agrees to $1.2 bn fund for Ecuador', *Financial Times*, 21 February.

110 World Bank (2021) 'Bolivian Product Exports and Imports to China 2017', World Integrated Trade Solution (WITS), https://wits.worldbank.org/CountryProfile/en/Country/BOL/Year/2017/TradeFlow/EXPIMP/Partner/CHN/Product/all-groups. See also WITS (n.d.) 'Bolivia Import

in thousand US$ for All Products China between 2005 and 2019', World Bank', https://wits.worldbank.org/CountryProfile/en/Country/BOL/StartYear/2005/EndYear/2019/TradeFlow/Import/Indicator/MPRT-TRD-VL/Partner/CHN/Product/Total; Emily Achtenberg (2017) 'Financial Sovereignty or a New Dependency? How China is remaking Bolivia', NACLA, 8 October, https://nacla.org/blog/2017/08/11/financial-sovereignty-or-new-dependency-how-china-remaking-bolivia.

111 Benjamin Kohl (2010) 'Bolivia under Morales, Part 1: consolidating power, initiating decolonization', *Latin American Perspectives* 37 (3): 114–17.

112 Ibid.

113 Ana Cristina Delgado (2017) 'The TIPNIS Conflict in Bolivia', *Contexto International* 39 (2): 373–91.

114 Natalya Naqvi (2019) 'Renationalizing Finance for Development: policy space and political economic control in Bolivia', *Review of International Political Economy*, doi: 10.1080/09692290.2019.1696870, 9–19.

115 Benjamin Kohl (2010) 'Bolivia under Morales, Part 1: Consolidating Power, Initiating Decolonization', *Latin American Perspectives* 37 (3): 117.

116 Germano Mendes de Paul (2012) 'Bolivia's El Mutun Ore Development Has Lost Its Window of Opportunity', *Steel Times* 36 (8): 10; Siliva Antonioli (2012) 'Jindal seeks alternative to Bolivia deal', *Reuters*, 20 June, https://in.reuters.com/article/steel-jindal/jindal-looking-at-coal-iron-ore-projects-chairman-idINDEE85J0GW20120620.

117 Vijay Prashad (2019) 'Chinese links with Morales figure in Bolivian coup', *Asia Times*, 13 November, https://www.asiatimes.com/2019/11/opinion/chinas-links-with-morales-figure-in-bolivia-coup/.

118 Benjamin Kohl (2010) 'Bolivia under Morales, Part 1: consolidating power, initiating decolonization', *Latin American Perspectives* 37 (3): 109–11.

119 Ibid., 111.

120 Emily Achtenberg (2013) 'Bolivia: the unfinished business of land reform', NACLA, 31 March, https://nacla.org/blog/2013/3/31/bolivia-unfinished-business-land-reform.

121 Interview by authors with leading entrepreneurs at the Bolivian Camara de Industria y Comercio (CAINCO), 18 May 2017. Santa Cruz, Bolivia. See also 'Nevado Illimani Entregado a Intereses Mineros', PPT 2017, https://www.cedib.org/wp-content/uploads/2017/03/04-Mineria-en-nevados.pdf.

122 Emily Achtenberg (2017) 'Financial Sovereignty or a New Dependency? How China is remaking Bolivia', NACLA, 8 October, https://nacla.org/blog/2017/08/11/financial-sovereignty-or-new-dependency-how-china-remaking-bolivia. This is not unique to Bolivia, China offered Argentina 'a $10 billion loan at 600 basis points above the London Interbank Offered Rate (LIBOR)'; see Kevin Gallagher and Amos Irwin (2015) 'China's Economic Statecraft in Latin America: Evidence from China's Policy Banks', *Pacific Affairs* 88 (1): 105.

123 Interview by authors with leading entrepreneurs at the Bolivian Camara de Industria y Comercio (CAINCO), 18 May 2017. Santa Cruz, Bolivia.
124 Stephen B. Kaplan (2021) *Globalizing Patient Capital: The Political Economy of Chinese Finance in the Americas*, Cambridge: Cambridge University Press.
125 Vivian Herrera Vargas (2019) 'Cuaderno de Coyuntura 25: Empresas chinas en Bolivia: Denuncias sobre derechos de los trabajadores y situación ambiental. Periodo 2015–2019', *Cedal, La Paz, Bolivia*: 1–8.
126 See Daniel Agramont and Gustavo Bonifaz (2018) 'The Growing Chinese Presence in Latin America and its (Geo)Political Manifestations in Bolivia', *LSE Global South Unit Working Paper Series* 2, 38.
127 Rachael Bale (2017) 'On the Trail of Jaguar Poachers', *National Geographic*, December, https://www.nationalgeographic.com/magazine/2017/12/on-the-trail-of-jaguar-poachers/; Roberto Navia (2018) 'Fang trafficking to China is putting Bolivia's jaguars in jeopardy', *Mongabay*, 26 January, https://news.mongabay.com/2018/01/fang-trafficking-to-china-is-putting-bolivias-jaguars-in-jeopardy/.
128 Plurinational State of Bolivia (2015) *Economic and Social Development Plan, 2016–2020 within the Framework of Integrated Development for Living Well: towards the patriotic agenda 2025*. La Paz, http://www.planificacion.gob.bo/uploads/PDES_INGLES.pdf.
129 Cited in Daniel Agramont and Gustavo Bonifaz (2018) 'The Growing Chinese Presence in Latin America and its (Geo)Political Manifestations in Bolivia', *LSE Global South Unit Working Paper Series* 2, 23.
130 Raquel Carvalho (2018) 'In Latin America, big brother China is watching you', *South China Morning Post*, 21 December, https://www.scmp.com/week-asia/geopolitics/article/2178558/latin-america-big-brother-china-watching-you; *Xinhua* (2016) 'Chinese technology to help Bolivia public security system', 15 December, http://www.china.org.cn/world/Off_the_Wire/2016-12/15/content_39920552.htm.
131 Chris Burt (2019) 'Chinese biometric surveillance technology deployed internationally amid criticism', *Biometric Update*, 23 October, https://www.biometricupdate.com/201910/chinese-biometric-surveillance-technology-deployed-internationally-amid-criticism.
132 Daniel Agramont and Gustavo Bonifaz (2018) 'The Growing Chinese Presence in Latin America and its (Geo)Political Manifestations in Bolivia', *LSE Global South Unit Working Paper Series* 2, 22–3.
133 Vivian Herrera Vargas (2019) 'Cuaderno de Coyuntura 25: Empresas chinas en Bolivia: Denuncias sobre derechos de los trabajadores y situación ambiental. Periodo 2015–2019', *Cedal, La Paz, Bolivia*: 1–6.
134 Daniel Agramont and Gustavo Bonifaz (2018) 'The Growing Chinese Presence in Latin America and its (Geo)Political Manifestations in Bolivia', *LSE Global South Unit Working Paper Series* 2, 23.
135 Keith Johnson and James Palmer (2019) 'Bolivia's lithium isn't the new oil', *Foreign Policy*, 19 November, https://foreignpolicy.com/2019/11/13/coup-morales-bolivia-lithium-isnt-new-oil/.

136 Andrew Polk (2009) 'Could Bolivia be the Saudi Arabia of lithium?', *Foreign Policy*, 4 September, https://foreignpolicy.com/2009/02/04/could-bolivia-be-the-saudi-arabia-of-lithium/.
137 TeleSur (2018) 'Bolivia's Morales and China's Xi sign strategic partnership', 19 June, https://www.telesurenglish.net/news/Bolivias-Morales-Chinas-Xi-Sign-Strategic-Partnership-20180619-0038.html.
138 Emily Achtenberg (2017) 'Why is Evo Morales Reviving Bolivia's Controversial TIPNIS Road?', NACLA, 21 August, https://nacla.org/blog/2017/08/22/why-evo-morales-reviving-bolivia%E2%80%99s-controversial-tipnis-road.
139 *Reuters* (2019) 'Bolivia picks Chinese partner for $2.3 billion lithium projects', 6 February, https://www.reuters.com/article/us-bolivia-lithium-china/bolivia-picks-chinese-partner-for-2-3-billion-lithium-projects-idUSKCN1PV2F7.
140 Sonia Sanchez Manzanaro, Rafa Cereceda and Sandrine Amiel (2019) 'Was Bolivia's ousting of Evo Morales a coup by the US for lithium?', *Euronews*, 11 November, https://www.euronews.com/2019/11/21/does-bolivia-s-ouster-of-morales-have-anything-to-do-with-lithium.
141 *Reuters* (2019) 'Bolivia picks Chinese partner for $2.3 billion lithium projects', 6 February, https://www.reuters.com/article/us-bolivia-lithium-china/bolivia-picks-chinese-partner-for-2-3-billion-lithium-projects-idUSKCN1PV2F7.
142 Keith Johnson and James Palmer (2019) 'Bolivia's lithium isn't the new oil', *Foreign Policy*, 19 November, https://foreignpolicy.com/2019/11/13/coup-morales-bolivia-lithium-isnt-new-oil/.
143 See debates in various sources, including Vijay Prashad (2019) 'Chinese links with Morales figure in Bolivian coup', *Asia Times*, 13 November, https://www.asiatimes.com/2019/11/opinion/chinas-links-with-morales-figure-in-bolivia-coup/; Sonia Sanchez Manzanaro, Rafa Cereceda and Sandrine Amiel (2019) 'Was Bolivia's ousting of Evo Morales a coup by the US for lithium?', *Euronews*, 11 November, https://www.euronews.com/2019/11/21/does-bolivia-s-ouster-of-morales-have-anything-to-do-with-lithium.
144 Irene Mia (2020) 'Bolivia's New Government: many challenges, one big opportunity', IISS Blog, 5 November, https://www.iiss.org/blogs/analysis/2020/11/bolivias-new-government; Sergio Held (2020) 'Bolivia eyes path back to boom years', *China Daily*, 28 October, http://global.chinadaily.com.cn/a/202010/28/WS5f98d71ea31024ad0ba8178c.html.
145 For instance, CHEN Yuanting, Chinese Academy for Social Sciences (CASS), said this blatantly at an international conference on China-Latin America, 30 November 2018, Brussels: http://irelac.be/wp-content/uploads/2018/12/Programme_China-Latin-America-ULB.pdf.
146 Interview by the authors with Chinese diplomat, 5 May 2018. San Jose, Costa Rica.

Chapter 5

1. Interview with former Foreign Minister and Defence Minister of Brazil, Celso Amorim, 12 February 2017. London.
2. BRICS, originally coined by Jim O'Neil at Goldman Sachs in 2001 to refer to the leading emerging economies in the coming decade, was refashioned by Russia, China, Brazil and India into a global strategic partnership in 2009. South Africa was invited to join in December 2010. See Francis Kornegay and Narnia Bohler-Muller (2013) *Laying the BRICS of a New Global Order: from Yekaterinburg 2009 to Ethekwini 2013*. Tswane: Africa Institute of South Africa.
3. The Petrobras scandal is a political corruption scheme where millions of dollars were given to company officials and politicians to award contracts at exorbitant prices. Dozens of prominent officials, including former President Lula were dragged into the corruption scandal; see Fernando Henrique Cardoso (2016) 'What is the Petrobras scandal that is engulfing Brazil?', *Financial Times*, 31 March, https://www.ft.com/content/6e8b0e28-f728-11e5-803c-d27c7117d132.
4. C. Hiratuka (2018) 'Chinese infrastructure projects in Brazil: two case studies', in E. Dussel-Peters et al. (eds), *Building Development for a New Era: China's infrastructure projects in Latin America and the Caribbean*. Pittsburgh: University of Pittsburgh, 122–43.
5. Robert Conrad (1975) 'The Planter Class and the Debate over Chinese Immigration to Brazil, 1850–1893', *International Migration Review* 9 (41), doi: 10.2307/3002529.
6. Alexandre Ratsuo Uehara (2013) 'China's Foreign Policy and Bilateral Relations with Brazil', in Leila da Costa Ferreira and Jose August Gulhon Albuquerque (eds), *China and Brazil: challenges and opportunities*. São Paulo: Annablume, 33.
7. Ibid.
8. Central Intelligence Agency (n.d.) 'Protest, Condemn, Demand: a world-wise Chinese Communist propaganda operation against Brazil', report https://www.cia.gov/readingroom/document/cia-rdp78-03062a000800030005-6.
9. Roberto Abdenur (2011) 'Brazil and its Strategic Relations with China, Germany and the United States', *Latin American Policy* 2 (1): 59, https://doi-org.gate3.library.lse.ac.uk/10.1111/j.2041-7373.2010.00008.x.
10. CEBRI (2019) *Relatório 45 Anos Relações Diplomáticas Brasil-China* (Rio de Janeiro: CEBRI), 5; Daniel Cardoso (2012) 'China-Brazil: a strategic partnership in an evolving world order', *East Asia* 29 (4): 9.
11. Daniel Cardoso (2012) 'China-Brazil: a strategic partnership in an evolving world order', *East Asia* 29 (4): 9–10; Probe International (n.d.) 'Who is behind China's Three Gorges Dam?', https://journal.probeinternational.org/three-gorges-probe/who-is-behind-chinas-three-gorges-dam/.

12 *Wikileaks* (2004) 'The Trip of the Century', 14 May, https://wikileaks.org/plusd/cables/04BRASILIA1185_a.html.
13 Interestingly, the head of Lula's governing party, the Partido dos Trabalhdores (PT), had visited Beijing in April the same year and signed a cooperative agreement with its counterpart, the Chinese Communist Party. *Wikileaks* (2004) 'The Trip of the Century', 14 May, https://wikileaks.org/plusd/cables/04BRASILIA1185_a.html.
14 As in the case of Argentina this is simply an acknowledgment that has no bearing in the actual status of China as a market economy. In reality this cannot happen until Members of WTO agree to do so. It is very unlikely to happen as countries like the US are not in favour of doing so.
15 Ministry of Foreign Affairs, PRC (2004) 'Brazil recognizes China's market economy status in memo', 13 November, https://www.mfa.gov.cn/ce/cgsf/eng/xw/t170382.htm; *Wikileaks* (2004) 'Brazil's One Note Samba', 24 November, https://wikileaks.org/plusd/cables/04BRASILIA2885_a.html.
16 *Wikileaks* (2004) 'Brazil's One Note Samba', 24 November, https://wikileaks.org/plusd/cables/04BRASILIA2885_a.html.
17 *Wikileaks* (2004) 'Brazil's One Note Samba', 24 November, https://wikileaks.org/plusd/cables/04BRASILIA2885_a.html; also see J. Mohan Malik (2005) 'Security Council Reform: China signals its veto', *World Policy Journal* 22 (1): 21; Mariana Pimenta Oliveira Baccarini (2018) 'Informal Reform of the United Nations Security Council', *Contexto Internacional* 40 (1): 97–114.
18 *Wikileaks* (2004) 'The Trip of the Century', 14 May, https://wikileaks.org/plusd/cables/04BRASILIA1185_a.html; *Wikileaks* (2004) 'Brazil's One Note Samba', 24 November, https://wikileaks.org/plusd/cables/04BRASILIA2885_a.html.
19 'New Era of China-Brazil Cooperation' (2014), *China Oil & Gas* 3: 60–3.
20 Interview with Andre Soares (2019) 'What's driving new changes in Brazil-China trade ties?', *The Dialogue*, 14 February, https://www.thedialogue.org/analysis/whats-driving-new-changes-in-brazil-china-trade-ties/.
21 Itamaraty (2012) '2nd meeting of the Chinese Brazilian High Level Coordination and Cooperation Commission – COSBAN – February 13 2012', 8 February, https://www.gov.br/mre/pt-br/media/ata-v-reuniao-cosban-portugues.pdf.
22 Maria Cristina Pereira de Melo, Jair do Amaral Filho and Frutusos Santana (2015) 'The Political Economy of Brazil-China Trade Relations, 2000–2010', *Latin American Perspectives* 42 (6): 75.
23 World Bank (2021) 'Brazilian Product exports and imports to China 2009', World Integrated Trade Solution (WITS), https://wits.worldbank.org/CountryProfile/en/Country/BRA/Year/2009/TradeFlow/EXPIMP/Partner/all/Product/Total; see also IPEA (2011) 'As Relacoes Bilaterais Brasil-China

a ascensao da China no system mundial e os desafios para Brasil', 85: 4–6; Carlos Pereira João Augusto de Castro Neves (2011) 'Brazil and China: South-South partnership or North-South competition?', *Policy Paper* 26. Washington, DC: Brookings, 3.
24 Maria Cristina Pereira de Melo, Jair do Amaral Filho and Frutusos Santana (2015) 'The Political Economy of Brazil-China Trade Relations, 2000–2010', *Latin American Perspectives* 42 (6): 75–6.
25 Ibid., 78–9.
26 Eduardo Costa Pinto (2011) 'O eixo Sino-Americano e insercao externa Brasileira: antes e depois da crise', *IPEA* 48, https://www.ipea.gov.br/portal/images/stories/PDFs/TDs/td_1652.pdf.
27 Maria Cristina Pereira de Melo, Jair Do Amaral Filho and Frutusos Santana (2015) 'The Political Economy of Brazil-China Trade Relations, 2000–2010', *Latin American Perspectives* 42 (6): 81–22.
28 Lourenço S. Paz (2016) 'The China Shock Impact on Brazil's Manufacturing Labour Market', unpublished, 6–7.
29 Carlos Pereira João Augusto de Castro Neves (2011) 'Brazil and China: South-South partnership or North-South competition?', *Policy Paper* 26. Washington, DC: Brookings, 6–7.
30 Maria Cristina Pereira de Melo, Jair Do Amaral Filho and Frutusos Santana (2015) 'The Political Economy of Brazil-China Trade Relations, 2000–2010', *Latin American Perspectives* 42 (6): 64–87.
31 By 2011, even senior diplomats were complaining in public about the negative impact that the trade relationship was having, such as the former Brazilian ambassador to China. Roberto Abdenur (2011) 'Brazil and its Strategic Relations with China, Germany and the United States', *Latin American Policy* 2 (1): 59, https://doi-org.gate3.library.lse.ac.uk/10.1111/j.2041-7373.2010.00008.x.
32 Interview with former Minister of External Affairs and Minister of Defence of Brazil, Celso Amorim, 12 February 2017. London.
33 Carlos Pereira João Augusto de Castro Neves (2011) 'Brazil and China: South-South partnership or North-South competition?', *Policy Paper* 26. Washington, DC: Brookings, 4–5.
34 'New Era of China-Brazil Cooperation' (2014) *China Oil & Gas* 3: 62.
35 Carlos Pereira João Augusto de Castro Neves (2011) 'Brazil and China: South–South partnership or North–South competition?', *Policy Paper* 26. Washington, DC: Brookings, 4–6.
36 'Visita a Pequim esvaziada', *O Estado de Sao Paulo* 19 May 2009, https://opiniao.estadao.com.br/noticias/geral,visita-a-pequim-esvaziada,373139.
37 Jean-Marc Blanchard (2019) 'Brazil's Samba with China: economics brought them together but failed to ensure their tango', *Journal of Chinese Political Science* 24: 586.
38 See Tulio Cariello (2019) 'Chinese Investments in Brazil 2018: the Brazilian framework in a global perspective'. Rio de Janeiro, Brazil: CEBC, https://

www.cebc.com.br/arquivos_cebc/investimentos-chineses/ChineseInvestmentsInBrazil2018_6set_.pdf.
39 Ibid., 8.
40 Ibid., 9.
41 Ibid.
42 Gaston Fornes and Álvaro Méndez (2018) *The China-Latin America Axis: emerging markets and their role in an increasingly globalised world*, 2nd edn. New York, NY: Palgrave Macmillan, 138.
43 Pedro da Motta Veiga and Sandra Poilonia Rios (2019) 'China's FDI in Brazil: recent trends and policy debate', *Policy Brief* 19/20, Policy Center for the New South, June, 5.
44 Ibid., 6.
45 Ibid.
46 Philip Fearnside and Antonio M. R. Figuereido (2015) 'China's Influence on Deforestation in Brazilian Amazonia: a growing force in the state of Mato Grosso', *Discussion Paper* 3-2015. Global Economic Governance Initiative, Boston University, 1–51.
47 IPEA (2011) 'As Relacoes Bilaterais Brasil-China a ascensao da China no system mundial e os desafios para Brasil' 85: 8; Pedro da Motta Veiga and Sandra Poilonia Rios (2019) 'China's FDI in Brazil: recent trends and policy debate', *Policy Brief* 19/20, Policy Center for the New South, June, 6.
48 Pedro da Motta Veiga and Sandra Poilonia Rios (2019) 'China's FDI in Brazil: recent trends and policy debate', *Policy Brief* 19/20, Policy Center for the New South, June, 6.
49 *Wikileaks* (n.d.) 'BRAZIL/CHINA/GV – President Rousseff said in a speech to businessmen and Chinese authorities that the prosperity of a nation cannot be achieved at the expense of others, and said she was inaugurating a new chapter of Brazil/China relations', https://wikileaks.org/gifiles/docs/19/1986842_brazil-china-gv-president-rousseff-said-in-a-speech-to.html; also see Rousseff's comments in Jose-Augusto Guilhon-Albuquerque (2014) 'Brasil, China EUA: uma relacao trangular', *Revista Brasilira de Politica Internacional* 57: 108–20.
50 'New Era of China-Brazil Cooperation' (2014) *China Oil & Gas* 3: 60–3.
51 MacauHub (2015) 'Brazil and China create production cooperation fund worth $20 billion', 29 June, https://macauhub.com.mo/2015/06/29/brazil-and-china-create-production-cooperation-fund-worth-us20-billion/.
52 Ibid.
53 Mariana Branco (2017) 'Brazil-China fund now operational with $20 billion', *Agencia Brasil*, 26 June, https://agenciabrasil.ebc.com.br/en/economia/noticia/2017-06/brazil-china-fund-now-operational-20-billion.
54 Xinhuanet (2017) 'China-Brazil investment fund launched to promote productive capacity', 31 May, http://www.xinhuanet.com//english/2017-05/31/c_136328445.htm.

55 Embassy of China in Brazil (2017) 'China incentiva que empresas invistam no Brasil', 9 March, https://www.mfa.gov.cn/ce/cebr/por/zbgx/t1489499.htm.
56 MacauHub (2018) 'Brazil-China Cooperation Fund selects five projects for analysis', 10 May, https://macauhub.com.mo/2018/05/10/pt-fundo-brasil-china-de-cooperacao-selecciona-cinco-projectos-para-analise/; Jake Spring (2018) 'Brazil-China Fund greenlights 2.4 bln in potential loans', *Reuters*, 9 May, https://www.reuters.com/article/brazil-china-investment/brazil-china-fund-greenlights-24-bln-in-potential-loans-idUSL4N1RI4YT.
57 *Wikileaks* (2013) 'Chinese Railway Project in Colombia Research', *Stratfor*, https://wikileaks.org/gifiles/docs/19/1980670_-latam-chinese-railway-project-in-colombia-research-.html.
58 Eva Grey (2018) 'Bi-Oceanic Corridor: a new railway to rival maritime freight?', *Railway Technology*, 30 April, https://www.railway-technology.com/features/the-bi-oceanic-corridor-a-new-railroad-to-rival-maritime-freight/.
59 Kamilia Larichi (2015) 'Chinese investment flood threat to Brazil's environment', *South China Morning Post*, 25 May, https://www.scmp.com/comment/insight-opinion/article/1808452/chinese-investment-flood-threat-brazils-environment.
60 MacauHub (2018) 'Brazil suggests an alternative route for the transoceanic railway', 9 February, https://macauhub.com.mo/2018/02/09/pt-brasil-sugere-percurso-alternativo-para-a-ferrovia-transoceanica/.
61 Milton Leal (2016) 'Fears raised over new Amazon railroad', *China Dialogue*, 31 August, https://chinadialogue.net/en/transport/9200-fears-raised-over-new-amazon-railroad/
62 Milton Leal (2016) 'Belo Monte's power line passes through Brazil's Amazon and Cerrado Savannah', *China Dialogue*, 22 September, https://chinadialogue.net/en/energy/9266-belo-monte-power-line-passes-through-brazil-s-amazon-and-cerrado-savannah/.
63 Shanna Handbury (2019) 'As Bolsonaro meets with Xi, China silent on Brazil environmental crisis', *Mongabay*, 28 October, https://news.mongabay.com/2019/10/as-bolsonaro-meets-with-xi-china-silent-on-brazil-environmental-crisis/.
64 Philip Fearnside and Antonio M. R. Figuereido (2015) 'China's Influence on Deforestation in Brazilian Amazonia: a growing force in the state of Mato Grosso', *Discussion Paper* 3-2015. Global Economic Governance Initiative, Boston University, 19.
65 Will Connors (2015) 'How Brazil's "Nine Horsemen" Cracked a Bribery Scandal', *The Wall Street Journal*, 6 April.
66 Globo.com (2017) 'Governo prevê arrecadar R$ 20 bilhões com 25 leilões até o fim do ano', 12 September, https://g1.globo.com/economia/noticia/governo-preve-arrecadar-r-20-bilhoes-com-25-leiloes-ate-o-fim-do-ano.ghtml.

67. Robert Muggah and Adriana Erthal Abdenur (2017) 'China's Strategic Play in Brazil', *Americas Quarterly*, 27 September, https://americasquarterly.org/article/chinas-strategic-play-in-brazil/.
68. World Bank (2021) 'Brazilian Product Exports and Imports to China 2017', World Integrated Trade Solution (WITS), https://wits.worldbank.org/CountryProfile/en/Country/BRA/Year/2017/TradeFlow/EXPIMP/Partner/CHN/Product/all-groups.
69. Claire Salisbury (2016) 'Top scientists: Amazon's Tapajós Dam Complex 'a crisis in the making', *Mongabay*, 28 November, https://news.mongabay.com/2016/11/top-scientists-amazons-tapajos-dam-complex-a-crisis-in-the-making/.
70. Dave Makichuk (2021) 'Huawei hires a former president to advise on 5G', published online 31 January, https://asiatimes.com/2021/01/huawei-hires-a-former-president-to-advise-on-brazil/.
71. Yan Hairong, Chen Yiyuan and Ku Hok Bun (2016) 'China's Soybean Crisis: the logic of modernization and its discontents', *Journal of Peasant Studies* 43 (2): 375.
72. Ibid., 378–80.
73. Ibid., 382.
74. Nilay Yildiz (2020) 'Effects of US-China trade disputes on global trade relations case study: Latin America', *Transnational Corporations Review* 12 (2): 203–14.
75. Yan Hairong, Chen Yiyuan and Ku Hok Bun (2016) 'China's Soybean Crisis: the logic of modernization and its discontents', *Journal of Peasant Studies* 43 (2): 384.
76. Revista Café Point (2010) 'Delfim Netto: a China está tentando comprar o Brasil', 3 August, https://www.cafepoint.com.br/noticias/giro-de-noticias/delfim-netto-a-china-esta-tentando-comprar-o-brasil-64859n.aspx.
77. Gustavo de L.t. Oliveira (2018) 'Chinese Land Grabs in Brazil? Sinophobia and foreign investments in Brazilian soybean agribusiness', *Globalizations* 15 (1): 118–19.
78. *O Estado do Sao* Pauo (2010) 'China comprar terras no Brasil', 3 August, https://opiniao.estadao.com.br/noticias/geral,china-compra-terras-no-brasil-imp-,589697; Revista Café Point (2010) 'Delfim Netto: a China está tentando comprar o Brasil', 3 August, https://www.cafepoint.com.br/noticias/giro-de-noticias/delfim-netto-a-china-esta-tentando-comprar-o-brasil-64859n.aspx.
79. Gustavo de L.t. Oliveira (2018) 'Chinese Land Grabs in Brazil: sinophobia and Chinese investment in Brazilian soybean agribusiness', *Globalizations* 15 (1): 123–4; also see Jean-Marc Blanchard (2019) 'Brazil's Samba with China: economics brought them together but failed to ensure their tango', *Journal of Chinese Political Science* 24: 596.
80. Daniel Ren (2017) 'Shanghai Pengxin sets sights on importing more Brazilian soybean', *South China Morning Post* 25 September, https://

www.scmp.com/business/companies/article/2112688/shanghai-pengxin-sets-sights-importing-more-brazilian-soybean; Ana Mano (2019) 'Brazil's Fiagril turnaround on track after investor burned – exec' *Reuters*, 14 May, https://www.reuters.com/article/fiagril-turnaround/brazils-fiagril-turnaround-on-track-after-chinese-investors-burned-exec-idUSL2N22M1IE.

81 Gustavo de L.t. Oliveira (2018) 'Chinese Land Grabs in Brazil? Sinophobia and foreign investments in Brazilian soybean agribusiness', *Globalizations* 15 (1): 120.
82 Ibid., 117–18.
83 Alan Chua (2020) 'Is Embraer-China tie up an inevitable marriage or a case of strange bedfellows?' *Flight Global*, 30 April, https://www.flightglobal.com/aerospace/is-embraer-china-tie-up-an-inevitable-marriage-or-case-of-strange-bedfellows/138155.article.
84 R. Chadrakanth (2016) 'Tianjin Airlines-Embraer, perfect fit for China's regional expansion', *SP's Aviation*, 16 December, http://www.sps-aviation.com/news/?id=521&catId=4&h=MRJ-Engine-First-Run-Photos.
85 Lawrence Brainard and John Welch (2012) 'Brazil and China: clouds on the horizon', *Americas Quarterly*, 24 January, https://www.americasquarterly.org/article/brazil-and-china-clouds-on-the-horizon/.
86 Carlos Pereira João Augusto de Castro Neves (2011) 'Brazil and China: South-South partnership or North-South competition?', *Policy Paper* 26, Washington, DC: Brookings, 6; Henrique Altemani de Oliveira (2010) 'Brazil and China: From South-South Cooperation to Competition?' in Alex E. Fernández Jilberto and Barbara Hogenboom (eds), *Latin America Facing China: South-South Relations beyond the Washington Consensus*, 47–8, New York, NY: Berghahn Books.
87 Richard Alboulafia (2020) 'China won't rescue Embraer. Boeing may remain its best hope', *Forbes*, 3 May, https://www.forbes.com/sites/richardaboulafia/2020/05/03/china-wont-rescue-embraer-boeing-may-remain-its-best-hope/.
88 Luciano Nacimento (2019) 'Brazil China agree to deepen exchange, cooperation', *Agencia Brasil*, 29 May, https://agenciabrasil.ebc.com.br/en/internacional/noticia/2019-05/brazil-china-agree-deepen-exchange-cooperation.
89 *Automotive World* (2014) 'China's Development in Brazil: steady work, constant progress', 26 August, https://www.automotiveworld.com/news-releases/cherys-development-brazil-steady-work-constant-progress/.
90 Yan Pei (2011) 'Chery wins temporary tariff exemption in Brazil', China.org.cn, 28 September, http://www.china.org.cn/business/2011-09/28/content_23512340.htm.
91 MacauHub (2017) 'Chinese group Chery Automobile Company puts Brazilian subsidiary up for sale', 18 October, https://macauhub.com.mo/2017/10/18/pt-grupo-chines-chery-automobile-company-coloca-a-venda-subsidiaria-do-brasil/.

92 Xinhuanet (2018) 'China's automaker Chery bets on Brazil's economic recovery to gain market share', 30 March, http://www.xinhuanet.com/english/2018-03/30/c_137077012.htm.
93 euroénergie (2009) 'Petrobras signs partnerships with Chinese companies', 21 February, https://www.euro-energie.com/petrobras-signs-partnerships-with-chinese-companies-n-886.
94 Erica Downs (2011) *Inside China, Inc: China Development Bank's cross-border energy deals*, John L. Thornton China Center, Brookings Institution: Washington, DC, 46–8.
95 Ibid., 46–8, 78–9.
96 Chen Yuan, cited in ibid., ii, 81.
97 *Reuters* (2019) 'Huge Brazil oil round disappoints as only Petrobras and Chinese bid', 6 November, https://www.reuters.com/article/us-brazil-oil-auction/huge-brazil-oil-round-disappoints-as-only-petrobras-and-chinese-bid-idUSKBN1XG2AX.
98 Anthony Boadle (2017) 'Brazil's Petrobras, China Development Bank sign cooperation deal', *Reuters*, 2 September, https://www.reuters.com/article/us-brazil-china-petrobras/brazils-petrobras-china-development-bank-sign-cooperation-deal-idUSKCN1BD0OU.
99 Offshore Energy (2017) 'Petrobras in $5 billion financing deal with Chinese bank', 6 December, https://www.offshore-energy.biz/petrobras-in-5-billion-financing-deal-with-chinese-bank/.
100 Richard Lapper (2019) 'Bolsonaro took aim at China. Then reality struck', *Americas Quarterly*, 23 April, https://www.americasquarterly.org/article/bolsonaro-took-aim-at-china-then-reality-struck/.
101 *Argus Media* (2018) 'Chinese companies diving into downstream Brazil', 13 September, https://www.argusmedia.com/en/news/1753982-chinese-companies-diving-into-downstream-brazil.
102 *Oil and Gas Journal* (2020) 'Brazil's downstream divestment program offers opportunities, risks', 4 May, https://www.ogj.com/refining-processing/article/14175642/brazils-downstream-divestment-program-offers-opportunities-risks.
103 Brazil Energy Insight (2019) 'Petrobras reports on debt pre-payment to China Development Bank', 14 August; Anthony Boadle (2019) 'Petrobras repays $5 billion China Development Bank loan due in 2027', *Reuters*, 16 December, https://www.reuters.com/article/us-petrobras-china/petrobras-repays-5-billion-china-development-bank-loan-due-in-2027-idUSKBN1YK23X.
104 Richard Lapper (2019) 'Bolsonaro took aim at China. Then reality struck', *Americas Quarterly*, 23 April, https://www.americasquarterly.org/article/bolsonaro-took-aim-at-china-then-reality-struck/.
105 MacauHub (2017) 'State Grid controls 94.76% of Brazil's CPFL Energia', 1 December, https://macauhub.com.mo/2017/12/01/pt-grupo-china-state-grid-controla-9476-do-capital-da-brasileira-cpfl-energia/.

106 David Winning (2010) 'China's State Grid to buy seven Brazilian power firms', *Market Watch*, 21 December, https://www.marketwatch.com/story/chinas-state-grid-to-buy-seven-brazil-power-firms-2010-12-21.

107 Jake Spring (2018) 'China's State Grid to invest $38 billion in Brazil power sector', *Reuters*, 30 May, https://www.reuters.com/article/us-brazil-power-state-grid-corp/chinas-state-grid-to-invest-38-billion-in-brazil-power-sector-idUSKCN1IV2SR.

108 Zhao Yan (2019) 'Spotlight: Chinese power line projects in Brazil put environment first' Xinhuanet, 4 April, http://www.xinhuanet.com/english/2019-04/05/c_137952512.htm; Milton Leal (2016) 'Belo Monte's power line passes through Brazil's Amazon and Cerrado Savannah', *China Dialogue*, 22 September, https://chinadialogue.net/en/energy/9266-belo-monte-power-line-passes-through-brazil-s-amazon-and-cerrado-savannah/.

109 Christian Poirier (2018) 'Mega-Dams may be history in the Brazilian Amazon', *Diálogo Chino*, 26 January, https://dialogochino.net/en/climate-energy/10554-mega-dams-may-be-history-in-the-brazilian-amazon/.

110 Claudio Fischtak and Andre Soares (2012) 'Brazilian Companies in China: presence and experience', presentation to the Conselho Empresarial Brasil-China, October, see http://www.redalc-china.org/monitor/images/pais/Brasil/investigacion/271_BRZ_2012_Companies_Presence_Experience_PPT.pdf.

111 Ibid.

112 Marcos Caramuru de Paiva, Clarissa Lins and Gujihuilme Ferreira (2019) *Brasil-China: o estado de relaçoes, Belt and Road, e liçoes para of futuro* (Rio de Janeiro: CEBRI), 35.

113 MacauHub (2012) 'Chinese group Wuhan Iron Steel gives up project to build steel works in Brazil', 12 November, https://macauhub.com.mo/2012/11/12/chinese-group-wuhan-iron-steel-gives-up-project-to-build-steel-works-in-brazil-2/; *China Daily* (2006) 'Brazil Steel Company Eyes China Deal', 10 January, www.china.org.cn/english/BAT/154599.htm.

114 Lawrence Brainard and John Welch (2012) 'Brazil and China: clouds on the horizon', *Americas Quarterly*, 24 January, https://www.americasquarterly.org/article/brazil-and-china-clouds-on-the-horizon/.

115 Chris Alden and Marco Antonio Vieira (2005) 'The New Diplomacy of the South: South Africa, Brazil, India, and Trilateralism', *Third World Quarterly* 26 (7): 1077–95.

116 Henrique Altemani de Oliveira (2010) 'Brazil and China: From South-South Cooperation to Competition?' in Alex E. Fernández Jilberto and Barbara Hogenboom (eds), *Latin America Facing China: South-South Relations beyond the Washington Consensus*, 36. New York, NY: Berghahn Books.

117 Marco Cepik, Fabrício H. Chagas-Bastos and Rafael R. Ioris (2021) 'Missing the China factor: evidence from Brazil and Mexico', *Economic and Political Studies* 9 (3): 358–77.

118 Interview by one of the authors with NDB's former President, K.V. Kamath, 27 May 2019. Shanghai, China.
119 Yijia Jing, Álvaro Méndez and Yu Zheng, eds (2020) *New Development Assistance: emerging economies and the new landscape of development assistance*, Governing China in the 21st Century. Basingstoke, UK: Palgrave Macmillan, 111.
120 See Francis Kornegay and Narnia Bohler-Muller (2013) *Laying the BRICS of a New Global Order: from Yekatrinburg to Ethekwini*. Tswane: Africa Institute of South Africa.
121 Daniel Cardoso (2012) 'China-Brazil: a strategic partnership in an evolving world order', *East Asia* 29 (4): 45.
122 Song Xiaoping (2015) 'China and Latin America in a World in Transition: a Chinese perspective', in Adrian Bonilla and Paz Milet, *Latin America, the Caribbean and China: sub-regional scenarios*, 55. San José, Costa Rica: FLASCO/CAF.
123 Richard Lapper (2019) 'Bolsonaro took aim at China. Then reality struck', *Americas Quarterly*, 23 April, https://www.americasquarterly.org/article/bolsonaro-took-aim-at-china-then-reality-struck/.
124 Keegan Elmer (2019) 'China-basher or bridge builder? What can we expect when Brazilian President Jair Bolsonaro visits Beijing?' *South China Morning Post*, published online 24 October, https://www.scmp.com/news/china/diplomacy/article/3034291/china-basher-or-bridge-builder-what-can-we-expect-when.
125 France 24 (2019) 'Brazil's Bolsonaro to walk diplomatic tightrope at BRICS', 12 November, https://www.france24.com/en/20191112-brazil-s-bolsonaro-to-walk-diplomatic-tightrope-at-brics; *Agencia EFE* (2017) 'Temer proposes BRICS Intelligence Forum to fight terrorism', 4 September, https://www.efe.com/efe/english/portada/temer-proposes-brics-intelligence-forum-to-fight-terrorism/50000260-3369681.
126 Fabio Zanini (2019) 'BRICS under the new Brazilian president', *India Times*, 6 February, https://economictimes.indiatimes.com/news/international/world-news/brics-under-new-brazilian-president/articleshow/67862185.cms.
127 Richard Lapper (2019) 'Bolsonaro took aim at China. Then reality struck', *Americas Quarterly*, 23 April, https://www.americasquarterly.org/article/bolsonaro-took-aim-at-china-then-reality-struck/.
128 Luciano Nacimento (2019) 'Brazil China agree to deepen exchange, cooperation', *Agencia Brasil*, 29 May, https://agenciabrasil.ebc.com.br/en/internacional/noticia/2019-05/brazil-china-agree-deepen-exchange-cooperation.
129 Itamaraty, 'Ata da Quinta da Reuniao Plenaria da Commisao Sino-Brasileira de Alto-Nivel de concertacao e cooperacao', https://www.gov.br/mre/pt-br/media/ata-v-reuniao-cosban-portugues.pdf.
130 Sergio Ley López and Salvador Suárez Zaizar (2020) 'Deal Making with China Amid Global Economic Uncertainty: opportunities, risks

and recommendations for Latin America and the Caribbean', *Research Report*, 16 December, https://www.atlanticcouncil.org/in-depth-research-reports/dealmaking-with-china-amid-global-economic-uncertainty-opportunities-risks-and-recommendations-for-latin-america-and-the-caribbean/.

131 MacauHub (2019) 'China has $100 billion to invest in projects in Brazil', 18 November, https://macauhub.com.mo/2019/11/18/pt-china-tem-100-mil-milhoes-de-dolares-para-aplicar-em-projectos-no-brasil/.

132 *South China Morning Post* (2019) 'China part of Brazil's future, Jair Bolsonaro says as he and Xi Jinping sign transport and investment agreements', 14 November, https://www.scmp.com/news/world/americas/article/3037631/china-part-brazils-future-jair-bolsonaro-says-he-and-xi-jinping.

133 Brazil Economia (2020) 'Liberal? Bolsonaro "trava" privatizações de maiores estatais brasileiras', 17 August, https://economia.ig.com.br/2020-08-17/liberal-bolsonaro-trava-privatizacoes-de-maiores-estatais-brasileiras.html.

134 Luciano Nacimento (2019) 'Brazil China agree to deepen exchange, cooperation', *Agencia Brasil*, 29 May, https://agenciabrasil.ebc.com.br/en/internacional/noticia/2019-05/brazil-china-agree-deepen-exchange-cooperation. The New Development Bank (NDB) is also known as the BRICS Bank. In 2021, the NDB launched an expansion drive and was able to increase its membership by 80% in one. Bangladesh, the United Arab Emirates (UAE), Uruguay, and Egypt joined the Bank, see: Mendez, A. (2022) 'The New Development Bank and Uruguay: A Win-Win Deal', Global Policy: Emerging Global Governance Project Available at: https://www.globalpolicyjournal.com/blog/13/06/2022/new-development-bank-and-uruguay-win-win-deal.

135 CEBRI (2019) *Relatório 45 Anos Relações Diplomáticas Brasil-China* (Rio de Janeiro: CEBRI), 5; Daniel Cardoso (2012) 'China-Brazil: a strategic partnership in an evolving world order', *East Asia* 29 (4): 8.

136 Ibid., 8.

137 Ibid.; Ibid., 14.

138 Gary Kavanaugh (2020) 'Chinese "recommendation" backfires as Brazilians rush to congratulate Taiwanese president', *RIPT*, 26 May, https://gript.ie/chinese-recommendation-brazil/.

139 Maricio Santoro (2020) 'Opinion: the Bolsonaros troubled relationship with China', *Diálogo Chino*, 26 March, https://dialogochino.net/en/trade-investment/the-bolsonaros-relationship-with-china-coronavirus/.

140 Pedro da Motta Veiga and Sandra Poilonia Rios (2019) 'China's FDI in Brazil: recent trends and policy debate', *Policy Brief* 19/20, Policy Center for the New South, June, 6; Margaret Myers and Kevin Gallagher (2017) 'Chinese Finance to LAC in 2016', *China-Latin America Report*, The Dialogue/Global Economic Governance Initiative, February, 1.

Chapter 6

1 Fabricio A. Fonseca (2018) 'Looking For a Platform in North America: Taiwan, Mexico and Cross-Strait Relations', *UNISCI Journal* 46 (January).
2 Ana Swanson and Jim Tankersley (2020) 'Trump Just Signed the U.S.M.C.A. Here's What's in the New NAFTA', *The New York Times*, 29 January, https://www.nytimes.com/2020/01/29/business/economy/usmca-deal.html.
3 The CPTPP is a free-trade agreement (FTA) between eleven countries around the Pacific Rim: Canada, Mexico, Peru, Chile, New Zealand, Australia, Brunei, Singapore, Malaysia, Vietnam and Japan. After the US withdrew from the TPP, the remaining eleven countries rapidly amended the text of the agreement to get the TPP going (without the US). Institute for Government (2021) 'Comprehensive and Progressive Agreement for Trans-Pacific Partnership (CPTPP)', published online 2 February, https://www.instituteforgovernment.org.uk/explainers/trade-cptpp.
4 SER (2009) *Manual de Organización de la Embajada de México en Chinaii*, https://sre.gob.mx/images/stories/docnormateca/manexte/embajadas/moemchina.pdf.
5 Ibid.
6 Vanni Pettinà (n.d.) 'Mexican-Soviet Relations 1958–1964: the limits of engagement', e-dossier No. 65, Cold War International History Project, Wilson Center, Washington, DC, https://www.wilsoncenter.org/publication/mexican-soviet-relations-1958-1964-the-limits-engagement.
7 Ibid.
8 Julia Sloan (2009) 'Carnivalising the Cold War: Mexico, the Mexican Revolution and Events of 1968', *European Journal of American Studies* 4 (1) Spring, https://doi.org/10.4000/ejas.7527.
9 Only six binational commission meetings had been held between 2004 and 2019. Government of Mexico (2019) 'Foreign Secretary Marcelo Ebrard concludes visit to China', 2 July, https://www.gob.mx/sre/prensa/foreign-secretary-marcelo-ebrard-concludes-visit-to-china; Government of Mexico (2017) 'Mexico and China strengthen their political dialogue and strategic partnership', 4 May, https://www.gob.mx/sre/en/prensa/mexico-and-china-strengthen-their-political-dialogue-and-strategic-partnership.
10 Liang Xizhi and Chen Yin (2013) 'Interview: Xi's visit to further promote China-Mexico relations: ambassador', Qiushi, 3 June, http://en.people.cn/90883/8268499.html.
11 Romer Cornejo, Francisco Javier Haro Narvejas and Jose Luis Leon-Manriquez (2013) 'Trade Issues and Beyond: Mexican perceptions of contemporary China', *Latin American Policy* 4 (1): 57–75.
12 Maquiladoras being industrial parks on the Mexico-US border which benefited from incentives on investment, labour costs and tariff exemptions. Jorge Alberto Lopez, Oscar Rodil and Saul Valdez (2014) 'The Impact of China's Incursion into the North American Free Trade Agreement (NAFTA) on Intra-Industry Trade', *CEPAL Review* 114. Santiago: Chile, 88.

13. Ibid., 86–7.
14. Roberto Hernandez Hernandez (2012) 'Economic Liberalization and Trade Relations between Mexico and China', *Journal of Current Chinese Affairs* 4 (1): 80.
15. See Eduardo Lora (2005) '¿Debe América Latina temerle a la China?', Documento de Trabajo 536 (IDB).
16. World Bank (2022) 'Mexico Export in Thousand US$ for All Products United States between 1999 and 2012', World Integrated Trade Solution (WITS), https://wits.worldbank.org/CountryProfile/en/Country/MEX/StartYear/1999/EndYear/2012/TradeFlow/Export/Indicator/XPRT-TRD-VL/Partner/USA/Product/Total.
17. Jorge Eduardo Mendoza (2010) 'The Effect of the Chinese Economy on the Mexican Maquiladora Employment', *Journal of International Trade* 24 (1): 64, 74, 77.
18. Ibid., 74–5.
19. World Bank (2022) 'Mexico Product Imports from China in US$ Thousand 2001–2018', World Integrated Trade Solution (WITS), https://wits.worldbank.org/CountryProfile/en/Country/MEX/StartYear/2001/EndYear/2018/TradeFlow/Import/Indicator/MPRT-TRD-VL/Partner/CHN/Product/all-groups; Roberto Hernandez Hernandez (2012) 'Economic Liberalization and Trade Relations between Mexico and China', *Journal of Current Chinese Affairs* 41 (1): 72.
20. Sergio Ley López and Salvador Suárez Zaizar (2020) 'Deal Making with China Amid Global Economic Uncertainty: opportunities, risks and recommendations for Latin America and the Caribbean', Research Report, 16 December, https://www.atlanticcouncil.org/in-depth-research-reports/dealmaking-with-china-amid-global-economic-uncertainty-opportunities-risks-and-recommendations-for-latin-america-and-the-caribbean/.
21. Jorge Alberto Lopez, Oscar Rodil and Saul Valdez (2014) 'The Impact of China's Incursion into the North American Free Trade Agreement (NAFTA) on Intra-Industry Trade', *CEPAL Review* 114. Santiago: Chile, 88.
22. Also see Jorge Dominguez (2006) 'China's Relations with Latin America: Shared Gains, Asymmetric Hopes', Weatherhead Center for International Affairs.
23. M. Colpan, T. Hikino and R. Lincoln (2010) 'The Business Group in Mexico', in T. Hishino (ed.), *Business Groups*, 424–59. Oxford: Oxford University Press.
24. Enrique Dussel Peters and Kevin Gallagher (2013) 'NAFTA's Uninvited Guest: China and the disintegration of North American trade', *CEPAL Review* 110. Santiago: Chile; Jorge Alberto Lopez, Oscar Rodil and Saul Valdez (2014) 'The Impact of China's Incursion into the North American Free Trade Agreement (NAFTA) on Intra-Industry Trade', *CEPAL Review* 114. Santiago: Chile, 93.

25 Roberto Hernandez Hernandez (2012) 'Economic Liberalization and Trade Relations between Mexico and China', *Journal of Current Chinese Affairs* 41 (1): 73.
26 Ibid., 77.
27 IFC (n.d.) 'China-Mexico Fund', https://www.ifcamc.org/funds/china-mexico-fund.
28 Enrique Dussel Peters (2016) 'Chinese Investment in Mexico: the contemporary context and challenges', *Asian Perspective* 40: 632.
29 Enrique Dussel Peters (2011), 'México: hacia una agenda estratégica en el corto, mediano y largo plazo con China. Propuestas resultantes de las labores del Grupo de Trabajo México-China (2009–2010)', Cuadernos de Trabajo del Cechimex Número 1, 2011.
30 Adrián Bonilla and Paz Milet (2015) 'China's Impact on the International Relations of Latin America and the Caribbean', in Adrian Bonilla and Paz Milet (eds), *Latin America, the Caribbean and China: sub-regional scenarios*, 9–20. San José, Costa Rica: FLASCO/CAF.
31 Song Xiaoping (2015) 'China and Latin America in a World in Transition: a Chinese perspective', in Adrian Bonilla and Paz Milet (eds), *Latin America, the Caribbean and China: sub-regional scenarios*, 56. San José, Costa Rica: FLASCO/CAF.
32 Myles Udland (2105) 'The "Made in China" story is falling apart', *Business Insider*, 5 December, https://www.businessinsider.com/cost-of-china-manufacturing-against-brazil-and-mexico-2015-12?r=US&IR=T.
33 Statista (2020) 'Manufacturing labour costs per hour for China, Vietnam, Mexico: 2016–2020', https://www.statista.com/statistics/744071/manufacturing-labor-costs-per-hour-china-vietnam-mexico/; North American Production Sharing, Inc. (2019) 'Mexico versus China manufacturing: how the two countries compare', NAPS International, 30 September, https://napsintl.com/manufacturing-in-mexico/mexico-vs-china-manufacturing-comparison/.
34 Jennifer Alsever (2013) 'Is Mexico the new China?', *INC*, June, https://www.inc.com/magazine/201306/jennifer-alsever/manufacturing-in-mexico.html.
35 Juan Carlos Moreno-Brid (2013) 'Industrial Policy: A Missing Link in Mexico's Quest for Export-led Growth', *Latin American Policy* 4 (2).
36 BBC News (2015), 'Mexico to pay China rail firm for cancelling project', 22 May, https://www.bbc.co.uk/news/business-32840712.
37 *Railway Gazette* (2020) 'Sino-Portuguese consortium to build first section of tren maya network', 28 April, https://www.railwaygazette.com/news/sino-portuguese-consortium-to-build-first-section-of-tren-maya-network/56366.article.
38 VTC (n.d.) 'Special Economic Zones in Mexico', 6–7, 14–17.
39 See, for example, critique levelled by Viridiana Rios (2016) 'Mexico's Special Economic Zones: White Elephants?', Mexico Institute, Woodrow Wilson Institute, 5 July.

40 *Mexico News Daily* (2019) 'Cancelling Special Economic Zones risks losing billions', 28 March, https://mexiconewsdaily.com/news/cancelling-special-economic-zones-risks-losing-billions/.
41 *El Herado de Mexico* (2019) 'Adiós a las zonas económicas', 27 March, https://heraldodemexico.com.mx/economia/2019/3/27/adios-las-zonas-economicas-84311.html.
42 Cecilia Sanchez (2015) 'Mexico halts Chinese megamall project after damage to environment', *Los Angeles Times*, 28 January, https://www.latimes.com/world/mexico-americas/la-fg-mexico-closing-chinese-megamall-20150128-story.html.
43 *Environmental Law Alliance Worldwide* (2017) 'Mega development project in Mexico canceled forever', 20 April, https://elaw.org/mega-development-project-mexico-canceled-forever.
44 Alejandro Gomez Tamez (2018) 'Mexico's Trade Relations with NAFTA partners and with China from the Perspective of the Mexican Footwear Industry', in Enrique Dussel Peters (ed), *The Renegotiation of NAFTA and China?*, 77–8. Mexico City: UNAM.
45 Sergio Ley López and Salvador Suárez Zaizar (2020) 'Dealmaking with China Amid Global Economic Uncertainty: opportunities, risks and recommendations for Latin America and the Caribbean', Research Report, 16 December, https://www.atlanticcouncil.org/in-depth-research-reports/dealmaking-with-china-amid-global-economic-uncertainty-opportunities-risks-and-recommendations-for-latin-america-and-the-caribbean/.
46 *El Universal* (2019) 'Corona comienza a producirse fuera de México', 10 October, https://www.eluniversal.com.mx/cartera/corona-comienza-producirse-fuera-de-mexico; *Just Drinks* (2019) 'Anheuser-Busch Inbev takes Corona production out of Mexico with China move', 18 October, https://www.just-drinks.com/news/anheuser-busch-inbev-takes-corona-production-out-of-mexico-with-china-move-analyst_id129533.aspx.
47 Roberto Hernandez Hernandez (2012) 'Economic Liberalization and Trade Relations between Mexico and China', *Journal of Current Chinese Affairs* 41 (1): 77.
48 Luis Fernando Lozano (2020) 'Cómo Bimbo Se Convirtió En La Segunda Panificadora En China', *Forbes Mexico*, 14 January, https://www.forbes.com.mx/como-bimbo-se-convirtio-en-la-segunda-panificadora-en-china/.
49 Mexico Now (2018) 'Nuevo Leon based Katcon to open three plants in China, US', 30 April, https://mexico-now.com/nuevo-leon-based-katcon-to-open-three-plants-in-china-us/.
50 Henny Sender (2015) 'Group Alfa close to $6.5 bn buyout of Pacifico Rubiales', *Financial Times*, 20 May, https://www.ft.com/content/7a3248b8-feb8-11e4-84b2-00144feabdc0.
51 *El Pais* (2015) 'Campofrío se queda solo en manos mexicanas: Sigma controla el 100 per cent', 4 June, https://elpais.com/economia/2015/06/04/actualidad/1433415167_987852.html.

52 Roberto Hernandez Hernandez (2012) 'Economic Liberalization and Trade Relations between Mexico and China', *Journal of Current Chinese Affairs* 41 (1): 77.
53 Barbara Taylor et al. (2017) 'Extinction is imminent for Mexico's endemic porpoise unless fishery bycatch is eliminated', *Conservation Letters* September/October 10 (5): 588–95.
54 Rebecca Wong (2019) *The Illegal Wildlife Trade in China: understanding the distribution networks*. Basingstoke: Palgrave, 50–1; *CBS News* (2019) 'Violent battle playing out to save vaquitas, the world's most endangered porpoise', 7 March, https://www.cbsnews.com/news/vaquitas-endangered-battle-sea-of-cortez-mexico-baja-california-sea-shepherd/.
55 Alejandro Gomez Tamez (2018) 'Mexico's Trade Relations with NAFTA Partners and with China from the Perspective of the Mexican Footwear Industry', in Enrique Dussel Peters (ed.), *The Renegotiation of NAFTA and China?*, 73. Mexico City: UNAM.
56 Jack Caporal and William Reinsch (2018) 'From NAFTA to USMCA: what's new and what's next?', CSIS Briefing, 3 October, https://www.csis.org/analysis/nafta-usmca-whats-new-and-whats-next; ' *El Financiero* (2017) 'AMLO gana y se queda T-MEC como nombre para aquerdo comercial trilateral', 17 October, https://www.elfinanciero.com.mx/economia/amlo-gana-y-se-queda-t-mec-como-nombre-para-acuerdo-comercial.
57 *Reuters* (2017) 'China open to free trade agreement with Mexico: Xinhua', 29 June, https://www.reuters.com/article/us-china-mexico-trade-idUSKBN19K01Z.
58 Ministry of Foreign Affairs, PRC (2017) 'Xi Jinping meets with President Enrique Pena Nieto of Mexico', 4 September, https://www.fmprc.gov.cn/mfa_eng/zxxx_662805/t1490482.shtml.
59 *Reuters* (2020) 'Foxconn, other Asian firms consider Mexico as China risks grow', 24 August, https://www.reuters.com/article/us-mexico-china-factories-exclusive-idUSKBN25K17X.
60 Chris Ludwig (2017) 'Mexico's Giant Motors to build and export Chinese SUVs beyond NAFTA', *Automotive Logistics*, 29 March, https://www.automotivelogistics.media/mexicos-giant-motors-to-build-and-export-chinese-suvs-beyond-nafta/17889.article; also see Sergio Ley López and Salvador Suárez Zaizar (2020) 'Deal Making with China Amid Global Economic Uncertainty: opportunities, risks and recommendations for Latin America and the Caribbean', Research Report, 16 December, https://www.atlanticcouncil.org/in-depth-research-reports/dealmaking-with-china-amid-global-economic-uncertainty-opportunities-risks-and-recommendations-for-latin-america-and-the-caribbean/.
61 *Mazatlan Post* (2020) 'At least 10 companies from China seek to move to Mexico every month', 20 February, https://themazatlanpost.com/2020/02/20/at-least-10-companies-from-china-seek-to-move-to-

mexico-every-month/; TECMA (n.d.) 'Why is China manufacturing moving to Mexico?', https://www.tecma.com/china-manufacturing-moving-to-mexicowhy-is-chinese-manufacturing-moving-to-mexico/.
62 Shaun Polczer (2018) 'USMCA designed to keep Canada from China's orbit', *Petroleum Economist*, 9 November, http://admin.pemedianetwork.com/petroleum-economist/articles/geopolitics/2018/usmca-designed-to-keep-canada-from-china-s-orbit; José Carlos Ramírez Sánchez and Ricardo Massa Roldán (2020) 'Mexico's Energy Regulatory Reform in the Context of a New Trilateral Agreement (NAFTA-USMCA)', *The International Trade Journal* 34 (1): 55–73.
63 Ann Deslandes (2020) 'Ganfeng announces lithium battery recycling plant in Mexico', *Diálogo Chino*, 2 December.
64 Pablo Hernandez (2019) 'Mexico exports sorghum to China amidst national crisis', *Diálogo Chino*, 12 June.
65 Daina Beth Solomon (2018) 'Mexico far from goal on Alibaba e-commerce deal: official', *Reuters*, 24 August.
66 *Agencia EFE* (2020) 'GINgroup firma convenio con Alibaba.com "Atomic88", para generar nuevos líderes de transformación digital', 28 August, https://www.efe.com/efe/cono-sur/comunicados/gingroup-firma-convenio-con-alibaba-com-atomic88-para-generar-nuevos-lideres-de-transformacion-digital/50000772-MULTIMEDIAE_4330213.
67 Haibin Niu (2018) 'A Strategic Analysis of Chinese Infrastructure Projects in Latin America and the *Caribbean*', in Enrique Dussel Peters et al. (eds), *Building Development for a New Era: China's infrastructure projects in Latin America and the Caribbean*, 180–94. Pittsburgh, PA: University of Pittsburgh. Also see Jorge Blazquez-Lidoy, Jorge Rodriguez and Javier Santiso (2006) 'Angel or Devil? China's Trade Impact on Latin American Emerging Markets', OECD Development Centre Working Papers, No. 252, OECD Publishing, Paris, https://doi.org/10.1787/422232033888.

Chapter 7

1 ECLAC (2005) *Foreign Investment in Latin America and the Caribbean 2005*, 23–6.
2 *Jamaica Observer* (2018) 'China looks towards deepening trade with CARICOM', 23 January, http://www.jamaicaobserver.com/latestnews/China_looks_towards_deepening_trade_with_CARICOM?profile=1228.
3 Mark Wenner and Dillon Clarke (2016) 'China's Rise in the Caribbean: what does it mean for Caribbean stakeholders?' Inter-American Development Bank, Technical Note No. IDB-TN 1073, Washington, DC, July, 6–7.
4 Richard Bernal (2016) 'Chinese Foreign Direct Investment in the Caribbean: potential and prospects', Inter-American Development Bank, Technical Note No. IDB-TN 1113, Washington, DC, July, 7–8.

5   *Wikileaks* (2009) Charge d'Affairs, Zuniga-Brown, US Embassy, 'China offers "golden opportunities" to the Bahamas', 15 September, 090Nassau560_a; *Wikileaks* (2009) Charge d'Affairs, Zuniga-Brown, US Embassy, 'China agrees to finance resort projects in the Bahamas', 19 March, 090Nassau180_a.
6   *The Habari Network* (2019) 'Grenada considers adopting Chinese development plan', 11 January, http://www.thehabarinetwork.com/grenada-considers-adopting-chinese-development-blueprint.
7   Stephen Chen (2017) 'China set to move into United States' backyard with national development plan for Grenada', *South China Morning Post*, 19 December, https://www.scmp.com/news/china/diplomacy-defence/article/2124925/china-set-move-united-states-backyard-national; also see excerpt from radio interview with the prime minister, *The Barnacle News* (2018) 'PM Mitchell: China's National Development Plan for Grenada was in response to request for help', 6 February, https://www.thebarnaclenews.com/pm-mitchell-chinas-national-development-plan-grenada-response-request-help/.
8   The Belt Road Initiative (BRI) president is Xi Jinping's co-prosperity plan, which was initially announced as the Silk Road Belt in September 2013 in Kazakhstan. For a detailed discussion on how the BRI was extended to Latin America, see Álvaro Méndez and Chris Alden (2021) 'China in Panama: From Peripheral Diplomacy to Grand Strategy', *Geopolitics* 26 (3): 838–60.
9   Zhou Yongchen, China's Ambassador to Grenada (2019) 'Belt and Road Initiative outlines blueprint: China-Grenada cooperation embraces new opportunity', Embassy of the People's Republic of Grenada, 5 February, http://gd.china-embassy.org/eng/gywm_1/dsjhjwz/t1660231.htm.
10 R. Evan Ellis (2019) 'China's Engagement in Trinidad and Tobago', *Global Americans*, 26 March, https://theglobalamericans.org/2019/03/chinas-engagement-with-trinidad-and-tobago/.
11 Richard Bernal (2015) 'The Growing Economic Presence of China in the Caribbean', *The World Economy*, 1429, https://onlinelibrary.wiley.com/doi/pdf/10.1111/twec.12204?casa_token=8iVDNAeQF0UAAAAA:aGUH2xP3yIoGff1yh_ppLP87yNlLNUB6lKInPkWuvyhH5wcGlPHEduNlzY181ncA0nX48tET7Cyz6yY.
12 Richard Bernal (2010) 'The Dragon in the Caribbean: China-CARICOM Economic Relations', *The Round Table* 99 (408): 289. See also Gaston Fornes and Álvaro Méndez (2018) *The China-Latin America Axis: Emerging Markets and their Role in an Increasingly Globalised World*, 2nd edn. London: Palgrave Macmillan.
13 Richard Bernal (2015) 'The Growing Economic Presence of China in the Caribbean', *The World Economy*, 1409–37, https://onlinelibrary.wiley.com/doi/pdf/10.1111/twec.12204?casa_token=8iVDNAeQF0UAAAAA:aGUH2xP3yIoGff1yh_ppLP87yNlLNUB6lKInPkWuvyhH5wcGlPHEduNlzY181ncA0nX48tET7Cyz6yY.

14. R. Evan Ellis (2019) 'China's Engagement in Trinidad and Tobago', *Global Americans*, 26 March, https://theglobalamericans.org/2019/03/chinas-engagement-with-trinidad-and-tobago/.
15. Nicholas Muller (2019) 'Nicaragua's Chinese-financed canal project still in limbo', *The Diplomat*, 20 August, https://thediplomat.com/2019/08/nicaraguas-chinese-financed-canal-project-still-in-limbo/.
16. Annita Montoute (2013) 'Caribbean-China Economic Relations: what are the implications? *Caribbean Journal of International Relations and Diplomacy* 1 (1): 121.
17. Richard Bernal (2010) 'The Dragon in the Caribbean: China-CARICOM Economic Relations', *The Round Table* 99 (408): 289–90.
18. Mark Wenner and Dillon Clarke (2016) 'China's Rise in the Caribbean: what does it mean for Caribbean stakeholders?' Inter-American Development Bank, Technical Note No. IDB-TN 1073, Washington, DC, July, 7; Neil Hartnell (2020) 'Judge slams CCA over Sarkis papers', *The Tribune*, 10 November, http://m.tribune242.com/news/2020/nov/10/judge-slams-cca-over-sarkis-papers/. Also see Muhammed Cohen (n.d.) 'How China Rescued – then ruined – the [not just the Bahamas] but the Caribbean's largest resort project – the Baha Mar a 1,000-acre resort complex on the island of New Providence in the Bahamas, close to its capital Nassau', *Forbes*, https://www.abacoescape.com/China/BahaMar.html.
19. Rashad Rolle (2020) 'Pointe's Chinese workers fly home', *The Tribune*, 13 October, http://m.tribune242.com/news/2020/oct/13/pointes-chinese-workers-fly-home/.
20. Jared Ward (2019) 'China's Presence in the Bahamas: a greater role after Hurricane Dorian?' *China Brief* 19 (20), Jamestown Foundation, http://jamestown.org/program/chinas-presence-in-the-bahamas-a-greater-role-after-hurricane-dorian/.
21. Mckinsey (2018) *Chinese Tourists: dispelling the myth: an in-depth look at China's outbound tourist market*, https://www.mckinsey.com/~/media/mckinsey/industries/travel%20logistics%20and%20infrastructure/our%20insights/huanying%20to%20the%20new%20chinese%20traveler/chinese-tourists-dispelling-the-myths.pdf.
22. Richard Bernal (2010) 'The Dragon in the Caribbean: China-CARICOM Economic Relations', *The Round Table* 99 (408): 295; Mordechai Chaziza (2019) 'China in the Middle East: tourism as a stealth weapon', *Middle East Quarterly* 26 (4): 1–8.
23. Caribbean Council (2014) 'Is the Chinese tourism market illusory?', https://www.caribbean-council.org/chinese-tourism-market-illusory-2/.
24. Mckinsey (2018) *Chinese Tourists: dispelling the myth: an in-depth look at China's outbound tourist market*, https://www.mckinsey.com/~/media/mckinsey/industries/travel%20logistics%20and%20infrastructure/our%20insights/huanying%20to%20the%20new%20chinese%20traveler/chinese-tourists-dispelling-the-myths.pdf.

25 Darren Lim, Victor Ferguson and Rosa Bishop (2020) 'Chinese Outbound Tourism as an Instrument of Chinese Statecraft', *Journal of Contemporary China* 29 (126): 916–33; Anu Anwar (2019) 'How China is using tourists to realise its geopolitical goals', East Asia Forum, 19 September, https://www.eastasiaforum.org/2019/09/19/how-china-is-using-tourists-to-realise-its-geopolitical-goals/; Mordechai Chaziza (2019) 'China in the Middle East: tourism as a stealth weapon', *Middle East Quarterly* 26 (4): 8.

26 *The Gleaner* (2019) 'Caribbean urged to tap Chinese market', 1 February, http://jamaica-gleaner.com/article/news/20190201/caribbean-urged-tap-chinese-tourism-market.

27 Muhammed Cohen (n.d.) 'How China Rescued – then ruined – the [not just the Bahamas] but the Caribbean's largest resort project – the Baha Mar a 1,000-acre resort complex on the island of New Providence in the Bahamas, close to its capital Nassau', *Forbes*, https://www.abacoescape.com/China/BahaMar.html.

28 Richard Bernal (2010) 'The Dragon in the Caribbean: China-CARICOM Economic Relations', *The Round Table* 99 (408): 281–302.

29 Ministry of Foreign Affairs (2005) 'Zeng Quinghong attends "China-Caribbean Economic and Trade Cooperation Forum" and delivers speech', Beijing, PRC, 3 February, http://ee.china-embassy.org/eng/dtxw/t184238.htm; Richard Bernal (2010) 'The Dragon in the Caribbean: China-CARICOM Economic Relations', *The Round Table* 99 (408): 283.

30 Yuan Li (2015) *Dominican Republic and P.R. China: exchange, trade and investment*. Washington, DC: GFDD, 28.

31 OECD/ECLAC/CAF (2015) *Latin American Economic Outlook 2016: towards a new partnership with China*. Paris: OECD, 102.

32 Richard Bernal (2010) 'The Dragon in the Caribbean: China-CARICOM Economic Relations', *The Round Table* 99 (408): 294.

33 Richard Bernal (2015) 'The Growing Economic Presence of China in the Caribbean', *The World Economy*, 1414–19.

34 Farhan Haq (1997) 'The Veto: a Case Study – The China Veto and the Guatemala Peace Process', Global Policy Forum, https://archive.globalpolicy.org/security-council/39935-the-veto-a-case-study.html.

35 Johanna Mendelson Forman and Susanna Moreira (2008) 'Taiwan-China Balancing Act in Latin America', *ARI* 154, Real Instituto Elcano, 26 November, 2.

36 Taiwan Commercial Guide website (n.d.) 'Taiwan trade agreements', https://www.export.gov/article?id=Taiwan-Trade-Agreements.

37 Gabriel Aguilera Peralta (2010) 'Central America between Two Dragons: relations with the Two Chinas', in Alex Fernandez Jilberto and Barbara Hoegnboom (eds), *Latin America Facing China*, 173–4. Oxford and New York, NY: Berghahn Books.

38 Ibid., 170.

39 Ibid.

40 Nicaragua has moved to recognize the PRC as the only legitimate China. They had done that already in 1985 and re-switched to Taiwan in 1990; see Álvaro Méndez (2021) 'Beijing and Taipei: The Latin American Geopolitical Connection', China Africa Project, published online 17 December, https://chinaafricaproject.com/analysis/beijing-and-taipei-the-latin-american-geopolitical-connection/.

41 *Taipei Times* (2019) 'Government confirms US$100 loan to Nicaragua', 21 February, https://www.taipeitimes.com/News/taiwan/archives/2019/02/21/2003710135.

42 Gabriel Aguilera Peralta (2010) 'Central America between Two Dragons: relations with the Two Chinas', in Alex Fernandez Jilberto and Barbara Hoegnboom (eds), *Latin America Facing China*, 174. Oxford and New York, NY: Berghahn Books.

43 Currently there are eight countries in Latin America that still recognize Taiwan diplomatically. This is more than 50 per cent of all countries that recognize Taipei globally. These countries are the following: Belize, Guatemala, Haiti, Honduras, Paraguay, Saint Lucia, St. Kitts and Nevis, St. Vincent and the Grenadines; see Álvaro Méndez (2021) 'Geopolitics in Central America: China and El Salvador in the 21st Century', in Thierry Kellner and Sophie Wintgens (eds), *China-Latin America and the Caribbean: Assessment and Outlook*, 207–21. Abingdon, UK: Routledge.

44 Interview with senior Costa Rican minister, May 2017; Colin R. Anderson (2014) *China and Taiwan in Central America: engaging foreign publics in diplomacy*. Basingstoke: Palgrave, footnote 3, 205.

45 Johanna Mendelson Forman and Susanna Moreira (2008) 'Taiwan-China Balancing Act in Latin America', *ARI* 154, Real Instituto Elcano, 26 November, 3.

46 Gabriel Aguilera Peralta (2010) 'Central America between Two Dragons: relations with the Two Chinas', in Alex Fernandez Jilberto and Barbara Hoegnboom (eds), *Latin America Facing China*, 171. Oxford and New York, NY: Berghahn Books.

47 Czeslaw Tubilewicz and Alain Guilloux (2011) 'Does Size Matter? Foreign aid in Taiwan's diplomatic strategy, 2000-2008', *Australian Journal of International Affairs* 65 (3): 326; Liu Shih-chung (2008) 'Now Ma must find a diplomatic strategem', *Tapei Times*, 17 May, https://www.taipeitimes.com/News/editorials/archives/2008/05/17/2003412212.

48 Czeslaw Tubilewicz and Alain Guilloux (2011) 'Does Size Matter? Foreign aid in Taiwan's diplomatic strategy, 2000–2008', *Australian Journal of International Affairs* 65(3): 334. Other sources report $122 million in economic assistance over six years; see Kerry Dumbaugh and Mark Sullivan (2005) 'China's Growing Interest in Latin America', CSIS Report for Congress, 20 April, 4.

49 Gabriel Aguilera Peralta (2010) 'Central America between Two Dragons: relations with the Two Chinas', in Alex Fernandez Jilberto and Barbara Hoegnboom (eds), *Latin America Facing China*, 168. Oxford and New York, NY: Berghahn Books.
50 Lowell Dittmer (2017) 'Taiwan and the Waning Dream of Reunification', in Lowell Dittmer (ed.), *Taiwan and China: fitful embrace*, 209. Berkley, CA: University of California Press; Czeslaw Tubilewicz and Alain Guilloux (2011) 'Does Size Matter? Foreign aid in Taiwan's diplomatic strategy, 2000–2008', *Australian Journal of International Affairs* 65 (3): 322–3.
51 Interview by the authors with Leonel Fernandez, former president of the Dominican Republic: 1996–2000, 2004–2012, 16 January 2016. London, UK.
52 *Financial Times* (2019) 'El Salvador halts Taiwan FTA cancellation as China ties probed', 14 March, https://www.ft.com/content/cfe52d72-45ed-11e9-b168-96a37d002cd3.
53 OECD/ECLAC/CAF (2015) *Latin American Economic Outlook 2016: towards a new partnership with China*. Paris: OECD, 102.
54 Ignacio Gonzalez Siles, Johan Espinoza Rojas and Andres Mendez Marnco (2016) '"El Silicon Valley Latinoamericano?" La produccion de Technologia de Comunicaion en Costa Rica (1950–2016)', *Anuario de Estudios Centroamericanos* 42: 411–41.
55 Ibid., 414–17.
56 Jaime Lopez (2014) 'Exit Costa Rica: the beginning of the end for Intel?', *The Costa Rica Star*, 10 April, https://news.co.cr/exit-costa-rica-the-beginning-of-the-end-for-intel/34260/; *The Tico Times* (2014) 'Intel to close Costa Rica chip assembly plant, lay off 1,500 workers', 8 April, http://ticotimes.net/2014/04/08/intel-to-close-costa-rica-chip-assembly-plant-lay-off-1500-workers.
57 Gabriel Aguilera Peralta (2010) 'Central America between Two Dragons: relations with the Two Chinas', in Alex Fernandez Jilberto and Barbara Hoegnboom (eds), *Latin America Facing China*, 175. Oxford and New York, NY: Berghahn Books.
58 Alex Leff (2011) 'Costa Rica inches towards coveted APEC membership', *Americas Quarterly*, 22 June.
59 Interview by the authors with Bruno Stagno, Minister of Foreign Affairs of Costa Rica from 2006 to 2010, 4 May 2017, San José, Costa Rica.
60 Ibid.
61 Johanna Mendelson Forman and Susanna Moreira (2008) 'Taiwan-China Balancing Act in Latin America', *ARI* 154, Real Instituto Elcano, 26 November, 1.

62 Czeslaw Tubilewicz and Alain Guilloux (2011) 'Does Size Matter? Foreign aid in Taiwan's diplomatic strategy, 2000–2008', *Australian Journal of International Affairs* 65 (3): 332–3.
63 Colin R. Anderson (2014) *China and Taiwan in Central America: engaging foreign publics in diplomacy*. Basingstoke: Palgrave, footnote 28, 208.
64 Daniel Erikson and Janice Chen (2007) 'China, Taiwan and the Battle for Latin America', *The Fletcher Forum of World Affairs* 31 (2): 69–89.
65 Monica Dehart (2012) 'Remodeling the Global Development Landscape: the China Model and South-South Cooperation in Latin America', *Third World Quarterly* 33 (7): 1362, 1369–70. Also see Monica Dehart (2018) 'The Impact of Chinese Anti-Corruption Policies in Costa Rica: emerging entrepreneurialism', *Journal of Latin American Geography* 17 (2).
66 Zhiqun Zhu (2013) *China's New Diplomacy: rationale, strategies and significance*, 2nd edn. Farnham, UK: Ashgate Publishing Ltd, 188; Andrew Baston (2008) 'China used reserves to sway Costa Rica', *Wall Street Journal*, 13 September, https://www.wsj.com/articles/SB122121919505927749.
67 *UN News* (2007) 'Five non-permanent Security Council members elected for seats starting next year', 16 October, https://news.un.org/en/story/2007/10/236062-five-non-permanent-security-council-members-elected-seats-starting-next-year.
68 Sophie Wintgrens (2018) 'China's Increasing Presence in Costa Rica and Nicaragua: from strategic issues to national impacts', conference paper, May.
69 Alex Leff (2011) 'Costa Rica inches towards coveted APEC membership', *Americas Quarterly*, 22 June.
70 Richard Harris (2015) 'China's Relations with the Latin American and Caribbean Countries: peaceful panda bear instead of a roaring dragon', *Latin American Perspectives* 42 (6): 173; OECD/ECLAC/CAF (2015) *Latin American Economic Outlook 2016: towards a new partnership with China*. Paris: OECD, 124.
71 Richard Harris (2015) 'China's Relations with the Latin American and Caribbean Countries: peaceful panda bear instead of a roaring dragon', *Latin American Perspectives* 42 (6): 173.
72 For a comprehensive view of the projects of San José and Beijing, see Monica DeHart (2018) 'China-Costa Rica Infrastructure Projects', in E. Dussel Peters, Ariel Armony and Shoujun Cui (eds), *Building Development for a New Era? China's Infrastructure Projects in Latin America and the Caribbean*, 3–23. Asian Studies Center at University of Pittsburgh Center for International Studies.
73 Interview by the authors with Bruno Stagno, Minister of Foreign Affairs of Costa Rica from 2006 to 2010, 4 May 2017, San José, Costa Rica. The visa regulations stipulated that if you had a US, Canadian or Schengen visa, you could automatically travel to Costa Rica under the same restrictions.

74 Richard Harris (2015) 'China's Relations with the Latin American and Caribbean Countries: peaceful panda bear instead of a roaring dragon', *Latin American Perspectives* 42 (6): 174.
75 *Tico Times* (2013) 'Costa Rica, China sign cooperation agreements worth nearly $2 billion', 1 June, https://ticotimes.net/2013/06/02/costa-rica-china-sign-cooperation-agreements-worth-nearly-2-billion.
76 Interview by the authors with Oscar Arias, president of Costa Rica 1966–1990, 2006–2010, 22 November 2017, San José, Costa Rica.
77 See John Booth (2008) 'Democratic Development in Costa Rica', *Democratization*, 15 (4): 714–32; also John Booth and Mitchel Seligsen (2005) 'Political Legitimacy and Participation in Costa Rica: evidence of arena shopping', *Political Research Quarterly* 58 (4): 537–50.
78 Diego Arguedes Ortiz (2014) 'Oil alliance between China and Costa Rica comes to life again', *Inter Press Service*, 30 July, http://www.ipsnews.net/2014/07/oil-alliance-between-china-and-costa-rica-comes-to-life-again/.
79 Ibid.
80 Interview by the authors with Oscar Arias, president of Costa Rica 1966–1990, 2006–2010, 22 November 2017, San José, Costa Rica.
81 Procomer (2010), cited in Colin R. Anderson (2014) *China and Taiwan in Central America: engaging foreign publics in diplomacy*. Basingstoke: Palgrave, footnote 5.
82 R. Evan Ellis (2014) *China on the Ground in Latin America: Challenges for the Chinese and Impacts on the Region*. London: Palgrave Macmillan.
83 Interview by one of the authors with Marco Vinicio Ruiz, Foreign Trade Minister of Costa Rica 2006–2010, 22 November 2017, San José, Costa Rica. See also Maria Cecilia Calello and Huey-Rong Chen (2013) 'Taiwan, China and Central American Allies: a discourse analysis of the Costa Rican diplomatic shift news coverage', *Taiwan International Studies Quarterly* 9(1): 139–78, 147.
84 Gregory T. Chin and Kevin P. Gallagher (2019) 'Coordinated Credit Spaces: The Globalization of Chinese Development Finance', *Development and Change* 50 (1): 250.
85 Kevin Gallagher (2020) 'Chinese Development Finance in the Americas', in Diana Barraclough, Kevin Gallagher and Richard Kozul-Wright (eds), *Southern-Led Development Finance: Solutions from the Global South*, 123–2, London: Routledge.
86 Interview by one of the authors with Marco Vinicio Ruiz, Foreign Trade Minister of Costa Rica 2006–2010, 22 November 2017, San José, Costa Rica.
87 *South China Morning Post* (2015) 'Chinese firms gain foothold in Costa Rica under new agreement', 7 January, www.scmp.com/news/china/article/1675976/china-costa-rica-agree-strengthen-ties.

88 Council on Hemispheric Affairs (2008) 'Costa Rica's Arias surprises no one by turning his back on the Dali Lama', 21 August, http://www.coha.org/costa-ricas-arias-surprises-no-one-by-turning-his-back-on-the-dalai-lama/.
89 Matt Youkee (2019) 'The Panama Canal could become the center of the U.S.-China trade war', *Foreign Policy*, 27 May, https://foreignpolicy.com/2019/05/07/the-panama-canal-could-become-the-center-of-the-u-s-china-trade-war/.
90 Keith Wallis (1997) 'Hutchinson completes Panama Canal deal', *South China Morning Post*, 4 March, https://www.scmp.com/article/186992/hutchison-completes-panama-canal-deal. Hutchinson-Whampoa moved into telecommunications in a joint venture with Cable and Wireless and CITI in 1990.
91 See, for example, Richard DelGaudio (1998) *Peril in Panama: China as the gatekeeper of the Panama Canal threatens new missile crisis*. Washington, DC: National Security Centre. For a defence of the Carter-Torrijos deal, see Thomas McNamara (1999) 'The phony China scare in Panama', *Washington Post*, 11 November, https://www.washingtonpost.com/wp-srv/WPcap/1999-11/11/016r-111199-idx.html.
92 Johanna Mendelson Forman and Susanna Moreira (2008) 'Taiwan-China Balancing Act in Latin America', *ARI* 154, Real Instituto Elcano, 26 November, 1.
93 Author's conversation with Juan Carlos Varela, president of Panama 2014–2019, 15 May 2018, London, UK; also see Evan Ellis (2018) 'The evolution of Panama-PRC Relations since recognition and their strategic implications for the US and the region', *Global Americans*, 21 September, https://theglobalamericans.org/2018/09/the-evolution-of-panama-prc-relations-since-recognition-and-their-strategic-implications-for-the-u-s-and-the-region/.
94 China.org.cn (2015) 'Huawei opens Latin American distribution center in Panama', 2 October, http://www.china.org.cn/world/Off_the_Wire/2015-10/02/content_36731925.htm; Enrique Dussel Peters (2016) 'Chinese Investment in Mexico: the contemporary context and challenges', *Asian Perspective* 40: 632.
95 Huawei (2017) 'President of Panama meeting in Beijing', 18 November, https://www.huawei.com/en/news/2017/11/president-panama-meeting-beijing.
96 *The Guardian* (2017) 'Panama cuts diplomatic ties with Taiwan in favour of China', 13 June, https://www.theguardian.com/world/2017/jun/13/panama-cuts-diplomatic-ties-with-taiwan-in-favour-of-china.
97 R. Evan Ellis (2019) 'China's Engagement in Trinidad and Tobago', *Global Americans*, 26 March, https://theglobalamericans.org/2019/03/chinas-engagement-with-trinidad-and-tobago/.
98 Álvaro Méndez (2018) 'Panama could soon become China's gateway to Latin America thanks to an imminent free trade agreement', LSE Blogs, 5 December, https://blogs.lse.ac.uk/latamcaribbean/2018/12/05/panama-could-soon-become-chinas-gateway-to-latin-america-thanks-to-an-imminent-free-trade-agreement/.

99 *Global Construction Review* (2017) 'Panama deal likely to finally "scupper" Nicaragua canal: Chinese state media', 26 June, http://www.globalconstructionreview.com/news/panama-deal-likely-fin7ally-scup7per-nicaragua/.
100 Álvaro Méndez and Chris Alden (2021) 'China in Panama: From Peripheral Diplomacy to Grand Strategy', *Geopolitics* 26 (3): 838838–60, doi: 10.1080/14650045.2019.1657413; Elido Morena (2018) 'Panama, China sign accords on Xi visit after diplomatic ties start', *Reuters*, 3 December, https://www.reuters.com/article/us-panama-china/panama-china-sign-accords-on-xi-visit-after-diplomatic-ties-start-IdUSKBN1O22PE.
101 Interview by the authors with Nestor Gonzalez, Vice-Minister of Foreign Trade of Panama 2014–2018, 8 May 2018, Panama City, Panama.
102 *Agencia EFE* (2019) 'China estimates cost of Panama high speed rail line at $4.1 bn', 15 March, https://www.efe.com/efe/english/business/china-estimates-cost-of-panama-high-speed-rail-line-at-4-1-bn/50000265-3926478.
103 *Hong Kong Free Press* (2018) 'Panama awards China $1.4 billion to build bridge for Belt and Road Initiative', 5 December, https://www.hongkongfp.com/2018/12/05/panama-awards-china-us1-4-billion-build-bridge-belt-road-initiative/.
104 Zawya (2018) 'Destination Dragon Mart as Nakheel hosts President of the Republic of Panama', 28 February, https://www.zawya.com/en/press-release/destination-dragon-mart-as-nakheel-hosts-president-of-the-republic-of-panama-during-visit-to-the-uae-nzkto5co
105 Interview by the authors with Nestor Gonzalez, Vice-Minister of Foreign Trade of Panama 2014–2018, 8 May 2018, Panama City, Panama.
106 Proponents like Varela argued for its 'social profitability'. *Agencia EFE* (2019) 'China estimates cost of Panama high speed rail line at $4.1 bn', 15 March, https://www.efe.com/efe/english/business/china-estimates-cost-of-panama-high-speed-rail-line-at-4-1-bn/50000265-3926478.
107 Will Fitzgibbon and M. Hudson (2021) 'Five years later, Panama Papers still having a big impact', International Consortium of Investigative Journalists, 3 April, https://www.icij.org/investigations/panama-papers/five-years-later-panama-papers-still-having-a-big-impact/.
108 Elida Moreno (2019) 'Panama's new president takes office, pledges end to corruption', *Reuters*, 1 July, https://www.reuters.com/article/us-panama-politics-idUSKCN1TW3ZN.
109 Matt Youkee (2020) 'Has China's winning streak in Panama ended?', *Diálogo Chino*, 25 March, https://dialogochino.net/en/trade-investment/34472-has-chinas-winning-streak-in-panama-ended/.
110 *Panamá América* (2020) 'Gobierno anuncia a Panama Ports que la auditará', 2 December, https://www.panamaamerica.com.pa/nacion/gobierno-anuncia-panama-ports-que-la-auditara-1156287.

111 Matt Youkee (2020) 'Has China's winning streak in Panama ended?', *Diálogo Chino*, 25 March, https://dialogochino.net/en/trade-investment/34472-has-chinas-winning-streak-in-panama-ended/.
112 See Patrick Bryan (2004) 'The Settlement of the Chinese in Jamaica: 1854–c.1970', *Caribbean Quarterly* 50 (2): 15–25.
113 Jacqueline Levy (1986) 'The Economic Role of the Chinese in Jamaica: the grocery retail trade', *Jamaican Historical Review* 15: 31–49.
114 Howard Johnson (1982) 'The Anti-Chinese Riots in Jamaica in 1918', *Caribbean Quarterly* 28 (3):19–32; Patrick Bryan (2004) 'The Settlement of the Chinese in Jamaica: 1854–c.1970', *Caribbean Quarterly* 50 (2): 17–19.
115 Jake Johnston (2013) *The Multilateral Debt Trap in Jamaica*, Centre for Economic and Policy Research, Issue Brief, June, 1.
116 International Monetary Fund (2019) 'Jamaica and the IMF: the power of partnership and ownership', *IMF Lending Case: Jamaica*, May, https://www.imf.org/en/Countries/JAM/jamaica-lending-case-study.
117 World Bank (2021) 'Jamaican Product Exports and Imports to China 2000; and 2017', World Integrated Trade Solution (WITS).
118 OEC World (2017) 'What does China import from Jamaica (2017)', https://oec.world/en/visualize/tree_map/hs92/import/chn/jam/show/2017/.
119 Dionne Rose (2010) 'COMPLANT to build Jamaican homes backed by J$6.5b Chinese loan', *Jamaica Gleaner*, 5 December, https://gleaner.newspaperarchive.com/kingston-gleaner/2010-12-05/page-31/.
120 Dong Xiaojun (2015) 'Jamaica, China must seize moment for industry links', *Jamaica Gleaner*, 19 June, https://jamaica-gleaner.com/article/focus/20150621/jamaica-china-must-seize-moment-industry-links.
121 Tiffany Foxcroft (2019) 'Jamaica has China to thank for much-needed infrastructure – but some locals say it has come at a price' *CBC: Radio-Canada*, 28 November, https://www.cbc.ca/news/world/china-power-belt-and-road-caribbean-jamaica-1.5374967.
122 Jake Johnston (2013) *The Multilateral Debt Trap in Jamaica*, Centre for Economic and Policy Research, Issue Brief, June, 1. Simpson Miller's government ultimately privatized the Kingston Container Terminal and handed it over to CMA-CGM group, a French consortium, to manage.
123 Andrea Braham (2013) 'Jamaica and China sign four agreements', *Jamaica Information Service*, 21 August, https://jis.gov.jm/jamaica-and-china-sign-four-agreements/.
124 Dong Xiaojun, China's ambassador to Jamaica (2015) 'China's Role in Jamaica: no strings attached', *Jamaica Gleaner*, 30 April, http://jamaica-gleaner.com/article/focus/20150503/china%E2%80%99s-role-jamaica-no-strings-attached.
125 Nanyang Technical University (2013) 'A Study to Position Jamaica as a Bunkering Location in the Caribbean Region: final report', https://www.micaf.gov.jm/sites/default/files/pdfs/FINAL%20Bunkering%20Hub%20Report%2020130331.pdf.

126 See debates in the Jamaican media at the time regarding the Chinese support. Mark Wignall (2012) 'This single dry dock project could transform Jamaica's economy', *Jamaica Observer*, 9 December, http://jamaica-gleaner.com/article/focus/20150503/chinaE2%80%99s-role-jamaica-no-strings-attachedhttps://www.jamaicaobserver.com/columns/this-single-dry-dock-project-could-transform-jamaicas-economy/.
127 Sandra Lavell (2015) 'Beijing Highway: $600 million road just the start of China's investments in the Caribbean', *The Guardian*, 24 December, https://www.theguardian.com/world/2015/dec/24/beijing-highway-600m-road-just-the-start-of-chinas-investments-in-caribbean.
128 *Construction Week* (2013) 'China to invest $1.2bn in new Jamaican port', 5 May, https://www.constructionweekonline.com/business/article-22271-china-to-invest-12bn-in-jamaican-port-project
129 Jerome Reynolds (2013) 'No transshipment Port at Fort Augusta', *Jamaica Gleaner*, 30 April, http://jamaica-gleaner.com/power/44520.
130 *The Maritime Executive* (2016) 'Jamaica to relocate planned port facility', 13 October, https://www.maritime-executive.com/article/jamaica-to-relocate-planned-port-facility; *Jamaica Observer* (2016) 'Environmentalists welcome scrapping of Goat Island project', 28 September, https://library.iucn-isg.org/documents/2016/Anonymous_2016_Jamaica_Observer-2.pdf.
131 Caribbean Council (n.d.) 'Chinese investment in Jamaica and region growing', https://www.caribbean-council.org/chinese-investment-jamaica-region-growing/; Vicki Cann (2018) 'Celebrating 46 years: the Jamaica-China connection', *Asia Dialogue*, University of Nottingham, 30 November, https://theasiadialogue.com/2018/11/30/celebrating-46-years-the-jamaica-china-connection/.
132 Caribbean Council (n.d.) 'Chinese investment in Jamaica and region growing', https://www.caribbean-council.org/chinese-investment-jamaica-region-growing/.
133 Sandra Lavell (2015) 'Beijing Highway: $600 million road just the start of China's investments in the Caribbean', *The Guardian*, 24 December, https://www.theguardian.com/world/2015/dec/24/beijing-highway-600m-road-just-the-start-of-chinas-investments-in-caribbean.
134 Albert Han (2019) 'Why Jamaica wants to call time on Chinese borrowing', *South China Morning Post*, 17 November, https://www.scmp.com/news/china/diplomacy/article/3038095/why-jamaica-wants-call-time-chinese-borrowing.
135 Kirk Semple (2020) 'China extends reach in the Caribbean, unsettling the U.S.', *New York Times*, 8 November, https://www.nytimes.com/2020/11/08/world/americas/china-caribbean.html.
136 CGTN (2018) 'Chinese province eyes billion-dollar Jamaica investment', 16 February, https://news.cgtn.com/news/776b544e33677a6333566d54/share_p.html.
137 Ibid.

138 Jevon Minto (2019) 'Jamaica issues enforcement orders against Chinese mining giant', *Diálogo Chino*, 19 April, https://dialogochino.net/en/extractive-industries/26051-jamaica-issues-enforcement-orders-against-chinese-mining-giant/; Jevon Minto (2019) 'Aluminium refinery sickens Jamaicans', *Diálogo Chino*, 22 March,https://dialogochino.net/en/extractive-industries/25227-aluminium-refinery-sickens-jamaicans/.

139 Caribbean Council (n.d.) 'China and Jamaica agree a "strategic framework" for economic relations', https://www.caribbean-council.org/china-and-jamaica-agree-a-strategic-framework-for-economic-relations/.

140 Albert Han (2019) 'Why Jamaica wants to call time on Chinese borrowing', *South China Morning Post*, 17 November, https://www.scmp.com/news/china/diplomacy/article/3038095/why-jamaica-wants-call-time-chinese-borrowing.

141 Ibid.; Caribbean Council (n.d.) 'China and Jamaica agree a "strategic framework" for economic relations', https://www.caribbean-council.org/china-and-jamaica-agree-a-strategic-framework-for-economic-relations/.

142 *Loop Jamaica* (2020) 'CHEC says upcoming projects not affected by coronavirus travel ban', 14 February, https://jamaica.loopnews.com/fr/node/446312; Jamaica Information Service (2019) 'HAJ and CHEC partner to build 1,650 houses', 16 October, https://jis.gov.jm/haj-and-chec-partner-to-build-1650-houses/.

143 Alphea Sanders (2020) 'Southern highway project won't stall', *Jamaica Observer*, 23 June, http://301-joweb.newscyclecloud.com/news/southern-highway-project-won-t-stall-government-says-it-s-now-in-negotiations-with-chec-for-restructuring_196865?profile=&template=PrinterVersion; Balford Henry (2020) 'NEPA keeping an eye on changes to south coast highway', *Jamaica Observer*, 12 September, https://www.jamaicaobserver.com/news/nepa-keeping-an-eye-on-changes-to-south-coast-highway/.

144 *Loop Caribbean News* (2020) 'Grenada receives US$200M in aid over past 15 years', 23 October, https://caribbean.loopnews.com/content/grenada-received-us200m-aid-china-over-past-15-years.

145 Nelson Renteria (2019) 'China signs on for "gigantic" investment in El Salvador infrastructure', *Reuters*, 3 December, https://www.reuters.com/article/us-el-salvador-china-idUSKBN1Y7266.

146 Mark Wenner and Dillon Clarke (2016) 'China's Rise in the Caribbean: what does it mean for Caribbean stakeholders?' Inter-American Development Bank, Technical Note No. IDB-TN 1073, Washington, DC, July, 21.

147 Larry Smith (2016) 'Chinese fishing proposal – what it means for The Bahamas', *Bahama Pundit*, 7 November, https://www.bahamapundit.com/2016/11/chinese-fishing-proposalwhat-it-means.html.

148 Richard Bernal (2010) 'The Dragon in the Caribbean: China-CARICOM Economic Relations', *The Round Table* 99 (408): 296.

149 *Rollcall* (2019) 'Caribbean islands become hotspots for Chinese investment', 25 March, https://www.rollcall.com/news/congress/caribbean-islands-becoming-hot-spots-for-chinese-investment.

150 Walter LaFeber (1993) *Inevitable Revolutions: the United States in Central America*, 2nd edn. New York, NY: W. W. Norton & Co., 5. Also see William M. LeoGrande (1998) *Our Own Backyard: the United States in Central America, 1977–1992*. Chapel Hill, NC: University of North Carolina Press; Greg Anderson (2014) 'The Political Economy of Post-9/11 US Security in Latin America: Has Anything Really Changed?,' in W. Andy Knight, Julian Castro-Rea and Hamid A. Ghany (eds), *Re-mapping the Americas: trends in region-making*, 205–30. Farnham, UK: Ashgate.
151 *Rollcall* (2019) 'Caribbean islands become hotspots for Chinese investment', 25 March, https://www.rollcall.com/news/congress/caribbean-islands-becoming-hot-spots-for-chinese-investment.
152 Scott MacDonald (2019) 'The Return of the Cold War in the Caribbean', *Global Americans*, 22 April, https://theglobalamericans.org/2019/04/the-return-of-the-cold-war-in-the-caribbean/.

Chapter 8

1 On practices in contemporary Spain and Portugal, see Charles Penty (2018) 'Debt collectors are wearing new hats in Spain', *Bloomberg*, 14 February, https://www.bloomberg.com/news/articles/2018-02-14/spanish-debt-collectors-in-top-hats-adopt-new-guise-for-recovery#xj4y7vzkg; *The Times* (2018) 'No more superhero costumes, Portugal tells debt collectors', 18 January, www.thetimes.co.uk/article/no-more-superhero-costumes-portugal-tells-debt-collectors-xqczjxh2w. On private lenders in nineteenth-century Peru, see Luis Philippe Zegara (2016) 'Private Lenders, Banks and Mortgage lenders in Peru: evidence from notarized loans', *Revista de Historia Economic/Journal of Iberian and Latin American Economic History* 35 (1): 105–46.
2 Jorn Dosch and David S.G. Goodman (2012) 'China and Latin America: complementarity, competition and globalisation', *Journal of Current Chinese Affairs* 41 (1): 12.
3 Miwa Hirono and Marc Lanteigne (2011) 'Introduction: China and UN Peacekeeping', *International Peacekeeping* 18 (3): 245–6.
4 Song Xiaoping (2015) 'China and Latin America in a World in Transition: a Chinese perspective', in Adrian Bonilla and Paz Milet, *Latin America, the Caribbean and China: sub-regional scenarios*, 60. San José, Costa Rica: FLASCO/CAF.
5 Gaston Fornes and Álvaro Méndez (2018) *The China-Latin America Axis: emerging markets and their role in an increasingly globalised world*, 2nd edn. London: Palgrave Macmillan.
6 Available in English: http://www.fmprc.gov.cn/mfa_eng/zxxx_662805/t1418254.shtml; and in Spanish: http://www.fmprc.gov.cn/esp/zxxx/t1418256.shtml.

7   Rebecca Ray and Kevin Gallagher (2017) 'China-Latin America Economic Bulletin (Discussion Paper). Working Group on Development and Environment in the Americas, 1, https://www.bu.edu/pardeeschool/files/2014/11/Economic-Bulletin.16-17-Bulletin.Draft_.pdf. See also Gaston Fornes and Álvaro Méndez (2018) *The China-Latin America Axis: emerging markets and their role in an increasingly globalised world*, 2nd edn. London: Palgrave Macmillan.
8   Álvaro Méndez (2019) 'Latin America and the AIIB: Interests and Viewpoints', *Global Policy* 10 (4). Also see Álvaro Méndez and Mariano Turzi (2020) *The Political Economy of China–Latin America Relations: the AIIB membership*. New York: Palgrave Pivot.
9   Personal anonymous communication with one of the authors, undisclosed location, 2 October 2014.
10 *Wikileaks* (2005) 'Chinese activities in the Bahamas', Charge d'Affaires, Brent Hardt, 8 September, Cable: 05NASSAU1601_a, wikileaks.org.
11 Subcommittee Hearing (6 April 2005) *China's Influence in the Western Hemisphere*, http://commdocs.house.gov/committees/intlrel/hfa20404.000/hfa20404_0f.htm.
12 Robert Evan Ellis (2014) *China on the Ground in Latin America: challenges for the Chinese and impacts on the region*. London: Palgrave Macmillan.
13 Authors' Private Roundtable with four unnamed former Peruvian Ministers of Foreign Affairs, 5 May 2017, Lima, Peru.
14 Authors' Roundtable at the Chilean Diplomatic Academy 'Andrés Bello', 10 May 2016, Santiago, Chile. Also see Diego Leiva Van de Maele (2017) 'Xi Jinping and the Sino-Latin American Relations in the 21st Century: facing the beginning of a new phase?, *Journal of Contemporary International Relations* 5 (1); Martín Dinatale (2016) 'La base militar china en Neuquén no podrá usarse con fines militares', *La Nación*, http://www.lanacion.com.ar/1934729-la-base-militar-china-enneuquen-no-podra-usarse-con-fines-militares.
15 US Department of Defence (2018) *Summary of the 2018 National Defense Strategy of the United States*. Washington, DC.
16 Charles Dunlap produced the founding definition in 2001, while subsequent work has elaborated upon this. See Lawfare (n.d.) 'Lawfare: a history of the term and the site', https://www.lawfareblog.com/about-lawfare-brief-history-term-and-site.
17 Matt Youkee (2020) 'Has China's winning streak in Panama ended?', *Diálogo Chino*, 25 March, https://dialogochino.net/en/trade-investment/34472-has-chinas-winning-streak-in-panama-ended/.
18 FAO, Agreement on Port State Measures, www.fao.org/en.
19 Mike Pompeo, US State Department (2020) 'On China's Predatory Fishing Practices in the Galapagos', press statement issued 2 August, https://www.state.gov/on-chinas-predatory-fishing-practices-in-the-galapagos/.

20 Kurt Campbell and Ely Ratner (2018) 'The China Reckoning: how Beijing defied American expectations', *Foreign Affairs* March/April, www.foreignaffairs.com/articles/china/2018-02-13/china-reckoning.
21 Moises Naim (2008) 'Rogue Aid', *Foreign Policy* 159: 95–6.
22 Mario Castillo and Antonio Martins Neto (2016) 'Premature Deindustrialization in Latin America', *ECLAC, Productive Development Series no. 205*, Santiago, Chile, June.
23 Dani Rodrik (2016) 'Premature Deindustrialization', *Journal of Economic Growth* 21: 1–33; Paul Cooney (2016) 'Reprimarization: implications for the environment and development in Latin America – the cases of Argentina and Brazil,' *Review of Radical Political Economies* 48 (4):) 553–61; also see P. Cooney and W. Sacher (2015) 'Reprimarización en Argentina y Brasil y la relevancia del concepto de "acumulación por desposesión"', presented at the VIII JEC, Rio Cuarto, Argentina.
24 Daniel Cardoso (2012) 'China-Brazil: a strategic partnership in an evolving world order', *East Asia* 29 (4): 16.
25 Roberto Russell and Juan Gabriel Tokatlian (2011) 'Beyond Orthodoxy: asserting Latin America's new strategic options toward the United States', *Latin American Politics and Society* 53(4): 127–46.
26 MercoPress (2006) 'Bolivia elected president woos China,' 8 January, https://en.mercopress.com/2006/01/08/bolivian-elected-president-woos-china.
27 Manuel Sutherland, director of Center for Research and Workers Training, Caracas, cited in Alicia Hernández (2020) 'China remains quiet and pragmatic on Venezuela crisis', *Diálogo Chino*, 20 January, https://dialogochino.net/en/trade-investment/32971-china-remains-quiet-and-pragmatic-on-venezuela-crisis/.
28 Robert Soutar (2020) 'China continues to cut back Latin America loans', *China Dialogue*, 28 April, https://chinadialogue.net/en/business/11982-china-continues-to-cut-back-latin-america-loans/.
29 Yang Chenxu (2020) 年:世界不会平静,但乱中有治 04-国际-解放日报, jfdaily.com, 2 January, originally sourced from https://dialogochino.net/en/trade-investment/32971-china-remains-quiet-and-pragmatic-on-venezuela-crisis/.
30 According to Statista, in the smartphones market alone Samsung has a 38 per cent market share, Motorola 15.5 per cent and Huawei 12.9 per cent, as of 2019, https://www.statista.com/statistics/271496/global-market-share-held-by-smartphone-vendors-since-4th-quarter-2009/.
31 Cheng Ting-Fang and Lauly Li (2020) 'Huawei enters a new world: how the US ban will affect global tech', *Nikkei Asia*, 14 September, www.nikkei.com/spotlight/uawei-enters-a-new-world-how-us-ban-will-affect-global-tech.htm.

32. BNAmericas (2020) 'How geopolitics shaped Chile's trans-pacific cable route', 31 July, https://www.bnamericas.com/en/analysis/how-geopolitics-shaped-chiles-trans-pacific-cable-route; *Financial Times* (2020) 'Chile picks Japan's trans-Pacific cable route in snub to China', 11 August.
33. Lisanadra Paraguassu (2020) 'Brazil looks for legal options to ban China's Huawei: sources', *Reuters*, 8 December, https://www.reuters.com/article/brazil-huawei-tech-idINL1N2IO0YR.
34. Kim Eun-jin (2020) 'Chinese smartphone makers begin to penetrate Latin American markets', *Business Korea*, 22 December, http://www.businesskorea.co.kr/news/articleView.html?idxno=57260.
35. Paul Amar (2020) 'Diplomacy of Masks: China and the crisis of populism in South America', *Global-e* 13 (60), 4 September, https://globaljournal.org/global-e/september-2020/diplomacy-masks-china-and-crisis-populism-south-america.
36. *The Guardian* (2020) 'China outraged as Brazilian minister suggests COVID 19 is part of "plan of world domination"',7 April, www.theguardian.com/world/202007april/china-outraged-after-brazil-miminister-suggests-covid-19-is-part-of-plan-for-world-domination.htm; Bryan Harris and Andres Schipani (2020) 'Brazil China ties strained by social media war,' *Financial Times*, 21 April, https://www.ft.com/content/606067af-7c06-4df2-848c-fd2e231c2ca9.
37. Wilson Center (2021) *Aid From China and the U.S. to Latin America Amid the Covid-19 Crisis*, https://www.wilsoncenter.org/aid-china-and-us-latin-america-amid-covid-19-crisis.
38. Cynthia Sanborn (2020) 'Latin America and China in Times of Covid-19', Wilson Center, 4.
39. Peter Beaumont (2020) 'Jair Bolsonaro claims "victory" after suspension of Chinese vaccine trial', *The Guardian*, 10 November, https://www.theguardian.com/world/2020/nov/10/jair-bolsonaro-claims-victory-after-suspension-of-chinese-covid-vaccine-trial.
40. Cynthia Sanborn (2020) 'Latin America and China in Times of Covid-19,' Wilson Center, 7.
41. *Latin American Advisor* (2019)'Is China going to help El Salvador develop faster?,' *The Dialogue*, 19 December, https://www.thedialogue.org/analysis/is-china-going-to-help-el-salvador-develop-faster/; *The Week* (2018) 'Why China is wooing El Salvador', 9 November, https://www.theweek.co.uk/97661/why-china-is-wooing-el-salvador.
42. Cited in Kirk Semple (2020) 'China extends reach in Caribbean, unsettling US', *New York Times*, 8 November, https://www.nytimes.com/2020/11/08/world/americas/china-caribbean.html.
43. Rosemary Foot (2020) *China, the UN, and Human Protection: beliefs, power, image*. Oxford: Oxford University Press.
44. Carlos Díaz Alejandro (1970) *Essays on the Economic History of the Argentine Republic*. New Haven, CT, and London: Yale University Press.

45 Cited in Sebastian Castaneda (2011) 'CHINESE TAKE-OVER OF SOUTH AMERICA?' Foreign Policy in Focus, 18 April, https://fpif.org/chinese_take-over_of_south_america/. See also: Carlos Pereira João Augusto de Castro Neves (2011) 'Brazil and China: South-South partnership or North-South competition?', *Policy Paper* 26, Washington, DC: Brookings, 6.
46 Yves Dezalay and Bryant G. Garth (2002) *The Internationalization of Palace Wars: lawyers, economists, and the contest to transform Latin American States*. Chicago, IL: University of Chicago Press.

Appendices

1 ECLAC, *Foreign Direct Investment in Latin America and the Caribbean 2021*. Santiago, Chile: Economic Commission for Latin America and the Caribbean, 2021. The ECLAC states that the countries for which information on the origin of FDI is available are Argentina (up to 2016), Brazil (excluding reinvested earnings), Chile, Colombia, Costa Rica, the Dominican Republic, Ecuador, El Salvador, Guatemala, Honduras, Mexico, Nicaragua (until 2013), Panama (until 2018), Paraguay, the Plurinational State of Bolivia and Uruguay.

Further Reading

Books and Edited Books

Dussel Peters, Enrique, ed. 2019. *China's Foreign Direct Investment in Latin America and the Caribbean: conditions and challenges*. Mexico, DF: Universidad Autonoma de Mexico.

Ellis, Robert Evan. 2014. *China on the Ground in Latin America: challenges for the Chinese and impacts on the region*. New York, NY: Palgrave Macmillan.

Fisher, John Robert. 1997. *The Economic Aspects of Spanish Imperialism in America, 1492–1810*. Liverpool: Liverpool University Press.

Fornes, Gaston, and Álvaro Méndez. 2018. *The China-Latin America Axis: emerging markets and their role in an increasingly globalised world*. 2nd edn. New York, NY: Palgrave Macmillan.

Gallagher, Kevin. 2016. *The China Triangle: Latin America's China boom and the fate of the Washington Consensus*. New York, NY: Oxford University Press.

Jenkins, Rhys. 2019. *How China is Reshaping the Global Economy: development impacts in Africa and Latin America*. Oxford: Oxford University Press.

Kellner, Thierry, and Sophie Wintgens, ed. 2021. *China-Latin America and the Caribbean: assessment and outlook*. Oxford: Taylor & Francis.

Méndez, Álvaro, and Mariano Turzi. 2020. *The Political Economy of China–Latin America Relations: the AIIB Membership*. New York, NY: Palgrave Pivot.

Myers, Margaret, and Carol Wise, ed. 2016. *The Political Economy of China-Latin America Relations in the New Millennium: brave new world*. Oxford: Taylor & Francis.

Stallings, Barbara. 2020. *Dependency in the Twenty-First Century? The political economy of China-Latin America relations*. Cambridge: Cambridge University Press.

Wise, Carol. 2020. *Dragonomics: How Latin America is Maximizing (or Missing Out On) China's International Development Strategy*. New Haven, CT: Yale University Press.

Journal Articles and Book Chapters

Flynn, Dennis O., and Arturo Giráldez. 1995. 'Born with a "Silver Spoon": The Origin of World Trade in 1571.' *Journal of World History* 6 (2): 201–21.

Heine, Jorge and Beal, Anders. (2018). The Strategy behind China's diplomatic offensive in Latin America. *Americas Quarterly*, 14.

Heine, Jorge. 2018. 'Chinese inroads in Panama: Transport hubs and BRI in the Americas.' *Global Americans* (26 June). https://theglobalamericans.org/2018/06/chinese-inroads-in-panama-transport-hubs-and-bri-in-the-americas/.

Heine, Jorge. 2021. 'Still Trailblazing? The Chile-China relationship at fifty.' *China Foresight at LSE IDEAS* (23 August). https://blogs.lse.ac.uk/cff/2021/08/23/still-trailblazing-the-chile-china-relationship-at-fifty/.

Jorge Heine. 2020. "Chile-China Relations: Half a Century of Continuity and Complementarity." *Journal of Latin American Studies Beijing*, Volume 42, Issue 5, pp. 13–25 (12).

Méndez, Álvaro. 2021. 'Geopolitics in Central America: China and El Salvador in the 21st Century.' In *China-Latin America and the Caribbean: assessment and outlook*, edited by Thierry Kellner and Sophie Wintgens, 207–21. Abingdon, UK: Routledge.

Méndez, Álvaro, and Francisco Javier Forcadell. 2022. 'China y America Latina. Diplomacia, comercio y geopolítica.' In *América Latina Hoy*, edited by Gaspard Estrada, 174–91. Madrid, Spain: Fundación Felipe Gonzales.

Méndez, Álvaro, and Chris Alden. 2021. 'China in Panama: from peripheral diplomacy to grand strategy.' *Geopolitics* 26 (3), 838–60. doi: 10.1080/14650045.2019.1657413.

Myers, Margaret, and Rebecca Ray. 2022. 'What Role For China's Policy Banks in LAC?' *China-Latin America Report*, March. https://www.thedialogue.org/wp-content/uploads/2022/03/Chinas-policy-banks-final-mar22.pdf.

Salama, Pierre Salama. 2018. 'China-Brasil: industrialização e "desindustrialização precoce".' *Cadernos do Desenvolvimento* 7 (10): 229–51.

Song, Xiaoping. 2015. 'China y América Latina en un mundo en transformación: una visión desde China.' In *China en América Latina y el Caribe: Escenarios estratégicos subregionales*, edited by Adrian Bonilla Soria and Paz Milet Garcia, 51–74. Costa Rica: FLACSO and CAF.

Vadell, Javier A. 2019. 'China in Latin America: South-South cooperation with Chinese characteristics.' *Latin American Perspectives* 46 (2): 107–25. doi: 10.1177/0094582x18815511.

Wise, Carol. 2016. 'China and Latin America's Emerging Economies: new realities amid old challenges.' *Latin American Policy* 7 (1): 26–51. doi: 10.1111/lamp.12087.

Other Resources

Diálogo Chino. China, Latin America & the environment. https://dialogochino.net/en/.

FMPRC. 2008. *China's Policy Paper on Latin America and the Caribbean*. Ministry of Foreign Affairs of the People's Republic of China. https://www.fmprc.gov.cn/ce/cein/eng/zgbd/t521025.htm.

FMPRC. 2016. *China's Policy Paper on Latin America and the Caribbean*. Ministry of Foreign Affairs of the People's Republic of China. http://www.fmprc.gov.cn/mfa_eng/wjdt_665385/2649_665393/t1418254.shtml.

The Dialogue. China-Latin America Finance Databases. https://www.thedialogue.org/map_list/.

Wilson Center. (2021). *Aid From China and the U.S. to Latin America Amid the Covid-19 Crisis*. https://www.wilsoncenter.org/aid-china-and-us-latin-america-amid-covid-19-crisis.

Index

Please note that page references to Tables will be in *italics*; those representing Figures will be in **bold**. References to Notes will contain the letter 'n' and Note number.

ADM 115
Administration Commission (SASAC), China 44
agency 9–11, 170–1
  bottom-up 10
  policy expressions 10
  running along two axes 10
Agreement on Port State Matters, UN 168
ALBA (Alianza Bolivariana para los Pueblos de Nuestra América) 79, 82, 96
  Social Movements Council 81
Alejandro, Carlos Díaz 175
Alfonsín, Raúl 68
Alianza Pais party, Ecuador 95
Alibaba Foundation 173
Alibaba Group 74, 137
Allende, Salvador 37, 39, 52
Alvarez, Luis F. 48
Amorim, Celso 108, 110, 185n16
Andean Pact (1968) 61–2
Andean Trade Preferences Act (1991) 90
Andes mountain range, South America 3
Angolan civil war (1975–1976) 39
Anning, Chen 118
anti-dumping 68
APEC *see* Asia-Pacific Economic Cooperation (APEC)
Araújo, Ernesto 123
Arce, Luis 103
Argentina
  see also Buenos Aires, Argentina
  agricultural supply infrastructure projects 69–70
  Comprehensive Strategic Partnership 69, 71, 73
  'cross default' clauses, loan contracts 73
  default by (2001–2002) 68
  democracy in 68
  elite consortium (Shima) 72–3
  foreign reserves 74
  hydropower sector 72
  indebtedness of 3, 12
  infrastructure projects 69–70, 71, 72, 73, 75
  liquidity problems 73–4, 75
  neo-liberalism 69
  Paraná River, 'grain superhighway' on 69, 70
  Peronist politicians 67, 68, 69, 75–6
  relations with China 15, 67–76, 77
    Binational Commission 69
    Comprehensive Strategic Partnership 69
    development finance 72–3
    economic ties 69–72
    history and diplomacy 67–76
    'recalibration' of Argentina-China relations 73–5
    recognition of China's official market economy status 68, 83
    Strategic Partnership 68–9
  resources 69
  Rio Negro provincial government 69
  San Martin infrastructure projects project 71
  soyabean imports 67, 70, 115
  successive financial crises 51

Arias, Óscar 150, 153
Arreaza, Jorge 87
ASEAN-China FTA 131
Asian and Pacific Regions Peace Conference (1952) 36–7
Asian Development Bank 82
Asian Infrastructure projects Investment Bank (AIIB) 75
Asia-Pacific Economic Cooperation (APEC) 6, 47, 150
  'China strategy' 62
  summits 62, 69
Assange, Julian 92, 97

Bachelet, Michelle 53, 174
Baha Mar 143
Bahamas 142
Banco del Sur 81
Bank of China 44, 93
Bannon, Steve 123
Baosteel 48
Barbados 143
Beidahuang Nongken (Chinese firm), Argentina 69
Beidahuang-Heilongjiang State Farm, Brazil 116
Beijing 3, 7–12, 14, 25, 29, 35, 37, 40, 47, 48, 103, 104, 140, 142
  see also China; People's Republic of China (PRC)
  and Argentina 67, 68, 69, 71, 73, 74, 75, 77
  Asian and Pacific Regions Peace Conference (1952) 36–7
  Belt and Road Summit (2017) *see* Belt and Road Initiative (BRI)
  bid for leadership of the 'Third World' 39
  and Bolivia 79, 80
  and Brazil 4, 105, 106, 107, 108, 110, 112, 115, 121, 123, 125, 126
  and Chile 51, 52, 53, 54, 58
  and Costa Rica 149, 150, 151
  and Cuba 37, 38
  and Ecuador 90, 92, 93, 95
  and Hong Kong 154
  and Jamaica 157, 159
  and Mexico 128, 131, 135, 137
  and Panama 155
  and Peru 61, 62, 66, 76
  and Taipei 3, 144, 146, 148, 154
  and Venezuela 82, 83, 84, 86, 87, 89
Belaúnde, Fernando 61
Belgrano Cargas (Argentine freight and logistics company) 71–2, 75
Belt and Road Initiative (BRI) 7, 74, 142, 154, 163, 180
  Belt and Road Summit (2017) 114
Beneficencia China 66
Bielsa, Rafael 68
Bi-Oceanic Corridor *see* Trans-Oceanic Railway, proposals for
BNDES (Banco Nacional de Desenvolvimento Econômico e Social), Brazil 112
'Boao Asia Forum,' China 53
Bolivar, Simon 26, 82
Bolivia 3, 97–103
  see also Morales, Evo
  Communist Party 40
  Framework Law on Autonomous Regions (2009) 98
  lithium deposits 102–103, 224n135
  National Development Plan (2016–2020) 100
  nationalism 15
  neo-liberalism 80
  physical features 99–100
  Plurinational State of Bolivia 98
  relations with China 97–103
  trade and investment 99–101
  republics 11
Bolsonaro, Jair 4, 105, 115, 120, 123–5, 173

Brazil 105–126
  see also Da Silva, Lula; Rousseff, Dilma; Temer, Michel
  agricultural sector 4, 111, 115–16
  aviation and automobiles 117–18
  bid for seat on UN Security Council 4
  energy sector, focus on 118–20
  expansive cooperation, era of 107–110
  farmland 116
  infrastructure projects development 4
  Itamaraty (Ministry of External Affairs) 110, 125
  manufacturing and technology sector 4, 117–18
  Ministry of Planning and Development 113
  multinationals 107
  relations with China 4, 106–110
    Brazilian companies in China 120–1
    China-Brazil Business Council 107, 111, 112
    China-Brazil Earth Resources Satellite programme 107
    China-Brazil Fund for Expansion of Production Capacity 112, 113, 114, 120, 125
    China-Brazil High Level Coordination and Cooperation Commission (COSBAN) 107, 108–109, 112
    China-Brazil Human Rights Commission 107
    Comprehensive Strategic Partnership, building 110–21
    global and regional diplomatic dimension 121–3
    trade, investment and competition 107–110
    trade missions 109
  São Luiz do Tapajós river basin 120
  slavery, abolition of 106
  soyabean imports 115
BRICS (Brazil, Russia, India, China and South Africa) 105, 112, 123
  Summits 122, 123
Bridas (Argentine partner company) 70
Bronstein, Hugh 210n134
buen vivir ('good living') philosophy 90–2, 95
  and Chinese development models 95–6
Buenos Aires, Argentina 24, 51, 71–5, 213n163
Bukele, Nayib 161
Bunting, Peter 160
Burton, Dan 166
Bush, George W. 91

Caixa Economical Federal 112
Calderón, Felipe 130, 131
Campbell, Kurt 168
Canton, 'Thirteen Factories' system (1757) 25
Cantonese immigrants 2, 5, 66
capitalism 5, 52, 53, 81
Caracas Company 25, 82, 83, 86, 87, 89, 215n9
Cargill 115
Caribbean Community and Common Market (CARICOM) 144, 145
Caribbean region *see* Central America and the Caribbean; Latin America and the Caribbean (LAC)
Caribbean-Canadian Trade Agreement 144
carracks (Portuguese vessels) 18

Carter, Jimmy 2, 154
Castro, Fidel 38, 39, 128, 198n22
Cauchari-Olaroz lithium mine 71
Cayman Islands 158
CCCME *see* China Chamber of Commerce for Import and Export of Machinery and Electronic Products (CCCME)
CDB *see* China Development Bank (CDB)
CELAC (*Comunidad de Estados Latinoamericanos y Caribeños*)
  and 1 + 3 + 6 164–5
  China-CELAC Forum 7
Central America and the Caribbean 3, 16, 139–62
  Costa Rica 149–53
  development finance for infrastructure projects, resources and tourism 139–45
  dollar diplomacy 145–61
  economic engagement 139–45
  Jamaica 157–61
  Panama 153–6
Central American Free Trade Area plus the Dominican Republic (CAFTA-DR) 144, 146
Cerén, Salvador Sánchez 149
Chaing Kai-shek 106
Chamber of Deputies, Brazilian members 125
Chávez, Hugo 80, 82–3, 84, 85, 215n6
  Misións Bolivarianos programme 81
Che Guevara 128
CHEC *see* China Harbour Engineering Company (CHEC)
Chery Automotive Company (CAC) 117, 118

Chicago School 52
Chile 3, 51–9, 76–7, 197n9
  see also Santiago, Chile
  agricultural sector 56, 58
  cell phone market 59
  Chinese firms in 57–8
  Communist Party 40, 52
  corporate tax rate 57
  FTAs *see under* Free Trade Agreements (FTAs)
  infrastructure projects 59
  manufacturing and services sector 56–7
  National Assembly 53
  open economy 57
  relations with China 15, 51–9
    economic ties 54–7, 58
    export credits from China 52
    exports to China 56
    'first mover' advantage 55, 76
    history and diplomacy 52–4
    military cooperation 54
  Socialist Party 52
  telecoms sector 59
  training programmes 54
  UNCTAD Conference (1971) 39
  wine industry 56
Chile-China Cultural Association, Santiago 37, 52
China
  see also Beijing; Imperial China and Latin America; People's Republic of China (PRC); Republic of China (RoC)
  accession to the WTO (2001) 55, 175
  agricultural sector 46
  agro-industrial firms 116
  authoritarian rule 11
  Belt and Road Initiative (BRI) 7, 74, 114, 142, 154
  'Boao Asia Forum' 53
  China-LAC relationship 176

Index

China-Latin America
  Cooperation Forum 122
Chinese communities in Latin
  America 31–3, 66–7, 120–1
Cold War in Latin America
  35–42
contemporary 17
dependency on Latin
  American silver 5, 25
'going out' policy and Latin
  America 46–8
Maoism and Latin American
  revolutionaries 40–2
response of Latin America
  to China's deepening
  involvement in 15
trade figures 178, 179f
*see also under relations with
  individual countries below*
civil war 36
Confucius Centres 6, 54, 67
construction firms 119
Cultural Revolution 35, 40, 41, 52
diplomatic recognition and 'Two
  Chinas' 36–8
economic expansion/reforms
  6, 43
end of revolutionary phase 42
expansion of interests/power 6,
  8, 11, 73
finished goods 8
foreign direct investment (FDI) 4
FTAs *see* Free Trade Agreements
  (FTAs)
Global China *see* Global China
global growth 42–8
imports of copper 54
legacy in shaping Latin America 33
loans from 9, 11, 12, 27, 52, 84,
  85, 87, 92, 93, 97, 98, 100,
  101, 125, 140, 141, 145,
  158, 161, 169, 173, 175
loans-for-oil *entente* 84
media instruments, Peru 66

Ming Dynasty (1368–1644) 5,
  19, 22
  collapse of 17, 25
Ministry of Commerce 83, 113
Ministry of Foreign Affairs 142
motivation for interests in Latin
  America 14
niche markets 134
nuclear programme 38
'One China policy' 147, 180
'opening and reform,' state-
  directed policy 52–3
People's Bank of China 44, 72
Qing Dynasty (1644–1911) 5,
  25–6, 27, 60
recognition as an official market
  economy 47, 68, 83, 107,
  131
relations with Argentina 15,
  67–76, 77
  Argentina's recognition of
    China's official market
    economy status 68, 83
  Binational Commission 69
  Comprehensive Strategic
    Partnership 69
  development finance 72–3
  economic ties 69–72
  history and diplomacy 67–76
  'recalibration' of Argentina-
    China relations 73–5
  Strategic Partnership 68–9
relations with Bolivia 97–103
  trade and investment 99–101
relations with Brazil 4, 106–110
  Brazilian companies in China
    120–1
  China-Brazil High Level
    Coordination and
    Cooperation Commission
    (COSBAN) 107, 108–109,
    112
  China-Brazil Business Council
    107, 111, 112

China-Brazil Earth Resources
  Satellite programme 107
China-Brazil Fund for
  Expansion of Production
  Capacity 112, 113, 114,
  120, 125
China-Brazil Human Rights
  Commission 107
Comprehensive Strategic
  Partnership, building
  110–21
  global and regional diplomatic
    dimension 121–3
  trade, investment and
    competition 107–110
  trade missions 109
relations with Chile 15, 51–9
  Chinese firms in Chile 57–8
  economic ties 54–7, 58
  export credits from China 52
  exports to China 56
  'first mover' advantage 55, 76
  history and diplomacy 52–4
  military cooperation 54
relations with Ecuador 90–2
relations with Mexico 15
  bilateral trade 130
  Binational Commission 128
  Chinese companies in Mexico
    133–5
  competition and collaboration
    3–4, 129–31
  diplomatic 128–35
  evolving economic ties 129–31
  Mexico-China Strategy
    Agenda 131
  trade and investment 131–2
relations with Peru 15, 59–67
  Chinese community in Peru
    66–7
  Chinese mining firms in Peru
    64–5
  Chinese-Peruvian Friendship
    Centre 66
  history and diplomacy 60–3
  Imperial China, official ties
    with 60
  'late comer advantage' 77
  trade and investment 62, 63–6
relations with Venezuela 82–6
  bilateral trade 83
Sino-Soviet split and Latin
  America 38–42
small and medium-sized
  enterprises (SMEs) 9
State Grid Corporation 120
state-owned enterprises (SOEs)
  see state-owned enterprises
  (SOEs), Chinese
as a 'strategic competitor' 13,
  167–8
technocratic leadership 11
Tiananmen Square massacre
  (1989) 43, 107
tourism 143
US-China trade war (2018) 63–4,
  124, 137, 139
China Aviation Industry Corporation
  (AVIC II) 117
China Communication
  Construction Company
  (CCCC) 70, 155
China Construction Bank (CCB) 44
China Council for the Promotion of
  International Trade 37
China Development Bank (CDB) 44,
  66, 72, 84, 93, 99–100, 118,
  119, 141–2, 145, 152
China Export-Import (Exim) Bank
  44, 66, 72, 85, 93, 94, 99,
  141, 143, 158, 160
China Harbour Engineering
  Company (CHEC) 48, 59,
  142, 158, 159, 160
China Machine Engineering
  Corporation (CMEC) 72
China Metallurgical Corporation
  (CMC) 70

China National Cereals, Oils and Foodstuffs (COFCO) 69, 114, 116
China National Complete Plant Import and Export Company (Complant) 157–8
China National Electric Engineering Company (CNEEC) 94
China National Electronics Import and Export Corporation 96
China National Overseas Oil Company (CNNOC) 44
China National Petroleum Company (CNPC) 44, 48, 64, 85, 88, 89, 93, 130
China National Technical Import-Export Corporation 70
China National Tourism Administration 143
China Railway Construction Corporation (CRRC) 75–6, 85, 93, 132
China Railway Engineering Corporation (CREC) 85, 113
China Railway Group 59
China Soybean Industry Association 115
China-Caribbean Business Council 144
China-Caribbean Forum (CCF) 144
China-Caribbean Trade and Economic Cooperation Forum Meeting, Santiago (2018) 141
China-CELAC Forum (2014) 13, 165
China-Latin America and Caribbean Friendship Association (CHILAC) 37, 40
China-Latin American Countries and Caribbean States Cooperation Plan (2015–2019) 165
China-Latin Forum 164
Chinalco mining, Peru 65
China-Mercosur Dialogue Forum (1998) 69
China-Venezuela Fund 84, 85
China-Venezuela High-Level Joint Commission 84
Chinese Academy for Social Sciences (CASS) 225n145
Chinese Commission of Enquiry (1873) 29
Chinese Foreign Ministry, White Papers on Latin America 7, 11, 12
Chinese People's Association for Friendship with Foreign Countries (CPAFFC) 37
chinos 20
Chonn Ching, Victoria 65
Chow Tai Fook 143
Círculos Bolivarianos 81
CITGO (US-based subsidiary of PDVSA) 83–4
CITIC (Chinese sovereign wealth fund) 72, 134, 141, 142
civil war, China 36
Clinton, Hillary 110
CNOOC (Chinese oil giant) 70, 83, 119
CNPC (Chinese petroleum SOE) *see* China National Petroleum Company (CNPC)
cobrador del frac 163
Coca Codo Sinclair hydroelectric dam project 94
Codelco (state-owned mining company) 54, 57
COFCO *see* China National Cereals, Oils and Foodstuffs (COFCO)
Cold War 2, 10, 15, 145, 175
  China's involvement in LAC during 35–42
  Peruvian-Chinese relations 60, 61

Colombia 10
colonialism 4
commodity supercycle 8, 79–80
Communist Party of China (CPC) 14, 36, 38, 41, 43, 49, 60, 145, 174
  founding of PRC under 145–6
  Party Congress (2017) 148
Comprehensive and Progressive Agreement for Trans-Pacific Partnership (CPTPP) 137, 237n3
Comprehensive Strategic Partnership
  Argentina 69, 71, 73
  Brazil 110–21
  Mexico 128
  Peru 62
  Venezuela 87
Confucius Centres 6, 54, 67, 140
CONIE (Confederación de Nacionalidades Indígenas del Ecuador) 95
Contingency Reserve Fund, Brazil 122
'coolies' 5, 17, 27, 30
Cooney, Paul 169
Cooperative Partnership (China-Chile), 2004 53
Corporate Social Responsibility 65–6
Corporation for the Promotion of Production (Corfo) 58
Correa, Rafael 90, 91, 92, 95–7, 171
corruption 115, 119
Cortizo, Laurentino 156
COSBAN (Comissão Sino-Brasileira de Alto Nível de Concertação e Cooperação) 108–109, 112, 124, 125
'Cosco Shipping Panama' (Chinese merchant vessel) 2
Costa Rica 16, 29, 143, 144, 147
  dollar diplomacy 149–53
  Foreign Ministry 150
  FTA with China (2011) 9, 149
Countering America's Adversaries through Sanctions Act (CAATSA) 167
COVID-19 pandemic 143, 172–4
CPC see Communist Party of China (CPC)
CPEL (Companhia Paulista Força e Luz) 120
CRRC see China Railway Construction Corporation (CRRC)
Cuba 10, 38–9, 145
Cuban missile crisis (1962) 38
Cultural Revolution 35, 40, 41, 52

Da Silva, Lula 4, 105, 107–110, 118, 121, 125
Dalai Lama 153
de Paiva, Marcos Caramuru 176
debt-to-GDP ratio 157
'debt-trap diplomacy' 12, 168, 188n49
Defense Studies Institute, Changping 54
Democratic People's Party 147
Deng Xiaoping 39, 42, 43, 51, 79, 154
Desalay, Yves 176
Development Bank of Latin America (CAF) 122, 128
development finance
  Argentina 72–3
  Central America and the Caribbean 139–45
  Venezuela 83
Diario Chino Latinoamericano (newspaper for Chinese immigrants in Panama) 2
Diaz, Porfirio 30
Dickens, Charles 29
dollar diplomacy 145–61
drug cartels 62

Economic and Trade Committee (Argentina-China) 74
economic statecraft 12

EcuaCorriente 93, 94
Ecuador 3, 90–7, 103
  see also Quito, Ecuador
  Bolivarian nationalism in 15
  Chinese immigration to 95
  Exclusive Economic Zone 94
  indebtedness of 12, 92
  neo-liberalism 80
  protests by indigenous
    communities and
    environmental activities 10
  relations with China 90–2
  sovereign bonds 91
  trade 92–5
El Salvador 146, 149
Electric Corporation of Ecuador
  (CELEC) 94
elites
  and agency 10
  Argentina 72–3
  Latin American 176
  Panama 1
  Peru 66
Ellis, Evan 13, 143, 166
EnCana (Canadian firm) 48, 93
entrepreneurs 53
Environmental Impact Assessment
  72
Esmeralda (training vessel) 54
Estatal Venezolana de
  Telecomunicaciones 85
Eurocentrism 197n1
European Partnership Agreements
  (2008) 144
Executive Decrees 96
Extractive Industries Transparency
  Initiatives (EITI) 65

FDI *see* foreign direct investment
  (FDI)
FEMSA (Fomento Económico
  Mexicano) 134
Fernández, Alberto 75
Flynn, Dennis 19
Fischtak, Claudio 120

foreign direct investment (FDI) 4,
  8–9, 55, 57, 61, 82, 111,
  190n61
  see also investment, Chinese
  statistics 179
Free Trade Agreements (FTAs) 3, 146
  bilateral 9, 55, 64
  China-Chile (2016) 9, 55
    impact in Chile 56
    renegotiating/extending
      (2006) 58–9
    signature (2005) 55
    WTO rules 55–6
  China-Costa Rica (2011) 9, 149
  China-Peru (2009) 9, 60, 62, 76
    renegotiating to 'optimize' 63–4
  Costa-Rica-Singapore (2013) 152
  discussions in Panama 2
  regional 9, 91
  US-Chile (2003) 55
  US-Ecuador (2004) 9, 91
Free Trade Area of the Americas
  (FTAA) 11, 82
Fuerabamba, Peru 65
Fujianese immigrants 5, 66
Fujimori, Alberto 61, 62

G20 122, 123, 128
  Argentina Summit (2018) 73
Gage, Thomas 20, 192n18
Gama, Vasco de 18
Gámiz, Arturo 41
Ganfeng Lithium 71, 136, 211n143,
  242n63
Garcia, Alan 66
Garcia, Enrique 128
Garth, Bryant G. 176
General Agreement on Tariffs and
  Trade (GATT) 62, 129
geopolitics 12–13
  agency 9–11, 170–1
  diplomatic and geopolitical
    matters 180–3
  Huawei and COVID diplomacy
    172–4

new geopolitics of Latin America 168–74
re-evaluation of risk in Latin America and the Caribbean by China 171–2
reframing of development 168–70
Giant Motors 136
Global China 35, 42–9, 163–77
    New Silk Road and remaking of Latin America 174–7
    rise of 15, 16
    strategic partnerships and regional forums 164–5
global financial crisis (GFC) 4, 105, 130
global value chains 56–7
globalization 4, 51, 62, 169
    historical 174
    US-led 13
Giráldez, Artur 19
González, Anabel 150
Goulart, João 106
Grupo Modelo, Mexico 133–4
Guaidó, Juan 87, 89
Guatemala 146
Guillermo-Solís, Luis 153
Guzmán, Abimael 41

Hakka migrants 2, 66
Hausmann, Ricardo 86
Havana 215n9
Hebei Wenfeng 57
Heshen 26, 193n53
Hierro Peru, Shougang's acquisition of (1992) 64
High-Level Coordination and Co-operation Commission, Brazil *see* COSBAN (Comissão Sino-Brasileira de Alto Nível de Concertação e Cooperação)
history and diplomacy
    Argentina 67–76

Chile 52–4
Peru 60–3
Honduras 146
Hong Kong 154
Hutchison-Whampoa 85
Hu Jintao 6, 68, 72, 82, 107, 150
    visit to China (2004) 53, 109
Hualong-I reactor 74
Huanqiu Contracting and Engineering Corporation (HCEC) 152
Huawei (Chinese telecom company) 59, 134, 140, 172
    and COVID diplomacy 172–4
Human Rights Commission 107
Human Rights Council (UN) 89, 174
Hutchison-Whampoa, Hong Kong 85, 134, 141, 154, 156
hydroelectric dams 3

IIRSA (Integración de la Infraestructura Regional Sudamericana) 74
Imperial China and Latin America
    see also China; People's Republic of China; silver
    Chinese communities in Latin America 5–6, 31–3
    Chinese legacy in shaping Latin America 33
    long-distance sea voyages 18–19
    'Manila galleon trade' 21, 23
    Mexico 128
    official ties with Peru 60
    shipbuilding 23–4
    silver, demand for 5, 19, 22–3, 25
    trade routes, opening up 17–27
India, Brazil and South Africa Forum (IBSA) 121
Industrial and Commercial Bank of China (ICBC) 44, 72
infrastructure projects
    Argentina 69–70, 71, 72, 73, 75

Brazil 4
Central America and the
  Caribbean 139–45
Chile 59
Mexico 131–2
mining 96
Peru 60
Inter-American Development Bank
  (IDB) 9, 89, 92, 164
International Monetary Fund (IMF)
  3, 74, 86, 97, 122
investment, Chinese 3, 4, 7, 9, 11,
  12, 14, 59, 105, 142, 155,
  169
  see also foreign direct investment
    (FDI); infrastructure
    projects; trade and
    investment
  and Argentina 68, 71, 72
  bilateral investment funds 113
  and Brazil 111, 124, 125
  and Chile 57
  and Global China 46, 47
  infrastructure projects 111
  and Mexico 130
  and Peru 64–5, 67, 76
  and Venezuela 83, 84, 89

JAC Motors 136
Jamaica 16, 142, 143, 144, 157–61
  indebtedness of 12
Jiang Zemin 53
Jimenez, Perez 88
Jiuquan Iron and Steel Company
  (JISCO) 159, 160
João VI, Emperor of Brazil 106
Joint High-Level Commission
  (Venezuela and China) 87
Ju Yijie 83

Khrushchev, Nikita 38
Kirchner, Cristina Fernández de 68,
  69, 71, 72, 73, 75, 87, 171
Kirchner, Néstor Carlos 68

KMT (Chinese Nationalist Party)
  36, 148
Koster, Richard 154
Kuczynski, Pedro Pablo 62

la trata amarilla ('yellow traffic')
  28, 30
LAC *see* Latin America and the
  Caribbean (LAC)
Lagos, Ricardo 53
Landbridge Group (China) 3, 154
Lapeña, Jorge 73
Las Bambas copper mine, Peru 65
Latin America/Latin America and
  the Caribbean (LAC)
  see also Argentina; Bolivia; Brazil;
    Cayman Islands; Chile;
    Costa Rica; Ecuador;
    El Salvador; Honduras;
    Jamaica; Mexico; New
    Spain; Nicaragua; Peru
  Cantonese immigrants 5
  Chinese communities in 5–6,
    31–3
  Chinese legacy in shaping 33
  dependency on export of
    commodities to China 8–9
  development 7–9, 27–31
  MNCs 7
  new geopolitics of 168–74
  revolutionaries 40–2
  select states on global stage 13
  state autonomy, struggle for 9–10
  China-LAC relationship 13, 42,
    176
  China-Latin America
    Cooperation Forum 122
  Chinese communities in Latin
    America 5–6, 31–3, 66–7,
    120–1
  Chinese dependency on Latin
    American silver 5, 25
  Cold War in Latin America
    35–42

'going out' policy 46–8
Maoism and Latin American
  revolutionaries 40–2
and the PRC 36–7
response of Latin America
  to China's deepening
  involvement in 15
see also China
development 7–9
Fujianese immigrants 5
'New Left' 36
and Panama 3
re-evaluation of risk by China
  171–2
and Taiwan 38
US response to China 166–8
White Paper 7, 11, 12
Laufer, Ruben 72
League of Nations 106
Lee Tsinghua 147
Léon-Manriquez, Jose Luis 48
Li Ka-Shing 154
Li Keqiang 113, 153
Li Peng 83
liberalism
  see also neo-liberalism
  liberal economics 83
  liberal market capitalism 35, 81
liberalization 42, 130
  economic 133
  market 43
  policy/political 43, 129
  trade 169
Lima, Peru 24, 28, 30–2, 51, 60, 61,
  63, 64, 67, 175
Lin Hua 74
lithium 64, 67, 102–103, 175
  see also Cauchari-Olaroz lithium
    mine; Tianqi Lithium
  batteries, demand for 58–9, 71
  Bolivia 102–103, 224n135
  Chile 205n52
  deposits 102–103, 136, 224n135
  global resources 58

Hanaq's investments in 71
mining 102
processing of 59, 71
reserves 101
loans 3, 83, 87, 89, 92, 100, 101,
  188n49
  Chinese 8, 9, 11, 12, 27, 52, 84, 85,
    87, 92, 93, 97, 98, 100, 101,
    125, 140, 141, 145, 158,
    161, 169, 173, 175
  commercial 145
  commodity-backed 84
  concessional 3, 113, 140–1, 146–7
  IMF 86, 97
  infrastructure projects 60, 71, 72,
    77, 140, 145, 173
  Inter-American Development
    Bank (IDB) 9
  large-scale 8, 9, 12, 27, 71, 140
  loans-for-oil 84
  oil-backed 85, 97
  regional banks 86
  soft 53
  Western 100
  World Bank 9, 82, 92
Louis Dreyfus (multinational) 115

Macau, Portuguese colony 5
McCauley, Diana 159
Macri, Mauricio 69, 72, 73–5, 77
macro-economic policy 86
Maduro, Nicolás 80, 85–6, 87, 88, 89
Malaysia 149
Mandarin language 6, 54
Mao Zedong 35, 38, 51, 82, 128
  death of (1976) 39, 40
  Red Guards 42
  'Three Worlds Theory' of
    international relations 39
Maoism 36, 40–2, 48, 61
maquiladoras (industrial parks)
  238n12
Maritime Authority of the Panama
  Canal 1

MAS (Movimiento al Socialismo-
      Instrumento Político por la
      Soberanía de los Pueblos)
      98, 99, 103
   Unity Pact 102
Mateos, López 128
Medrano, Florencio 41
Meiggs, Henry 30
Menem, Carlos 68
mercury 22
mergers and acquisitions, Chinese-
      financed 4, 69
neo-liberalism 68
Mexico 20–1, 32, 127–37, 156
   see also New Spain
   Chamber of Commerce 133
   Communist Party 40
   economy 185n14
   exports 129
   expulsion of Chinese people
      (1931) 6
   failed high-speed railway project
      3–4
   footwear industry 133
   mining interests 5
   National Development Plan 130
   relations with China 15, 128–35
      bilateral trade 130
      Binational Commission 128
      Chinese companies in Mexico
         133–5
      competition and collaboration
         3–4, 129–31
      diplomatic 128–35
      evolving economic ties 129–31
      Mexican companies in China
         133–5
      Mexico-China Strategy
         Agenda 131
      trade and investment 131–2
   textiles, footwear and electronics 3
   trade and investment
      infrastructure projects 131–2
      retail sector 133
   Special Economic Zones
      (SEZs) 132–3
   trade wars 135–7
Minas Gerais, Brazil 106
Ming Dynasty (1368–1644) 5, 19, 22
   collapse of 17, 25
mining sector 27, 46, 60, 71, 76, 90,
      91, 99
   Chile 57
   Chinese firms/interests 65–6, 86,
      101
   conglomerates 102
   costs of sector 77
   infrastructure projects project 95
   Orinoco Mining Arc 86
   Peru 5, 47–8, 60, 64, 65–6
   silver 5, 18, 19, 21–2
   Venezuela 86
Minmetals (MMG, Chinese SOE) 57,
      58, 107
   joint venture with Jiangxi 65
Miraflores, Peru 1
Moín oil refinery, Caribbean coast
      152
Monroe Doctrine 89
moral hazards 175–6
Morales, Evo 10, 79, 97–103
Moreno, Lenin 90, 94, 96, 97
Morococha, Peru 65
Mourão, Hamilton 124
multilatinas (MNCs) 7
Myers, Margaret 70, 211n137

NAFTA *see* North American
      Free Trade Agreement
      (NAFTA)
National Bank of Bolivia 101
National Development Bank
      (BANDES) 84
National Development Foundation
      (FONDEN), Venezuela 84
National Development Reform
      Commission (NDRC),
      China 43, 63

Nationalist Party (Kuomintang/ KMT), China 36, 148
NDB *see* New Development Bank (NDB), Brazil
NDRC *see* National Development Reform Commission (NDRC), China
neo-extractivism 11, 169
neo-liberalism 11, 61, 80, 90
 Argentina 68, 69
 US-led 7, 176
Neruda, Pablo 37
Netto, Antonio Delfim 116
New Development Bank (NDB), Brazil 124, 128
New International Economic Order 39
New Spain 5, 18–20, 22–6, 31
 see also Mexico
Nicaragua 145, 147, 148, 246n40
Nieto, Enrique Peña 131, 132, 133, 135
Nixon, Richard 38, 52
Noble Group 69
Noriega, General Manuel 2
North American Free Trade Agreement (NAFTA) 55, 127, 129, 130, 135–7
 renegotiating 136
Nuclear Security Summit, Washington (2016) 74

Obama, Barack 88, 166
Obrador, Andrés Manuel López 132
Occidental Petroleum 91
oil 4, 10, 45, 47, 48, 60, 64, 73
 companies *see* oil companies
 'full oil sovereignty' 81
 oil-backed loans 85
 prices *see* oil prices
 refineries 85, 151, 152
 soya 68, 73
 Venezuela 81, 82, 83, 84, 85
  oil-for-loan deal 88

oil companies 10, 81, 108
 Chinese 118–20
 US 90, 91
oil prices
 collapsing 86–7
 falling 70, 88, 118, 119
 price-fixing 119
 rising 81–2
'One China policy' 147, 180
opium 28
Organization of American States (OAS) 96, 164
Orinoco Mining Arc 86
Overseas Chinese Affairs Office 6, 32–3
Oviedo, Eduardo Daniel 73

Pacheco, Abel 150
Pacific Alliance (2011) 62, 74, 131, 177
Panama 16, 142, 146
 breaking of ties with Taiwan (2017) 3
 Cantonese migrants 2
 Chinese communities 6
 dollar diplomacy 153–6
 Hakka migrants 2
 Maritime Authority of the Panama Canal 1
 Panama City 1
 'Panama Papers' (2016) 156
 Panama-China Maritime Agreement (2018) 1
 trade negotiations 2
 US forces, withdrawal (1977) 2
 US invasion (1989) 2
Panama Canal 143
 financing of Canal Zone 153, 154
 symbol of American hegemony 2
 widening of (2016) 85
Pannunzio, Antonio Carlos 110
Parian (emporium) 20
Parker, Matthew 12
PDVSA 81, 84, 87, 88

People's Bank of China 44, 72
People's Republic of China (PRC) 150
    see also China; Imperial China
        and Latin America
    conflict with Republic of China
        (ROC) 36–7
    diplomatic relations with Chile 52
    establishment 36
    formal recognition (1971) 61
    and Latin America and the
        Caribbean 36–7
    and Peru 60–1
Peru 3, 59–67, 76–7
    see also Lima, Peru
    accession to the WTO (1998) 62
    Andean Pact (1968) 61–2
    Callao (Peruvian port) 59
    Chinese community 66–7
    Communist Party 40, 41
    as a 'Comprehensive Strategic
        Partner' (2013) 62
    Comprehensive Strategic
        Partnership 62
    foreign policy 62
    FTA with China (2009) see under
        Free Trade Agreements
        (FTAs)
    infrastructure projects 60
    iron ore mine, Marcona 59–60
    military regimes 10, 61
    mining sector 5, 47–8, 60, 64,
        65–6
    relations with China 15, 59–67
        Chinese community in Peru
            66–7
        Chinese mining firms in Peru
            64–5
        Chinese-Peruvian Friendship
            Centre 66
        history and diplomacy 60–3
        Imperial China, official ties
            with 60
        'late comer advantage' 77
        trade and investment 62, 63–6

resources 60, 65
'soft power' 66
Petrobras (Brazilian SOE) 64, 98,
    105, 107, 119, 120, 226n3
Petro Ecuador 91
Petróleos de Venezuela (PSDVA) 81
Pham, Peter 13
Pinera, Sebastian 59
Pinochet, General Augusto 52–3, 107
Pompeo, Mike 88, 163
populism 12, 13, 68, 95, 171
    leftist 73, 79, 90
Portilla, Alfonso 147
Portugal, Portuguese Empire 15
Potosí, Bolivia 101
    silver in 5, 22, 101
Prado, Manuel 30
pragmatism 74, 80, 82, 154
'progressive extractivism,' Venezuela
    79–80
PSUV (Partido Socialista Unificado
    de Venezuela) 86
PT (Partido dos Trabalhadores) 109,
    115

Qing Dynasty (1644–1911) 5, 25–6,
    27, 60
Qingbao, Niu 160
Qiu Xiaoqi 135
Quito, Ecuador 90, 92, 93, 95, 96

railways 5, 31, 60, 99, 137, 140, 169
    Argentina 70, 71, 72
    Central Brazil railroad project 106
    China Railway Construction
        Company 75–6, 85, 93, 132
    China Railway Engineering
        Corporation (CREC) 85,
        113
    China Railway Group 59
    failed high-speed railway project,
        Mexico 3–4
    Mexico 131, 142
    Panama 30

between Panama and Costa Rica 142, 156
Peru 30
reconstruction 75–6
between Santiago and Valparaíso 59
trans-Isthmus 153
Trans-Oceanic Railway, proposals for 59, 76, 113, 205n58
'Two Oceans Railway' initiative 8
Ratner, Ely 168
regional forums, and strategic partnerships 164–5
regionalism 10, 62
new regionalism 62
relational autonomy 10
reprimarization 105, 109
Repsol Argentina 70
Repsol-YPF 70
Republic of China (RoC), conflict with PRC 36–7
research approach 13–15
resource nationalism 123, 171
resources
Argentina 69
development finance (Central America and the Caribbean) 139–45
Latin American, Chinese demand for 8, 54–5
lithium *see* lithium
mineral 65, 70–1
Peru 60, 65
pursuit of opportunities 8
silver *see* silver
of Venezuela 86
Rio de Janeiro, Brazil 106
Rio+20 Summit (2012) 122
Robinson, St. John 195n72
Robinson, Thomas 196n1
Rodrik, Dani 169
Rothwell, Matthew 40, 41, 197n1
Rousseff, Dilma 112, 114, 124, 125
Rubio, Marco 162

Russell, Roberto 10, 169
Russian-Cuban active measures 88

Sanborn, Cynthia 65
Sanhe Hopefull Grain & Oil (SOE) 72
Santiago, Chile 51, 55, 56, 59, 172
Chile-China Cultural Association 37, 52
China-Caribbean Trade and Economic Cooperation Forum Meeting (2018) 141
São Paulo, Brazil 106
Sarney, José 106
Schmidt, Luis 58
SCM (*Sociedad Química y Minera de Chile*) 58
Security Council, UN *see* UN Security Council
Shambaugh, David 196n1
Shandong (Chinese SOE) 70–1
Shanghai Dredging Company 70
Shankun, Yang 52
'Shining Path' (*Sendero Lumunoso*), self-styled Maoist revolutionary movement 41, 61
guerrilla war techniques 42
'People's War' (1980) 41–2
Shougang-Hierro Peru (Chinese SOE) 64–5
silver 93, 174, 175, 193n53
demand/flows in Imperial China 3, 5, 8, 19–20, 22–3, 25
discovery of, in Zacatecus (1548) 22
exchange of for Chinese goods 5, 17, 18, 19–20, 21
extraction of 21, 22
global trade 5, 22
ingots and coins 19, 22, 23
mining 5, 18, 19, 21–2
New World 18, 20, 23
ore 21, 22
Potosí as source 5, 22, 101

pure 19
refining factories 21
Silver Route 5, 18
Spanish galleons 20, 21, 192n25
Sinohydro 94
Sino-Macau-Nagasaki trade route 20
Sino-PDVSA JV 84
Sinopec (Chinese oil giant) 44, 70, 88, 89, 107, 119
Sino-Soviet split and Latin America 36, 38–42, 48
slavery, abolition of 106
Slim, Carlos 136
small and medium-sized enterprises (SMEs) 9, 63, 111, 121, 137, 147
Snowden, Edward 92
Soares, Andre 120
Song Xiaoping 6
Soong Mei-ling 106
South Africa 186n18
South America
    see also Latin America/ Latin America and the Caribbean (LAC)
    Andes mountain range 3
    China's 'gateway' to markets 76
    Jiang Zemin's tour of (2001) 53
South Korea 144
soya oil products 68, 73
soyabeans 48, 69, 100, 168
    see also China Soybean Industry Association
    Argentine 67, 70
    Brazilian 8, 114–16, 124
    US 115
Spain
    conquistadors 4–5
    Crown 24
    Spanish Empire 5, 15
    Spanish galleons 20, 21, 192n25
    unrest in colonies 24–5
Special Economic Zones (SEZs) 132–3

Spring Festival celebrations 56
Sri Lanka 169
State Grid Corporation, China 120
state-owned enterprises (SOEs), Chinese 43–9, 54, 57, 103, 107, 121, 134, 136, 140–2, 169, 175
    agro-industry 69
    breaking up/restructuring 44
    in Chile's resource sector 58
    in Ecuador 93–4
    energy 82, 130, 134
    in mining 176
    penetration of international markets 45
    strategic planning 45
    in Venezuela 83
strategic partnerships and regional forums 164–5
Sun Yat-sen 36, 128
Surinam 175
System of Central American Integration (SIECA) 147

Taboada, Ernesto Fernández 77
Taiping Rebellion (1851–1865) 26
Taiwan 3, 35, 36, 38
    recognition 185n13, 246n43
    Taipei 147
Temer, Michel 114, 115, 120, 124
'Thirteen Factories' system, Canton 25
Three Gorges Dam project 107
'Three Worlds Theory' of international relations 39
Tiananmen Square massacre (1989) 43, 107
Tianqi Lithium 58, 205n52
TIPNIS (Isiboro Sécure National Park and Indigenous Territory) 102
Tokatlian, Juan Gabriel 10, 169
Toledano, Vincente Lombardo 40–1
Toledo, Alejandro 61

Toledo, Francisco de 21
Tongling Non-Ferrous Metals Group 93
Tordesillas Treaty (1494) 18
Torrijos, Omar 154
trade and investment
  changing patterns 13
  Ecuador 92–5
  liberal policies 62
  Mexico
    infrastructure projects 131–2
    retail sector 133
    Special Economic Zones (SEZs) 132–3
  Peru 62, 63–6
  trade wars 135–7
trade unions 143
trade wars 13
  US-China trade war (2018) 63–4, 124, 137, 139
Trans-Oceanic Railway, proposals for 59, 76, 113, 205n58
Trans-Pacific Partnership (TPP) 11, 137, 166
  US summary withdrawal from 53
Tricontinental Conference, Havana (1966) 38–9
Trinidad and Tobago 142, 143
Trump, Donald 11, 13, 88, 135–7, 162, 168
  'America First' policies 13, 135
Tsai Ing-wen 148
Túpac Amaru rebellion (1780) 26
tusan (people of mixed Chinese origin), Peru 32
'twenty-first-century Socialism' 82
'Two Oceans Railway' initiative 8

UN General Assembly 39, 128, 164
UN Security Council 4, 36, 108, 121, 128, 146, 151
UNCTAD Conference, Chile (1971) 39
unipolarity 11

United States
  globalization 13
  hegemony 80, 169
  neo-liberalism, US-led 7, 11
  and Panama 2
  response to China 166–8
  Security Strategy 13
  soyabeans 115
  summary withdrawal from TPP 53
  US-China trade war (2018) 63–4, 124, 137, 139
  US-Ecuador FTA (2004) 9
UNOCAL (US oil company) 70
UNSCH (Universidad Nacional de San Cristóbal de Huamanga) 41
USMCA (US-Mexico-Canada Agreement) 127, 135, 136

vaccine diplomacy 173
Varela, Juan Carlos 148–9, 154
Velasco, General Juan 61
Venezuela 3, 13, 79, 80–9, 103, 171
  see also Chávez, Hugo; Maduro, Nicolás
  ALBA Social Movements Council 81
  authoritarianism 80
  Bolivarian nationalism in 15
  Bolivarian Republic of, building 81–2
  commodity supercycle 79–80
  Comprehensive Strategic Partnership 87
  Confederación de Trabajadores de Venezuela 81
  currency devaluation 86
  Fifth Republic Movement 81
  foreign and economy policy 81–2
  indebtedness of 88–9
  National Development Bank (BANDES) 84
  oil 85, 86–7, 88

opposition politics 87–8
'progressive extractivism'
    79–80
pursuit of energy by China 47–8
relations with China 82–6
    bilateral trade 83
    development finance 83
    substantial Chinese
        investment 83–4
    resources 86
    strategic partner of China 82
Vietnam 149
Villegas, Carlos 169

Walker, Ignacio 204n45
Walton Look Lai 194n60
Wang Jin 143
Wang Xiaoshen 136
Wang Yi 89
War of the Pacific (1879–1884), Peru and Chile 60
Wen Jiabao 112, 164
Western Hemisphere 2, 11, 13, 18, 20–2, 26, 27, 30, 31, 164, 166, 170, 174
World Bank 9, 82, 92, 167

World Health Organization (WHO) 150
World Trade Organization (WTO) 43
    China's accession to (2001) 55
    dispute settlement 110
    Peru's accession to (1998) 62
W.R. Grace and Company 28, 30, 174

Xi Jinping 62, 69, 87, 94, 135, 152, 165, 180
Xinhua News Agency 96
Xinjiang TBEA Group 102

Yang Chengxu 171
Yang Shangkun 107
Yasuni-ITT National Plan 93
YLB (Yacimientos de Litio Bolivianos) 102
Yunnan Chinhong 100

Zhang, Yujing 1–2
Zhao Ziyang 43
Zhejiang Fudi Agriculture Company 116
ZTE (Chinese firm) 134, 140, 172